THE POWER OF Positive Psychology & Mindfulness

Rehabilitation and Mental Health Counseling

Michele M. Mahr, PhD

innovativeink PUBLISHING
A Division of Kendall Hunt

innovativeink PUBLISHING
A Division of Kendall Hunt

www.innovativeinkpublishing.com
Send all inquiries to:
4050 Westmark Drive
Dubuque, IA 52004-1840

Print ISBN: 979-8-3851-5480-7
Ebook ISBN: 979-8-3851-5481-4

Published in the United States of America

Contents

Foreword

David S. Pfaff, PhD, LPC

I find it intriguing when counseling clients profess to being "realistic" or a "realist" when evaluating their individual experiences. When asked for elaboration, clients offer markedly similar explanations bolstering pessimism and hopelessness as "just the way things really are." While maybe coincidental or simply my own compartmentalized experience, there seems a bourgeoning trend of equating pervasive negativity to "realism." I am hard-pressed to recall when optimism or hopefulness factor into this "realism" equation. And yet, a genuinely "realistic" approach to life embraces a full spectrum of human experiences, the positives included. Of course, the age-old axiom of "taking the good with the bad" is far easier said than done. Exposures to stress, adversity, trauma, and emotional hardships serve to reinforce notions of life being a minefield of negativity and hopelessness. The intent is not casting dispersions upon notions of what is "realistic" or not. On the contrary, the point is demonstrating life is never wholly negative or positive but that it is a mixture of both. That and living reality to its fullest require accepting both.

This anecdote is one of many testaments to the clinical benefits of positive psychology and mindfulness-based practices. Both modalities appreciate the role of negative experiences, though within the broader context of cultivating well-being and meaning (Hart, 2021). Operating from a wellness-based model, positive psychology and mindfulness promote hopefulness, optimism, and flexibility to elevate functioning and well-being (Hart, 2021; Peseschkian & Remmers, 2021; Seligman, 2018). This textbook delves into the benefits of positive psychology and mindfulness-based practices within clinical counseling. After introducing principal concepts, the textbook guides readers through the application of positive psychology and mindfulness-based intervention for a variety of presenting problems. Chapters within this text are authored by trained and experienced professionals within their respective clinical and academic fields.

Now, are positive psychology and mindfulness-based practices ideal for all counseling clients? Of course not, and sweeping statements or overgeneralizations attesting to the unbridled effectiveness of any therapeutic modality are suspect at best. The problem is sweeping statements and overgeneralizations make for attractive prospects. Human beings are not only prone to generalizations but also neurologically hardwired for them (Taylor et al., 2022). And why not, overgeneralizations require less effort than deliberately parsing among the possible variations (Taylor et al., 2022). In a word, overgeneralizations are efficient. Nonetheless, they come at the risk of advancing cognitive inflexibility, oversimplification, and stereotyping (Dweck, 2007; Peters et al., 2022). In a few more words, overreliance on generalizations drowns all-important nuances and uniqueness.

Practitioners are no exception to the pitfalls of overgeneralizations. For instance, it is common for practitioners to form habits within their clinical practice that, if gone unchecked, could manifest in rigidity and one-size-fits all approaches. Some practitioners might get hooked into overgeneralizations while pursuing a mythological one-right-way of clinical practice and intervention. Perhaps others assume evidence-based practices must always be used and applied the same across all clients and contexts. Nevertheless, evidence-based practice is by no means a warranty of service, and performing a modality perfectly pales in comparison to the individual needs and characteristics of clients. Overgeneralizing means practitioners overlook client uniqueness, which invalidates their individual experiences, perspective, background, and problem variations. Instead, client uniqueness and individuality merit clinical acknowledgment and celebration. Everything from a client's cultural background to their personal history, experiences, values, and so forth yields invaluable knowledge for properly helping and supporting them. Even in the face of similarity or universality, a client's worldview remains undeniably their own. All this is to say, effective practitioners adapt their clinical stylings to account for client uniqueness and meet them where they are.

Speaking of integrating individuality in counseling, a client's unique change process is worthy of special consideration. In a profession focused on tackling presenting problems, we must not forget the significance of therapeutically addressing the client's unique change process along the way. Certainly, therapeutic change is easier to grasp when conceived as a logical and linear process beginning at conceptualization and culminating in successful outcomes. My years as a clinical mental health counselor have taught otherwise though, with behavioral change rarely being so straightforward. Nevertheless, there are no shortage of catch phrases and clichés like "change is hard ... growth and comfort do not coexist ... just embrace change" diluting the complexities of the change process. Lofty expectations ranging from "I can change anything if I try hard enough" to "what doesn't kill you makes you stronger" sound motivating at first, only to feel defeating when change is not so easy. The at times bitter but fulfilling reality is enduring behavioral change is a challenging process achieved via committed action, patience, and compassion.

The *well-worn path* metaphor poetically illustrates this point while demonstrating the biopsychosocial undercurrents that flow through behavioral change. For this metaphor, imagine starting and ending your day by walking the same unkept woodland. Each day you choose the exact same pathway, inevitably wearing a distinct trail in the dense grass and undergrowth. Naturally, you become increasingly comfortable with this same pathway, coming to know the nuances and obstacles of the landscape by heart. With enough time and repetition, traversing this pathway becomes second nature with the very thought of attempting another failing to cross your mind. And why would it? Your well-worn path obviously serves a function and purpose. But what if problems began arising with this pathway to the degree of impeding or slowing travel?

Simply changing pathways sounds simple enough. But human beings tend to be creatures of habit, thanks to a brain forming neural pathways around routines and habits (Mendelsohn, 2020). The more you rely on the same woodland pathway, the more engrained that neural pathway comes. And the more engrained the neural pathway, the greater effort required to change it. That means changing your woodland pathway is not only challenging but is also stressful on the brain and body (Wisse & Sleebos, 2016). Given the brain's design for efficiency and survival, it makes sense it would try avoiding the stresses of change by harkening back to the safety and comfort of old routines and habits (Hanson & Mendius, 2009). Enter the human propensities for comfort-zone biases, illusions of control, and cognitive dissonance (Ersche et al., 2017; Russo-Netzer & Cohen, 2022). There is also something to be said for finding comfort within discomfort, miring in comfortable ruts, or choosing the *devil I know*. The underlying theme is the belief that familiar distress is more palatable than the unknowns of change. As for changing paths within the woodlands, there are possibilities for getting lost within thick undergrowth, encountering dangerous wildlife, or unwittingly wandering off a ledge. In the event previous attempts at changing paths did not go well, there could also be negative expectations or learned hopelessness for future changes (Duckworth et al., 2005). Let us also not forget the social effects of behavioral change. What will others think of your new woodland pathway? Will they agree, judge negatively, or outright reject this change? Or worse, will there be feelings of loneliness or isolation in taking a new woodland path? Change seldom occurs within a vacuum, and the probability is high that practicing new behaviors will resonate through social interactions and relationships (DiClemente & Graydon, 2020; Greaney et al., 2018). Considering these social effects, it is reasonable to worry how family, friends, partners, and/or others will react to change.

Paradoxically, these biopsychosocial undercurrents provide subtle clues that change could prove advantageous. The problem is that recognizing that is hard when confronting the worries and stressors of change. Still, shouldn't change be easier within counseling settings; that's why people go to counseling, right? Logically wanting change is one thing, but navigating the stress and discomfort of the process is another. Clients can vacillate and struggle as they engage in the change process. Let us not forget that relapses, backsliding, and resistance are parts of the behavioral change process as well. Acting upon and maintaining change is a constant two-step-forward, one-step-back process. Practitioners are important supporters within this process, with their approach and attitudes regarding change consequential to the client's success. Practitioners' demonstrating understanding and hopefulness for a client's unique process goes a long way in clients' pursuit of newfound fulfilling pathways as opposed to remaining stuck in comfortable ruts (DiClemente & Graydon, 2020; Gallagher et al., 2019; Laranjeira & Querido, 2022; Tzur Bitan et al., 2022).

Therapeutically addressing the change process begins at the earliest stages of conceptualization and carries through to the end at client termination. Not doing so risks disregarding an important and unique feature within the client's therapeutic process. Practitioners may wonder how to go about therapeutically approaching the client's change process. Counseling theories afford differing perspectives on change, with some modalities criticized as convoluted or ambiguous with respect to the process (DiClemente & Graydon, 2020). Contrasting theoretical stances and constructs regarding change also make it difficult for practitioners to collaborate or consult on the process (DiClemente & Graydon, 2020).

Fortunately, there are therapeutic modalities tailored specifically to the behavioral change process, many of which are designed for integration with existing theoretical orientations (DiClemente & Graydon, 2020; Hagger et al., 2020). Some of these change-centric modalities are even hypothesized to integrate well with positive psychology and mindfulness-based interventions (Stuntz, 2017). Take the Transtheoretical Model/Stages of Change (TTM/SOC), a well-established and comprehensive model for change (Abo Hamza et al., 2023; Prochaska & Velicer, 1997; Raihan & Cogburn, 2023; Stuntz, 2017). Stuntz (2017) suggests positive psychology's emphasis on utilizing strengths, hope, and optimism is conducive to progressing throughout the TTM/SOC processes of change. Additionally, Abo Hamza et al. (2023) concluded mindfulness-based interventions promoted the insights and attitudes necessary for elevating readiness to change and advance through the TTM/SOC stages. If you are not already familiar with the TTM/SOC, the modality has a robust literature and research base. As is the case with any therapeutic modality, the TTM/SOC is not perfect and has its share of limitations. If anything, see the TTM/SOC as a starting point for reflecting upon your own therapeutic approach to change. And should the TTM/SOC not be suitable, there are a number of other available modalities for further study (Hagger et al., 2020b).

Last and certainly not least, this textbook provides valuable insights for utilizing positive psychology and mindfulness-based interventions. Just remember it does so while painting with a broad brush. And why not—this is a textbook after all? And while studying this text, it is important to reflect upon such individual applications as the *who, what, when*, and *where* of utilizing positive psychology and mindfulness-based intervention. This includes considering what positive psychology and mindfulness may look like for the population groups and treatment contexts you practice within. Additionally, identify which individual and unique client characteristics you feel need to be at the forefront of integration into the counseling process. Also think of ways for adapting these modalities to meet the needs of individual. In doing so, remember to accentuate the unique change process as well. Counseling is about effecting meaningful change, meaning effective practitioners take the role of change agents. Consider ways of implementing positive psychology and mindfulness-based interventions to facilitate the change process. Ask yourself whether some positive psychology and mindfulness interventions are better than others for meeting these ends. And with that, best regards on your own journey of change as you learn and adapt valuable concepts from this textbook.

References

Abo Hamza, E., Yoon, A., Liu, L., Garg, A., Richard, Y., Frydecka, D., Helal, A., & Moustafa, A. A. (2020). The relationship between mindfulness and readiness to change in alcohol drinkers. *International Journal of Environmental Research and Public Health, 20*(9), 5690. https://doi.org/10.3390/ijerph20095690

DiClemente, C. C., & Graydon, M. M. (2020). Changing behaviors using the transtheoretical model. In M. S. Haggaer, L. D. Cameron, K. Hamilton, N. Hankonen, & T. Lintunen (Eds.). *The handbook of behavior change* (pp. 136–149). Cambridge University Press.

Duckworth, A. L., Steen, T. A., & Seligman, M. E. P. (2005). Positive psychology in clinical practice. *Annual Review of Clinical Psychology, 1*, 629–651. https://doi.org/10.1146/annurev.clinpsy.1.102803.144154

Dweck, C. S. (2007). *Mindset: The new psychology of success (updated ed.).* Ballantine Books.

Ersche, K. D., Lim, T. V., Ward, L. H. E., Robbins, T. W., & Stochl, J. (2017). Creature of Habit: A self-report measure of habitual routines and automatic tendencies in everyday life. *Personality and Individual Differences, 116*, 73–85. https://doi.org/10.1016/j.paid.2017.04.024

Gallagher, M. W., Long, L. J., Richardson, A., D'Souza J., Boswell, J. F., Farchione, T. J., & Barlow, D. H. (2019). Examining hope as a transdiagnostic mechanism of change across anxiety disorders and CBT treatment protocols. *Behavior Therapy, 51*(1), 190–202. https://doi.org/10.1016/j.beth.2019.06.001

Greaney, M. L., Puleo, E., Sprunck-Harrild, K., Haines, J., Houghton, S. C., & Emmons, K. M. (2018). Social support for changing multiple behaviors: Factors associated with seeking support and the impact of offered support. *Health Education & Behavior, 45*(2), 198–206. https://doi.org/10.1177/1090198117712333

Hagger, M. S., Cameron, L. D., Hamilton, K., Hankonen, N., & Lintunen, T. (2020a). Changing behavior: A theory- and evidenced-based approach. In M. S. Haggaer, L. D. Cameron, K. Hamilton, N. Hankonen, & T. Lintunen (Eds.), *The handbook of behavior change* (pp. 136–149). Cambridge University Press.

Hagger, M. S., Cameron, L. D., Hamilton, K., Hankonen, N., & Lintunen, T. (Eds.). (2020b). *The handbook of behavior change*. Cambridge University Press.

Hanson, R., & Mendius, R. (2009). *Buddha's brain: The practical neuroscience of happiness, love, and wisdom*. New Harbinger Publications.

Hart, R. (2021). *Positive psychology: The basics*. Routledge.

Laranjeira, C., & Querido, A. (2022). Hope and optimism as an opportunity to Improve the "positive mental health" demand. *Frontiers in Psychology, 13*. https://doi.org/10.3389/fpsyg.2022.827320

Mendelsohn, A. I. (2020). Creatures of habit: The neuroscience of habit and purposeful behavior. *Biological Psychiatry, 85*(11), e49–e51. https://doi.org/10.1016/j.biopsych.2019.03.978

Peseschkian, H., & Remmers, A. (2021). Positive psychotherapy: An introduction. In E. Messias, H. Peseschkian, & C. Cagande (Eds.), *Positive psychiatry, psychotherapy, and psychology*. Springer.

Peters, U., Krauss, A., & Braganza, O. (2022). Generalization bias in science. *Cognitive Science, 46*(9). https://doi.org/10.1111/cogs.13188

Prochaska, J. O., & Velicer, W. F. (1997). The transtheoretical model of behavioral change. *American Journal of Health Promotion, 12*(1), 38–48. https://doi.org/10.4278/0890-1171-12.1.38

Raihan, N., & Cogburn, M. (2023). *Stages of change theory*. StatPearls. https://www.ncbi.nlm.nih.gov/books/NBK556005/

Russo-Netzer, P., & Cohen, G. L. (2022). "If you're uncomfortable, go outside your comfort zone": A novel behavioral "stretch" intervention supports the well-being of unhappy people. *The Journal of Positive Psychology*, *18*(3), 394–410. https://doi.org/10.1080/17439760.2022.2036794

Seligman, M. E. (2018). *The hope circuit: A psychologist's journey from helplessness to optimism*. Public Affairs.

Stuntz, C. P. (2017). Linking positive psychology and the transtheoretical model: How character strengths and processes of change relate to each other and to exercise. *Journal of Positive Psychology and Wellbeing, 1*(2), 85–108.

Taylor, J. E., Cortese, A., Barron, H. C., Pan, X., Sakagami, M., & Zeithamova, D. (2022). How do we generalize? *Neuron Behavioral Data Analysis and Theory, 1*. https://doi.org/10.51628/001c.27687

Tzur Bitan, D., Shalev, S., & Abayed, S. (2022). Therapists' views of mechanisms of change in psychotherapy: A mixed-method approach. *Frontiers in Psychology, 13*. https://doi.org/10.3389/fpsyg.2022.565800

Wisse, B., & Sleebos, E. (2016). When change causes stress: Effects of self-construal and change consequences. *Journal of Business and Psychology, 31*, 249–264. https://doi.org/10.1007/s10869-015-9411-z

1

Introduction to Positive Psychology

Michele M. Mahr
Elina Saeki

KEYWORDS AND DEFINITIONS:

Social support: Providing assistance to others often to help them cope with stressors (APA).

Spirituality: A concern for God or a higher power and sensitivity to religious experience, which may not only include the practice of a particular religion but may also exist without such practice (APA).

Toxic positivity: The idea of overemphasizing happiness and joy while remaining positive by ignoring negative emotions.

Tragic optimism: The search for meaning among the inevitable adversities of human existence, seeking for something that is more logical and realistic within troubling periods (Kaufman, 2021).

Well-being: A state of happiness and contentment, with low levels of distress, overall good physical and mental health and outlook, or good quality of life.

LEARNING OBJECTIVES:

1. Identify the key components to positive psychology.
2. Explain the difference between positive psychology and toxic positivity.
3. Describe positive psychology assessments that may be applicable for use with clients in the mental health field.
4. Discuss the different theoretical frameworks and models within the positive psychology realm.
5. Give an example of how principles of positive psychology could be applied in various settings.

Overview of the Book

The purpose of this book is to educate, inform, and provide tangible strategies based on the core principles of positive psychology and mindfulness that can be implemented into the treatment plan when assisting individuals with chronic conditions. Throughout this textbook, the authors of each chapter have outlined the etiology of the condition, current research relevant to the topic, and how positive psychology and mindfulness are treatment modalities that can be used to assist in the treatment plan for each condition. Furthermore, each chapter will have at least one case study or activity that relates to the implementation of these natural therapies. The textbook can be utilized in the classroom setting as well as a valuable resource for practitioners in the field, specifically rehabilitation and mental health counselors. Of course, not all conditions in the *DSM-6* have been noted in this textbook; however, the authors and contributors have dedicated time to research the most common conditions that are often noted in the field of counseling.

Introduction to Positive Psychology

Positive psychology can be defined as the examination of positive experiences and positive individual characteristics, human strengths, and optimal functioning, and the elements that foster the development of these traits (Duckworth et al., 2005; Seligman & Csikszentmihalyi, 2000). The framework of positive psychology provides an attractive approach for mental health practitioners, rehabilitation counselors, and human service providers to consider when working with individuals with emotional, psychological, developmental, or physical challenges. Within the mental health field, positive psychology can be a viable and effective concept to employ when providing services within the treatment plan.

Historically, psychology as a field has focused on the assessment, identification, and treatment of psychopathology and disease. Positive psychology emerged as a challenge to the predominant approach of focusing on deficits and pathology in understanding human behavior. Positive psychologists endorse that the strong focus of many psychologists on relatively uncommon negative behavior produced concepts, theories, methods, and treatments that ignored the universal positive qualities and characteristics of human beings (Seligman & Csikszentmihalyi, 2000). Additionally, the facilitation of positive emotion and the strengthening of character may assist—both directly and indirectly—to reduce suffering and to undo its root causes (Duckworth et al., 2005).

Individuals who are struggling with mental health issues, chronic conditions, dual diagnosis, and other health-related concerns may find that positive psychology is a natural treatment modality to assist in improving their overall health. The unique aspect of positive psychology is that, specially, Seligman and colleagues advanced to a different lens than what has been deemed as "normal" in psychology by focusing on the dysfunction, whereas positive psychology specifically focuses on the positive (Lomas et al., 2020).

According to Seligman,

> Psychology is not just the study of disease, weakness, and damage; it also is the study of strength and virtue. Treatment is not just fixing what is wrong; it also is building what is right. Psychology is not just about illness or health; it also is about work, education, insight, love, growth, and play. And in this quest for what is best, positive psychology does not rely on wishful thinking, self-deception, or hand waving; instead, it tries to adapt what is best in the scientific method to the unique problems that human behavior presents in all its complexity. (Seligman, 2002, p. 2)

With this approach, mental health practitioners, psychologists, and rehabilitation counselors can employ and integrate positive psychology into the treatment plan for individuals from an optimistic viewpoint. The overall goal is to focus on the strengths and positive assets, as this may alter their mindset during treatment. Furthermore, positive psychology's focus on human capacities (actual and potential) recognizes a valuable viewpoint through which to understand how people can cope with and flourish during times of crisis (Waters et al., 2022). One example of how positive psychology may have been useful was during the crisis situation of the global pandemic, COVID-19.

Dual-Factor Model of Mental Health

The traditional model of wellness and psychopathology has placed these two constructs on two ends of a single continuum, with psychopathology on one end and well-being on the other. In contrast, the dual-factor model of mental health posits that putting the two on the same continuum does not adequately capture the complex nature of psychological functioning because the absence of disease is not adequate to determine that an individual is mentally healthy (Diener et al., 2002). Mental health consists not merely of the absence of illness or disorder but also involves the presence of positive factors such as life satisfaction, positive emotions, and accomplishment (Cowen, 1994; Keyes, 2007).

The dual-factor model of mental health includes traditional negative indicators of mental health (e.g., psychopathology) as well as positive indicators of mental health (e.g., subjective well-being) and describes individuals on a continuum of both positive and negative indicators (Greenspoon & Saklofske, 2001; Suldo & Shaffer, 2008). An individual could not only exhibit low levels of psychopathology, or an absence of psychopathology, but also exhibit low levels of subjective well-being, experiencing few positive emotions, poor life satisfaction, and unhappiness. Individuals who are flourishing (i.e., low on psychopathology and high on subjective well-being) function better than individuals with moderate mental health, who in turn function better than individuals who are languishing (i.e., high on psychopathology and low on subjective well-being; see, for example, Keyes, 2007). One of the practical goals of positive psychology is to support individuals' development of psychological well-being and help them create opportunities in order for them to experience a flourishing state of being.

Mindfulness-Based Positive Psychology

Mindfulness is the practice of conscious nonjudgmental awareness to the present and is associated with increased psychological well-being (Branstrom et al., 2011). In recent years, PPIs that incorporate mindfulness have shown some promising outcomes. Mindfulness-based PPIs have been found to improve life satisfaction, well-being, gratitude, compassion, and help individuals find and/or create meaning in life (Allen et al., 2021).

Connection/Social Support

Sense of belonging, connectedness, and social support are positively associated with many physical, psychological, and social health outcomes. Research suggests that social connectedness provides positive benefits such as subjective well-being (Liao & Weng, 2018), mental health (Saeri et al., 2018), and life satisfaction (Chin et al., 2021). Individuals with limited social connectedness have poorer physical and mental health and die earlier than those with strong connectedness (Holt-Lunstad et al., 2010).

Interestingly, social connectedness and mental health appear to have a bidirectional relationship (Saeri et al., 2018). When people engage in social interaction or experience a sense of connectedness with others, they experience better mental health, and when people experience better mental health, they seek out more social interactions or have a greater sense of connectedness with others. Thus, positive psychologists may consider interventions that focus on improving social connectedness and support as a way to improve overall mental health.

Religion, Spirituality, and Positive Psychology

Although positive psychology as a subfield of psychology was developed in the 1990s, the core concepts of positive psychology have existed throughout history. Socrates, Plato, and Aristotle, all sought to understand the "good life." The pursuit of happiness, gratitude, and resilience are common themes in many major religions and spiritual practices around the world. Spirituality and religion both have history related to mental health and specific treatment modalities. Specifically, for the purpose of this chapter, we will provide a brief overview of how religion, spirituality, and positive psychology are connected.

There are many definitions for religion; however, Koenig et al. (2020) defined religion as a set of beliefs, practices, and rituals related to the "transcendent"—also known as God—where the "transcendent" in Western and Eastern customs and traditions is recognized to be the final truth, reality, or enlightenment. Religion can be practiced alone and privately; however, religion is often rooted in a tradition that grows from a group of people with common beliefs and practices related to the "transcendent" (Koenig et al., 2020). Similar to the notion of using social connectedness as a strength and resource, clients may use religion and spirituality as a resource to cope with their mental illness and to promote optimal functioning.

Toxic Positivity

Toxic positivity is defined as the concept of over-emphasizing happiness and believing that remaining positive by ignoring negative emotions is the right solution to coping with issues (Putra et al., 2023). However, this misinterpretation about the concept of remaining positive is certainly not as a result that negative feelings are dismissed in human life (Putra et al., 2023). It is important to recognize when toxic positivity can be detrimental to the well-being of clients. Some scholars suggest that although positivity fosters growth and promotes resilience, it may be counterproductive in certain situations. Toxic positivity is the belief in excessive positive concepts, demanding a person to always be positive in all circumstances and all situations, ignoring negative emotions (Putra et al., 2023). According to Dr. Jaime Zuckerman, a licensed clinical psychologist and trained cognitive behavior therapist, it is "the assumption, either by one's self or others, that despite a person's emotional pain or difficult situation, they should only have a positive mind set or positive vibes" (Council for Relationships, 2021).

Another perspective to consider is tragic optimism. This term was developed by Viktor Frankl, a recognized humanistic psychologist and survivor of the holocaust. Tragic optimism encompasses the search for meaning among the inevitable adversities of human existence, seeking out for something that is more logical and realistic within troubling periods (Kaufman, 2021). Frankl (1985) proposed that individuals could maintain a positive view on life in spite of adversity and tragedy if they believe that humans are capable of transforming life's adversity and tragedy into positives. However, positive psychologists are cautioned not to overemphasize the positives and minimize or dismiss the negatives for individuals experiencing trauma. By focusing only on the positives, mental health practitioners might hinder client's opportunity for growth that comes from a full exploration of their negative experiences and emotions and also simplifies the complexity of clients' experiences to a narrow focus on positives (Wong, 2011). Clients' sharing their negative emotions is an important part of the healing process, even when adopting a positive psychology framework.

Research Supporting the Use of Positive Psychology

There has been an increase in evidence supporting the effectiveness of positive psychology interventions (PPIs) over the last several decades and, particularly, randomized controlled trials involving multicomponent positive psychology interventions (MPPIs) over the last decade. PPIs are interventions aimed at increasing positive feelings, behaviors, and cognitions with theoretical and empirical strategies to promote well-being (e.g., Bolier et al., 2013) and focus on improving one component of well-being, such as gratitude interventions or engaging in acts of kindness. In contrast, MPPIs are interventions that focus on improving two or more well-being components that are conducted in one integrated program, such as the PERMA™ Model (Positive Emotion, Engagement, Relationships, Meaning, and Accomplishment—PERMA™; Seligman, 2018) that focuses on building positive emotions, engagement, relationships, meaning, and accomplishment. PPIs and MPPIs have become increasingly popular in applied settings, with many developed and validated to facilitate positive emotional states, character strengths, and positive relationships (e.g., Quoidbach et al., 2015; Shankland & Rosset, 2017). Meta-analytic studies have found both PPIs and MPPIs to have small to moderate effect sizes for subjective well-being, psychological well-being, anxiety, depression, burnout, and stress (Carr et al., 2021; Hendriks et al., 2020; Sin & Lyubomirsky, 2009), and effects are fairly sustainable, as follow-up studies have shown long-term improvements (Bolier et al., 2013).

Research shows promising effects of PPIs in various settings. For example, PPIs for families build on family strengths and work to enhance the growth of each individual family member (Conoley & Conoley, 2009) and can be delivered to all types of families. School-based PPIs have been shown to significantly increase youths' subjective well-being and psychological well-being and decrease symptoms of depression, and these effects remain significant over time (Tejeda-Gallardo et al., 2020). PPIs in schools can be implemented by classroom teachers and integrated into the curriculum and can also be delivered by school-based mental health practitioners such as school psychologists and school counselors. The concepts of positive psychology, including strengths, adaptability, and empowerment, can also be infused in career or vocational counseling contexts. Studies have found that strengths-based career counseling, such as those that target empowerment, contributed to participants making greater progress toward their goals (Chronister & McWhirter, 2006) and that the participants had greater self-esteem and higher rates of employment than the comparison groups (Littman-Ovadia et al., 2014). Last, positive psychology may also be applied in the rehabilitation counseling setting. The principles of positive psychology resonate well with the philosophy of rehabilitation counseling by refocusing on the individuals' strengths to promote psychosocial adjustment to disability (Lee et al., 2022). Rehabilitation scholars have an opportunity to apply forgiveness as a positive coping strategy that is learned, developed, and/or encouraged as it can foster overall optimism and well-being as well as serve as a positive therapeutic strategy (Stuntzner et al., 2019). Specifically, this intervention strategy can be a positive option that is applicable to the diverse set of surrounding factors for people with disabilities (Stuntzner et al., 2019). The aim of a strength-based paradigm in positive psychology is to allow for initiatives in research programs that will educate evidence-based practices in rehabilitation (Lee et al., 2022).

Implications for Practice

Mental health practitioners who embrace positive psychology help individuals thrive and flourish, but they do not completely ignore problems in life or focus only on the positives. Positive psychologists view mental illness as malleable and amenable to change and improvements and seek to uncover what works for people as they work to reduce psychopathology and pursue optimal functioning (Magyar-Moe et al., 2015). Clients often seek out psychological help due to a lack of, or a recent decrease in, well-being; therefore, mental health practitioners can work with clients to both remediate problems and promote growth and well-being.

Positive Psychology Interventions

Mental health practitioners can implement positive psychology interventions (PPIs) as standalone treatments or incorporate positive psychology strategies to augment treatment-as-usual depending on clients' presenting concerns (Magyar-Moe et al., 2015). Several formal positive psychology therapy models have been described in the scholarly literature, including Strength-Based Counseling (Smith, 2006), Well-being Therapy (Fava, 2016), Quality of Life Therapy (Frisch, 2006), and Positive Psychotherapy (Rashid, 2015). These therapeutic models can be used as a framework for providing mental health services for clients seeking to reduce symptoms of mental illness as well as those seeking to improve subjective well-being, or both. For example, the Quality of Life Therapy is a comprehensive and manualized intervention to promote well-being and happiness, in which clients are taught strategies to help them identify, pursue, and fulfill their goals and wishes leading them to experience well-being and happiness (Frisch, 2006).

A number of PPIs have been developed over the years, including but not limited to:

- Thinking and writing about positive experiences (Burton & King, 2009)
- Keeping a gratitude journal (Seligman et al., 2005)
- Focusing on blessings (Emmons & McCullough, 2003)
- Engaging in acts of kindness (Lyubomirsky et al., 2005).

The "Three Good Things" exercise involves clients writing every day about three good things that happened to them and why they happened. In the "Using Your Strengths" exercise, individuals are given feedback about their best strengths and are told to use a different strength in a new way every day. Seligman and colleagues (2005) found that a 1-week intervention using these exercises did not increase happiness and decrease depressive symptoms compared to the no-intervention group, but they were significantly happier and less depressed than the no-intervention group at the 1-, 3-, and 6-month follow-ups. Further analysis revealed that participants who voluntarily continued their positive psychology exercises beyond the required 1-week period were more likely to experience the continued benefits of the exercises (Seligman et al., 2005).

Positive Psychology Assessments

As mental health practitioners adopt a positive psychology framework and implement positive psychology interventions and strategies, there is a need to assess baseline levels of subjective well-being as well as the extent to which their practices are having a positive impact on their clients. As such, the utility of the positive psychology framework extends to the assessment and evaluation process. Many assessment instruments, including multi-informant questionnaires and rating scales, observation tools, interview protocols, and review of records, typically focus on uncovering client deficits and dysfunction to determine the presence or absence of mental illness. Assessment tools aligned with the positive psychology framework focus on the opposite: the presence of well-being factors in clients' lives. There are several empirically validated positive psychology assessments and tools, including but not limited to

- Satisfaction with Life Scale (SWLS; Diener et al., 1985)
- Quality of Life Inventory (QOLI; Frisch, 2013)
- Meaning in Life Questionnaire (MLQ; Steger et al., 2006)
- Student Subjective Wellbeing Questionnaire (SSWQ; Renshaw et al., 2015)
- Subjective Happiness Scale (SHS; Lyubomirsky & Lepper, 1999)
- PERMA-Profiler (Butler & Kern, 2016)

The College Student Subjective Wellbeing Questionnaire (CSSWQ) has been developed for use among college-level students, consisting of 15 items and measuring 4 dimensions of well-being: academic efficacy, academic satisfaction, school connectedness, and college gratitude (Renshaw, 2018). This questionnaire can be used in schools and colleges to assess students' school-specific positive psychological functioning. This is in direct contrast to the traditional tools used in schools and colleges to assess student problem behaviors, risk, and psychopathology, and this questionnaire can be a useful tool to evaluate the effectiveness of school-based PPIs. It can also be used as a population-based screening tool for assessing, responding to, and monitoring college students' mental health.

Conclusion

Since the inauguration of positive psychology (also commonly referred to as 'PP' in the mental health field), the literature has confirmed several advantages and potential opportunities for positive psychology to be an effective treatment modality when working with individuals in mental health, school, and rehabilitation counseling settings. The current research and information presented in this chapter have solidified authors' observation that there are specific PPIs that can be implemented into the treatment plan for counselors, practitioners, and mental health professionals to tap into when working with diverse populations. Hendriks et al. (2020) define PPIs as mediations targeting to enhance positive feelings, behaviors, and cognitions and, at the same time, applying theoretically and empirically based strategies to improve overall wellness. Essentially, it is at the discretion of both the client and the counselor on how and when to utilize positive psychology treatment models and tools during the treatment process. The relationship between the client and the counselor is most important before implementing any specific strategy while also providing a safe, open, trusting space for the client to feel their most authentic self. The concept of rapport has been connected with the obtaining and maintaining of the therapeutic relationship (Freire et al., 2020). By allowing the rapport and relationship to develop naturally, counselors can make executive decisions as to when they should begin to use positive psychology models–based treatment strategies without jeopardizing the trust and boundaries of the client. It is important to not minimize traumas, crisis, or other adversities that the client is presenting to the counselor by not acknowledging their feelings. However, it may be even more applicable and in the best interest of the client for counselors to assist in reframing the mental state of focusing on the strengths, assets, and gratitude, which are all key components of positive psychology.

Case Study

Melinda is a 35-year-old single woman who was diagnosed with depression and anxiety 6 months ago. After she experienced the loss of her fiancé in a car accident, she fell into a very dark space mentally and began seeking mental health care. She and her fiancé were both in the car driving to pick out the venue for their wedding location when a drunk driver ran into their car on the freeway, killing her fiancé, while Melinda survived the crash. Melinda began expressing to her therapist that she feels many emotions since the loss of her fiancé, such as hopelessness, grief, emptiness, guilt, and anger. She has also noted that there are times when she really does not see how she can move on with her life and feels very stuck. She is constantly repeating—"I lost the love of my life, how can I ever be happy again?" Melinda has been prescribed an antidepressant, Zoloft, to help her with symptoms related to her anxiety and depression. She has often talked about lack of sleep and appetite as well as feeling very nervous around social situations. This all began after the accident which has escalated within the last 2 months.

Fortunately, Melinda is quite independent financially and has a degree in kinesiology, in addition to certification as a personal trainer. She maintains her own business as a personal trainer and also works at her local gym. However, since her recent diagnosis and the accident, she has not been motivated to meet with her clients at her own business or at the gym. Her social support is quite limited because her family of origin resides in a different state, and she would consider herself estranged from them on many levels.

Critical Thinking Questions

- What are some specific strategies or interventions based on positive psychology principles you would implement to begin to assist Melinda?
- What are some assessment tools that might be useful or most relevant for Melinda at this time?
- What questions would you ask Melinda regarding her future goals in general?
- How might you help Melinda implement positive psychology to reevaluate her business and career goals as a personal trainer?
- How might you suggest Melinda to seek out social support, other than her family of origin, during this critical time period for her?
- What resources could you offer for Melinda that could contribute to her self-care?

References

Allen, J. G., Romate, J., & Rajkumar, E. (2021). Mindfulness-based positive psychology interventions: A systematic review. *BMC Psychology, 9*(116), 1–18. https://doi.org/10.1186/s40359-021-00618-2

Bolier, L., Haverman, M., Westerhof, G. J., Riper, H., Smit, F., & Bohlmeijer, E. (2013). Positive psychology interventions: A meta-analysis of randomized controlled studies. *BMC Public Health, 13*(119), 1–20. http://www.biomedcentral.com/1471-2458/13/119

Branstrom, R., Duncan, L. G., & Moskowitz, J. T. (2011). The association between dispositional mindfulness, psychological well-being, and perceived health in a Swedish population-based sample. *British Journal of Health Psychology, 16*, 300–316. https://doi.org/10.1348/135910710X501683

Burton, C. M., & King, L. A. (2009). The health benefits of writing about positive experiences: The role of broadened cognition. *Psychology & Health, 24*(8), 867–879. https://doi.org/10.1080/08870440801989946

Butler, J., & Kern, M. L. (2016). The PERMA-Profiler: A brief multidimensional measure of flourishing. *International Journal of Wellbeing, 6*(3), 1-48. https://doi.org/10.5502/ijw.v6i3.526

Carr, A., Cullen, K., Keeney, C., Canning, C., Mooney, O., Chinseallaigh, E., & O'Dowd, A. (2021). Effectiveness of positive psychology interventions: A systematic review and meta-analysis. *The Journal of Positive Psychology, 16*(6), 749–769. https://doi.org/10.1080/17439760.2020.1818807

Chin, A. S., Lin, G., & Yang, H. (2021). Staying connected: Effects of social connectedness, cultural intelligence, and socioeconomic status on overseas students' life satisfaction. *International Journal of Intercultural Relations, 83*, 151–162. https://doi.org/10.1016/j.ijintrel.2021.06.002

Chronister, K. M., & McWhirter, E. H. (2006). An experimental examination of two career interventions for battered women. *Journal of Counseling Psychology, 53*(2), 151–163. https://doi.org/10.1037/0022-0167.53.2.151

Conoley, C. W., & Conoley, J. C. (2009). *Positive psychology and family therapy: Creative techniques and practical tools for guiding change and enhancing growth.* John Wiley & Sons.

Council for Relationships. (2021). *Toxic positivity: It's ok to not be ok all of the time.* https://councilforrelationships.org/toxic-positivity-its-ok-to-not-be-ok-all-of-the-time/

Cowen, E. L. (1994). The enhancement of psychological wellness: Challenges and opportunities. *American Journal of Community Psychology, 22*, 149–179. https://doi.org/10.1007/BF02506861

Diener, E., Emmons, R. A., Larsen, R. J., & Griffin, S. (1985). The satisfaction with life scale. *Journal of Personality Assessment, 49*(1), 71–75. https://ssrn.com/abstract=2199190

Diener, E., Lucas, R. E., & Oishi, S. (2002). Subjective well-being: The science of happiness and life satisfaction. In C. R. Snyder & S. Lopez (Eds.), *Handbook of positive psychology* (pp. 463–473). Oxford University Press.

Duckworth, A. L., Steen, T. A., & Seligman, M. E. P. (2005). Positive psychology in clinical practice. *Annual Review of Clinical Psychology, 1*(1), 629–651. https://doi.org/10.1146/annurev.clinpsy.1.102803.144154

Emmons, R. A., & McCullough, M. E. (2003). Counting blessings versus burdens: An experimental investigation of gratitude and subjective well-being in daily life. *Journal of Personality and Social Psychology, 84*(2), 377–389. https://doi.org/10.1037/0022-3514.84.2.377

Fava, G. A. (2016). Well-being therapy: Current indications and emerging perspectives. *Psychotherapy and Psychosomatics, 85*(3), 136–145. https://doi.org/10.1159/000444114

Frankl, V. (1985). *Man's search for meaning: Revised and updated.* Washington Square.

Freire, C., Ferradás, MdM., Regueiro, B., Rodríguez, S., Valle, A., & Núñez, J. C. (2020). Coping strategies and self-efficacy in university students: A person-centered approach. *Frontiers in Psychology, 11*(841), 1–11. https://doi.org/10.3389/fpsyg.2020.00841

Frisch, M. B. (2006). *Quality of Life Therapy: Applying life satisfaction approach to positive psychology and cognitive therapy.* Wiley.

Frisch, M. B. (2013). Evidence-based well-being/positive psychology assessment and intervention with Quality of Life Therapy and Coaching and the Quality of Life Inventory (QOLI). *Social Indicators Research, 114*, 193–227. https://doi.org/10.1007/s11205-012-0140-7

Greenspoon, P. J., & Saklofske, D. H. (2001). Toward an integration of SWB and psychopathology. *Social Indicators Research, 54*, 81–108. https://doi.org/10.1023/A:1007219227883

Hendriks, T., Schotanus-Dijkstra, M., Hassankhan, A., de Jong, J., & Bohlmeijer, E. (2020). The efficacy of multi-component positive psychology interventions: A systematic review and meta-analysis of randomized controlled trials. *Journal of Happiness Studies, 21*, 357–390. https://doi.org/10.1007/s10902-019-00082-1

Holt-Lunstad, J., Smith, T. B., & Layton, J. B. (2010). Social relationships and mortality risk: A meta-analytic review. *PLoS Medicine, 7*(7), e1000316. https://doi.org/10.1371/journal.pmed.1000316

Kaufman, S. B. (2021). The opposite of toxic positivity. *The Atlantic, 18.* https://medium.com/the-atlantic/the-opposite-of-toxic-positivity-6ebaf2470d68

Keyes, C. L. M. (2007). Promoting and protecting mental health as flourishing: A complementary strategy for improving national mental health. *American Psychologist, 62*(2), 95–108. http://dx.doi.org/10.1037/0003–066X.62.2.95

Koenig, H. G., Al-Zaben, F., & VanderWeele, T. J. (2020). Religion and psychiatry: Recent developments in research. *BJPsych Advances, 26*(5), 262–272. https://doi.org/10.1192/bja.2019.81

Lee, H., Pena, J., Lee, B., & Sung, C. (2022). Promoting well-being in individuals with autism: Applying positive psychology in rehabilitation counseling. *Rehabilitation Research, Policy & Education, 36*(4), 276–291. http://dx.doi.org/10.1891/RE-21-19

Liao, K. Y.-H., & Weng, C.-Y. (2018). Gratefulness and subjective well-being: Social connectedness and presence of meaning as mediators. *Journal of Counseling Psychology, 65*(3), 383–393. https://doi.org/10.1037/cou0000271

Littman-Ovadia, H., Lazar-Butbul, V., & Benjamin, B. A. (2014). Strengths-based career counseling: Overview and initial evaluation. *Journal of Career Assessment, 22*(3), 403–419. https://doi.org/10.1177/1069072713498483

Lomas, T., Waters, L., Williams, P., Oades, L. G., & Kern, M. L. (2020). Third wave positive psychology: Broadening towards complexity. *The Journal of Positive Psychology, 16*(5), 660–674. https://doi.org/10.1080/17439760.2020.1805501

Lyubomirsky, S., & Lepper, H. S. (1999). A measure of subjective happiness: Preliminary reliability and construct validation. *Social Indicators Research, 46*(2), 137–155. https://doi.org/10.1023/A:1006824100041

Lyubomirsky, S., Sheldon, K. M., & Schkade, D. (2005). Pursuing happiness: The architecture of sustainable change. *Review of General Psychology, 9*(2), 111–131. https://doi.org/10.1037/1089-2680.9.2.111

Magyar-Moe, J. L., Owens, R. L., & Conoley, C. W. (2015). Positive psychological interventions in counseling: What every counseling psychologist should know. *The Counseling Psychologist, 43*(4), 508–557. https://doi.org/10.1177/0011000015573776

Putra, R. P., Ramadhanti, A., Rahajeng, A. S., Fadil, A., & Salsyabila, N. (2023). Toxic positivity in adolescents: An attitude of always being positive in every situation. *Journal of Psychology and Instruction, 7*(1), 11–21. https://doi.org/10.23887/jpai.v7i1.60616

Quoidbach, J., Mikolajczak, M., & Gross, J. J. (2015). Positive interventions: An emotion regulation perspective. *Psychological Bulletin, 141*(3), 655–693. https://doi.org/10.1037/a0038648

Rashid, T. (2015). Positive psychotherapy: A strength-based approach. *The Journal of Positive Psychology, 10*(1), 25–40. https://doi.org/10.1080/17439760.2014.920411

Renshaw, T. L. (2018). Psychometrics of the revised College Student Subjective Wellbeing Questionnaire. *Canadian Journal of School Psychology, 33*(2), 136–149. https://doi.org/10.1177/0829573516678704

Renshaw, T. L., Long, A. C., & Cook, C. R. (2015). Assessing adolescents' positive psychological functioning at school: Development and validation of the Student Subjective Wellbeing Questionnaire. *School Psychology Quarterly, 30*(4), 534–552. https://doi.org/10.1037/spq0000088

Saeri, A. K., Cruwys, T., Barlow, F. K., Stronge, S., & Sibley, C. G. (2018). Social connectedness improves public mental health: Investigating bidirectional relationships in the New Zealand Attitudes and Values Survey. *Australian & New Zealand Journal of Psychiatry, 52*(4), 365–374. https://doi.org/10.1177/0004867417723990

Saeri, A. K., Cruwys, T., Barlow, F. K., Stronge, S., Sibley, C. G. (2018). Social connectedness improves public mental health: Investigating bidirectional relationships in the New Zealand attitudes and values survey. *Australian & New Zealand Journal of Psychiatry, 52*(4), 365-374. doi:10.1177/0004867417723990

Seligman, M. (2018). PERMA and the building blocks of well-being. *The Journal of Positive Psychology, 13*(4), 333–335. https://doi.org/10.1080/17439760.2018.1437466

Seligman, M. E. (2002). Positive psychology, positive prevention, and positive therapy. In C. R. Snyder & S. J. Lopez (Eds.), *Handbook of positive psychology* (pp. 3–12). Oxford University Press.

Seligman, M. E. P., & Csikszentmihalyi, M. (2000). Positive psychology: An introduction. *American Psychologist, 55*, 5–14. http://dx.doi.org/10.1037/0003-066X.55.1.5

Seligman, M. E. P., Steen, T. A., Park, N., & Peterson, C. (2005). Positive psychology progress: Empirical validation of interventions. *American Psychologist, 60*(5), 410–421. https://doi.org/10.1037/0003-066X.60.5.410

Shankland, R., & Rosset, E. (2017). Review of brief school-based positive psychological interventions: A taste for teachers and educators. *Educational Psychology Review, 29*, 363–392. https://doi.org/10.1007/s10648-016-9357-3

Sin, N. L., & Lyubomirsky, S. (2009). Enhancing well-being and alleviating depressive symptoms with positive psychology interventions: A practice-friendly meta-analysis. *Journal of Clinical Psychology, 65*(5), 467–487. https://doi.org/10.1002/jclp.20593

Smith, E. J. (2006). The strength-based counseling model. *The Counseling Psychologist, 34*(1), 13–79. https://doi.org/10.1177/0011000005277018

Steger, M. F., Frazier, P., Oishi, S., & Kaler, M. (2006). The Meaning in Life Questionnaire: Assessing the presence of and search for meaning in life. *Journal of Counseling Psychology, 53*(1), 80–93. https://doi.org/10.1037/0022-0167.53.1.80

Stuntzner, S., Dalton, J. A., & MacDonald, A. (2019). Application of forgiveness in rehabilitation psychology: A positive option for change. *International Physical Medicine & Rehabilitation Journal, 4*(4), 184–191. https://doi.org/10.15406/ipmrj.2019.04.00196

Suldo, S. M., & Shaffer, E. J. (2008). Looking beyond psychopathology: The dual-factor model of mental health in youth. *School Psychology Review, 37*(1), 52–68. https://doi.org.10.1080/02796015.2008.12087908

Tejeda-Gallardo, C., Blasco-Belled, A., Torrelles-Nadal, C., & Alsinet, C. (2020). Effects of school-based multicomponent positive psychology interventions on well-being and distress in adolescents: A systematic review and meta-analysis. *Journal of Youth and Adolescence, 49*, 1943–1960. https://doi.org/10.1007/s10964-020-01289-9

Waters, L., Algoe, S. B., Dutton, J., Emmons, R., Fredrickson, B. L., Heaphy, E., Moskowitz, J. T., Neff, K., Niemiec, R., Pury, C., & Steger, M. (2022). Positive psychology in a pandemic: Buffering, bolstering, and building mental health. *The Journal of Positive Psychology, 17*(3), 303–323. https://doi.org/10.1080/17439760.2021.1871945

Wong, P. T. P. (2011). Positive psychology 2.0: Towards a balanced interactive model of the good life. *Canadian Psychology, 52*(2), 69–81. http://dx.doi.org/10.1037/a0022511

Introduction to Mindfulness

2

Michele M. Mahr
Sherry Rosenblad
David Gary II

KEYWORDS AND DEFINITIONS:

Awareness: The recognition and understanding of events or internal conditions, such as thoughts and emotions, and externally in the surrounding environment.

Breath: The inhaling and exhaling air from the lungs, used in mindfulness practices to help focus attention and achieve a sense of calm.

Compassion: The awareness of distress in oneself or others and a desire to alleviate it through kindness and understanding to promote well-being.

Focus: A point of concentration often used in mindfulness to increase mental clarity.

Meditation: The practice of focusing attention and engaging in contemplation to achieve spiritual, emotional, or mental clarity and awareness.

Presence: Being fully aware and engaged in the current moment with perception and focus.

Relaxation: A state of freedom from tension and stress, often achieved through mindfulness practices.

LEARNING OBJECTIVES:

1. Describe primary concepts of mindfulness to include origins, key points, and potential practices.
2. Identify the benefits of mindfulness implementation as related to emotional, psychological, physiological, biological, and spiritual states of being.
3. Understand and name proper implementation techniques for integrating mindfulness within a counseling practice.
4. Recognize the application strategies for emotional regulation and stress management.

Overview of the Chapter

This chapter will expand on the operational definition of mindfulness, specific strategies of mindfulness, spirituality and mindfulness, and personal reflections on how mindfulness has been implemented into daily practice. The term "mindfulness" has received much attention in the field of counseling as well as in other human service professions. We hope to provide an in-depth explanation of the components related to mindfulness, tenets that have been identified with mindfulness, a case study, and personal reflections on how the authors have used mindfulness in their own practice. We aim to assist the reader in expanding their current knowledge related to mindfulness while at the same time allowing room for growth and adaptations based on the client's individual needs.

What Is Mindfulness?

At the core, mindfulness has its foundation in Eastern contemplative traditions and is typically connected with the official practice of mindfulness meditation (Shapiro et al., 2006). According to Kabat-Zinn (2009), mindfulness means paying attention in a specific way: with intention and in the present moment while remaining nonjudgmental. This concept is universal and does not oppose or conflict with other religious or scientific beliefs or customs (Kabat-Zinn, 2015). Mindfulness is often connected with meditation rituals, targeted at developing the skills for present-moment awareness as a mental habit (e.g., similar to physical exercise to assist the body to become healthier even beyond exercise sessions—meditation or mindfulness practices strive to foster healthy psychological awareness and wellness, extending beyond the exercises themselves) (Henriksen et al., 2020). The act of being mindful helps us to focus our attention (Kabat-Zinn, 2015). Approximately 50% of the time, our minds wander; however, when we practice being mindful, we use our attention muscles, and this forces us to begin to develop a mentally fit mind (Kabat-Zinn, 2015).

Mindfulness has three elements that characterize its operational definition: (1) our natural ability of attention to direct our awareness to the experience; (2) the operation of attending to target the present-moment experiences, without judgment of pleasant or unpleasant, *good* or *bad*; and (3) perception with specific qualities that come forth as a *result* of applying the process that comprises of openness, willingness, open-mindedness, and stillness allowing for the individual to hold any *movement* within it, which may include thoughts, emotions, or any extrinsic stimuli derived from our senses (Antonova et al., 2021). As individuals or clients begin to face their repressed feelings or allow their thoughts to come forth, the lack of judgment is fundamental as it provides a space for letting the feelings, thoughts, and emotions *just be* without labeling. The approach of mindfulness promotes the acceptance of the uncomfortable, challenging, and unpleasant experiences, allowing them to simply be, feeling them as they are without discernment, remaining in the deep cognitive thoughts until we are ready to let them go, and this allows the mental space to open for potential experiences and new possibilities (Antonova et al., 2021).

Research Supporting Mindfulness and Mental Health

Mindfulness consistently gains momentum in research, academia, and clinical applications in revealing positive mental health outcomes. For example, in a study that examined the reporting of positive results for mindfulness-based interventions on mental health, out of the 124 studies utilizing randomized controlled studies, 90% reported positive results (Coronado-Montoya et al., 2016). A vast majority of mindfulness research has explored its potential to modulate stress and increase cognitive, emotional, and interpersonal performance (Sedlmeier et al., 2012). Mindfulness-based interventions, or MBI, are specifically developed to target fixed mental concerns and may be combined with other treatment modalities (Kabat-Zinn, 2003). Research supports the positive effects of mindfulness training for both clinical and nonclinical populations (Gál et al., 2021). One of the advantages of mindfulness is that it can be applied by anyone, regardless of the situation. Moreover, being mindful is a practice that may lead to positive benefits on an individual's overall well-being and quality of life.

Regarding nonclinical settings, scholars Galante et al. (2021) published a systemic meta-analysis review examining the impact of mindfulness-based programs (MBPs) on individuals in nonclinical settings. The findings of this study suggested that MBPs may be a successful treatment to increase positive mental health compared to taking no action. However, the authors also note that it cannot be assumed that MBPs will constantly be effective in every nonclinical setting. Furthermore, the results of this review also demonstrated that the effects of MBPs in the United States were lower than those studies in the UK. Based on the results of this meta-analysis, it appears that MBPs implemented within a variety of cultures and contexts by different agents while also aiming at different categories within specific communities may have altering effects (Galante et al., 2021). As always, counselors must be mindful and considerate of individual characteristics that may also impact how clients incorporate mindfulness into their lives. For example, individuals who lack resources, are overly stressed, are challenged with adversity, and are struggling with self-love may find mindfulness programs hard to integrate easily versus someone who happens to be in a healthy place within their lives.

Other topics that have gained popular attention within the counseling discipline are self-compassion, compassion fatigue, and self-care for health professionals. Mindfulness may be a viable practice for healthcare professionals to reflect upon their own self-care and well-being while serving others. One definition of compassion fatigue is when individuals experience tension because of perennial or long-drawn preoccupation with clients who have experienced trauma, and their experience of compassion fatigue becomes more pronounced/acute when they are re-experiencing the traumatic events and trying to avoid the client and memories of their own trauma, which, in turn, leads to their lack of interest and ability to be there for others (Figley, 2002). Healthcare professionals (HCPs) are a unique group that is at high risk for increased burnout and compassion fatigue (Conversano et al., 2020). HCPs can implement self-compassion and mindfulness into their own lives, which may combat the fatigue and exhaustion often associated with their desire to assist others. Essentially, compassion is a feeling that is filled with warmth and care versus cold and judgmental, and it also denotes a strong desire to help others rather than harm (Neff, 2023). Learning how to remain with uncomfortable experiences, suffering, or hardship may include becoming mindful. Neff (2023) suggested that in order to experience compassion, individuals must be willing to lean into suffering, regardless of the pain. Finally, a foundation for feeling compassion is connecting with others who are struggling versus remaining isolated from them in times of darkness (Neff, 2023). As HCPs focus on compassion for others, they also need to remember to uphold self-compassion.

Self-compassion is not an option, but it is necessary in order for HCPs to remain the most effective in their careers when assisting others. Self-compassion is operationally defined as being supportive toward oneself when experiencing pain; however, this suffering may have occurred due to personal choices or external life stressors (Neff, 2023). Self-compassion has currently obtained increased awareness, specifically in the examination of psychological well-being when individuals are living with daily life stressors (Ewert et al., 2021). Within the mental state of self-compassion comes self-kindness. Self-kindness is comprised of forgiveness, empathy, sensitivity, warmth, and patience directed at oneself during experiences of pain or hardship, with total acceptance of one's own mistakes or choices and a passion for caring for oneself despite the pain (Ewert et al., 2021). If HCPs are able to become mindful of these feelings for themselves, perhaps they may demonstrate more compassion to others as well in times of need. Moreover, self-compassion, self-care, and self-love could foster individuals' resilience and mental toughness, leading to less burnout and compassion fatigue as they continually assist others.

As counselors and HCPs continue to recognize and practice the need for self-care, this may lead to more sustainable and satisfying careers and increased overall well-being for the individual. Fortunately, counselor educators and members of professional counseling organizations have recognized the need for self-care to assist counselors (Dye et al., 2019). It is true that there is only a minimal number of counseling organizations that target self-care or wellness; however, there are several that include a statement in their code of ethics mandating that counselors evaluate themselves and/or others for health concerns—sometimes caused by stress, compassion fatigue, or burnout—with encouragement to seek assistance to manage the mental, emotional, or physical challenges that diminish or cripple their ability to provide effective and appropriate services to clients (Dye et al.,

2019). Fortunately, mental health training programs and professional organizations hold the power to cultivate and foster an attitude of self-care in the field of mental health work (Posluns & Gall, 2019). Moreover, a positive approach to self-care and mindfulness on the part of the counselors can promote relaxation, a heightened sense of well-being with the mind–body connection, recognition of the benefits of mindfulness, and, ultimately, an increase in effective service to our clients.

Mindful Spirituality

Spirituality's role in mental health is increasingly recognized in contemporary culture. Yuniarwati et al. (2020) stated, "Spirituality helps individuals to live at peace with themselves, to love God and their neighbor, and to live in harmony with the environment" (p. 208). Religious and spiritual practices serve as effective coping mechanisms, supporting mental health and resilience against life's stressors (Hannabuss, 2021; Verghese, 2008; Weber & Pargament, 2014). Studies show that psychological well-being improves when individuals engage in spiritual practices and focus on nurturing the mind and the spirit (Bożek et al., 2020; Garssen et al., 2020). Mental health professionals are increasingly integrating spiritual assessments and addressing spiritual needs in therapy to enhance therapeutic outcomes (Hadzic, 2011; Milner et al., 2019; Moreira-Almeida et al., 2014; Verghese, 2008).

PatrickAssale/Shutterstock.com

Mindful meditation has been shown to enhance spiritual well-being by cultivating inner peace and strengthening connections with God, others, and the environment. Incorporating meditation is linked to increased hope, self-acceptance, and a deeper sense of life's purpose (Yuniarwati et al., 2020). Meditation's roots go back to ancient religions, with some of the earliest records found in Hindu and Buddhist traditions in India, Jewish practices in Palestine, and Taoist traditions in China (Basham, 1991; Nash, 2019; Paramahamsa, 2007). Over time, meditation was also adopted by more contemporary religious traditions, including the Eastern Orthodox Christian sect (Nash, 2019).

Ancient Indian beliefs held that humans consist of the physical body, inner consciousness and intellect, and the deep inner self. Meditation functions as a bridge between these aspects, promoting benefits that encompass every facet of life, including spiritual well-being (Sharma, 2015). Hindu meditation aims to still the body, senses, and mind to attain a thought-free state of consciousness, achieved through controlled breathing and sensory withdrawal (Tomasino et al., 2014; Wernicke-Olesen, 2019).

Trance-like states and visions are frequently referenced in ancient Jewish texts (Persico, 2022). Biblical books like Psalms, Exodus, and Ezekiel describe practices such as meditation, concentration, contemplation, and sensory techniques to achieve union with God and elevated consciousness or enlightenment (Scott, 2002). As organized religion evolved, focused attention on the divine became more common, with prayer serving as a form of meditative practice (Persico, 2022). In modern Jewish practice, Buddhist mindfulness techniques, especially insight meditation, have been integrated to deepen Jewish prayer and address existential anxieties stemming from Jewish suffering (Niculescu, 2015, 2017, 2019).

holysiam/Shutterstock.com

Buddhist mindfulness meditation emphasizes focused attention on the body, breath, and thoughts to attain a state of emptiness and self-transcendence (Anālayo, 2020; Tomasino et al., 2014). This mindfulness can be cultivated through various practices, including sitting, walking, eating, chanting, and other devotions aimed at spiritual growth (Bielefeldt, 1988; Shaw, 2021). In Chinese Buddhism, meditation may also involve visualizing bodily decay to foster detachment from the physical self (Bianchi, 2021) or concentrating on themes of rebirth (Griffiths & Gregory, 1988). Contemporary Chinese Buddhist mindfulness has even merged with psychoanalytic approaches to aid in depression treatment (Lau, 2021), while Taoist meditation focuses on achieving a state of purity and quietness.

The Jesus Prayer, an ancient Eastern Orthodox prayer often attributed to the early monk Evagrius Ponticus (d. 339), takes the form: "Lord Jesus Christ, Son of God, have mercy on me, a sinner." This prayer later spread beyond Eastern Orthodoxy, influencing Byzantine Hesychasm, Roman Catholicism, Protestant Christianity, Buddhism, and Hinduism. In the 13th century, practitioners began pairing the Jesus prayer with deep breathing techniques (Britannica, 2017; Molleur, 2011). By the 20th century, a revival of Christian meditation, notably the centering prayer inspired by Fr. Thomas Keating and fellow Trappist monk Thomas Merton, was embraced across Europe, Canada, Australia, and the United States and taught by Episcopal priest Cynthia Bourgeault (Nash, 2019).

Sansoen Saengsakaorat/Shutterstock.com

Incorporating mindful meditation has been integral to religious and spiritual practices across cultures for millennia, offering a path to deepen connections with the divine, the self, and others. This practice, rooted in diverse traditions, emphasizes inner peace, self-awareness, and spiritual growth. In therapeutic contexts, integrating clients' spiritual beliefs with mindfulness techniques can enhance resilience, facilitate coping, and promote healing. As mental health professionals increasingly recognize the value of spirituality in therapy, mindful meditation serves as a powerful tool for supporting clients' psychological and spiritual well-being.

Doidam 10/Shutterstock.com

Selected Mindfulness Interventions

In this section, selected mindfulness interventions will be explored as an overview to pave the way for further investigation of specific mindfulness practices generally utilized unilaterally within the mentioned interventions. It should be noted that the interventions and practices included in the following list are not exhaustive. These interventions and practices are more of a basis for foundational acquisition of mindfulness modality adoption. Students and other mental health professionals are encouraged to absorb core fundamentals to develop a more profound understanding, thereby potentially assimilating these constructs within their future counseling practice endeavors. By investigating areas further, students and other mental health professionals could achieve an increased potential to establish a continuum of erudition for improved best practices and client care.

Mindfulness Interventions Overview

Mindfulness-Based Stress Reduction

Mindfulness-based stress reduction (MBSR) was initially designed for detailed guidance of individuals through prescribed meditation and moments with the purpose of growing awareness within ourselves. As mentioned earlier in the chapter, ***mindfulness*** is constructing an established practice focused on cognizance surrounding the openness of experiential present moments (Hazlett-Stevens et al., 2019; Kriakous et al., 2021; Sadooghiasl et al., 2022). A majority of MBSR programs tend to run for about 8 weeks (Hazlett-Stevens et al., 2019; Kriakous et al., 2021; Sadooghiasl et al., 2022), but there is also research showing valid efficacy in programs implementing a more brief timeline for an increase in areas such as distress tolerance, self-compassion, emotional regulation, and mindfulness (Krisakous et al., 2021). Mindfulness-based stress reduction programs have utility in an assortment of settings and possess the ability to assist a diverse population.

Krisakous et al. (2021) performed a systematic review investigating MBSR's efficacy in improving psychological areas in healthcare workers. Their findings suggested MBSR as an effective means for reducing stress, burnout, anxiety, and depression and improving mental well-being, self-compassion, and mindfulness traits among healthcare providers from different disciplines and settings. Similarly, Hazlett-Stevens et al. (2019) reviewed random control trials concerning the effectiveness of MBSR in older adults. Findings from this review point toward MBSR's positive outcomes for older adults striving to reduce sleep disturbances, reduce anxiety and depressive symptoms, improve executive function and memory, and increase positive affect. Sadooghiasl et al. (2022) implemented an MBSR study involving a randomized control trial exploring the mental well-being of COVID-19 patients. This study showed positive outcomes with patient well-being in areas related to "autonomy, mastery of the environment, personality development, positive relationships with others, purpose in life, and self-acceptance" (Sadooghiasl et al., 2022, p. 444). The authors suggested MBSR programs be included in conjunction with medical treatments for patients suffering from COVID-19. The aforementioned study and reviews of the body of research suggest MBSR programs maintain effective outcomes for individuals spanning various populations, demographics, and professional fields, instilling a sense of hope about its potential benefits.

Dialectical Behavior Therapy

Dialectical behavior therapy (DBT) was initially developed to treat borderline personality disorder and has shown significant success in this area (Linehan, 2015). While some counselors may not immediately recognize DBT as a mindfulness-based intervention, it incorporates core components of mindfulness practices, such as what and how skills. These skills are not just theoretical concepts but practical tools that guide clients toward greater self-awareness of the present, including detailed descriptions of feelings, emotions, objects, or themselves. How skills enable clients to develop mindfulness skills to effectively change negative responses to various experiences (Hunnicutt & Lenz, 2018). This process often involves the client learning to notice and accept a range of thoughts and emotions. For instance, journaling thoughts and emotions can help build inner self-awareness of the present moment.

DBT is also heavily based on building effective emotional self-regulation strategies, including mindfulness, interpersonal effectiveness, and distress tolerance skills (Linehan, 2015; Hunnicutt & Lenz, 2018). ***Emotion regulation*** is typically regarded as a person's ability to navigate daily stressors while effectively managing emotions and thus adhering to proper situational action or inaction (Clarke et al., 2020; Giordano et al., 2023).

Mindfulness-Based Cognitive Therapy

Mindfulness-based cognitive therapy (MBCT) purports substantial similarities with MBSR, as both are typically 8-week programs. In addition, MBCT and MBSR utilize the following techniques: meditation, psychoeducation, breath work, and physical movement, designed to assist clients with increasing present-moment awareness nonjudgmentally. However, MBCT goes a step further by incorporating cognitive therapy aspects centered around meta-consciousness increase while decreasing depressive thinking (Kraines et al., 2022). One key feature of MBCT is assisting individuals with becoming aware of continual negative thoughts and learning to identify such thoughts, thereby being able to accept these thoughts on a nonjudgmental plane (Hanssen et al., 2024; Kraines et al.,

2022; MacKenzie & Kocovski, 2016). Research has shown that like MBSR, MBCT also has applications with diverse populations and mental health issues.

MacKenzie and Kocovski (2016) reviewed current trends and developments in MBCT for depression, including efficacy, change mechanisms, and treatment-outcome moderators. Their review concluded there to be substantial efficacy for the use of MBCT with reduction of depressive thoughts. Furthermore, the authors concluded that mechanisms of change underlying MBCT include increased mindfulness, decreased negative repetitive thoughts, self-compassion, and cognitive reactivity. Similarly, Kraines et al. (2022) performed a systematic review of both MBSR and MBCT, investigating the cognitive outcomes of individuals with depression. Their findings show results varied across studies, with some showing significant improvements in specific cognitive functions post-treatment, while others did not find significant changes in cognitive measures. Whereas not all results yielded significant findings, the importance of these findings lies in understanding the impact of mindfulness-based interventions on cognitive functions in different populations with varying levels of depression symptoms. Hanssen et al. (2024) performed a study investigating potential treatment effect moderators concerning MBCT and positive psychology interventions (PPIs) with individuals having bipolar disorder.

Specifically, the study involved two multicenter randomized controlled trials focusing on exploring moderators of treatment effects of MBCT or PPI compared to treatment as usual (TAU) and MBCT compared to PPI on depressive symptoms and well-being in patients with bipolar disorder. Results showed the following variables increased response due to interventions, "higher baseline anxiety, lower well-being, lower levels of self-focused positive rumination, well-being, and self-compassion" (Hanssen et al., 2024, p. 79). Again, the above-mentioned body of research suggests MBCT is effectively utilized in various settings and with an assortment of mental health issues. These were a small example of the literature concerning MBCT, and students are encouraged to search deeper within the research to gain a complete understanding.

Yoga

Yoga has existed for over 3,500 years and mindfulness practices have their roots within yoga (Sadooghiasl et al., 2022). Primarily in Western society, Hatha yoga is the main form, encompassing several styles of yoga, focusing on breath work, movement, physical postures, and meditation, working to align the body physically, mentally, and spiritually (Capon et al., 2019). Research has shown benefits from using yoga in the form of improved mood and emotional self-regulation, as noted by Dossett et al. (2022), potentially due to activation of the parasympathetic nervous system. At this point, yoga has not been accepted as an evidence-based independent counseling method, but there is research suggesting yoga's utility in conjunction with or adjacent to evidence-based prac-

BearFotos/Shutterstock.com

tices such as cognitive behavior therapy (CBT). The following is a sample of research pertaining to legitimizing yoga's effectiveness with various mental health issues.

Capon et al. (2021) looked at the utilization of yoga adjunct with CBT, in their study involving 36 participants having depression and anxiety issues. Participants reported the use of yoga along with CBT had a tendency to enhance their experiences, with the study reporting improvements in areas such as critical evaluation of irrational thoughts and implementation of positive behavioral habits. Similarly, Deepeshwar and Kumar (2022) completed a study with participants in one group performing yoga and another group receiving counseling concerning stress for 2 weeks. The study reported significant decreases in anxiety and depression for the yoga group compared to the control group. Another study by Dossett et al. (2022) investigated yoga's effectiveness with patients having serious mental health issues and thus being admitted to psychiatric units. This study reported that yoga intervention participants experienced significant reductions in anxiety and improved feelings of mood post-yoga intervention, along with an increased ability for participants to calm themselves post-yoga. The use of yoga appears to have gained research traction for investigating effects concerning the mental well-being of clients, and clinicians are strongly encouraged to delve further into the body of research for themselves.

Ecotherapy

Prostock-studio/Shutterstock.com

Ecotherapy is essentially defined as using outdoor, within-nature interventions to improve individual psychological well-being (Wilson et al., 2008), thereby allowing counselors to think outside the confines of the traditional office setting. Ecotherapy uses natural settings to assist individuals in managing emotional self-regulation. Ecotherapy provides an avenue to solidify relationships in a positive and creative manner (Duffy et al., 2020; Richardson et al., 2020; Sackett, 2010; Tekavc, 2024) and is more than simply resolving an issue. As we take a brief look into a small sample of research, students are encouraged to explore how such a practice could be incorporated into various counseling settings. The following presented research explores the use of ecotherapy in an assortment of settings to include youth programs, counselor education, supervision, and integrative therapy.

In the study performed by Richardson et al. (2020), a number of youth from a YMCA program were given the opportunity to experience a nature-based program. The purpose was to investigate the effects of various outdoor environments on the well-being of the participants. The study's participants reported enhanced abilities with relationship formation, growth in self-worth, greater sense of self, and practical skills development. In another setting, Duffy et al. (2020) explored the ecotherapy experiences of several counselor-in-training and the impact on counselor development. Several of the participants' studies concluded that there was greater cohesiveness between their peers. It was also reported that participating in nature-based activities allowed the group to attain considerable realization surrounding their emotional, physical, and rational states within themselves. In a supervision setting, Tekavc (2024) utilized metaphors and symbolism within a nature-based supervision model on a weekly basis with her supervisees. Within her illustrations of supervision, each supervisee essentially arrived at their own conclusions or problem resolutions. Concerning sessions with clients, the author suggested using imagery in the office setting to build client/therapist rapport and then solidifying with nature-based real-time imagery (i.e., grounding exercise coupled with tactile stimuli). There appear to be an assortment of settings and populations in which ecotherapy could be beneficial and research of the subject matter continues to grow. Again, clinicians are encouraged to seek more research and explanations for any counseling modality they choose to practice; moving forward into the counseling field demands growth in all areas of counselor development and professional identity.

Mindfulness Practices

Mindful Breathing

Antonio Guillem/Shutterstock.com

Buddhist breath meditation includes 16 steps designed to cultivate both a broad mental state and focused attention, often using breath counting to strengthen concentration (Anālayo, 2019). In Hindu practices, breath is central to meditation (Green, 2008), while Zen Buddhism begins with focused attention on the breath, progressing to awareness of other bodily sensations to unify the mind and body, thus enhancing vitality (Ashton, 2023). In Indo-Tibetan traditions, yogic breathing is essential for health and spiritual growth, serving as both a meditative practice and preparation for deeper meditation.

Mindful breathing techniques are shown to alleviate symptoms of stress, depression, anxiety, and posttraumatic stress by calming the autonomic nervous system and promoting relaxation (Brown & Gerbarg, 2009; Brown et al., 2013; Cheng et al., 2019; Ma et al., 2017; Perciavalle et al., 2017). Engaging in deep breathing practices also contributes to overall mental health and well-being, supporting healthier lifestyle choices and behaviors (Melnyk et al., 2020). Furthermore, research indicates that these practices enhance cognitive performance by improving attention, mental clarity, and processing speed, making mindful breathing a versatile tool for both emotional and cognitive resilience (Soni et al., 2015).

Progressive Muscle Relaxation

siriratsavett/Shutterstock.com

Progressive muscle relaxation (PMR) is a technique that involves systematically tensing and then relaxing specific muscle groups to promote deep relaxation throughout the body. Tensing each muscle group briefly increases electrical activity, creating a contrast effect; upon release, muscle tension drops below baseline levels, leading to an enhanced state of relaxation. This method has been shown to not only achieve greater physiological relaxation (Toussaint et al., 2021) but also to significantly reduce symptoms of stress, anxiety, and depression, contributing to improved mental well-being and emotional resilience (Li et al., 2015; Merakou et al., 2019; Sepideh, 2012; Toussaint et al., 2021). PMR is commonly used in therapeutic settings and has proven to be a simple yet effective tool for both physical and psychological relaxation.

Visualization

Visualization involves mentally creating a safe, peaceful setting to induce calm and relaxation. This technique, often called guided imagery, has been shown to promote tranquility while effectively reducing stress and anxiety (Bennett, 2022; Margolin et al., 2011; Toussaint et al., 2021). In trauma treatment, visualization can also address sleep-related issues, helping to reduce insomnia and extend sleep duration, which are common challenges for individuals with posttraumatic stress (Aldahadha & Mustafa, 2022). By engaging the senses in a vividly imagined setting, visualization not only supports emotional regulation but also fosters a greater sense of control and safety, making it a valuable tool in therapeutic practices for stress and trauma recovery.

insta_photos/Shutterstock.com

Mindfulness Practice Examples

Progressive Muscle Relaxation

The following is an abbreviated example of what can be utilized within client sessions. Begin with instructing the client to sit in a position that is relaxing to them. This example will also incorporate the use of mindfulness breath work. It is encouraged for clients to use the breath work daily and progressive muscle relaxation a few times a week while lying in bed to enhance their ability to induce sleep.

1. Place yourself in a relaxing seated position and allow your arms to fall down to your side or in your lap as you close your eyes.
2. Slowly exhale all the air in your lungs through your mouth and then slowly breathe in through your nose, taking at least 6 to 7 seconds for the lungs to fill and, at the end, take a quick breath in. Hold for 1, 2, and 3, and exhale slowly through your mouth as though blowing through a straw.
3. Continue on your own, repeating the same breathing process as you breathe in. Begin tensing the facial muscles until they are tight at the last breath-in, hold for 1,2,3,4, and then exhale as before, allowing facial muscles to relax and allow the relaxation to run down through the body as you exhale.
4. As you breathe in, begin tensing your neck and shoulder muscles, as before they are tight at your last breath-in, and hold for 1,2,3,4, and again exhale slowly through your mouth. Remember blowing through a straw. Again, allow the relaxation to travel down through the body.

These steps are repeated with muscle groups in a descending order, ending with the feet. Typically clients report having an extreme relaxed and calming effect. There may also be appearances of being tired by evidence of yawning. Some clients have reported this exercise becoming foundational to their daily sleep hygiene.

Group Yoga Session

This is an abbreviated example of a group counseling yoga therapy (GCYT) session lasting approximately 20 to 25 minutes. The following is an example yoga flow.

The Yoga Flow

- Begin with mindfulness breathwork: 2 minutes
- Basic yoga poses (movements)
  - Right side of body: 5 to 7 minutes
- Group reflection period: 3 minutes
- Basic yoga poses (movements)

    - Left side of body: 5 to 7 minutes
- Ends with breathwork: 2 minutes
- Group reflection period – 3 minutes

The basic premise within this example is to start with breathwork to allow clients to begin to calm their body and travel toward a higher sense of emotional regulation ability. Then we move into simple Hatha yoga poses, which are typically slower-paced and more beginner-friendly, on one side of the body. There is then a period of group reflection where participants voice thoughts without prompts as in many counseling groups. Once this is concluded, the process is repeated in reverse starting with yoga poses to target the other side of the body and ending with group reflection.

This section does not qualify any mental health professional to use yoga in their individual or group practice. With the use of yoga, it is imperative and an ethical practice to ensure that any mental health professional wishing to implement yoga into individual or group counseling must be properly trained. The requirement for yoga education may vary depending on the level of delivery and job settings in which professionals work.

BearFotos/Shutterstock.com

Focused 5, 4, 3, 2, 1 Grounding Exercise

A typical grounding exercise involves using localized visualizations within the client's current environment, but a different approach includes the client utilizing visualizations of an imagined or real safe and calming place. This technique draws clients further out of their negative since they are visualizing their safe and calm place.

1. This part will begin the same as the progressive muscle relaxation, with the client sitting in a relaxing position and progressing through a few cycles of breath work with the eyes closed.
2. With the client partially relaxed and progressing through the breath work on their own, begin to visualize a safe and calming place. It does not matter if it is real or fantasy. Some people think of beaches, rivers, mountains, and so forth.

Dmytro Buianskyi/Shutterstock.com

3. Allow them a couple of breaths and then ask if they have a place in mind.
4. Have them take a deep breath in. As they exhale, have them say five things that they can see while they are there. (They will list five things.)
5. Have them take another breath in and as they exhale and say four things they can touch in that place. (They will list four things.)
6. Again, have them take in a breath and when they exhale, tell about three things they can hear in that place right now. (They will list three things.)
7. Continuing on and breathing, have them tell two things they can smell or taste in that safe and calm place as they breathe out. (They will list two things).
8. For the final breath, make it the slowest, longest, and deepest breath possible and hold for 1, 2, 3, 4. As they exhale, allow their relaxation to flow downward throughout their body.
9. At the conclusion, have them open their eyes and describe their thoughts and feelings.

The examples above are not an exhaustive list of the exact ways in which to implement mindfulness practices. Mindfulness practices are highly adaptive to individuals, groups, and practice needs.

Conclusion

To summarize, utilizing mindfulness interventions and practices is not merely limited to the aforementioned interventions but may be adaptable cross-theoretically and across vast counseling modalities. As mentioned earlier in this chapter, counselors-in-training and other mental health professionals must continue growing within their respective fields, as this may directly affect client care. Exploring an assortment of interventions and practices, of course, assists clients and may also provoke mental health professionals to practice self-care and well-being.

Personal Reflections

Where Were You When It Happened—David

Riding in the back of the ambulance, still on an adrenaline high, we were returning from a 911 call when I received the call where things began to change forever. My wife informed me she had seen an ENT (Ear, Nose, and Throat) doctor and, in the process of the visit, was given one of two possibilities: multiple sclerosis (MS) or a brain tumor. We both remember thinking at that moment, "God let it be MS," not knowing the type of evil MS actually becomes. The year was 2003, and I cannot recall the month, but it was hot enough for asphalt to have a liquid state in Texas, so likely July. Eventually, we both hung up the phone, and my heart was pounding; the feeling was as though I had been pummeled by a raging buffalo, and my breathing was erratic. A short time later, after the call, a fellow EMT noticed my emotional distress and walked me through focused deep breathing techniques and expressing gratitude for what I have. My first thought was, "This is bullshit," but I went along to at least entertain their muse, and surprisingly, it worked. This was my first recall of an introduction to mindfulness work, unrealized at the time, as it was a long road ahead before I began contemplating becoming a counselor or practicing yoga.

Currently, as a counselor, I employ a multitude of mindfulness-based practices on a daily to weekly basis. I have learned to be intentionally consistent with my practices, having essentially created an automatic response to daily life stressors. This intentionality has heightened my distress tolerance and outlook on life, and my family has commented on various times being grateful for the 180-degree change in attitude on many levels.

Personal Reflection—Sherry

As I have utilized these practices in counseling, I have learned to implement a rating scale both before and after mindfulness techniques. Clients often expect immediate and complete relief of symptoms, and anything less can be perceived as a failure. To address this, I use rating scales as a psychoeducational tool to facilitate realistic and achievable change. I ask clients to rate their symptoms on a scale from 1 to 10, where 1 represents *no symptoms*, and 10 represents the *worst imaginable symptoms*. The areas assessed include present pain level, muscle tension, irritability, depression, worry, anger, and stress level.

This method is grounded in the principles of cognitive-behavioral therapy, which underscores the importance of incremental progress and realistic goal-setting. By rating each area before and after mindfulness exercises, clients can observe gradual changes. Even a one-point reduction in any symptom area can be significant and provide relief. Clients often experience substantial alleviation of symptoms or at least notable improvements across multiple areas. The rating scale enables clients to recognize these improvements, validating the efficacy of mindfulness practices and helping them manage their expectations more effectively. Consistent use of the scale, with clear client education on its purpose, ensures reliable and meaningful data. Additionally, the insights gained from these ratings inform subsequent sessions and treatment plans, further enhancing the therapeutic process.

Personal Reflection—Michele

My own experience with mindfulness is now a significant part of my daily activity. I actually wait for the moments of silence to sit and reflect on two specific occasions. I often do this in the morning after my morning run and then again at night before I retreat to bed. Mindfulness provides so much clarity for me. As busy as we all are in this modern world, I think it is important to just "be." I will share two words that are very impactful for me during my mindfulness practice, "intentionality" and "gratitude." Sometimes I am intentional about being grateful, and other days I am grateful that I am intentional. When I speak of intentionality, I naturally find myself being grateful for the simple pleasures of my life: trees, health, silence, and even sleep. Looking back on my life, I feel as if I have been implementing mindfulness at an early age without even knowing that I was practicing it. I feel most at peace in my mind and body during times of silence, which provides a safe space for me to stop and reflect. I embrace and lean into the ability to just be in my own without any judgment, guidelines, rules, and complete acceptance. Mindfulness allows me to focus on what I am grateful for in my life without questioning the reasoning or logic behind every experience that I have and will continue to have on my life journey.

Case Study

Crystal, a 40-year-old marketing manager, has been experiencing significant stress for several weeks, largely due to ongoing staff conflicts at work. She reports tension between team members and a lack of support from her colleagues. Her work stress has started to spill over into her personal life, causing tension with her spouse and children, increased irritability, and major disruptions to her sleep, including bouts of insomnia. Feeling overwhelmed, Crystal sought counseling to better manage her stress. After the intake session, the counselor recommended mindfulness exercises to help Crystal regulate stress and enhance her overall well-being. Before starting these exercises, Crystal rated her initial symptoms as follows: pain 2, muscle tension 7, irritability 5, depression 6, worry 8, anger 6, and stress 10. Valuing a Christian perspective, she consented to incorporate it into the practice and selected specific statements to guide the exercises.

Counselor: OK. Let's begin. I want you to get as comfortable as you can with both feet on the floor. You can close your eyes if you feel comfortable. We will begin with Deep Breathing—as you breathe in, imagine your lungs are cups and you are filling them from the bottom, all the way to the top. And as you breathe out, empty your lungs completely. Breathe in, breathe out, breathe in, breathe out. As you are breathing in, say to yourself, Jesus Christ. As you breathe out, My Peace. Breathe in, Lead me beside quiet waters. Breathe out, Restore my soul. Breathe in, Jesus Christ. Breathe out, My Peace. Breathe in, Lead me beside quiet waters. Breathe out; restore my soul. Breathe in, Jesus Christ. Breathe out, My Peace. Breathe in, Lead me beside quiet waters. Breathe out; restore my soul. Breathe in, Jesus Christ. Breathe out, My Peace. Breathe in, Lead me beside quiet waters. Breathe out; restore my soul.

As you continue breathing deeply, I want you to tense the muscles in your feet as tight as you can and hold that. Notice how the muscles feel as they are tight. Take a deep breath in, and relax your feet, noticing how the muscles feel relaxed. Tense the muscles in your feet. Hold it. Deep breath in, and relax. Now tense the muscles in your legs and calves. Notice how the tension feels. Deep breath in, and relax. Noticing the difference between the tension and relaxation. Tense your legs and calves. Deep breath in, and relax. Now tighten the muscles in your abdomen, chest, and back. Pay attention to how the tension feels. Take a deep breath in, then release the tension as you exhale. Notice the contrast between the tension and relaxation. Tighten your abdomen, chest, and back again, take a deep breath, and relax. Tense the muscles in your arms and hands, and observe how the tension feels. Take a deep breath in, then let the tension go as you exhale. Feel the difference between the tightness and relaxation. Now, tense your arms and hands once more, breathe in deeply, and release. Tighten the muscles in your neck and shoulders, noticing the tension. Inhale deeply, then release the tension as you exhale. Feel the difference. Tighten your neck and shoulders again, take a deep breath in, and let go.

Now, choose the sensation you like the most: heavy, light, floating, warm, cool, or tingling. Imagine that sensation starting at the top of your head, filling your body with that feeling. Tension, stress, and worry are replaced by the pleasant sensation. This feeling moves down into your neck and shoulders, into your chest and back, removing pain and discomfort, and down into your arms; stress and tension leave your body out through your fingers. Finally, the sensation moves into your legs, and more stress and tension leave your body out through your toes, leaving that pleasant sensation and relaxation.

Now choose the emotion you prefer: calmness, joy, peace, or comfort. Imagine that emotion starting to fill up your heart. Once your heart is full of that pleasant emotion, it starts to overflow into the rest of you. That emotion fills your body and reaches your mind. The positive emotion covers over other negative emotions, leaving a peaceful heart, body, and mind.

Now imagine that your favorite-colored light is coming in through the top of your head and directing itself at the shape in your body. Let's pretend that the source of this light is energy: the more you see, the more you have available. The light directs itself at pain or a problem area and penetrates and permeates it, resonating and vibrating in and around it. As the light continues to direct itself to that area, you can then allow the light to come in and gently fill your entire head, easily and gently. Now allow it to descend through your neck, into your shoulders, and down your arms into your hands and out your fingertips. Now allow it to come down your neck and into the trunk of your body, easily and gently. Now allow it to descend through your legs, streaming down and flowing out your feet.

Your body is part of you, but your body is not the total you. You have feelings; they are part of you, but your feelings are not the total you. You are a thinking being; you have ideas, but your thoughts are not the total you. You have a center where all of these parts of you come together, a center of your being where you experience peace, wholeness, and strength; this center is an important part of you. In this center of yourself, think about all your strengths. (Pause). Think about the positive things in your life. (Pause). Praise yourself for your good work. (Pause).

Now imagine your favorite place. It can be real or made up. Maybe you are walking on the beach next to the waves, at the beginning of a quiet path in the woods or by a lake, in the crisp air of a majestic mountain retreat, a leaf floating down a river toward a quiet cove alone, at a wildlife preserve, hearing the birds sing, watching the animals at peace, or in a meadow surrounded by fragrant flowers. Wherever you are, you are completely safe, at peace, restful, and calm. As I count from 10 to 1, you walk through your peaceful place and become more relaxed, more at ease, more at peace, more of your stress and worry leaving. 10, 9, 8, 7, 6, 5, 4, 3, 2, 1—more deeply relaxed. In your place, look around you and see the colors of the animals or the trees. Smell the fragrance of the flowers or the crisp, clean air. Hear the sounds of the birds or the waves. Feel the wind on your face or the water on your hand. This is your place of refuge with God or alone. Completely relaxed.

As you are there in God's presence, notice you have a very heavy bag on your back. It is painful because it is so heavy. Your shoulders hurt. Your back hurts. You notice it is full of rocks. You take one rock out and you see written on it one of your worries. You notice it, acknowledge it, feel the heaviness of it. Then you give it to Jesus. You pull the next rock out and see another concern on it. You notice it, acknowledge it, feel the heaviness of it. Then you give it to Jesus. You continue to pull out rocks with different stressful images, emotions, worries, and thoughts, and you notice them, acknowledge them, and feel their heaviness. Then you hand each to Jesus until the bag is empty. Even though it is empty, you notice the bag itself is still heavy. You hand your bag to Jesus and he gives you his bag. An amazing thing happens when you put his bag on your back – instead of feeling weight from this new bag, you feel as though it is almost lifting you up. His bag is weightless and freeing.

You can return to this place anytime you need to feel refreshed, or you need to talk to God, or just to be still. Now as I count from 0 to 5, you take Jesus by the hand and walk with him from your special place back to here. With each count, you become more alert and refreshed. 0, 1, 2, 3, 4, 5. Alert and refreshed.

At the conclusion of the mindfulness exercises, Crystal rates her subsequent symptom levels as pain 1, muscle tension 1, irritability 1, depression 3, worry 2, anger 1, and stress 3.

Counselor: Do you see how all of your numbers went down? Even those that did not go down to 1 went down several points! In those exercises, we did deep breathing, progressive muscle relaxation (the tensing and releasing), progressive relaxation (pleasant sensation and emotion), light stream, centering, and visualization (favorite place). Which of those was your favorite or did you feel helped the most?

Crystal: The peaceful place.

Counselor: Did you have a second favorite?

Crystal: The floating.

Counselor: Any time you are stressed, you can take a deep breath and visit your favorite place. Or you can go to the bathroom, and spend a minute floating. You can do these almost anywhere and reduce your symptoms by at least a few points. Can you try this during the week?

Crystal: Yes! That was great. I haven't been this relaxed in several weeks! I even kind of liked the breathing prayer. Thank you!

Mindfulness Activity

Periodically, I have held sessions with clients outside, either just outside the clinic, at a hike and bike trail, or at a park. What I like to lead my clients through is a focused 5, 4, 3, 2, 1 grounding exercise. It is also important when working with clients outdoors that it is an appropriate environment; they understand that confidentiality cannot be guaranteed and reemphasize the boundaries of the professional relationship. The following is an example script:

1. Have the client initially stand in nature and guide them through a few deep breaths.
2. Instruct them to close their eyes and visualize everything they just saw walking to the meeting place.
3. With the client concentrating on their breath and this visualization, have them then open their eyes and name 5 things they can see.
4. Instruct them to again breathe in deep and then, after exhaling, name 4 things they can touch in nature and then have them touch those objects. Instruct them to then describe the feeling.
5. Again, the client will breathe in deeply and then instruct them to name 3 things they can hear in nature.
6. With the client focusing on breath, they then name 2 things they can either taste or smell in nature.
7. The 1 is for the client to close their eyes and visualize everything around them while taking in the longest breath possible, holding for at least 5 seconds, and as they exhale instruct them to relax their body moving from the neck down to the feet.
8. It is always good to have the client reflect on where their thoughts were before, during, and after the focused grounding exercise.

References

Aldahadha, B., & Bani Mustafa, M. (2022). Case Report: Visualization for treatment of insomnia, anxiety, and depression caused by PTSD. F1000Research, 11, 1155. https://doi.org/10.12688/f1000research.125801.1

Anālayo, B. (2019). Meditation on the breath: Mindfulness and focused attention. *Mindfulness, 10*, 1684–1691. https://doi.org/10.1007/S12671-019-01169-9

Anālayo, B. (2020). The centrality of mindfulness-related meditations in early Buddhist discourse. *Mindfulness*, 1–8. https://doi.org/10.1007/s12671-020-01381-y

Antonova, E., Schlosser, K., Pandey, R., & Kumari, V. (2021). Coping with COVID-19: Mindfulness-based approaches for mitigating mental health crisis. *Frontiers in Psychiatry*, *12*, 563417. https://doi.org/10.3389/fpsyt.2021.563417

Ashton, G. (2023). The somaesthetics of heaviness and Hara in Zen Buddhist meditation. *Poligrafi, 28*(111/112), 143–172. https://doi.org/10.35469/poligrafi.2023.397

Basham, A. L. (1991). *The origins and development of classical Hinduism*. Oxford University Press.

Bennett, J. (2022). Visual communication and mental health. *Visual Communication*, *22,* 46–70. https://doi.org/10.1177/14703572221130451

Bianchi, E. (2021). Revisiting Impurity in Republican China: An Evaluation of the Modern Rediscovery of Bujing guan 不淨觀. *Religions, 12*(10), 903. https://doi.org/10.3390/rel12100903

Bielefeldt, C. (1988). *Dogen's manuals of Zen meditation.* Ukraine: University of California Press. https://doi.org/10.2307/2719216

Bożek, A., Nowak, P., & Blukacz, M. (2020). The relationship between spirituality, health-related behavior, and psychological well-being. *Frontiers in Psychology*, *11*. https://doi.org/10.3389/fpsyg.2020.01997

Britannica, T. Editors of Encyclopaedia. (2017, August 24). *Jesus Prayer*. *Encyclopedia Britannica*. https://www.britannica.com/topic/Jesus-prayer

Brown, R., & Gerbarg, P. (2009). Yoga breathing, meditation, and longevity. *Annals of the New York Academy of Sciences*, 1172. https://doi.org/10.1111/j.1749-6632.2009.04394.x

Brown, R., Gerbarg, P., & Muench, F. (2013). Breathing practices for treatment of psychiatric and stress-related medical conditions. *The Psychiatric clinics of North America*, *36*(1), 121–140. https://doi.org/10.1016/j.psc.2013.01.001

Capon, H., O'Shea, M., Evans, S., & McIver, S. (2021). Yoga complements cognitive behaviour therapy as an adjunct treatment for anxiety and depression: Qualitative findings from a mixed-methods study. *Psychology & Psychotherapy: Theory, Research & Practice*, *94*(4), 1015–1035. https://doi-org.lib-e2.lib.ttu.edu/10.1111/papt.12343

Capon, H., O'Shea, M., & McIver, S. (2019). Yoga and mental health: A synthesis of qualitative findings. *Complementary Therapies in Clinical Practice*, *37*, 122–132. https://doi.org/10.1016/j.ctcp.2019.101063

Cheng, K., Croarkin, P., & Lee, P. (2019). Heart rate variability of various video-aided mindful deep breathing durations and its impact on depression, anxiety, and stress symptom severity. *Mindfulness*, 1–13. https://doi.org/10.1007/S12671-019-01178-8

Clarke, P. B., Lewis, T. F., Myers, J. E., Henson, R. A., & Hill, B. (2020). Wellness, emotion regulation, and relapse during substance use disorder treatment. *Journal of Counseling & Development*, *98*(1), 17–28. https://doi.org/10.1002/jcad.12296

Coronado-Montoya, S., Levis, A. W., Kwakkenbos, L., Steele, R. J., Turner, E. H., & Thombs, B. D. (2016). Reporting of positive results in randomized controlled trials of mindfulness-based mental health interventions. *PloS one*, *11*(4), e0153220. https://doi.org/10.1371/journal.pone.0153220

Deepeshwar, S. & Kumar, D. (2022). Beneficial effect of yoga-based lifestyle intervention on anxiety and depression in young adults: Non-randomized controlled study. *International Journal of Medicine & Public Health, 12*(1), 12–19. https://doi.org/10.5530/ijmedph.2022.1.3

Dossett, A., Smith, A., Gingerich, M. K., & Cullen, L. (2022). An evidence-based yoga practice for hospitalized adults on medical–psychiatric units. *American Journal of Nursing*, *122*(7), 28–36. https://doi.org/10.1097/01.NAJ.0000840304.76501.96

Duffy, J. T., Springer, S., Delaney, M., & Luke, M. (2020). Eco-education: Integrating nature into counselor education. *Journal of Creativity in Mental Health*, *15*(1), 55–68. https://doi.org/10.1080/15401383.2019.1640152

Dye, L., Burke, M. G., & Wolf, C. (2019). Teaching mindfulness for the self-care and well-being of counselors-in-training. *Journal of Creativity in Mental Health, 15*(2), 140–153. https://doi.org/10.1080/15401383.2019.1642171

Ewert, C., Vater, A., & Schröder-Abé, M. (2021). Self-compassion and coping: A meta-analysis. *Mindfulness*, *12*, 1063–1077. https://doi.org/10.1007/s12671-020-01563-8

Figley, C. R. (2002). Compassion fatigue: Psychotherapists' chronic lack of self care. *Journal of Clinical Psychology, 58*(11), 1433–1441. https://doi.org/10.1002/jclp.10090

Galante, J., Friedrich, C., Dawson, A. F., Modrego-Alarcon, M., Gebbing, P., Delgado-Suarez, I., Gupta, R., Dead, L., Dalgleish, T., White, I. R., & Jones, P. B. (2021). Mindfulness-based programmes for mental health promotion in adults in nonclinical settings: A systematic review and meta-analysis of randomized controlled trials. *PLoS Medicine, 18*(1), e1003481. https://doi.org/10.1371/journal.pmed.1003481

Gál, É., Ștefan, S., & Cristea, I. A. (2021). The efficacy of mindfulness meditation apps in enhancing users' well-being and mental health related outcomes: A meta-analysis of randomized controlled trials. *Journal of Affective Disorders*, *279*, 131–142. https://doi.org/10.1016/j.jad.2020.09.134

Garssen, B., Visser, A., & Pool, G. (2020). Does spirituality or religion positively affect mental health? Meta-analysis of longitudinal studies. *The International Journal for the Psychology of Religion*, *31*, 4–20. https://doi.org/10.1080/10508619.2020.1729570

Giordano, A. L., Schmidt M. K., & McCall J. (2023). Exploring adolescent social media and internet gaming addiction: The role of emotion regulation. *Journal of Addictions & Offender Counseling. 44*(1), 69–80. https://doi.org/10.1002/jaoc.12116

Green, N. (2008). Breathing in India, c. 1890. *Modern Asian Studies, 42*, 283–315. https://doi.org/10.1017/S0026749X07003125

Griffiths, P., & Gregory, P. (1988). Traditions of meditation in Chinese Buddhism. *The Journal of Asian Studies, 47*, 595–596. https://doi.org/10.2307/2056996

Hadzic, M. (2011). Spirituality and mental health: Current research and future directions. *Journal of Spirituality in Mental Health, 13*, 223–235. https://doi.org/10.1080/19349637.2011.616080

Hannabuss, S. (2021). Spirituality and mental health across cultures. *Journal of Mental Health, 31*, 445–446. https://doi.org/10.1093/med/9780198846833.001.0001

Hanssen, I., ten Klooster, P., Kraiss, J., Huijbers, M., Regeer, E., Kupka, R., Bohlmeijer, E., & Speckens, A. (2024). Predicting which intervention works better for whom: Moderators of treatment effect of mindfulness-based cognitive therapy and positive psychology intervention in patients with bipolar disorder. *Journal of Affective Disorders, 360*, 79–87. https://doi.org/10.1016/j.jad.2024.05.110

Hazlett-Stevens, H., Singer, J., & Chong, A. (2019). Mindfulness-based stress reduction and mindfulness-based cognitive therapy with older adults: A qualitative review of randomized controlled outcome research. *Clinical Gerontologist, 42*(4), 347–358. https://doi.org/10.1080/07317115.2018.1518282

Henriksen, D., Richardson, C., & Shack, K. (2020). Mindfulness and creativity: Implications for thinking and learning. *Thinking Skills and Creativity, 37*, 100689. https://doi.org/10.1016/j.tsc.2020.100689

Hunnicutt Hollenbaugh, K. M., & Lenz, A. S. (2018). An examination of the effectiveness of dialectical behavior therapy skills groups. *Journal of Counseling & Development, 96*(3), 233–242. https://doi.org/10.1002/jcad.12198

Kabat-Zinn, J. (2003). Mindfulness-based interventions in context: Past, present, and future. *Clinical Psychology: Science and Practice, 10*(2), 144–156.

Kraines, M. A., Peterson, S. K., Tremont, G. N., Beard, C., Brewer, J. A., & Uebelacker, L. A. (2022). Mindfulness-based stress reduction and mindfulness-based cognitive therapy for depression: A systematic review of cognitive outcomes. *Mindfulness, 13*(5), 1126–1135. https://doi.org/10.1007/s12671-022-01841-7

Kriakous, S. A., Elliott, K. A., Lamers, C., & Owen, R. (2021). The effectiveness of mindfulness-based stress reduction on the psychological functioning of healthcare professionals: A systematic review. *Mindfulness, 12*(1), 1–28. https://doi.org/10.1007/s12671-020-01500-9

Lau, N. (2021). Teaching transnational Buddhist meditation with vipassanā and mindfulness for healing depression in contemporary China. *Religion, 12*, 212. https://doi.org/10.3390/REL12030212

Li, Y., Wang, R., Tang, J., Chen, C., Tan, L., Wu, Z., Yu, F., & Wang, X. (2015). Progressive muscle relaxation improves anxiety and depression of pulmonary arterial hypertension patients. *Evidence-Based Complementary and Alternative Medicine: eCAM, 2015*, 1–8. https://doi.org/10.1155/2015/792895

Linehan, M. M. (2015). *DBT skills training manual* (2nd ed.). Guilford Press. Kindle Edition.

Ma, X., Yue, Z., Gong, Z., Zhang, H., Duan, N., Shi, Y., Wei, G., & Li, Y. (2017). The effect of diaphragmatic breathing on attention, negative affect and stress in healthy adults. *Frontiers in Psychology*, *8*. https://doi.org/10.3389/fpsyg.2017.00874

MacKenzie, M. B., & Kocovski, N. L. (2016). Mindfulness-based cognitive therapy for depression: Trends and developments. *Psychology Research and Behavior Management*, *2016*(9), 125–132. https://doi.org/10.2147/PRBM.S63949

Margolin, I., Pierce, J., & Wiley, A. (2011). Wellness through a creative lens: Meditation and visualization. *Journal of Religion & Spirituality in Social Work: Social Thought*, *30*, 234–252. https://doi.org/10.1080/15426432.2011.587385

Melnyk, B., Kelly, S., Stephens, J., Dhakal, K., McGovern, C., Tucker, S., Hoying, J., McRae, K., Ault, S., Spurlock, E., & Bird, S. (2020). Interventions to improve mental health, well-being, physical health, and lifestyle behaviors in physicians and nurses: A systematic review. *American Journal of Health Promotion*, *34*, 929–941. https://doi.org/10.1177/0890117120920451

Merakou, K., Tsoukas, K., Stavrinos, G., Amanaki, E., Daleziou, A., Kourmousi, N., Stamatelopoulou, G., Spourdalaki, E., & Barbouni, A. (2019). The effect of progressive muscle relaxation on emotional competence: Depression–anxiety–stress, sense of coherence, health-related quality of life, and well-being of unemployed people in Greece: An intervention study. *The Journal of Science and Healing*, *15*, 38–46. https://doi.org/10.1016/j.explore.2018.08.001

Milner, K., Crawford, P., Edgley, A., Hare-Duke, L., & Slade, M. (2019). The experiences of spirituality among adults with mental health difficulties: A qualitative systematic review. *Epidemiology and Psychiatric Sciences*, *29*. https://doi.org/10.1017/S2045796019000234

Molleur, J. (2011). A Hindu monk's appreciation of Eastern Orthodoxy's Jesus prayer: The "inner senses" of hearing, seeing, and feeling in comparative perspective. In T. Cattoi & J. McDaniel (Eds.), *Perceiving the divine through the human body*. Palgrave Macmillan. https://doi.org/10.1057/9780230339767_2

Moreira-Almeida, A., Koenig, H., & Lucchetti, G. (2014). Clinical implications of spirituality to mental health: Review of evidence and practical guidelines. *Revista Brasileira de Psiquiatria*, *36*(2), 176–182. https://doi.org/10.1590/1516-4446-2013-1255

Nash, J. (2019, May 27). *The history of meditation: Its origins & timeline*. PositivePsychology.Com. https://positivepsychology.com/history-of-meditation/

Neff, K. D. (2023). Self-compassion: Theory, method, research, and intervention. *Annual Review of Psychology*, *74*(1), 193–218. https://doi.org/10.1146/annurev-psych-032420-031047

Niculescu, M. (2015). Going online and taking the plane from San Francisco to Jerusalem. The physical and electronic networks of "Jewish Mindfulness." *Online-Heidelberg Journal of Religions on the Internet*, *8*. https://doi.org/10.11588/REL.2015.0.20326

Niculescu, M. (2017). Boundary crossers. The "Jewish Buddhists" and Judaism's symbolic boundaries in a global age. *Archives Des Sciences Sociales Des Religions*, 157–175. https://doi.org/10.4000/ASSR.29318

Niculescu, M. (2019). "Jewish Mindfulness" as spiritual didactics teaching Orthodox Jewish religion through mindfulness meditation. *Religion*, *11*, 11. https://doi.org/10.3390/rel11010011

Paramahamsa, K. R. (2007). *The philosophy of the Upanisads.* TotalRecall Publishing..

Perciavalle, V., Blandini, M., Fecarotta, P., Buscemi, A., Corrado, D., Bertolo, L., Fichera, F., & Coco, M. (2017). The role of deep breathing on stress. *Neurological Sciences*, *38*, 451–458. https://doi.org/10.1007/s10072-016-2790-8

Persico, T. (2022). Studying Jewish meditative techniques: A phenomenological typology and an interdisciplinary view. *Religions*, *13*(7), 648. https://doi.org/10.3390/rel13070648

Posluns, K., & Gall, T. L. (2019). Dear mental health practitioners, take care of yourselves: A literature review on self-care. *International Journal for the Advancement of Counseling*, *42*(1), 1–20. https://doi.org/10.1007/s10447-019-09382-w

Richardson, M., Richardson, E., Hallam, J., & Ferguson, F. J. (2020). Opening doors to nature: Bringing calm and raising aspirations of vulnerable young people through nature-based intervention. *Humanistic Psychologist*, *48*(3), 284–297. https://doi.org/10.1037/hum0000148

Sadooghiasl, A., Ghalenow, H. R., Mahinfar, K., & Hashemi, S. S. (2022). Effectiveness of mindfulness-based stress reduction program in improving mental well-being of patients with COVID-19: A randomized controlled trial. *Indian Journal of Critical Care Medicine*, *26*(4), 441–447. https://doi.org/10.5005/jp-journals-10071-24164

Sackett, C. (2010). Ecotherapy: A counter to society's unhealthy trend? *Journal of Creativity in Mental Health*, *5*(2), 134–141. https://doi.org/10.1080/15401383.2010.485082

Scott, L. (2002). A mystical explanation of the real historical Jesus. *Religion*, *32*, 273–276. https://doi.org/10.1006/reli.2002.0425

Sedlmeier, P., Eberth, J., Schwarz, M., Zimmermann, D., Haarig, F., Jaeger, S., & Kunze, S. (2012). The psychological effects of meditation: A meta-analysis. *Psychological Bulletin, 138*(6), 1139–1171. https://doi.org/10.1037/a0028168

Sharma, H. (2015). Meditation: Process and effects. *AYU, 36*, 233–237.

Shapiro, S. L., Carlson, L. E., Astin, J. A., & Freedman, B. (2006). Mechanisms of mindfulness. *Journal of Clinical Psychology*, *62*(3), 373–386. https://doi.org/10.1002/jclp.20237

Shaw, S. (2021, August 31). Buddhist meditation and contemplation. *Oxford Research Encyclopedia of Religion.* Retrieved 18 Feb. 2025, from https://oxfordre.com/religion/view/10.1093/acrefore/9780199340378.001.0001/acrefore-9780199340378-e-571

Soni, S., Joshi, L., & Datta, A. (2015). Effect of controlled deep breathing on psychomotor and higher mental functions in normal individuals. *Indian Journal of Physiology and Pharmacology*, *59*(1), 41–47.

Sepideh, H., Irah, A., Isa, P., Mehri, G., Reza, S., & Zohreh, S. (2012). Efficacy of progressive muscle relaxation training on anxiety, depression and quality of life in cancer patients undergoing chemotherapy at Tabriz Hematology and Oncology Research Center, Iran in 2010. *Middle East Journal of Cancer, 3*(1), 9–13.

Tekavc, M. Z. (2024). Nature in integrative psychotherapy and supervision. *International Journal of Integrative Psychotherapy*, *14*, 15–25. http://www.integrative-journal.com/index.php/ijip/article/view/332/144

Tomasino, B., Chiesa, A., & Fabbro, F. (2014). Disentangling the neural mechanisms involved in Hinduism- and Buddhism-related meditations. *Brain and Cognition*, *90*, 32–40. https://doi.org/10.1016/j.bandc.2014.03.013

Toussaint, L., Nguyen, Q., Roettger, C., Dixon, K., Offenbächer, M., Kohls, N., Hirsch, J., & Sirois, F. (2021). Effectiveness of progressive muscle relaxation, deep breathing, and guided imagery in promoting psychological and physiological states of relaxation. *Evidence-Based Complementary and Alternative Medicine: eCAM*, 2021. https://doi.org/10.1155/2021/5924040

Verghese, A. (2008). Spirituality and mental health. *Indian Journal of Psychiatry*, *50*, 233–237. https://doi.org/10.4103/0019-5545.44742

Weber, S., & Pargament, K. (2014). The role of religion and spirituality in mental health. *Current Opinion in Psychiatry*, *27*, 358–363. https://doi.org/10.1097/YCO.0000000000000080

Wernicke-Olesen, B. (2019). *Hinduism and meditation: Yoga.* Oxford University Press. https://doi.org/10.1093/oxfordhb/9780198808640.013.5

Wilson, N. W., Ross, M. K., Lafferty, K., & Jones, R. (2008). A review of ecotherapy as an adjunct form of treatment for those who use mental health services. *Journal of Public Mental Health*, *7*(3), 23–35. https://www.proquest.com/scholarly-journals/review-ecotherapy-as-adjunct-form-treatment-those/docview/212398675/se-2

Yuniarwati, Ardana, I. C., & Dewi, S. P. (2020). The Impact of meditation on the spiritual well-being. *Proceedings of the Tarumanagara International Conference on the Applications of Social Sciences and Humanities (TICASH 2019).* Tarumanagara International Conference on the Applications of Social Sciences and Humanities (TICASH 2019), Barat, Indonesia. https://doi.org/10.2991/assehr.k.200515.034

Traumatic Brain Injury: Positive Psychology and Mindfulness

3

Michele M. Mahr
Connie Mancera
Aldo Juarez
Anna Osipova

KEYWORDS AND DEFINITIONS:

Biopsychosocial model: The biopsychosocial model is an approach to understanding mental and physical health through a multi-systems lens, understanding the influence of biology, psychology, and social environment.

Blast brain injury: A blast-induced traumatic brain injury is caused by a complex pressure wave generated by an explosion.

Closed brain injury: This type of injury occurs when an external force impacts the head without penetrating the skull.

Open brain injury: This type of injury involves an object penetrating the skull which could cause damage to the areas surrounding the penetration site.

Spirituality: Spirituality is a worldview that suggests a dimension to life beyond what we experience on the sensory and physical levels.

LEARNING OBJECTIVES:

1. Identify the types of traumatic brain injuries (TBI), etiology, repercussions of injury, and severity levels
2. Be able to conceptualize TBI within the biopsychosocial model of well-being
3. Conceptualize how Positive Psychology can be applied to working with individuals with TBI
4. Learn how Mindfulness can be a viable treatment option solely or with other modalities when treating individuals with TBI

Overview of Traumatic Brain Injury

A traumatic brain injury (TBI) happens when an external force impacts the head with enough force that bypasses the brain's ability to protect itself, resulting in possible physical damage to the central nervous system (CNS) and further neurological issues (Borlongan et al., 2015). The severity of TBIs can depend on the type and effect, affecting an individual's cognitive, physical, and emotional health. TBI is a critical public health issue not only in the United States but also worldwide and contributes greatly to both mortality and long-term disabilities. According to the Centers for Disease Control and Prevention (CDC, 2024), there are over 214,000 hospitalizations and approximately 70,000 deaths related to TBI annually in the United States alone. Globally, around "64–74 million people sustain a TBI each year" (CDC, 2024; Haarbauer-Krupa et al., 2021). The economic burden is high when it comes to TBI, with costs exceeding $80 billion in the United States, due to covering healthcare expenses, productivity loss, and long-term care that may be required (Vella et al., 2017). Additionally, Zollman (2016) highlights that beyond immediate medical expenses, TBI affects long-term rehabilitation, social reintegration, and family dynamics, displaying impact in multiple areas of life.

Stigma associated with TBI can have profound effects on an individual's psychological health and their place in society. People with a TBI experience "invisible" impairments, such as cognitive and behavioral changes, which can lead to a lack of understanding from others, contributing to social stigma (Krahn, 2015). The stigma can manifest in a variety of ways, which may include enacted stigma (discriminatory attitudes and behaviors from others), and internalized stigma, developed when individuals accept negative societal attitudes about themselves. Ownsworth et al. (2024) also discuss how early post-injury stigma, particularly in the first year after the injury, can hinder community integration and exacerbate psychological distress that can have long-term consequences for social functioning.

A study by Simpson et al. (2011) highlighted how stigma may increase feelings of hopelessness in TBI patients, which adds to severe psychological outcomes, including increased risk for depression and even suicidal ideation. The difficulties of these effects necessitate supportive interventions to address stigma and foster positive community engagement. Tackling stigma as soon as possible could be essential for improving mental health and reducing barriers to social participation for TBI survivors. Moreover, misconceptions surrounding TBI, such as beliefs that recovery depends only on effort, are seen across various demographics, and this can hinder proper understanding and treatment (Block et al., 2016). Addressing the misconceptions by educating and spreading the word, as well as clinical guidance, can help reshape attitudes toward TBI management and recovery. Social anxiety and stigma are important issues when an individual reintegrates into their adjusted life after a TBI and can impact one's psychological health, thus making a positive support system essential (Curvis et al., 2018).

Many rehabilitation approaches can be used when helping someone with a TBI. Positive psychology is one approach that offers valuable strategies for supporting individuals with TBI by focusing on resilience, hope, and acceptance. Martz and Livneh (2016) mention that positive psychological constructs such as optimism as well as resilience play crucial roles in adapting to life with a disability and the changes that come with focusing on a strength-based perspective. Rauwenhoff et al. (2023) illustrate the use of Acceptance and Commitment Therapy (ACT) in helping patients with acquired brain injuries accept difficult emotions and engage with their values in a meaningful way, rather than resisting or avoiding these experiences. Furthermore, Bombardier et al. (2016) highlight the importance of addressing depression early post-TBI and emphasize that fostering hope and adopting proactive coping strategies can help reduce depressive symptoms over time. Positive psychology can contribute an empowering foundation, encouraging TBI patients to cultivate inner strengths, maintain hope, and find personal growth, regardless of their injuries.

Common Causes of TBI

Although there are many possible ways to acquire a TBI, some ways are more common than others. This section aims to discuss common types of TBI. Falls are the leading cause of TBI, especially among older adults and young children, and account for 35% of nonfatal TBIs in the United States (Nizamutdinov & Shapiro, 2017). Road traffic accidents represent approximately 17% of TBIs and are more common among adolescents and young adults aged 15 to 24 (Nizamutdinov & Shapiro, 2017). TBIs commonly known as concussions are frequently seen in contact sports like football, boxing, or soccer, particularly for younger individuals (Clark & Guskiewicz, 2016). Although concussions might not seem detrimental at first, Pavlovic et al. (2019) highlight that repeated mild TBIs in sports can lead to long-term neurocognitive and behavioral effects, which are linked to diffuse axonal injury, a condition where the brain turns inside the skull and axons are torn. Blast injuries are another type of TBI for which military personnel are at higher risk. This TBI is caused by the exposure to explosions, and the blast injuries account for a significant percentage of TBIs in combat zones (Falvo & Holland, 2018).

In addition to the abovementioned leading causes of TBI, domestic violence has been recently discussed as a critical but under-recognized cause of TBIs, particularly in women. Research indicates that up to 92% of physical assaults in intimate partner violence (IPV) involve the head, face, or neck, which raises the risk of TBI in this context (Colantonio & Valera, 2022). These injuries can occur through strangulation, blows to the head, or falls, which can lead to both acute and long-term cognitive and psychological impairments, including depression and posttraumatic stress disorder (PTSD) (Costello & Greenwald, 2022). It is really alarming that the prevalence of IPV-related TBI is estimated to be 11 to 12 times higher than the combined occurrence of TBIs in athletes and military personnel (Costello & Greenwald, 2022).

Socioeconomic status (SES) has also been researched to play a role in TBI risk and outcomes of post-preventative care. Research shows that lower SES has a higher correlation with experiencing TBI due to such risk factors as unsafe housing conditions, limited access to healthcare, and increased exposure to violence (Johnson & Diaz, 2023). The data also show that children from lower-SES households experience higher rates of TBIs and that their TBIs are of greater severity, often associated with longer hospital stays, more complications, and even increased mortality rates (Salik et al., 2022). Disparities in healthcare access and post-injury support exacerbate the long-term consequences of TBIs and have been shown to disproportionately affect marginalized groups (Crozes et al., 2024). Addressing these disparities through targeted healthcare interventions and policy reforms is an essential task to improving outcomes for the at-risk populations.

Types of TBI

TBIs are categorized by different types of injury, features, as well as severity, which is important in choosing appropriate treatment and rehabilitation strategies. A **closed head type of injury** occurs when an external force impacts the head without penetrating the skull. Common causes include motor vehicle accidents, falls, and sports activities. These injuries commonly result in widespread brain damage, affecting multiple regions of the brain (Ng & Lee, 2019). An **open or penetrating injury** involves an object penetrating the skull, which could cause damage to the surrounding areas (Ashina et al., 2021). Common causes include gunshot wounds, collision with sharp objects, or severe accidents. It is important to note that open injuries can lead to more severe complications and carry a higher risk of infection (Harrington et al., 2020). A **blast injury** is common among military personnel exposed to explosive devices, and Falvo and Holland (2018) noted that blast-related TBIs have become a distinct category in recent years.

Severity of TBI

The Glasgow Coma Scale (GCS) is the standard tool for assessing the severity of TBIs.

A mild TBI (mTBI) has a GCS score of 13 to 15. Mild TBIs represent about 58% to 88% of all TBI cases (Sussman et al., 2018). Although often seen as less severe due to the word "mild," the CDC suggests that mTBI involves brief confusion, disorientation, or loss of consciousness lasting less than 30 minutes (Pavlovic et al., 2019). Additionally, Sussman et al. (2018) and Wilson et al. (2017) discuss the importance of accurately diagnosing and treating mild TBIs, since many cases are overlooked, especially when symptoms are subtle.

A moderate TBI is characterized by a GCS score of 9 to 12. Moderate TBIs can result in significant neurological impairments, including confusion, memory loss, and potential physical deficits (Siebold et al., 2018). **Severe TBIs** have a GCS score of 3 to 8 and commonly lead to long-term or permanent disabilities. Severe TBIs may cause long moments of unconsciousness, comas, and at times even death. Capizzi et al. (2020) note that understanding the severity of TBI is crucial for predicting functional recovery and planning rehabilitation of an individual who has suffered this type of injury. Zollman (2016) emphasizes the need for personalized, multidisciplinary approaches to treatment for severe TBI, including a combination of not only physical rehabilitation but also cognitive and emotional support that may be needed to adjust to significant life changes.

Primary and Secondary Injuries

The effects of TBI can sometimes remain after the initial primary injury, with secondary injuries posing big risks to long-term recovery. A primary injury occurs at the moment of impact and results from the external force on the brain, often causing immediate damage, such as contusions, hemorrhages, or skull fractures (Galgano et al., 2017). On the other hand, secondary injuries develop over time, from minutes to days following the initial trauma, and can lead to other risks such as inflammation, oxidative stress, and excitotoxicity exacerbating brain damage (Galgano et al., 2017). Borlongan et al. (2015) **suggest that** the extended inflammatory response can contribute to long-term neurodegenerative changes and emphasize that early intervention is important to reduce secondary damage. Secondary injuries result in widespread effects that may be anywhere in the brain. Inflammation and oxidative stress not only affect the brain but can also lead to complications in peripheral organs (Sabet et al., 2021). TBI can also lead to chronic issues across cardiovascular, renal, and endocrine systems, which can complicate recovery and contribute to poor health outcomes.

TBI survivors are at increased risk for developing chronic conditions such as cardiovascular disease, diabetes, and mental health disorders. Izzy et al. (2023) found that TBI accelerates the risk of hypertension and diabetes, which usually occur within a few years post-injury. Moreover, Livingston et al. (2020) linked TBI to an increased risk of dementia and suggested that TBI can result in comorbid conditions such as depression and diabetes. Behavioral disturbances following a TBI can further complicate recovery. According to Timmer et al. (2020), approximately 50% to 60% of survivors experience issues such as irritability and disinhibition, which interfere with rehabilitation and long-term outcomes. These adverse post-TBI conditions highlight the importance of addressing both physical and psychological aspects of recovery.

Prevention is central to reducing the burden of secondary injuries and associated complications. Maas and colleagues (2022) emphasized that timely interventions and structured follow-ups, particularly after mild TBI, can improve recovery trajectories and reduce long-term complications. Public health initiatives targeting modifiable risk factors (e.g., promoting helmet use and reducing falls) can significantly lower TBI incidence (Fatuki et al., 2020).

Post-TBI survivors often engage in behaviors that exacerbate their vulnerability to further injury. Substance use disorder (SUD), while addressed more fully in the next section, is particularly concerning. Dams-O'Connor et al. (2023) identified SUD as a frequent issue in younger survivors, complicating the already significant challenges posed by secondary injuries. Additionally, Izzy et al. (2023) found that poor lifestyle behaviors post-TBI, such as physical inactivity and unhealthy diets, increase the risk of comorbid cardiovascular conditions.

TBI and SUD

It is important for counselors to recognize that TBI often contributes to the development of SUD due to the cognitive and emotional challenges that follow such injuries. As individuals with TBI experience impaired executive functioning, emotional regulation, and cognitive abilities, they are more likely to turn to substances as a coping mechanism (Chan et al., 2022). Studies have shown that a significant proportion of individuals with TBI develop substance use patterns, with one inpatient trauma center reporting that SUDs affect between 37% and 66% of TBI patients (Olsen & Corrigan, 2022). Moreover, the relationship between TBI and substance use is complex, as TBI can either precede SUDs or be a consequence of risky behaviors like intoxication, which increase the likelihood of sustaining a TBI (Weil et al., 2018).

Moreover, TBI can damage brain regions involved in impulse control and emotional regulation, which increases vulnerability to SUD. For instance, Howlett et al. (2022) highlight that TBI often results in affective symptoms, such as impulsivity and emotional instability, which contribute to substance misuse as a maladaptive coping strategy. Additionally, Cannella et al. (2019) found that early-life TBI disrupts the development of the brain's reward pathways, making adolescents who experienced TBI especially susceptible to SUD later in life. With this understanding, it's important to acknowledge how the structural and functional changes affect behavior when treating someone with these co-occurring conditions.

Sociodemographic factors, including race, age, and socioeconomic background, play a crucial role in the TBI–SUD relationship. For instance, Rosenthal et al. (2023) reported that young adults with TBI, especially those in minority groups, are at higher risk for substance misuse, with disparities in access to treatment further exacerbating this risk after a TBI. Jones et al. (2020) also highlighted that individuals in precarious housing or homelessness often face "trimorbidity" (mental health issues, substance use, and physical illness), which can further elevate the risk of TBI and subsequent SUD in these vulnerable populations. It is important to note the bidirectionality of the relationship between TBI and SUD. Eskander et al. (2020) discussed the bidirectional relationship between alcohol use disorder and TBI, noting that individuals with TBI are not only at higher risk of developing substance misuse but may also have poorer rehabilitation outcomes due to the compounding effects of SUD on cognitive recovery. Furthermore, Oliverio et al. (2020) note gender-based differences in the causes and impacts of TBI, such as IPV in women and sports-related injuries in men, which create distinct pathways to substance misuse.

Positive Psychology and TBI

Traditionally, interventions for TBI include methods such as physical rehabilitation, attention training, cognitive behavioral therapy (CBT), and mindfulness to improve the immediate and long-term outcomes stemming from TBI (Sharma, 2018). Some of the adverse effects from TBI include post-traumatic amnesia of which 70% of individuals report experiencing symptoms such as confusion, agitation, and lack of attention and self-awareness (Cho & Jang, 2021). Due to these adverse outcomes, individuals can face challenges engaging in meaningful activity, in feeling a sense of contribution to society, and in their overall life satisfaction (Payne et al., 2018). Although interventions address physical and cognitive symptoms associated with TBI and during recovery, not enough attention is directed to the psychosocial aspect of recovering and managing the long-term symptoms from TBI. In this context, positive psychology approaches can effectively address these existing gaps.

Positive psychology is defined as the scientific study of positive experiences and positive individual traits and is characterized as a field that is concerned with well-being and optimal functioning (Lee Duckworth et al., 2005). In a clinical setting, positive psychology is especially advantageous because it acts as a buffer against the impact of negative life events and promotes resilience. Positive psychology can potentially prevent the development of post-TBI disorders, and it can be fostered to treat clinical disorders (Wood & Tarrier, 2010). Posttraumatic growth (PTG) and its correlation with positive psychology are impactful in highlighting the benefits that positive psychology can have for individuals with TBI. Research shows that PTG is positively linked to themes bolstered through positive psychology, including personal meaning, life satisfaction, experiencing major life events, social support, and optimism (Martz & Livneh, 2016).

There are many positive psychology techniques that can be used in the population of individuals who have sustained TBI. For example, fostering resilience is a technique that can support individuals post-injury in creating a buffer against the traumatic aftermath of their injury and shifting the individual's focus on their well-being and quality of life. Research has shown that individuals with mild to severe brain injury can benefit from techniques such as learning resilience, as it can dramatically shape the course of rehabilitation for the client (Rapport et al., 2019).

Other researched positive psychology techniques for individuals with TBI include adaptive coping, positive affect, hope, and optimism (Rabinowitz & Arnett, 2018). The aftermath of TBI can be harrowing for individuals and their families. Even with appropriate medical intervention, individuals post-injury may face permanent damage to their cognitive, emotional, and physical health. Rabinowitz and Arnett (2018) found that higher levels of adaptive coping predict better psychosocial functioning after injury.

Although additional research is needed to further gauge the level of impact positive psychology techniques have on individuals with TBI post-injury, the studies thus far have shown very promising results, which warrants additional attention to positive psychology approaches in exploring how to best support the post-TBI population. The promise of positive psychology techniques is particularly critical in cases when vastly researched interventions such as CBT may have substantial limitations for individuals with TBI depending on the level of brain damage sustained.

To date, studies have found positive psychology interventions to be effective, and although research on the subject is still limited, results of the interventions appear to be promising (Tulip et al., 2020). For example, with regards to vocational rehabilitation counseling, return to work (RTW) is a major concern in supporting individuals recovering from TBIs. Positive psychology can be utilized in this context as an intervention to improve emotional regulation, effective communication, attending to and remembering new information, as well as facilitate recognition of one's strengths and limitations in the work environment (Mills & Kreutzer, 2016). Due to the pervasive and debilitating impact TBI can have on individuals' social, psychological, and emotional expression, positive psychology serves as a powerful tool to address the gaps in traditional treatments that are more focused on treating the physical and cognitive consequences following a TBI.

It is also important to note that interventions for individuals post-TBI should be tailored to support the unique challenges that individuals often face during the short acute phase as well as the chronic phase. The chronic phase is the aftermath and repercussions that typically occur during the 6 to 12 months after the TBI (Tsai et al., 2021). Studies examining the impact of individually tailored and goal-oriented intervention in the chronic phase of TBI demonstrate that participants were much more likely to show reduction in secondary outcomes of TBI and anxiety-related symptoms than in other treatment modalities (Borgen et al., 2023). In addition to reduced symptomatology, participants reported a higher sense of health-related quality of life (HRQOL), which is always a positive aspect of treatment.

Studies discussed in this section highlight the significance of providing a tailored approach to TBI patients, as each case is unique and entails differences in severity, affected brain areas, and the stages of rehabilitation. The fluctuations of improvement and deterioration in each individual case can last for months and even years following injury (Meyfroidt et al., 2022). Although positive psychology interventions have research to support their efficacy in populations that have sustained TBI, prospective practitioners in rehabilitation counseling should take heed in tailoring the intervention to meet each client in their own time. It can be assumed that providing ineffective treatment by giving the client too much homework or using treatment modalities that do not target important areas of their life may dissuade the client from continuing treatment altogether.

Spirituality and TBI

An additional intervention that pairs with positive psychology is spirituality, which also has been shown to have a promising impact on individuals recovering from TBI. Quantitative and qualitative research alike suggest that spirituality has the potential to play a positive role in recovery from TBI and in ultimately increasing one's quality of life and overall mental health (Versace et al., 2023). Individuals with TBI are known to be at an increased risk of developing symptoms of anxiety and depression, and researchers speculate that spirituality can serve as a vehicle to enhance an individual's sense of meaning and/or purpose in their life post-TBI (Sekely et al., 2019).

Adding on, spirituality can also play a prominent role during the stage known as PTG, which is defined as a stage of resilience, gratitude, and openness to new possibilities as well as a newfound sense of purpose and meaning (Gillespie, 2019). In these stages of PTG, research found that individuals with a stronger sense of spirituality had better self-perceived physical health 2 years after their injury. Furthermore, inpatient rehabilitation research that included participants with TBI discovered that patients were open to exploring themes of spirituality, seeing it as a means of finding meaning in life and as a source of spiritual strength (Jones et al., 2024). Presumably, like positive psychology, spirituality can play a strong role in providing hope, optimism, and meaning to individuals grappling with the pervasive health consequences stemming from TBI. As such, it is vital for practitioners to take this information into consideration when working with individuals who have long-term side effects from disability to ensure holistic treatment. Nonetheless, additional research is needed to identify the specific spiritual needs in individuals with TBI and how practitioners in the field can better support individuals in their journey toward recovery (Jones et al., 2018)

Mindfulness and TBI

Mindfulness is a practice that entails training the individual to focus on recognizing and perceiving specific experiences with full attention (Shapiro et al., 2006). There are three elements that make up the psychological training of this practice: intentions, attention, and attitude (Feng et al., 2024). Mindfulness may be a viable treatment modality by itself or as a supplemental treatment when assisting individuals who have experienced TBI. Fortunately, current treatment protocols are beginning to recognize mild traumatic brain injury (mTBI) as a rehabilitative injury, where patients can implement active measures to improve their condition versus waiting for submissive improvement to occur (Acabchuk et al., 2021). Due to TBIs having such a broad range of symptoms (which ultimately affects how each individual responds to the injury), it is important for healthcare professionals to make sure that the correct mindfulness technique is appropriate for the client.

A vast amount of literature suggests that meditation, yoga, and mindfulness-based interventions (MBIs) may be applicable for treating symptoms of chronic mTBI (Acabchuk et al., 2021). Some literature suggests that MBIs have targeted consequences on the mental fatigue and cognitive impairments for individuals; however, the impact on psychological symptoms and the ongoing efficaciousness widespread on all symptoms require further investigation (Feng et al., 2024). Increasing research on the subject implies that psychosocial interventions, specifically MBIs, may accelerate recovery prior to an mTBI (Lovette et al., 2022).

The following are MBIs that have been typically used in clinical and therapeutic settings: mindfulness-based stress reduction training (MBSR), mindfulness-based cognitive training (MBCT), acceptance and commitment therapy (ACT), and goal-oriented attention self-regulation (GOALS) (Feng et al., 2024). It is imperative that when implementing these techniques into the treatment plan for individuals with TBI that special consideration is taken regarding cognitive ability, emotional regulation, decision-making ability, and also the self-awareness of the individual. Although a TBI can alter all cognitive domains, it typically affects the individual's attention and awareness, processing speed, learning, memory, and executive functioning (Devi et al., 2020). Therefore, damage to specific areas of the brain can alter the individual's abilities to perform mindfulness techniques.

Caregivers for TBI Survivors

It is also important to consider the role of the caregiver for individuals who have experienced a TBI. It may be common for counselors and mental health professionals to have clients who are struggling psychologically due to extensive stress that they have taken on as the caregiver for someone with a TBI. Often, caregivers of individuals with moderate to severe TBIs encounter more challenges, adversities, and handicaps in comparison to those of survivors of mild TBI (Page et al., 2021). The recovery process for individuals with TBI typically impacts the caregiver's well-being and often can result in caregiver burnout (Devi et al., 2020). Caregivers of TBI survivors often experience a variety of challenges, and it is essential that future research aims to increase the development and ongoing plans for all inclusive and adaptable long-term support (Page et al., 2021). Another important consideration is that the impact on caregivers for children with TBI is different than for caregivers of TBI adult survivors. Notably, caregivers of children who survive TBI encounter alternative challenges and experiences given that the injury resulted when the brain was in developmental status (Anderson et al., 2001).

The correlation between TBI outcomes and the mental health of the caregiver suggests that there is a need for interventions that will directly support the caregivers' well-being (Coxe et al., 2021). As such, when in the home, caregivers are constantly upholding the majority of care for the TBI survivor, and this ultimately can lead to negative changes in the psychological and mental well-being for the caregiver (Devi et al., 2020). The impact of these changes may be relative to the needs of the survivor, resources, recovery process, severity level of the TBI, family adaptation, and other familial support (Devi et al., 2020).

Conclusion

This chapter provided a brief overview of defining TBI, types of TBIs, severity levels of TBIs, and some common etiology related to TBIs. Further exploration and recommendations were discussed on how both positive psychology and mindfulness may be efficacious practices to implement when assisting individuals with TBI. It is always essential for counselors, rehabilitation professionals, and healthcare professionals to also consider individual characteristics that may influence the repercussions of a TBI experience.

Furthermore, environmental, societal, familial, financial, and spiritual factors may highly alter the treatment plan for those coping with a TBI. It is encouraged for the support/rehabilitative team to also consider the impact that this condition may have on the caregiver. Caregivers often neglect their own health, work, or family obligations during acute care, hospital time, and post follow-up appointments for the survivor (Devi et al., 2020). Therefore, it is essential that we have an understanding of specific caregivers' experiences in order to create and implement effective and intentional strategies to accurately meet their needs and advance their quality of life (Page et al., 2021). It may be likely that counselors will be also assisting caregivers on how to handle the significant consequences that may have occurred due to the TBI. That said, a positive perspective that needs to be highlighted is that we have and will continue to have significant progress in a variety of approaches to rehabilitative treatments and supports for individuals with TBI. These approaches will shape how individuals with TBI can recover and lead healthy, positive, and high-quality lives.

Case Study 1

Hugo is a 37-year-old marketing specialist whose schedule is busy and involves working with multiple professional teams. He leads an active lifestyle and loves to travel. He is an avid athlete and has many hobbies, which include mountain biking, surfing, and motorcycle rallies. A year ago, Hugo was involved in a serious motorcycle accident that resulted in several broken ribs, broken shoulder, and a closed head TBI. He was hospitalized after the accident and received comprehensive medical treatment. He attended three months of physical therapy and is still working on his right-arm motion range due to the shoulder injury. His doctors characterize Hugo's lingering condition as a mild TBI.

Twelve months after his accident, Hugo decided to call in to inquire about rehabilitation counseling. Even though the medical team is satisfied with his recovery from TBI, Hugo is continuing to experience long-term TBI symptoms that negatively affect his professional and personal life. He continues to be prone to severe headaches and fatigue. He notices that his attention span and his short-term and long-term memory are significantly weaker than they used to be. Hugo reports being irritable but is not sure whether it is due to his disrupted sleep patterns, or due to his frustration with self. He comments that despite his return to the exercise routine, he gained some weight. He recently noticed that his everyday math skills have significantly declined. He is unable to calculate tax on some of his purchases, and even keeping track of time zones for his virtual work meetings is challenging. Hugo is worried about his career and is concerned about his low self-esteem and lack of motivation for anything in his life. He is also worried that he will never gain his motivation back to get on bike or get back with his friends who are into extreme sports. Hugo is wondering whether rehabilitation therapy may bring him "back to normal."

Critical Thinking Questions

1. What questions did you have about TBI before you read this chapter?
2. How is TBI different and similar to other conditions in this volume?
3. What are some ways in which TBI can be prevented?
4. What are some of the long-term effects of TBI on one's health, self-esteem, and daily life?
5. How can positive psychology be a resource for someone who is experiencing the long-term effects of TBI?

Case Study 2: TBI Caretaker Case Study: Hugo's Brother

Hugo and his younger brother Eric have always been very close. Eric grew up looking up to Hugo, seeing him as a role model. Eric recognized Hugo as a thriving professional, avid athlete, and as someone who was clearly enjoying life. When Eric heard about Hugo's motorcycle accident and TBI, his first reaction was shock and disbelief. Eric expected his brother to bounce back and quickly regain his physical strength and positive disposition. As he spent sleepless nights in the hospital with Hugo, Eric realized that the recovery would not be as fast as he hoped for. After hearing the doctors' prognosis that Hugo would take months if not longer to recover, Eric felt immense worry about his brother, not knowing what recovery would look like.

When Hugo was discharged from the hospital, it became Eric's duty to take him to therapy sessions and doctors' appointments. Eric also had to pick up Hugo's share of family responsibilities, as the brothers used to share caring for their elderly uncle. Taking care of Hugo has taken a physical and emotional toll on Eric: lack of sleep and chronic lack of time are becoming overwhelming, and Eric had to put his social interactions with friends on hold. In addition, he had to deal with stigma when friends and family suggested that Hugo's injury was caused by "having too much fun." As Eric continues to accompany his brother to appointments, he fears admitting to himself that his brother is no longer the same easygoing individual. Hugo's irritability, forgetfulness, and frequent lack of attention are frustrating and depressing to Eric. At one of Hugo's rehabilitation counseling sessions, the counselor checks in with Eric and suggests that he should also consider getting some counseling support. Eric is surprised and hopeful at the same time. He did not expect to be considered as someone who might be needing help. At the same time, he feels that caring for Hugo is a heavy task for him.

Critical Thinking Questions

1. Why might a caregiver of someone with TBI be referred to rehabilitation counseling?
2. What are some of the effects of TBI on one's caregiver's health and daily life?
3. How can positive psychology be a resource for someone who is a caregiver for an individual with TBI?

Resources

The resources listed below are specific resources that provide psychoeducation, techniques, and strategies that may be informative and useful for individuals with a TBI.

https://www.ninds.nih.gov/health-information/disorders/traumatic-brain-injury-tbi

https://www.ncbi.nlm.nih.gov/books/NBK580075/

https://www.dor.ca.gov/Home/TBIProgramSites

https://www.biausa.org

https://msktc.org/TBI

https://www.cdc.gov/traumatic-brain-injury/index.html

References

Acabchuk, R. L., Brisson, J. M., Park, C. L., Babbott-Bryan, N., Parmelee, O. A., & Johnson, B. T. (2021). Therapeutic effects of meditation, yoga, and mindfulness-based interventions for chronic symptoms of mild traumatic brain injury: A systematic review and meta-analysis. *Applied Psychology: Health and Well-being*, *13*(1), 34–62.

Anderson, V., Northam, E., Hendy, J., & Wrennall, J. (2001). Traumatic brain injury. In C. Code & D. Muller (Eds.), *Developmental neuropsychology a clinical approach* (pp. 125–184). East Sussex, United Kingdom: Psychology Press Ltd.

Ashina, H., Eigenbrodt, A. K., Seifert, T., Sinclair, A. J., Scher, A. I., Schytz, H. W., Lee, M. J., De Icco, R., Finkel, A. G., & Ashina, M. (2021). Post-traumatic headache attributed traumatic brain injury: Classification, clinical characteristics, and treatment. *The Lancet Neurology*, *20*(6), 460–469. https://doi.org/10.1016/S1474-4422(21)00094-6

Block, C. K., West, S. E., & Goldin, Y. (2016). Misconceptions and misattributions about traumatic brain injury: An integrated conceptual framework. *PM&R*, *8*(1), 58–68. https://doi.org/10.1016/j.pmrj.2015.05.022

Bombardier, C. H., Hoekstra, T., Dikmen, S., & Fann, J. R. (2016). Depression trajectories during the first year after traumatic brain injury. *Journal of Neurotrauma*, *33*(23), 2115–2124. https://doi.org/10.1089/neu.2015.4349

Borgen, I. M., Løvstad, M., Hauger, S. L., Forslund, M. V., Kleffelgård, I., Andelic, N., Sveen, U., Søberg, H., Sigurdardottir, S., Winter, L., Lindstad, M., Brunborg, C., & Røe, C. (2023). Effect of an individually tailored and home-based intervention in the chronic phase of traumatic brain injury: a randomized clinical trial. *JAMA Network Open*, *6*(5), e2310821–e2310821. https://doi.org/10.1001/jamanetworkopen.2023.10821

Borlongan, C., Acosta, S., De La Pena, I., Tajiri, N., Kaneko, Y., Lozano, D., & Gonzales-Portillo, G. (2015). Neuroinflammatory responses to traumatic brain injury: Etiology, clinical consequences, and therapeutic opportunities. *Neuropsychiatric Disease and Treatment*, 97–106. https://doi.org/10.2147/NDT.S65815

Cannella, L. A., McGary, H., & Ramirez, S. H. (2019). Brain interrupted: Early life traumatic brain injury and addiction vulnerability. *Experimental Neurology*, *317*, 191–201. https://doi.org/10.1016/j.expneurol.2019.03.003

Capizzi, A., Woo, J., & Verduzco-Gutierrez, M. (2020). Traumatic brain injury. *Medical Clinics of North America*, *104*(2), 213–238. https://doi.org/10.1016/j.mcna.2019.11.001

Centers for Disease Control and Prevention. (2024). *Traumatic brain injury and concussion*. U.S. Department of Health and Human Services. https://www.cdc.gov/traumatic-brain-injury/data-research/index.html

Chan, V., Toccalino, D., Omar, S., Shah, R., & Colantonio, A. (2022). A systematic review on integrated care for traumatic brain injury, mental health, and substance use. *PLOS ONE*, *17*(3), e0264116. https://doi.org/10.1371/journal.pone.0264116

Cho, M. J., & Jang, S. H. (2021). Relationship between post-traumatic amnesia and white matter integrity in traumatic brain injury using tract-based spatial statistics. *Scientific Reports, 11*(1), 6898. https://doi.org/10.1038/s41598-021-86439-0

Clark, M., & Guskiewicz, K. (2016). Sport-related traumatic brain injury. In D. Laskowitz & G. Grant (Eds.), *Translational research in traumatic brain injury*. CRC Press/Taylor and Francis Group. http://www.ncbi.nlm.nih.gov/books/NBK326721/

Colantonio, A., & Valera, E. M. (2022). Brain injury and intimate partner violence. *Journal of Head Trauma Rehabilitation*, *37*(1), 2–4 https://doi.org/10.1097/HTR.0000000000000763

Costello, K., & Greenwald, B. D. (2022). Update on domestic violence and traumatic brain injury: A narrative review. *Brain Sciences*, *12*(1), 122. https://doi.org/10.3390/brainsci12010122

Coxe, K. A., Pence, E. K., & Kagotho, N. (2021). Social work care in traumatic brain injury and substance use disorder treatment: A capacity-building model. *Health & Social Work*, *46*(4), 277–288. https://doi.org/10.1097/HTR.0000000000000587

Crozes, F., Delpierre, C., & Costa, N. (2024). Mapping the costs and socioeconomic characteristics involved in traumatic brain injuries: A scoping review. *Journal of Rehabilitation Medicine*, 56. https://doi.org/10.2340/jrm.v56.18311

Curvis, W., Simpson, J., & Hampson, N. (2018). Social anxiety following traumatic brain injury: An exploration of associated factors. *Neuropsychological Rehabilitation*, *28*(4), 527–547. https://doi.org/10.1080/09602011.2016.1175359

Dams-O'Connor, K., Juengst, S. B., Bogner, J., Chiaravalloti, N. D., Corrigan, J. D., Giacino, J. T., Harrison-Felix, C. L., Hoffman, J. M., Ketchum, J. M., Lequerica, A. H., Marwitz, J. H., Miller, A. C., Nakase-Richardson, R., Rabinowitz, A. R., Sander, A. M., Zafonte, R., & Hammond, F. M. (2023). Traumatic brain injury as a chronic disease: Insights from the United States Traumatic Brain Injury Model Systems Research Program. *The Lancet Neurology*, *22*(6), 517–528. https://doi.org/10.1016/S1474-4422(23)00065-0

Devi, Y., Khan, S., Rana, P., Dhandapani, M., Ghai, S., Gopichandran, L., & Dhandapani, S. (2020). Cognitive, behavioral, and functional impairments among traumatic brain injury survivors: Impact on caregiver burden. *Journal of Neurosciences in Rural Practice*, *11*(4), 629. https://doi.org/10.1055/s-0040-1716777

Eskander, N., Prabhudesai, S., Imran, H., Ceren Amuk, O., & Patel, R. S. (2020). Alcohol use disorder increases risk of traumatic brain injury-related hospitalization: Insights from 3.8 million children and adolescent inpatients. *Cureus, 12(6).* https://doi.org/10.7759/cureus.8740

Falvo, D. R., & Holland, B. (2018). *Medical and psychosocial aspects of chronic illness and disability* (6th ed.). Jones & Bartlett Learning.

Fatuki, T. A., Zvonarev, V., & Rodas, A. W. (2020). Prevention of traumatic brain injury in the United States: Significance, new findings, and practical applications. *Cureus, 12(10).* https://doi.org/10.7759/cureus.11225

Feng, Q., Huang, Z., Wang, Y., & Wang, B. (2024). The effects of mindfulness-based interventions on symptoms of mild traumatic brain injury: A systematic review. *International Journal of Mental Health Promotion*, *26*(6). https://doi.org/10.32604/ijmhp.2024.049010

Galgano, M., Toshkezi, G., Qiu, X., Russell, T., Chin, L., & Zhao, L.-R. (2017). Traumatic brain injury: Current treatment strategies and future endeavors. *Cell Transplantation*, *26*(7), 1118–1130. https://doi.org/10.1177/0963689717714102

Gillespie, E. (2019). A qualitative pilot study of spirituality in long-term recovery in acquired brain injury. *Journal of Pastoral Care & Counseling*, *73*(2), 96–105. https://doi.org/10.1177/1542305019853588

Haarbauer-Krupa, J., Pugh, M. J., Prager, E. M., Harmon, N., Wolfe, J., & Yaffe, K. (2021). Epidemiology of chronic effects of traumatic brain injury. *Journal of Neurotrauma*, *38*(23), 3235–3247. https://doi.org/10.1089/neu.2021.0062

Harrington, B. M., Gretschel, A., Lombard, C., Lonser, R. R., & Vlok, A. J. (2021). Complications, outcomes, and management strategies of non-missile penetrating head injuries. *Journal of Neurosurgery*, *134*(5), 1658–1666. https://doi.org/10.3171/2020.4.JNS20122

Howlett, J. R., Nelson, L. D., & Stein, M. B. (2022). Mental health consequences of traumatic brain injury. *Biological Psychiatry*, *91*(5), 413–420. https://doi.org/10.1016/j.biopsych.2021.09.024

Izzy, S., Grashow, R., Radmanesh, F., Chen, P., Taylor, H., Formisano, R., Wilson, F., Wasfy, M., Baggish, A., & Zafonte, R. (2023). Long-term risk of cardiovascular disease after traumatic brain injury: Screening and prevention. *The Lancet Neurology*, *22*(10), 959–970. https://doi.org/10.1016/S1474-4422(23)00241-7

Johnson, L. W., & Diaz, I. (2023). Exploring the social determinants of health and health disparities in traumatic brain injury: A scoping review. *Brain Sciences*, *13*(5), 707. https://doi.org/10.3390/brainsci13050707

Jones, A. A., Gicas, K. M., Seyedin, S., Willi, T. S., Leonova, O., Vila-Rodriguez, F., Procyshyn, R. M., Smith, G. N., Schmitt, T. A., Vertinsky, A. T., Buchanan, T., Rauscher, A., Lang, D. J., MacEwan, G. W., Lima, V. D., Montaner, J. S. G., Panenka, W. J., Barr, A. M., Thornton, A. E., & Honer, W. G. (2020). Associations of substance use, psychosis, and mortality among people living in precarious housing or homelessness: A longitudinal, community-based study in Vancouver, Canada. *PLoS Medicine*, *17*(7), e1003172. https://doi.org/10.1371/journal.pmed.1003172

Jones, K. F., Pryor, J., Care-Unger, C., & Simpson, G. K. (2018). Spirituality and its relationship with positive adjustment following traumatic brain injury: A scoping review. *Brain Injury*, *32*(13–14), 1612–1622. https://doi.org/10.1080/02699052.2018.1511066

Jones, K. F., Pryor, J., & Best, M. C. (2024). An exploration of spirituality and spiritual care with rehabilitation inpatients. *Disability and Rehabilitation*, 1–8. https://doi.org/10.1080/09638288.2024.2420848

Krahn, T. M. (2015). Traumatic brain injury and the use of documentary narrative media to redress social stigma. In J. Clausen & N. Levy (Eds.), *Handbook of neuroethics* (pp. 1501–1524). Springer Netherlands. https://doi.org/10.1007/978-94-007-4707-4_126

Lee Duckworth, A., Steen, T. A., & Seligman, M. E. (2005). Positive psychology in clinical practice. *Annual Review of Clinincal Psychology*, *1*(1), 629–651.

Livingston, G., Huntley, J., Sommerlad, A., Ames, D., Ballard, C., Banerjee, S., Brayne, C., Burns, A., Cohen-Mansfield, J., Cooper, C., Costafreda, S. G., Dias, A., Fox, N., Gitlin, L. N., Howard, R., Kales, H. C., Kivimäki, M., Larson, E. B., Ogunniyi, A., … Mukadam, N. (2020). Dementia prevention, intervention, and care: 2020 report of the Lancet Commission. *The Lancet, 396*(10248), 413–446. https://doi.org/10.1016/S0140-6736(20)30367-6

Lovette, B. C., Kanaya, M. R., Bannon, S. M., Vranceanu, A. M., & Greenberg, J. (2022). "Hidden gains"? Measuring the impact of mindfulness-based interventions for people with mild traumatic brain injury: A scoping review. *Brain Injury, 36*(9), 1059–1070. https://doi.org/10.1080/02699052.2022.2109745

Maas, A. I. R., Menon, D. K., Manley, G. T., Abrams, M., Åkerlund, C., Andelic, N., Aries, M., Bashford, T., Bell, M. J., Bodien, Y. G., Brett, B. L., Büki, A., Chesnut, R. M., Citerio, G., Clark, D., Clasby, B., Cooper, D. J., Czeiter, E., Czosnyka, M., … Zemek, R. (2022). Traumatic brain injury: Progress and challenges in prevention, clinical care, and research. *The Lancet Neurology, 21*(11), 1004–1060. https://doi.org/10.1016/S1474-4422(22)00309-X

Martz, E., & Livneh, H. (2016). Psychosocial adaptation to disability within the context of positive psychology: Findings from the literature. *Journal of Occupational Rehabilitation, 26*, 4–12. https://doi.org/10.1007/s10926-015-9598-x

Meyfroidt, G., Bouzat, P., Casaer, M. P., Chesnut, R., Hamada, S. R., Helbok, R., Hutchinson, P., Maas, A. I., Manley, G., Menon, D. K., & Newcombe, V. F. (2022). Management of moderate to severe traumatic brain injury: An update for the intensivist. *Intensive Care Medicine, 48*(6), 649–666. https://doi.org/10.1007/s00134-022-06702-4

Mills, A. L., & Kreutzer, J. S. (2016). Theoretical applications of positive psychology to vocational rehabilitation after traumatic brain injury. *Journal of Occupational Rehabilitation, 26*, 20–31. https://doi.org/10.1007/s10926-015-9608-z

Ng, S. Y., & Lee, A. Y. W. (2019). Traumatic brain injuries: Pathophysiology and potential therapeutic targets. *Frontiers in Cellular Neuroscience, 13*, 528. https://doi.org/10.3389/fncel.2019.00528

Nizamutdinov, D., & Shapiro, L. (2017). Overview of traumatic brain injury: An immunological context. *Brain Sciences, 7*(1), 11. https://doi.org/10.3390/brainsci7010011

Oliverio, R., Karelina, K., & Weil, Z. M. (2020). Sex, drugs, and TBI: The role of sex in substance abuse related to traumatic brain injuries. *Frontiers in Neurology, 11*, 546775. https://doi.org/10.3389/fneur.2020.546775

Olsen, C. M., & Corrigan, J. D. (2022). Does traumatic brain injury cause risky substance use or substance use disorder? *Biological Psychiatry, 91*(5), 421–437. https://doi.org/10.1016/j.biopsych.2021.07.013

Ownsworth, T., Mols, H., O'Loghlen, J., Xie, Y., Kendall, M., Nielsen, M., Mitchell, J., Jones, R., & Geraghty, T. (2024). Stigma following acquired brain injury and spinal cord injury: Relationship to psychological distress and community integration in the first-year post-discharge. *Disability and Rehabilitation, 46*(9), 1796–1806. https://doi.org/10.1080/09638288.2023.2205173

Page, T. A., Gordon, S., Balchin, R., & Tomlinson, M. (2021). Caregivers' perspectives of the challenges faced with survivors of traumatic brain injury: A scoping review. *NeuroRehabilitation*, *49*(3), 349–362. https://doi.org/10.3233/NRE-210099

Pavlovic, D., Pekic, S., Stojanovic, M., & Popovic, V. (2019). Traumatic brain injury: neuropathological, neurocognitive and neurobehavioral sequelae. *Pituitary*, *22*(3), 270–282. https://doi.org/10.1007/s11102-019-00957-9

Payne, L., Hawley, L., Ketchum, J. M., Philippus, A., Eagye, C. B., Morey, C., Gerber, D., Harrison-Felix, C., & Diener, E. (2018). Psychological well-being in individuals living in the community with traumatic brain injury. *Brain Injury*, *32*(8), 980–985. https://doi.org/10.1080/02699052.2018.1468573

Rabinowitz, A. R., & Arnett, P. A. (2018). Positive psychology perspective on traumatic brain injury recovery and rehabilitation. *Applied Neuropsychology: Adult*, *25*(4), 295–303.

Rapport, L. J., Wong, C. G., & Hanks, R. A. (2019). Resilience and well-being after traumatic brain injury. *Disability and Rehabilitation*, *42*(14), 2049–2055. https://doi.org/10.1080/09638288.2018.1552327

Rauwenhoff, J. C., Bol, Y., Van Heugten, C. M., Batink, T., Geusgens, C. A., Van Den Hout, A. J., Smits, P., Verwegen, C. R., Visser, A., & Peeters, F. (2023). Acceptance and commitment therapy for people with acquired brain injury: Rationale and description of the BrainACT treatment. *Clinical Rehabilitation*, *37*(8), 1011–1025. https://doi.org/10.1177/02692155231154124

Rosenthal, S. R., Sonido, P. L., Sammartino, C., Swanberg, J. E., & Noel, J. K. (2023). Brain injury and substance use in young adults: The need for integrating care. *Rhode Island Medical Journal (2013)*, *106*(3), 17–22.

Sabet, N., Soltani, Z., & Khaksari, M. (2021). Multipotential and systemic effects of traumatic brain injury. *Journal of Neuroimmunology*, *357*, 577619. https://doi.org/10.1016/j.jneuroim.2021.577619

Salik, I., Dominguez, J. F., Vazquez, S., Ng, C., Das, A., Naftchi, A., Spirollari, E., Subah, G., Zhang, A., Sukul, V., Pisapia, J. M., Muh, C., & Stewart, D. (2022). Socioeconomic characteristics of pediatric traumatic brain injury patients. *Clinical Neurology and Neurosurgery*, *221*, 107404. https://doi.org/10.1016/j.clineuro.2022.107404

Sekely, A., Xie, Y., Makani, A., Brown, T., & Zakzanis, K. K. (2019). Spiritual well-being as a predictor of emotional impairment following mild traumatic brain injury. *Journal of Clinical Psychology in Medical Settings, 27,* 859–866. https://doi.org/10.1007/s10880-019-09687-3

Sharma, B., Lawrence, D. W., & Hutchison, M. G. (2018). Branched chain amino acids (BCAAs) and traumatic brain injury: A systematic review. *The Journal of Head Trauma Rehabilitation*, *33*(1), 33–45.

Shapiro, S. L., Carlson, L. E., Astin, J. A., & Freedman, B. (2006). Mechanisms of mindfulness. *Journal of Clinical Psychology*, *62*(3), 373–386. https://doi.org/10.1002/jclp.20237

Siebold, L., Obenaus, A., & Goyal, R. (2018). Criteria to define mild, moderate, and severe traumatic brain injury in the mouse controlled cortical impact model. *Experimental Neurology, 310*, 48–57. https://doi.org/10.1016/j.expneurol.2018.07.004

Simpson, G. K., Tate, R. L., Whiting, D. L., & Cotter, R. E. (2011). Suicide prevention after traumatic brain injury: A randomized controlled trial of a program for the psychological treatment of hopelessness. *Journal of Head Trauma Rehabilitation, 26*(4), 290–300. https://doi.org/10.1097/HTR.0b013e3182225250

Sussman, E. S., Pendharkar, A. V., Ho, A. L., & Ghajar, J. (2018). Mild traumatic brain injury and concussion: Terminology and classification. In *Handbook of Clinical Neurology* (Vol. 158, pp. 21–24). Elsevier. https://doi.org/10.1016/B978-0-444-63954-7.00003-3

Timmer, M. L., Jacobs, B., Schonherr, M. C., Spikman, J. M., & Van Der Naalt, J. (2020). The spectrum of long-term behavioral disturbances and provided care after traumatic brain injury. *Frontiers in Neurology, 11*, 246. https://doi.org/10.3389/fneur.2020.00246

Tsai, Y. C., Liu, C. J., Huang, H. C., Lin, J. H., Chen, P. Y., Su, Y. K., Chen, C. T., & Chiu, H. Y. (2021). A meta-analysis of dynamic prevalence of cognitive deficits in the acute, subacute, and chronic phases after traumatic brain injury. *Journal of Neuroscience Nursing, 53*(2), 63–68. https://doi.org/10.1097/JNN.0000000000000570

Tulip, C., Fisher, Z., Bankhead, H., Wilkie, L., Pridmore, J., Gracey, F., Tree, J., & Kemp, A. H. (2020). Building wellbeing in people with chronic conditions: A qualitative evaluation of an 8-week positive psychotherapy intervention for people living with an acquired brain injury. *Frontiers in Psychology, 11*, 66. https://doi.org/10.3389/fpsyg.2020.00066

Vella, M. A., Crandall, M. L., & Patel, M. B. (2017). Acute management of traumatic brain injury. *Surgical Clinics of North America, 97*(5), 1015–1030. https://doi.org/10.1016/j.suc.2017.06.003

Versace, J., Tazrin, S., O'Connor, E., Sekibo, J., Morey, E., Kasinopoulou, A., O'Donoghue, D., & Simblett, S. K. (2023). The role of spirituality and identity formation in personal recovery from traumatic brain injury: A qualitative analysis through the personal experiences of survivors. *Neuropsychological Rehabilitation, 34*(8), 1110–1140. https://doi.org/10.1080/09602011.2023.2274624

Weil, Z. M., Corrigan, J. D., & Karelina, K. (2018). Alcohol use disorder and traumatic brain injury. *Alcohol Research: Current Reviews, 39*(2), 171–180.

Wilson, L., Stewart, W., Dams-O'Connor, K., Diaz-Arrastia, R., Horton, L., Menon, D. K., & Polinder, S. (2017). The chronic and evolving neurological consequences of traumatic brain injury. *The Lancet Neurology, 16*(10), 813–825. https://doi.org/10.1016/S1474-4422(17)30279-X

Wood, A. M., & Tarrier, N. (2010). Positive clinical psychology: A new vision and strategy for integrated research and practice. *Clinical Psychology Review, 30*(7), 819–829. https://doi.org/10.1016/j.cpr.2010.06.003

Zollman, F. S. (Ed.). (2016). *Manual of traumatic brain injury: Assessment and management* (2nd ed.). Demos Medical.

Addressing Chronic Pain Through Positive Psychology and Mindfulness

4

Sarah M. Roundtree
Robert Paul Maddox II
Dana Brickham

KEYWORDS AND DEFINITIONS:

Chronic pain: An unpleasant experience associated with tissue damage that persists beyond the expected healing process and significantly impacts a person's well-being (Davenport et al., 2017; International Association for the Study of Pain [IASP], 2020; Katz et al., 2015).

Comorbidity: The presence of two or more physical or mental health conditions.

Mindfulness: "The awareness that arises by paying attention on purpose, in the present moment, and non-judgmentally" (Kabat-Zinn, 2013, p. xxxv).

Positive psychology interventions (PPIs): Activities intended to foster feelings of gratitude, compassion, care, and meaningful life purpose (Hassett, 2018).

LEARNING OBJECTIVES:

1. Identify common challenges faced by individuals experiencing chronic pain
2. Be able to discuss how chronic pain may impact people
3. Describe various cultural components related to chronic pain and pain management
4. Understand how elements of positive psychology may interact with the experience of pain
5. Become familiar with multiple mindfulness-based interventions that can be useful for working with clients with chronic pain

Introduction

Pain is a difficult experience to quantify. Therefore, treating pain requires the ability of the person to first perceive the pain and then be able to describe the experience in a way that others can understand. The International Association for the Study of Pain (IASP, 2020) defines pain as "An unpleasant sensory and emotional experience associated with, or resembling that associated with, actual or potential tissue damage" (p. 2). Chronic pain is very common, affecting nearly 21% of adults in the United States (Rikard et al., 2023) and is identified as the third greatest healthcare problem in the country (Brodwin et al., 2020). Although there is no one solution to treating chronic pain, mindfulness-based practices are becoming increasingly popular, with the act of mindfulness being described as a protective factor (Brooks et al., 2018; Davenport et al., 2017; McKraken, 2005). People who experience chronic pain often develop high levels of resiliency and name characteristics such as being positive, having meaningful interpersonal relationships, and having strong self-management skills as some of their strengths (Aungst et al., 2019; Davenport et al., 2017; Kristjansdottir et al., 2018). There are many nuances within the realm of chronic pain that are important for rehabilitation professionals to understand in order to be truly empathetic to a client's experience and support them in maintaining a high quality of life. In this chapter, we hope that readers gain an understanding of (a) what chronic pain is and how it may impact people, (b) how elements of positive psychology such as connectedness to self and others may influence pain and vice versa, and (c) types of mindfulness-based interventions that can be useful for working with clients with chronic pain.

Chronic pain can be difficult to define, as it impacts each person differently (Brodwin et al., 2020; Falvo & Holland, 2018; Katz et al., 2015; Knoebel et al., 2021). Broadly, chronic pain can be described as pain that persists beyond the expected healing process and significantly impacts a person's well-being (Davenport et al., 2017; Katz et al., 2015). Many definitions, including those provided in the *Diagnostic and Statistical Manual of Mental Disorders* (*DSM-5TR*), have time constraints to constitute chronic pain, ranging from a minimum of 3 to 6 months (American Psychiatric Association [APA], 2022; Davenport et al., 2017; Falvo & Holland, 2018; Katz et al., 2015), though some researchers have argued that time limits such as this neglect certain aspects of chronic pain such as that some pain may remit and return (Katz et al., 2015; Raffaeli et al., 2021). Chronic pain varies in severity and frequency, with fluctuations that can occur over long periods of time or even within a given day (Davenport et al., 2017; Katz et al., 2015). With the severity of pain often being subjective, it can be misdiagnosed, challenging to treat, and prone to prejudice (Falvo & Holland, 2018; Katz et al., 2015; Knoebel et al., 2021). For instance, racial and ethnic disparities in chronic pain exist particularly among Black patients, due to identified factors such as biased provider communication and structural barriers that limit access to care (Knoebel et al., 2021). As such, it is important to understand what causes chronic pain and the biopsychosocial influences of pain to break down some of these barriers to chronic pain treatment for your clients.

People with chronic pain may identify with the diagnosis differently as well. Depending on the definitions being used, chronic pain might be considered a disability as it can significantly impact several core areas of daily life (Bogart & Dunn, 2019). Some folks with chronic pain may identify as disabled and associate themselves with disability culture, the pride of identifying as disabled and sharing a set of norms and experiences among other people with disabilities (Andrews & Forber-Pratt, 2022; Pierce, 2024). For others, they may not identify as having a disability even if they have chronic pain. As such, it's important to mirror the language that our clients use to talk about themselves.

While pain is a natural response to protect the body from danger, it can become pathological when it lasts beyond the useful purpose of bringing awareness to the threat (Falvo & Holland, 2018; Katz et al., 2015). Generalized causes of chronic pain include injury, illness, and stress and can be impacted by biological, psychological, and social factors. As there is no one explanation for chronic pain, etiologies related to specific conditions with different types of pain (e.g., nerve, musculoskeletal, inflammatory) are talked about in more depth in the following section.

Types of Chronic Pain Conditions

There are many different types of chronic pain conditions. Becoming familiar with some of the most common diagnoses can help us be attentive to our clients. Chronic pain is often overlooked in the medical field, and understanding how to bring clients alongside the treatment process helps alleviate some doubt in the efficacy of chronic pain treatments (Brodwin et al., 2020).

Arthritis. Arthritis is not only one of the most common chronic pain conditions, but it is also the leading cause of disability (Barbour et al., 2017; Brodwin et al., 2020). Two of the most prevalent types of arthritis (dependent on etiology) include rheumatoid arthritis and osteoarthritis. Rheumatoid arthritis affects the connective tissues of the body, primarily impacting the joints (Brodwin et al., 2020). Arthritis is sometimes discussed as a disorder that only older adults acquire, but that is not always true. Juvenile idiopathic arthritis, which falls under the category of rheumatoid arthritis, shows up in children and may last through adulthood. Osteoarthritis is distinct from rheumatoid arthritis in that it is degenerative and affects the cartilage lining of joints (Brodwin et al., 2020). Both types may show symptoms including pain, swelling, stiffness, and loss of motion, while rheumatoid arthritis may also show symptoms of inflammation such as redness and warmth (Brodwin et al., 2020). Though arthritis is mainly addressed through medications, mindfulness-based practices have been shown to be effective for people with rheumatoid arthritis as a complementary treatment (Zhou et al., 2020).

Fibromyalgia. Fibromyalgia is a complex rheumatic disease, mostly because there is a lot we do not know about its etiology. What we do know is that fibromyalgia manifests as chronic muscular pain, accompanied by the presence of other symptoms including sleep disturbances and headaches (Brodwin et al., 2020). Research has shown that fibromyalgia is a diagnosis particularly prone to biases, largely based on gender stereotypes and cognitive biases (Wolfe et al., 2018). However, because fibromyalgia is widely understudied, mindfulness-based interventions for fibromyalgia are only beginning to be explored; some research demonstrates promising results about the effectiveness of mindfulness in supporting people with fibromyalgia, though greater research is needed to draw significant conclusions (Gordon et al., 2022; Leca & Tavares, 2022).

Chronic migraine. Chronic migraine is a neurological disorder in which people experience severe headaches, often accompanied by other symptoms, for more days than not (Gibler, 2022; Hovaguimian & Roth, 2022). Chronic migraine impacts millions of children and is considered the leading cause of disability for people below 50 years of age (Gibler, 2022; Hovaguimian & Roth, 2022). Counselors should be educated on the biopsychosocial implications of migraine, the short- and long-term impacts of migraine medications, and how to navigate environmental triggers and make lifestyle changes to lessen the impact of migraine when possible (Gibler, 2022; Hovaguimian & Roth, 2022). The effectiveness of mindfulness-based interventions and chronic migraine reduction is beginning to be explored (Gibler, 2022; Grazzi et al., 2021; Hovaguimian & Roth, 2022; Wells et al., 2021).

Multiple sclerosis. Multiple sclerosis (MS) is a chronic autoimmune disorder that affects the central nervous system. Symptoms of MS vary widely from person to person and may include severe fatigue, sensitivity to heat, and pain (Brodwin et al., 2020). The progression of MS is fairly unpredictable and can change course depending on what type of MS someone has: relapsing-remitting, primary-progressive, or secondary-progressive (Brodwin et al., 2020). MS is identified once other diagnoses have been ruled out, meaning that the process of receiving a diagnosis in and of itself is time-consuming (Brodwin et al., 2020). By the time a client has a diagnosis of MS, they have already been dealing with symptoms for a significant period, in addition to now having to adjust and cope with a newfound disorder. For many years now, Mindfulness-Based Stress Reduction (MBSR) has been shown to be a helpful intervention for clients with MS in working toward managing pain and attaining a high quality of life (Senders et al., 2018; Younesi et al., 2020).

Spinal cord injuries. Spinal cord injuries are not one of the more common diagnoses globally, but they do show up frequently in rehabilitation counseling. The reason behind this is the wide range of biopsychosocial implications that come with having a spinal cord injury (Brodwin et al., 2020). Depending on the level of the injury, spinal cord injuries can impact mobility, strength, and the ability to regulate functions of the central nervous system such as temperature regulation or breathing (Brodwin et al., 2020). People with spinal cord injuries may also experience chronic pain near the site of the injury and/or due to overuse of other extremities to get around (Brodwin et al., 2020). Research on positive psychology and spinal cord injury has shown reductions in symptoms of depression and anxiety, improved overall quality of life, and the usefulness of mindfulness as a protective factor against pain (Bhattarai et al., 2024; Hearn & Cross, 2020). Continuing to study more specific and tailored mindfulness-based interventions in people with spinal cord injury and other types of chronic pain will be helpful for propelling treatment forward in the coming years.

Comorbidity

Chronic pain conditions overlap and interact greatly with other mental health diagnoses. Mental health conditions such as posttraumatic stress disorder (PTSD) and major depressive disorder are highly correlated with chronic pain (Katz et al., 2015). When multiple conditions are frequently seen in conjunction with one another, it is important to consider the impact of cultural, environmental, and biopsychosocial influences in your conceptualization of a client. For example, in response to the opioid epidemic in the United States, it has become more difficult for people to get access to pain management medications. Some opioid medications are highly necessary for people with chronic pain to function, and, therefore, people with chronic pain may self-medicate with other substances (Davenport et al., 2017). In this case, understanding the cultural context and lack of access can be important for seeing clients' strengths and strategies for coping. The comorbidity of chronic pain is complex, yet it can help counselors provide resources that positively influence clients' physical and mental health, while reassuring that both their chronic pain and additional diagnoses are valid experiences.

Key Components of Positive Psychology and Connections With Chronic Pain

Positive psychology interventions (PPIs) involve activities intended to foster feelings of gratitude, compassion, care, and meaningful life purpose (Hassett, 2018). With a resource-oriented focus, PPIs emphasize the importance of bolstering individual positive factors that can be beneficial in chronic pain management and treatment. Endeavoring to expand positive emotions, cognitions, and healthy behaviors, PPIs can be implemented in various forms ranging from brief interventions focused on one or more factors to more extensive, long-term therapeutic programs (Braunwalder et al., 2022). Through the practice of activities designed to increase components such as optimism and positive orientation (Sheldon et al., 2006), research indicates that PPIs may help in decreasing depressive symptoms and lowering overall psychological distress for clients (Bolier et al., 2013; Chakhssi et al., 2018). For those experiencing chronic pain, overall emotional functioning may be impacted, particularly in relation to emotions viewed as "negative," as such emotions often serve a protective role related to pain. With time, the consistent experience of negative emotions can lead to the development of long-term maladaptive and unhealthy coping habits in individuals. The engagement in unhealthy, maladaptive coping can worsen an individual's experience of chronic pain. However, emphasizing the positive aspects of one's experiences can strengthen needed psychosocial resources, improving their capacity to effectively manage and address chronic pain. This improved capacity can also lead to increased resiliency related to a person's experience with chronic pain.

Integrative Implementation

When addressing chronic pain, implementing PPIs in an integrative manner may be beneficial. Hassen et al. (2018) described how the utilization of PPIs in conjunction with other types of therapies and therapeutic approaches may assist clients with chronic pain and certain medical conditions to face challenges and stressors related to their pain in a more meaningful and effective manner. For example, through the aspects of awareness emphasized in mindfulness, the aim is not for happiness or positivity per say; rather, the aim is to move away from automatic reactions and ruminative thinking, the effects of which can be seen even on a neurological and biological level. When paired with PPIs, the emphasis on strengths and positivity in mindfulness-based practices may be more easily interwoven (Allen et al., 2021). Figure 4.1 demonstrates how integrative implementation can allow for synergetic connections between mindfulness-based interventions, PPIs, and potential points of intervention within the chronic pain cycle.

Key Components of Mindfulness and Chronic Pain

Kabat-Zinn describes mindfulness "as the awareness that arises by paying attention on purpose, in the present moment, and non-judgmentally" (Kabat-Zinn, 2013, p. xxxv). However, awareness may be the last thing people with chronic pain want to do—many people in pain use day-to-day strategies to escape or avoid the unpleasantness—through medication, distraction, overeating, and so on. However, research suggests that "… even short periods of formal practice can significantly modulate and alleviate the experience of pain" (Kabat-Zinn, 2023, p. 46). There are many ways to practice mindfulness, and it is important to be flexible and open-minded when looking at a strategy that will be supportive of each unique client and their specific experience with pain. Clinicians can support clients with multiple tools from the many techniques and strategies available in the mindfulness toolbox. Starting a mindfulness practice when experiencing pain may be difficult—it may feel daunting to sit still for an extended length of time, and a lot of "excuses" about why someone cannot start mindfulness meditation may even occur. However, it does not have to be such a major undertaking that feels overwhelming; a mindfulness practice could even be a simple moment of gratitude (Condon, 2022). This is pausing, dropping in, and considering what you are grateful for could be a start to a greater mindfulness practice that could grow and facilitate healing.

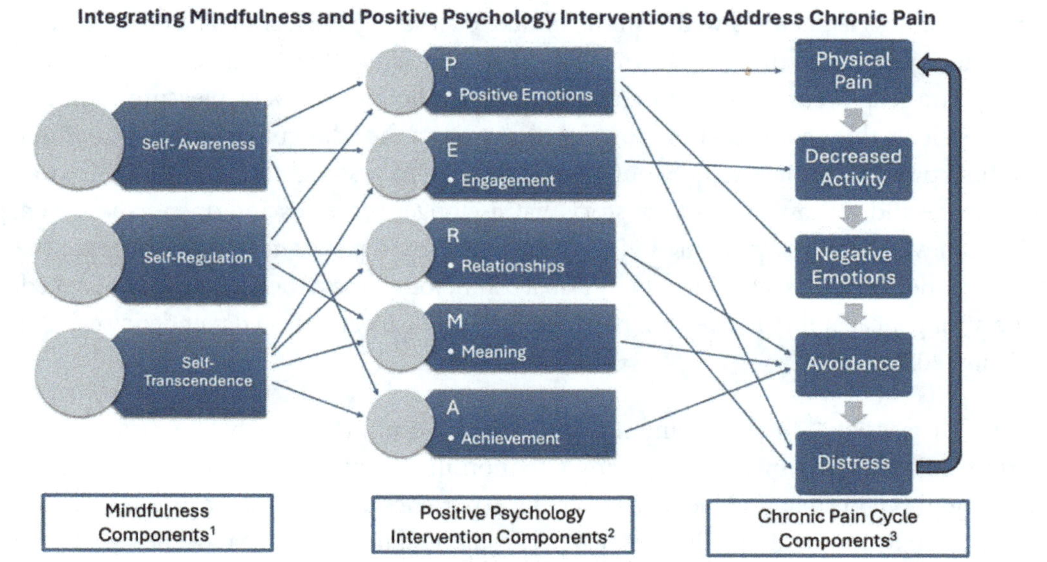

Note: [1]Mindfulness Components derived from: Vago, D. R., & Silbersweig, D. A. (2012). Self-awareness, self-regulation, and self-transcendence (S-ART): a framework for understanding the neurobiological mechanisms of mindfulness. *Frontiers in human neuroscience*, 6, 296. https://doi.org/10.3389/fnhum.2012.00296

[2] Positive Psychology Intervention Components derived from: Seligman, M. (2010). Flourish: Positive psychology and positive interventions. *The Tanner lectures on human values, 31*(4), 1-56.

AND

Liu, B., Guan, Y., Jing, H., Hofmann, S. G., & Liu, X. (2022). Mindfulness and PERMA Well-Being: Intervention Effects and Mechanism of Change. *Psychology, 13*(5), 675-704. Chicago.

[3] Chronic Pain Cycle Derived from: Yaugher, A., Voss, M., Swensen, K., & Condie, A. W. (2023, December 14). *Cognitive behavioral therapies for the management of chronic pain*. USU. https://extension.usu.edu/heart/research/cognitive-behavioral-therapies-for-chronic-pain-management

FIGURE 4.1. Integration of mindfulness and positive psychology interventions (PPIs) for chronic pain.

Furthermore, it is important to look at the forest from the trees when viewing pain. Kabat-Zinn says, "Pain is not just a 'body' problem, it is a whole-systems problem" (Gardner-Nix & Costin-Hall, 2009, p. 1). Emotions, trauma, stress, and genetics can all factor into the pain experience (Gardner-Nix & Costin-Hall, 2009). Van der Kolk writes, "In order to change, people need to become aware of their sensations and the way that their bodies interact with the world around them. Physical self-awareness is the first step in releasing the tyranny of the past" (van der Kolk, 2014, p. 103). Mindfulness meditation provides the interruption between what we are doing and what we are feeling, so that this awareness can occur (Stone, 2016).

Michael Stone, an internationally recognized Buddhist and meditation teacher, explains quite simply that mindfulness is ticking a wedge in the middle of what we are feeling and what we are doing (Stone, 2016). When something arises in this in-between space that is unpleasant, our reactivity of grasping and fear occur because biologically and psychology we want pleasure (Stone, 2016). Mindfulness slows this chain reaction down so that we can face difficulties and not hold onto our viewpoints so tightly (i.e., have to hold our desire to escape pain so tightly). Through this awareness comes a choice, and we can let go of the story that no longer serves us and open to a new chapter. The Mindfulness-Based Stress Reduction (MBSR) program, a program that has become the gold standard in mindfulness research created by Kabat-Zinn, found that when suffering is reduced, people have a stronger capability to live with pain and pain intensity and drug dependency can decrease (Kabat-Zinn, 2023).

Kabat-Zinn writes that "… the amazing thing, which you can find out only by *practicing* mindfulness fairly regularly over time, is that paying attention in a particular way to the very sensations, emotions, and thoughts that together constitute the experience of pain—in the present moment and as nonjudgmentally as possible (which may be very judgmental a good deal of the time)—actually has within it the seeds of freedom from suffering" (Gardner-Nix & Costin-Hall, 2009, foreword by Kabat-Zinn, p. vi). Bringing the attitude of "beginner's mind" to your practice allows us to have compassion and opens up many possibilities (Stone, 2016). We are also "befriending" our experience "at the level of the body and at the level of the mind and heart, and seeing what unfolds" (Gardner-Nix & Costin-Hall, 2009, foreword by Kabat-Ziin, vii). While bringing awareness to body sensations, we have a greater ability to turn toward unpleasant sensations. It's the "… thoughts and emotions [that] may actually compound the intensity and duration of pain" (Gardner-Nix & Costin-Hall, 2023, foreword by Kabat-Zinn, p. viii). As we see thoughts and emotions for what they really are, we can change our connection to bodily sensations.

On a biological level, mindfulness meditation is so powerful for people in chronic pain because the brain changes in response to experience—the brain is not fixed but fluid—and has the ability to modify its structure and function. Neurons can be created, and new connections can be made. This process is called neuroplasticity (Davidson & Lutz, 2008). Therefore, we can transform our brains, which can in turn transform our experience. We can change the relationship that we are having to pain by separating our behaviors and the experience. These changes may take time or may occur in as short as a few weeks (Treadway & Lazar, 2010). Grant et al. (2010) found that meditators had lower pain sensitivity and a thicker cortex after a meditation program, typically meaning more neurons and processing ability. A couple of different meta-analyses found moderate evidence that mindfulness-based interventions may affect the perception of pain, leading to improved functioning and quality of life (Hilton et al., 2016; Majeed et al., 2017).

Accommodations for Chronic Pain

There are several main barriers that can affect people who are in chronic pain when they engage in some PPIs or mindfulness-based interventions. The length of the activity can be an issue. Pain can be exacerbated with standing, sitting, and/or walking. Supportive measures and accommodations might be needed. Some of the unique barriers that people with chronic pain and related disabilities face when engaging in PPIs and mindfulness practices can include decreased self-efficacy, past reliance on external/extrinsic motivators, and perceived social role decline (National Disability Institute, 2021). To address the barriers faced by individuals with chronic pain, a variety of accommodations can be implemented to support people with disabilities and chronic pain and other health conditions. Gardner-Nix et al. (2009) recommend taking breaks and not trying to push through the activities; choosing times when pain is not at its very worst; and doing a little each day versus one long session. Anti-fatigue matting and wearable anti-fatigue matting, along with supports on chairs, can be helpful (Job Accommodation Network [JAN], n.d.). It is important to allow space for participants to change position and move as needed. Clinicians should withhold any judgments when these adjustments are made—and it is also important for the participant not to feel judgment toward themselves when they need to change positions. Part of the process related to PPIs and mindfulness-based activities for addressing pain is to acknowledge that it does not mean things will always be like this, but things are like this in the particular moment. Part of the practicing is just noticing what is coming up in the moment and bringing nonjudgmental awareness to what is being felt (Gardner-Nix & Costin-Hall, 2009). Furthermore, "... attempts to control pain are often at the heart of our difficulties .... Mindfulness practice helps us differentiate what we can fruitfully control from what we cannot ... we can control our behavior but not our symptoms" (Siegel, 2010, p. 191). Acceptance of how things are in the current moment is paradoxically the point at which physical abilities might improve (Gardner-Nix & Costin-Hall, 2009).

Cultural Components to Mindfulness Interventions

Much of the mindfulness meditation movement in the United States that we see today in major fields like counseling and psychology came out of the work of Dr. Jon Kabat-Zinn and Dr. Richard Davidson. It was in 1979 at the University of Massachusetts Medical School where Kabat-Zinn started a program that would become his formal Mindfulness-Based Stress Reduction (MBSR) program because he wanted to help patients with chronic stress and pain (Kabat-Zinn, 2013, p. 170; Mindful Leader, n.d.). At that time, there was a lot of skepticism within the Western medical community on meditation, so much so that Kabat-Zinn implemented his program in the basement of the hospital due to the lack of formal support. Furthermore, Kabat-Zinn secularized the work—making it more amenable to the Western crowd (Gates et al., 2009; Mindful Leader, n.d.).

In the early 1970s, when Kabat-Zinn was teaching at Brandeis, he became friends and practiced meditation with a grad student Richard Davidson at Harvard (Gates et al., 2009). Later, Dr. Davidson also faced intense scrutiny for wanting to investigate the positive effects of meditation on the brain through scientific means. It was through the work of Davidson and colleagues' landmark study (2003) using Kabat-Zinn's MBSR framework where Davidson et al. analyzed the effects on the immune system and brain. After the 8-week MBSR program, Davidson et al.'s research found participants had a significantly greater rise in antibodies, a significant increase of frontal lobe activation (the area associated with positive emotion), and a decrease of anxiety on immune markers (2003). The synergistic research combination of practice (Kabat-Zinn) and systematic study on the brain (Davidson) would forever change the trajectory of acceptance of meditation as a viable practice to help people who were chronically ill.

However, it would be quite remiss to not talk about the cultural and historical roots that extend far beyond Kabat-Zinn's and Richardson's work. The practice of meditation emerged in India over 2,500 years ago. Mindfulness meditation is taken from the Pali language word "sati" from India (and early Buddhism), which refers to a state of awareness, attention, and presence in the current moment (Alvear et al., 2022). There are many ties to mindfulness practices of spiritual and philosophical traditions in Buddhism, Hinduism, and Taoism. Kabat-Zinn was inspired by Eastern philosophies and Buddhist traditions that came from China, India, and Tibet. It was not until 1992 when Dr. Davidson met the Dalai Lama that he committed to the work and really began to actively do research and talk publicly about meditation (Gates et al., 2009).

So, the historical roots of mindfulness meditation originated from communities of color. There has been concern that the Westernized mindfulness that Kabat-Zinn started actually stripped away the cultural roots of mediation and cultural appropriation has occurred. There has also been a commercialization focused on mindfulness meditation where there are profits made off of apps and trainings. However, Kabat-Zinn has "been explicit in saying that his intent was never to exploit or decontextualize the dharma, but instead to recontextualize it so it was accessible for those who would never discover it through more traditional methods (and their insurance companies)" (Mindful Leader, n.d., para. 9). Other cultural considerations to the MBSR program are that many people may not be able to afford entrance into the MBSR program.

Conclusions

There is a lot of information about various chronic pain conditions that is still unknown. Research on chronic pain and positive psychology strategies is also mixed, but successful outcomes seem to be amplified when paired with other treatment modalities. Mindfulness meditation interventions can be adapted and modified to support people with chronic pain. Mindfulness and positive psychology could be further studied to see what components interrupt the chronic pain cycle.

Case Study

A client who is experiencing chronic migraine comes in for services. She is a Black woman recently employed as a high school teacher. She shares with you that she is having difficulties advocating for accommodations in her workplace and is feeling that others do not believe her pain is real. Though she has been living with chronic migraine for nearly a decade, she's beginning to wonder whether a career in teaching is "right" for her and why her usual methods of pain management (over-the-counter medication, icing, and rest) do not seem to be as effective.

Critical Thinking Questions

1. Considering what you know about the client's social identities, what factors may be coming into play with others' perceptions of her? What about self-perceptions?
2. What are some institutional barriers might she be facing in advocating for accommodations? How do these barriers connect to societal stigmas?
3. How might you incorporate positive psychology or mindfulness-based strategies in your treatment plan for this client? What questions might you ask her to see what interventions would be a good fit?

References

Allen, J. G., Romate, J., & Rajkumar, E. (2021). Mindfulness-based positive psychology interventions: A systematic review. *BMC psychology*, *9*, 1–18.

Alvear, D., Soler, J., & Cebolla, A. (2022). Meditators' non-academic definition of mindfulness. *Mindfulness, 13*(6), 1544–1554. https://doi.org/10.1007/s12671-022-01899-3

American Psychiatric Association. (2022). *Diagnostic and statistical manual of mental disorders* (5th ed., text rev.). https://doi.org/10.1176/appi.books.9780890425787

Andrews, E. E., & Forber-Pratt, A. J. (2022). Disability culture, identity, and language. In M. L. Wehmeyer & D. S. Dunn (Eds.), *The positive psychology of personal factors: Implications for understanding disability*. Lexington Books.

Aungst, H., Baker, M., Bouyer, C., Catalano, B., Cintron, M., Cohen, N. B., Gannon, P. A., Gilliam, J., Gullett, H., Hassmiller-Lich, K., Horner, S.C., Karmali, R. N., Kristjánsdóttir, Ó. B., Martukovich, R., Mirkovic, J., Misak, J. E., Moore, S. M., Ponyicky, N., Reichsman, A., . . . Yokie, J. (2019). *Identifying personal strengths to help patients manage chronic illness.* Patient-Centered Outcomes Research Institute. https://doi.org/10.25302/3.2019.CER.732

Barbour, K. E., Helmick, C. G., Boring, M., & Brady, T. J. (2017). Vital Signs: Prevalence of Doctor-Diagnosed Arthritis and Arthritis-Attributable Activity Limitation - United States, 2013-2015. MMWR. *Morbidity and mortality weekly report, 66*(9), 246–253. https://doi.org/10.15585/mmwr.mm6609e1

Bhattarai, M., McDaniels, B., Jin, Y., & Smedema, S. M. (2024). Pain and quality of life in persons with spinal cord injury: Mediating effects of mindfulness, self-efficacy, social support, and functional independence. *Journal of Clinical Psychology, 80*(2), 406–420. https://doi.org/10.1002/jclp.23616

Bogart, K. R., & Dunn, D. S. (2019). Ableism special issue introduction. *Journal of Social Issues, 75*(3), 650–664. https://doi.org/10.1111/josi.12354

Bolier, L., Haverman, M., Westerhof, G. J., Riper, H., Smit, F., & Bohlmeijer, E. (2013). Positive psychology interventions: A meta-analysis of randomized controlled studies. *BMC Public Health*, *13*, 1–20.

Braunwalder, C., Müller, R., Glisic, M., & Fekete, C. (2022). Are positive psychology interventions efficacious in chronic pain treatment? A systematic review and meta-analysis of randomized controlled trials. *Pain Medicine*, *23*(1), 122–136.

Brodwin, M. G., Sin, F. W., Howard, J., Brodwin, E. R., & Du, A. T. (Eds.). (2020). *Medical, psychosocial and vocational aspects of disability* (5th ed.). Elliott & Fitzpatrick, Inc.

Brooks, J. M., Iwanaga, K., Cotton, B. P., Deiches, J., Blake, J., Chiu, C., Morrison, B., & Chan, F. (2018). Perceived Mindfulness and Depressive Symptoms Among People with Chronic Pain. *Journal of rehabilitation, 84*(2), 33–39.

Chakhssi, F., Kraiss, J. T., Sommers-Spijkerman, M., & Bohlmeijer, E. T. (2018). The effect of positive psychology interventions on well-being and distress in clinical samples with psychiatric or somatic disorders: A systematic review and meta-analysis. *BMC Psychiatry, 18*, 1–17.

Condon, S. E. (2022). Gratitude and well-being in older adults with chronic pain: A brief gratitude intervention feasibility study. *ProQuest Dissertations & Theses* (No. 29326449).

Davenport, J., Koch, L. C., & Rumrill, P. D., Jr. (2017). Mindfulness-based approaches for managing chronic pain: Applications to vocational rehabilitation and employment. *Journal of Vocational Rehabilitation, 47*(2), 247–258. https://doi.org/10.3233/JVR-170899

Davidson, R. J., Kabat-Zinn, J., Schumacher, J., Rosenkranz, M. S., Muller, D, Santorelli, S. F., Urbanowski, F., Harrington, A., Bonus, K., & Sheridan, J. F. (2003). Alterations in brain and immune function produced by mindfulness meditation. *Psychosomatic Medicine*, *65*, 564–570.

Davidson, R. J., & Lutz, A. (2008). Buddha's brain: Neuroplasticity and meditation. *IEEE Signal Processing Magazine*, *25,* 176–174. https://doi.org/10.1109/msp.2008.4431873

Falvo, D., & Holland, B. E. (2018). *Medical and psychosocial aspects of chronic illness and disability* (6th ed.). Jones & Bartlett Learning.

Gardner-Nix, J., & Costin-Hall, M. (with Kabat-Zinn, J.). (2009). *The mindfulness solution to pain.* New Harbinger Publications, Inc.

Gates, B., Cullen, M., & Nisker, W. (2009). Interview with Richard Davidson, Daniel Goleman, & Jon Kabat-Zinn: Friends in mind, friends at heart. *Inquiring Mind, 25*(2). https://inquiringmind.com/article/2504_davidson-goleman_kabatzinn/

Gibler, R. C., Knestrick, K. E., Reidy, B. L., Lax, D. N., & Powers, S. W. (2022). Management of chronic migraine in children and adolescents: Where are we in 2022? *Pediatric Health, Medicine and Therapeutics, 13*(1), 309–323. https://doi.org/10.2147/PHMT.S334744

Gordon S, Brown R, Hogan M, Menzies V. Mindfulness as a Symptom Management Strategy for Fibromyalgia: An Integrative Review. *Journal of Holistic Nursing. 2023;41*(2):200-214. doi:10.1177/08980101221123833

Grazzi, L., Grignani, E., Raggi, A., Rizzoli, P., & Guastafierro, E. (2021). Effect of a mindfulness-based intervention for chronic migraine and high frequency episodic migraine in adolescents: A pilot single-arm open-label study. *International Journal of Environmental Research and Public Health, 18*(22), 11739.

Grant, J. A., Courtemanche, J., Duerden, E. G., Duncan, G. H., & Rainville, P. (2010). Cortical thickness and pain sensitivity in Zen meditators. *Emotion*, 10, 43–53. https://doi.org/10.1037/a0018334

Hassett, A. L. (2018). Remaining positive about positive psychological interventions for pain. *JAMA Network Open*, *1*(5), e182531–e182531.

Hearn, J. H., & Cross, A. (2020). Mindfulness for pain, depression, anxiety, and quality of life in people with spinal cord injury: A systematic review. *BMC Neurology, 20*(32), 1–11. https://doi.org/10.1186/s12883-020-1619-5

Hilton, L., Hempel, S., Ewing, B.A., Apaydin, E., Xenakis, L., Newberry, S., Colaiaco, B., Maher, A. R., Shanman, R. M., Sorbero, M. E., & Maglione, M. A. (2016). Mindfulness meditation for chronic pain: Systematic review and meta-analysis. *Annals Behavioral Medicine, 51*(2), 199–213. https://doi.org/10.1007/s12160-016-9844-2

Hovaguimian, A., & Roth, J. (2022). Management of chronic migraine. *The BMJ, 379*, 1–19. https://doi.org/10.1136/bmj-2021-067670

IASP. (2020, July 16). *IASP announces revised definition of pain.* https://www.iasp-pain.org/publications/iasp-news/iasp-announces-revised-definition-of-pain/

Job Accommodation Network. (n.d.). *Chronic pain.* https://askjan.org/disabilities/Chronic-Pain.cfm

Kabat-Zinn, J. (2013). *Full catastrophe living: Using the wisdom of your body and mind to face stress, pain, and illness.* Bantam Books.

Kabat-Zinn, J. (2023). *Mindfulness meditation for pain relief.* Sounds True.

Katz, J., Rosenbloom, B. N., & Fashler, S. (2015). Chronic pain, psychopathology, and *DSM-5* somatic symptom disorder. *The Canadian Journal of Psychiatry, 60*(4), 160–167. https://doi.org/10.1177/070674371506000402

Knoebel, R. W., Starck, J. V., & Miller, P. (2021). Treatment disparities among the Black population and their influence on the equitable management of chronic pain. *Health Equity, 5*(1), 596–605. https://doi.org/10.1089/heq.2020.0062

Kristjansdottir, O. B., Stenberg, U., Mirkovic, J., Krogseth, T., Ljoså, T. M., Stange, K. C., & Ruland, C. M. (2018). Personal strengths reported by people with chronic illness: A qualitative study. *Health Expectations, 21*(4), 787–795. https://doi.org/10.1111/hex.12674

Leça, S., & Tavares, I. (2022). Research in Mindfulness Interventions for Patients With Fibromyalgia: A Critical Review. *Frontiers in integrative neuroscience, 16*, 920271. https://doi.org/10.3389/fnint.2022.920271

Liu, B., Guan, Y., Jing, H., Hofmann, S. G., & Liu, X. (2022). Mindfulness and PERMA well-being: Intervention effects and mechanism of change. *Psychology, 13*(5), 675–704.

Majeed, M. H., Ali, A. A., & Sudak, D. (2017). Mindfulness-based interventions for chronic pain: Evidence and applications. *Asian Journal of Psychiatry, 32*, 79–83. https://doi.org/10.1016/j.ajp.2017.11.025

McCracken, L. M., Gauntlett-Gilbert, J., & Vowles, K. E. (2007). The role of mindfulness in a contextual cognitive-behavioral analysis of chronic pain-related suffering and disability. *Pain, 131*(1-2), 63–69. https://doi.org/10.1016/j.pain.2006.12.013

Mindful Leader. (n.d.). *Why was MBSR created?* https://www.mindfulleader.org/mbsr/why-was-mbsr-created

National Disability Institute. (2021, September 20). *Positive psychology.* National Disability Institute. https://www.nationaldisabilityinstitute.org/capacity-building/positive-psychology/

Pierce, K. L. (2024). Bridging the gap between intentions and impact: Understanding disability culture to support disability justice. *The Professional Counselor, 13*(4), 486–495. https://doi.org/10.15241/klp.13.4.486

Raffaeli, W., Tenti, M., Corraro, A., Malafoglia, V., Ilari, S., Balzani, E., & Bonci, A. (2021). Chronic pain: What does it mean? A review on the use of the term chronic pain in clinical practice. *Journal of Pain Research, 14,* 827–835. https://doi.org/10.2147/JPR.S303186

Rikard, S. M., Strahan, A. E., Schmit, K. M., & Guy, G. P. Jr. (2023). Chronic pain among adults—United States, 2019–2021. *Morbidity and Mortality Weekly Report, 72,* 379–385. http://dx.doi.org/10.15585/mmwr.mm7215a1

Seligman, M. (2010). Flourish: Positive psychology and positive interventions. *The Tanner Lectures on Human Values, 31*(4), 1–56.

Senders, A., Borgatti, A., Hanes, D., & Shinto, L. (2018). Association between pain and mindfulness in multiple sclerosis: A cross-sectional survey. *International Journal of MS Care, 20*(1), 28–34. https://doi.org/10.7224/1537-2073.2016-076

Sheldon, K. M., & Lyubomirsky, S. (2006). How to increase and sustain positive emotion: The effects of expressing gratitude and visualizing best possible selves. *The Journal of Positive Psychology, 1*(2), 73–82.

Siegel, R. (2010). *The mindfulness solution: Everyday practices for everyday problems.* The Guilford Press.

Stone, M. (2016, January). *Meditation Facilitation Mentorship Program with Michael Stone.* Program conducted at Hemma the Home of Yoga and Acupuncture, Victoria, BC, Canada.

Treadway, M. T., & Lazar, S. W. (2010). Meditation and neuroplasticity: Using mindfulness to change the brain. In R. A. Baer (Ed.), *Assessing mindfulness and acceptance processes in clients: Illuminating the theory and practice of change* (pp. 186–205). New Harbinger Publications, Inc.

Vago, D. R., & Silbersweig, D. A. (2012). Self-awareness, self-regulation, and self-transcendence (S-ART): A framework for understanding the neurobiological mechanisms of mindfulness. *Frontiers in Human Neuroscience, 6,* 296. https://doi.org/10.3389/fnhum.2012.00296

Van der Kolk, B. (2014). *The body keeps the score: Brain, mind and body in the healing of trauma.* Viking.

Wells, R. E., O'Connell, N., Pierce, C. R., Estave, P., Penzien, D. B., Loder, E., Zeidan, F., & Houle, T. T. (2021). Effectiveness of mindfulness meditation vs headache education for adults with migraine: A randomized clinical trial. *JAMA Internal Medicine, 181*(3), 317–328. https://doi.org/10.1001/jamainternmed.2020.7090

Wolfe, F., Walitt, B., Perrot, S., Rasker, J. J., & Häuser, W. (2018). Fibromyalgia diagnosis and biased assessment: Sex, prevalence and bias. *PLoS ONE, 13*(9), 1–14. https://doi.org/10.1371/journal.pone.0203755

Yaugher, A., Voss, M., Swensen, K., & Condie, A. W. (2023, December 14). *Cognitive behavioral therapies for the management of chronic pain.* USU. https://extension.usu.edu/heart/research/cognitive-behavioral-therapies-for-chronic-pain-management

Younesi, J., Kazemi, J., Khanjani, M. S., Dadkhah, A., Biglarian, A., & Ebrahimi Barmi, B. (2020). The effects of acceptance and commitment therapy on the sense of coherence, locus of control, and posttraumatic growth in patients with multiple sclerosis. *Iranian Rehabilitation Journal, 18*(4), 445–454. https://doi.org/10.32598/irj.18.4.1016.2

Zhou, B., Wang, G., Hong, Y., Xu, S., Wang, J., Yu, H., Liu, Y., & Yu, L. (2020). Mindfulness interventions for rheumatoid arthritis: A systematic review and meta-analysis. *Complementary Therapies in Clinical Practice*, *39*, 101088. https://doi.org/10.1016/j.ctcp.2020.101088

Applying Positive Psychology and Mindfulness: Substance Use Disorder

5

Michele M. Mahr
Monica Wilson
Tobias Zellner

KEYWORDS AND DEFINITIONS:

3,4-methyl-enedioxy-methamphetamine (MDMA): Also known as "Ecstasy" or "X," it is an entactogenic drug. Frequently used in the rave scene. Consumed orally.

Alcohol: Also known as ethanol.

Amphetamines: A stimulating drug also known as "Speed," it can be consumed by inhalation or intravenously or nasally.

Bath salts: Synthetic amphetamine, phenethylamine, or cathinone derivatives acting as stimulating drugs. These can be consumed intravenously or nasally. Bath salts have severe adverse effects and are extremely addictive.

Benzodiazepines/Z-substances: Sleeping medication like lorazepam (Ativan®), alprazolam (Xanax®), or diazepam (Valium®). Z-substance had the same mechanism of action and was marketed as less addictive; examples are zopiclone or zolpidem.

Cannabis: Also known as THC, it can be consumed orally, by inhalation, or nasally. Synthetic cannabinoid receptor agonists (SCRA) like "Spice" are more potent and cannot be detected easily.

Cocaine: A stimulating drug which can be consumed intravenously or nasally. Crack cocaine is the free base and can be smoked. Highly addictive.

Gamma hydroxybutyrate (GHB)/gamma butyrolactone (GBL): Also known as "liquid ecstasy" or date rape drugs. Fast wash-in and wash-out with unconsciousness and amnesia are some of the effects. These drugs are consumed orally.

Lysergic acid diethylamide (LSD): Also known as "Acid," it is a psychedelic drug that causes hallucinations and, in some cases, "horror trips" and can trigger psychosis and schizophrenia. The famous Beatles song "Lucy in the Sky with Diamonds" is said to describe an LSD trip. Consumed orally.

Methamphetamine: A stimulating drug also known as "Crystal" or "Crystal Meth." Famous from the TV series "Breaking Bad." It can be consumed by inhalation or intravenously or nasally and is highly addictive.

Nicotine: The most addictive drug known to mankind, in tobacco, cigarettes, and e-cigarettes.

Opiates and opioids: Naturally occurring and synthetically created opiates. Drugs like heroin and fentanyl belong to this group. Heroin is consumed by either inhalation or intravenously or nasally and is highly addictive

Psilocybin: Active hallucinogenic ingredient in "magic mushrooms" or "shrooms." Consumed orally.

Substance use disorder (SUD): Addiction, drug addiction, drug dependency, substance abuse, substance misuse, substance dependency, alcoholism, alcohol use disorder.

LEARNING OBJECTIVES:

1. Understand the operational definitions of substance use, tolerance, and addiction and how they are used interchangeably within the literature and the general public.
2. Understand the different substances, their pharmacokinetics and symptoms, and treatment options.
3. Conceptualize how positive psychology can be implemented into the treatment plan when working with individuals with an SUD.
4. Learn how mindfulness interventions can be viable and effective treatment modalities to assist individuals with SUD.
5. Apply the information provided in this chapter to answer the questions for the clinical case study provided pertaining to an individual struggling with SUD.

Introduction

In this chapter, the focus will be on substance use disorder (SUD). According to the *Diagnostic and Statistical Manual of Mental Disorders*, Fifth Edition, Text Revision (*DSM-5-TR*), SUD involves patterns of symptoms caused by using a substance that an individual continues taking despite its negative effects. The authors will first address the following substances: alcohol, nicotine, cannabis and synthetic cannabinoid receptor agonists (SCRA), opiates and opioids, benzodiazepines/Z-Substances, gamma hydroxybutyrate (GHB)/gamma butyrolactone (GBL), pregabalin, amphetamines, methamphetamine, cocaine, "bath salts," 3,4-methyl-enedioxy-methamphetamine (MDMA), lysergic acid diethylamide (LSD), and psilocybin (magic mushrooms). Following the overview of each substance, specific strategies within positive psychology and mindfulness will be suggested as potential treatment modalities for mental health and rehabilitation counselors working with SUD.

Overview of Substance Use Disorder

The Diagnostic and Statistical Manual of Mental Disorders, Fifth Edition, Text Revision (*DSM-5-TR*) defines SUDs as conditions characterized by a range of cognitive, behavioral, and physiological symptoms that indicate ongoing substance use despite significant related problems. SUDs involve underlying changes in brain circuits, which can persist even after detoxification, often leading to relapses and strong cravings. The diagnostic criteria for SUDs are organized into four main categories: impaired control, social impairment, risky use, and pharmacological criteria (including tolerance and withdrawal). The severity of the disorder is determined by the number of criteria met: 2 to 3 symptoms suggest a mild disorder, 4 to 5 indicate a moderate disorder, and 6 or more suggest a severe disorder (American Psychiatric Association, 2022).

According to the *DSM-5-TR*, SUDs can be diagnosed across 10 distinct classes of substances: alcohol, caffeine, cannabis, hallucinogens, inhalants, opioids, anxiolytics, stimulants, tobacco, and other (or unknown) substances, all of which can contribute to the development of SUD (American Psychiatric Association, 2022). The manual also highlights that these disorders are not limited to substance use itself but can include substance-induced disorders, such as intoxication, withdrawal, and other substance/medication-induced mental disorders. The *DSM-5-TR* emphasizes the importance of recognizing that each substance affects the brain differently due to its unique pharmacological mechanisms. These differences in how substances interact with the brain's reward system can make treatment and recovery more challenging. Additionally, the manual notes that SUDs are chronic conditions with a tendency to recur or relapse after a period of recovery. Therefore, treating SUDs requires a comprehensive, long-term approach rather than a short-term intervention.

The etiology of SUDs is complex, involving an interplay of biological, psychological, and social factors. The *DSM-5-TR* identifies the activation of the brain's reward system as a key biological factor, noting that all substances of abuse share this characteristic. This activation leads to the reinforcement of behaviors associated with substance use due to the intense pleasure or "high" these substances produce. The reward system's influence is so strong that it can overshadow other important activities and responsibilities, causing individuals to prioritize substance use over essential life functions. The *DSM-5-TR* also notes that individuals with lower levels of self-control, possibly due to impairments in brain inhibitory mechanisms, are more prone to developing SUDs. This suggests that certain neurobiological vulnerabilities may exist even before substance use begins, making some individuals more susceptible to addiction (American Psychiatric Association, 2022). Psychological factors, including personality traits and co-occurring mental health disorders, play a significant role in the development of SUDs, as do environmental factors such as peer pressure, stress, and early exposure to substances. Social factors like peer influence, socioeconomic status, and exposure to environments where substance use is common further contribute to the risk. The *DSM-5-TR* emphasizes that the etiology of SUDs is not due to a single cause but is the result of a combination of genetic, psychological, and environmental factors interacting to increase the likelihood of substance abuse (American Psychiatric Association, 2022).

Alcohol

Alcohol use disorder (AUD) is a chronic condition characterized by a problematic pattern of alcohol consumption that leads to significant impairment or distress. According to the *DSM-5--TR*, the diagnostic criteria for AUD are based on the presence of at least 2 of the following symptoms within a 12-month period: consuming alcohol in larger amounts or over a longer period than intended; a persistent desire or unsuccessful attempts to cut down or control alcohol use; spending a great deal of time obtaining, using, or recovering from the effects of alcohol; craving or a strong desire to use alcohol; and recurrent alcohol use resulting in failure to fulfill major role obligations at work, school, or home. Other symptoms include continued alcohol use despite social or interpersonal problems; giving up important activities in favor of alcohol use; using alcohol in physically hazardous situations; continuing alcohol use despite knowledge of having a physical or psychological problem likely caused or exacerbated by alcohol; developing tolerance (needing more alcohol to achieve the same effect); and experiencing withdrawal symptoms when not consuming alcohol (American Psychiatric Association, 2022).

The severity of AUD is classified as mild, moderate, or severe based on the number of symptoms present: mild (2–3 symptoms), moderate (4–5 symptoms), and severe (6 or more symptoms). The *DSM-5* provides specific International Classification of Diseases, Tenth Revision, Clinical Modification (ICD-10-CM) codes to represent these severity levels: F10.10 for mild AUD and F10.20 for moderate or severe AUD. Individuals with AUD may find it difficult to control their alcohol intake, experience cravings, and continue to use alcohol despite adverse consequences in their social, occupational, or personal life (American Psychiatric Association, 2022).

History and Epidemiology

The use of alcohol is deeply embedded in our culture. Although alcohol use can provide social connections, it can also be harmful, cause disease, and decrease lifespan. It is a toxic substance and is currently the fourth leading preventable cause of death in the United States (Fairbanks et al., 2020; Stahre et al., 2014). The pathologic use of alcohol impacts more than 2 billion people worldwide and results in nearly 6% of all deaths. Currently, the Western European countries have the largest alcohol per capita consumption worldwide with >12.5 L of pure alcohol per inhabitant per year (World Health Organization, 2018). Alcohol use causes fetal alcohol spectrum disorder (FASD), liver disease, hepatitis, cardiovascular disease (such as cardiomyopathy), polyneuropathy, dementia, and cancers such as breast cancer and head and neck cancer (especially laryngeal cancer). Excessive alcohol use is responsible for about 178,000 deaths in the United States each year, and it shortens the lives of those who die by an average of 24 years. Excessive alcohol use was associated with an economic cost of $249 billion in 2010 (U.S. Centers for Disease Control and Prevention, 2024). A diagnosis attributable to alcohol is associated with higher annual per-person healthcare expenditures in both commercially insured and Medicaid-insured participants by $14,918 (95% CI = $14,540, $15,297) and $4,823 (95% CI = $4,489, $5,158), respectively. As much as 60% to 75% of the additional costs of excessive alcohol use are driven by heart disease and stroke; conditions of the liver, gallbladder, and pancreas; and certain cancers as well as acute conditions that may be attributable to alcohol (Ozluk et al., 2022).

Pathophysiology, Pharmacology, and Effect of Alcohol

Alcohol causes central nervous system (CNS) depression. It is a positive $GABA_A$ modulator and is associated and related with decreased anxiety, decreased social inhibition, sedation; impairment of cognitive, memory, and sensory function; and cognitive, memory, motor, and sensory impairment. It slows and impairs cognition and reaction time and the cognitive skills; impairs judgment; interferes with motor function resulting in motor incoordination and numbness; impairs memory formation; and causes sensory impairment. Co-use with other CNS-depressant drugs increases the risk of adverse effects and is associated with a higher need for medical treatment, especially when combined with opiates/opioids or GHB/GBL (Heier et al., 2022).

Clinical Features

Alcohol intoxication, also known in overdose as alcohol poisoning or drunkenness, is the behavior and physical effects caused by a recent consumption of alcohol (Jung & Namkoong, 2014). In addition to the toxicity of alcohol, the main psychoactive component of alcoholic beverages, other physiological symptoms may arise from the activity of acetaldehyde, a metabolite of alcohol (Zakhari, 2006).

Alcoholics can suffer from alcohol withdrawal. This may cause alcohol withdrawal syndrome (AWS) with fatal outcomes. Severe alcohol withdrawal symptoms are withdrawal seizures and delirium tremens and may require intensive care treatment (Bramness et al., 2022; Mohan et al., 2023).

Diagnosis and Treatment

Alcohol can be measured via breath analyzers, also known as breathalyzers or alcohol meters (per mille, ‰). It can also be measured in serum to get the current alcohol level (g/l). Long-term markers in serum (carbohydrate deficient Transferrin [CDTR]) and in urine (ethyl glucuronide [EtG]) are available. AWS is diagnosed clinically, as is alcohol use disorder (AUD).

Alcohol intoxications are usually treated at home or at an emergency department. Vitamin B injections, antiemetic drugs, fluid replacement therapy, and monitoring are usually sufficient (Heier et al., 2022; Jung & Namkoong, 2014). After successful therapy of the acute intoxication, patients with AUD should be monitored for AWS. Patients with AWS should be treated in-hospital with benzodiazepines and prophylactic anticonvulsant therapy.

After successful alcohol detoxification, patients with AUD should be treated in out- or in-patient rehabilitation. Established treatment modalities are total abstinence or harm reduction also known as contingency management. Motivational interviewing (MI), first described in 1991 by Miller and Rollnick (1991), and cognitive behavioral therapy (CBT) are the psychotherapy modalities of choice (American Psychiatric Association, 2010) and can be used for both total abstinence and harm reduction. While total abstinence is the preferred goal, harm reduction is often the more realistic goal. For AUD, controlled drinking was first described by Pattison et al. as a treatment option (1977). Strange and Stimson established the concept of harm reduction or contingency management in the context of IV drug use by suggesting to hand out clean needles and syringes to drug users instead of following a strict zero-tolerance policy (Strang & Stimson, 1990). This concept was adapted for AUD; for example, Esser et al. described surveillance as an approach that may be viable to decrease excessive alcohol consumption and reduce harmful consequences (2020). Controlled drinking is taught in specialized programs and includes teaching patients the understanding of alcohol use patterns and effects. A recent meta-analysis showed that abstinence should not be seen as the only approach in the treatment of AUD. However, controlled drinking supported by specific psychotherapy appears to be a viable option when an abstinence-oriented approach is not applicable (Henssler et al., 2021).

Self-help groups such as Alcoholics Anonymous (AA) can support patients with AUD and their family members (Kelly et al., 2020). Patients can join AA meetings in every phase of their alcohol dependence, also while still actively drinking. Often caregivers, family members, students, donors, and so on will become AA members and might even attend AA meetings to gain valuable knowledge about AUD. While AA is the predominant self-help group in the United States, it is seen more critically or even negatively in other Western countries due to the strong focus on spirituality (Nelson, 2009).

Pharmacotherapy with disulfiram, naltrexone (oral and long-acting injectable), and acamprosate can be used to support alcohol abstinence or harm reduction (Fairbanks et al., 2020; Witkiewitz et al., 2019). Disulfiram therapy should always be accompanied by psychotherapy due to the severe or even life-threatening adverse event in case of alcohol relapse. While effective, this is the reason Disulfiram lost its approval in countries like Germany. Baclofen and Nalmefene can be used but are currently not approved by the FDA. Nalmefene is especially recommended for supporting controlled drinking since it reduces drinking amounts. Currently, it is largely unclear which treatment approach and medication should be implemented due to the variance in frequency and duration of drinking (Palpacuer et al., 2018).

Case study

An approximately 50-year-old male is delivered to the Emergency Department (ED) in December 2023. He was found unconscious on a park bench in Central Park. A jogger found him at 5 a.m. during her morning round covered by snow and called 911 after checking that he was still breathing. Emergency medical services found an unconscious, hypothermic patient with a strong stench of alcohol. He was clearly homeless and had vomited and soiled his pants.

In the ED, due to lack of information, the patient was designated John Doe, date of birth January 1, 1973. The patient's vitals were the following: Heart rate: 33 beats/minute. Blood pressure: 92/52 mmHg. Oxygen saturation: 92%. Temperature: 82° Fahrenheit. Alcohol serum level: 4.2 (g/l, a lethal level for non-alcoholics). Due to his critical heart rate and temperature, the patient was transferred to the Intensive Care Unit (ICU) for further treatment. There, he received intravenous Vitamin B_1, fluid resuscitation and was warmed up with an intravenous warming catheter inserted via a central venous catheter in his femoral vein.

After successful temperature management, the patient sobered up and instantly developed severe delirium tremens with hallucinations, agitation, and aggression. After assaulting the ICU personnel, he was sedated and received intravenous benzodiazepines (Midazolam), Dexmedetomidine (Precedex®), and haloperidol. He developed aspiration pneumonia and was treated with intravenous antibiotics. Treatment in the ICU was successfully concluded after 2 weeks. The patient was reoriented and stated that his name was Malcom Stone, date of birth March 23, 1972. He had no home, no job, and no health insurance. He is divorced and has two children from his previous marriage. He usually drinks one to two bottles of vodka but denies using drugs other than alcohol. He smokes two packs of cigarettes per day.

He was presented to Social Service, and, with the help of Motivational Interviewing, the client was convinced to join one of the local New York Alcoholics Anonymous groups. Due to his lack of insurance, professional rehabilitation was not an option. The patient left the hospital against medical advice (AMA) and with an enormous bill which added to his already substantial previous debt.

Fortunately, he attended AA while continuing to drink. He now presents approximately one year later for detoxification. He managed to achieve controlled drinking, enabling him to get a job with health insurance and an apartment. He still has debt, which causes anxiety and depression. He recently relapsed to heavier drinking endangering his job. This is his motivation for detoxification. He started alcohol withdrawal treatment, and Social Service got involved for organizing inpatient rehabilitation, which is covered by his Medicaid insurance plan.

Critical Thinking Questions

1. What are some questions that you would ask the patient regarding his current drinking status?
2. What techniques of Positive Psychology would you suggest for the client?
3. How might you encourage the client to implement mindfulness into their life to assist in relapse prevention?
4. What resources would you suggest to the client to facilitate social support, financial support, and emotional support during this difficult time?

Nicotine or Tobacco Use Disorder

Tobacco use disorder (TUD), as defined in the *DSM-5-TR*, is characterized by a problematic pattern of tobacco use that leads to significant impairment or distress. The diagnostic criteria for TUD require the presence of at least two of the following symptoms within a 12-month period: Tobacco is often taken in larger amounts or over a longer period than intended; there is a persistent desire or unsuccessful efforts to cut down or control tobacco use; a great deal of time is spent in activities necessary to obtain or use tobacco; craving or a strong desire to use tobacco; recurrent tobacco use resulting in a failure to fulfill major role obligations at work, school, or home; continued tobacco use despite having persistent or recurrent social or interpersonal problems caused or exacerbated by tobacco; important social, occupational, or recreational activities are given up or reduced because of tobacco use; recurrent tobacco use in physically hazardous situations; tobacco use continued despite knowledge of having a persistent or recurrent physical or psychological problem likely caused or exacerbated by tobacco; tolerance (a need for markedly increased amounts of tobacco to achieve the desired effect or a markedly diminished effect with continued use of the same amount); and withdrawal symptoms or use of tobacco to relieve or avoid withdrawal symptoms (American Psychiatric Association, 2022).

The severity of TUD is classified as mild, moderate, or severe depending on the number of symptoms present: mild (2–3 symptoms), moderate (4–5 symptoms), and severe (6 or more symptoms). The ICD-10-CM codes corresponding to these severity levels are Z72.0 for mild TUD, F17.200 for moderate, and F17.200 for severe. Additionally, the *DSM-5-TR* provides specifiers for remission, including "in early remission" and "in sustained remission" based on the duration of abstinence. The disorder is most commonly associated with cigarette smoking, although it can also occur with the use of other tobacco products. TUD is highly prevalent and often begins in adolescence, with a significant proportion of individuals attempting to quit multiple times before achieving long-term abstinence (American Psychiatric Association, 2022).

Pathophysiology, Pharmacology, and Epidemiology

After consuming nicotine, circulating levels of norepinephrine and epinephrine increase rapidly, and the bioavailability of dopamine is altered. Among the neuroendocrine effects are release of arginine vasopressin, beta-endorphin, adrenocorticotropic hormone, and cortisol. After inhalation, the reinforcing effects of the drug are maximized (Pomerleau, 1992). Cigarettes cause illnesses such as cancer, chronic obstructive pulmonary disease (COPD), heart disease, birth defects, and other health problems. Tobacco kills more than 8 million people each year, including an estimated 1.3 million nonsmokers who are exposed to secondhand smoke. In 2020, 22.3% of the world's population used tobacco: 36.7% of men and 7.8% of women (World Health Organization, 2023). Cigarette smoking cost the United States more than $600 billion in 2018, with more than $240 billion in healthcare spending (U.S. Centers for Disease Control and Prevention, 2022).

Treatment

As with AUD, total abstinence and harm reduction are the main treatment modalities for Tobacco Dependence. MI and CBT are the psychotherapy of choice. For harm reduction, electronic cigarettes (e-cigarettes) are a relatively new option: In the United Kingdom, the NHS guidance recommends e-cigarettes (also known as vapes) to people who wish to stop smoking or who are trying to cut down. E-cigarettes are used by many people to stay smoke-free after they have successfully quit smoking (King's College Hospital NHS Foundation Trust, 2022). The assumption is that e-cigarettes are 95% less toxic than normal cigarettes. If it were possible to get every smoker to switch to e-cigarettes, the morbidity and mortality caused by smoking should therefore be reduced by 95%.

Cannabis and Cannabinoid Receptor Agonists

Cannabis-Related Disorders

Cannabis use disorder (CUD) is defined in the *DSM-5-TR* as a problematic pattern of cannabis use that leads to significant impairment or distress. The diagnosis requires the presence of at least two symptoms within a 12-month period. These symptoms include using cannabis in larger amounts or over a longer period than intended; persistent desire or unsuccessful attempts to cut down or control use; spending a significant amount of time obtaining, using, or recovering from cannabis effects; experiencing cravings; and recurrent cannabis use leading to failure to fulfill major obligations at work, school, or home. Other criteria involve continued cannabis use despite social or interpersonal issues, giving up important activities in favor of cannabis, using cannabis in physically hazardous situations, and continuing use despite physical or psychological problems likely caused by cannabis. Tolerance and withdrawal are also recognized indicators (American Psychiatric Association, 2022).

The *DSM-5-TR* categorizes the severity of CUD as mild (2–3 symptoms), moderate (4–5 symptoms), or severe (6 or more symptoms). Corresponding ICD-10-CM codes are provided for each severity level: F12.10 for mild and F12.20 for moderate or severe. Specifiers for remission, including "early remission" and "sustained remission," are defined based on abstinence duration. Additionally, cannabis withdrawal, newly recognized in *DSM-5-TR*, is characterized by symptoms like irritability, anxiety, sleep difficulties, and decreased appetite, which may arise following the cessation of heavy use. Cannabis is typically consumed by smoking or, increasingly, by vaporization or ingestion.

While cannabis intoxication often produces euphoria, its effects can vary, leading to impairments in cognitive and motor functions that interfere with daily responsibilities. The disorder is highly comorbid with other SUDs, such as AUD or TUD, and is associated with increased risks of mental health issues, including anxiety, depression, and psychotic symptoms. Risk factors include early onset of cannabis use, conduct issues during childhood or adolescence, and environmental influences like family substance use or low socioeconomic status. The prevalence of CUD varies across age and demographic groups, with a notable concentration among adolescents and young adults. Males are generally more affected than females, though gender differences are less pronounced among adolescents. The disorder often develops gradually, typically beginning in adolescence or early adulthood. Cultural acceptance and the legal landscape surrounding cannabis use can influence patterns of use and the development of CUD.

History and Epidemiology

Marijuana from "cannabis sativa" with the active ingredients tetrahydrocannabinol (THC) and cannabidiol (CBD) has long been used as a recreational drug by smoking the dried marijuana. Hashish and hash oil can also be consumed either by inhalation or orally. It is either added to cigarettes, smoked pure, or nebulized in a vaporizer. Furthermore, synthetic cannabinoid receptor agonists (SCRA) have been synthesized with much greater potency. John W. Huffman, an organic chemist at Clemson University, was a pioneer in SCRA research and first described many SCRA like JWH-018. JWH-018 was first sold in Germany on December 15, 2008, with the brand name "spice" to circumvent the cannabis ban. Hexahydrocannabinol (HHC) was first synthesized 1940 and has recently become more prominent on the drug market. In the United States, cannabis is considered and remains a Schedule I drug at federal level and is regulated by the United Nations "Single Convention on Narcotic Drugs" of 1961, "Convention on Psychotropic Substances" of 1971, and "Convention against Illicit Traffic in Narcotic Drugs and Psychotropic Substances" of 1988. Some countries like Germany have effectively banned SCRA with the New Psychoactive Substances (NPS) legislation in November 2016 (Bundesministerium für Gesundheit, 2016). Recently, in countries like, for example, the Netherlands, the United States, Canada, and Germany, efforts were made to legalize cannabis (Manthey et al., 2023).

Pathophysiology, Pharmacology, and Effect

THC, CBD, HHC, and SCRA bind to the cannabinoid receptors called CB_1 and CB_2. While the CB1 receptor is mainly expressed in the CNS, it is also expressed in the lungs, liver, and kidneys. The CB_2 receptor is expressed in the immune system, in hematopoietic cells, and in the brain. The activation of CB_1 in the human body generally inhibits neurotransmitter release, controls pain, regulates metabolism, and monitors the cardiovascular system (Brent et al., 2017; Huang et al., 2020).

Clinical Features

Acute cannabis toxicity usually involves neurobehavioral changes like agitation/aggression, psychosis, anxiety, and vomiting (Brent et al., 2017; Dines, Wood, Galicia, et al., 2015). SCRA poisonings have statistically significantly higher rates of drowsiness, coma, agitation, seizures, and bradycardia at the time of presentation (Waters et al., 2024). Continuous use of cannabis has especially negative effects on individuals without full brain development, which is usually complete at the age of 25. In these individuals, it causes disrupted learning, impaired cognitive performance, reduced educational attainment and an increased risk of CUD, psychosis/schizophrenia, mood and anxiety disorders, and suicidal behaviors (Hoch et al., 2024).

Treatment

Most patients with acute cannabis poisoning require no medical treatment (Brent et al., 2017; Dines, Wood, Galicia, et al., 2015). Total abstinence and harm reduction are the main treatment modalities for CUD. MI and CBT are the psychotherapy of choice.

Legalization

In the United States, cannabis was first legalized as medical marijuana (MML) in some states and later legalized recreationally (recreational marijuana legalization [RML]) in some states. While cannabis availability and use increased in RML states, there has been no significant increase in CUD or psychosis. However, acute cannabis toxicity increased, especially in children (Manthey et al., 2023). In RML states, the black market for cannabis decreased with mixed results on cannabis-associated crime.

Opiate and Opioid Use Disorder

Opiate and opioid use disorders (OUD) are characterized by a problematic pattern of opioid use leading to significant impairment or distress, as outlined by the *DSM-5-TR*. The diagnostic criteria include at least 2 of the following symptoms occurring within a 12-month period: opioids are often taken in larger amounts or over a longer period than intended; there is a persistent desire or unsuccessful efforts to cut down or control opioid use; a great deal of time is spent in activities necessary to obtain, use, or recover from the effects of opioids; craving or a strong desire to use opioids; recurrent opioid use resulting in a failure to fulfill major role obligations at work, school, or home;

continued opioid use despite persistent or recurrent social or interpersonal problems; important social, occupational, or recreational activities are given up or reduced because of opioid use; recurrent opioid use in physically hazardous situations; continued opioid use despite knowledge of a physical or psychological problem likely caused or exacerbated by opioids; tolerance; and withdrawal symptoms (American Psychiatric Association, 2022).

The severity of OUD is categorized as mild if 2–3 symptoms are present, moderate if 4–5 symptoms are present, and severe if 6 or more symptoms are present. The ICD-10-CM codes associated with this disorder are F11.10 for mild cases, F11.20 for moderate cases, and F11.20 for severe cases. The *DSM-5-TR* highlights that individuals with this disorder often experience significant tolerance and withdrawal symptoms, indicating physiological dependence. Opioid use can lead to severe health issues, social problems, and a high risk of overdose, especially in cases where the substances are used without medical supervision. The course of the disorder is often chronic and relapsing, with individuals frequently planning their daily activities around obtaining and using opioids (American Psychiatric Association, 2022).

History and Epidemiology

Opiates are naturally occurring substances or derivatives of opium, a substance found in the plant *Papaver somniferum*. These are opium, morphine, codeine, thebaine, and heroin, all binding to opioid receptors in the brain causing central pain relief. All are regulated under the "Uniform Controlled Substances Act" of the United States. Opioids are synthetically manufactured opiate derivatives like fentanyl (100 times more potent than morphine), sufentanil (1,000 times more potent), and carfentanil (approx. 15,000 times more potent). Oxycodone (OxyContin®), hydrocodone (Dilaudid® or Vicodin®), buprenorphine, and methadone are also opioids. Synthetic opioids have been found on the drug market (European Drug Agency, 2024).

Pathophysiology, Pharmacology, and Effect

Opioid receptors are receptors in the CNS. The main receptor is the mu (μ) receptor responsible for analgesia, physical dependence, respiratory depression, miosis, euphoria, and reduced GI motility. The delta receptor is responsible for analgesia, antidepressant effects, convulsant effects, and physical dependence. The kappa receptor causes analgesia, anticonvulsant effects, depression, dissociative/hallucinogenic effects, diuresis, miosis, dysphoria, neuroprotection, sedation, and stress (Brent et al., 2017).

Opiates and opioids have different receptor affinities. Buprenorphine had an approximately 3,000 times stronger affinity than heroin and competitively displaces heroin from the receptors. Furthermore, most opiates are full agonists, causing the effects mentioned above. There are also opioids with partial agonistic/antagonistic effects like buprenorphine or full antagonists like naloxone, naltrexone, and nalmefene (Brent et al., 2017).

Opiates and opioids have different absorption properties. Heroin is not absorbed in the gastrointestinal tract; it needs to be smoked or injected intravenously. Opium needs to be smoked while morphine can be injected or consumed orally. The main antagonist naloxone is absorbed intravenously, intramuscularly, or intranasally. Some formulations are a mix of an opioid with naloxone. If consumed orally and correctly, the opioid is absorbed, and naloxone is not absorbed in the gastrointestinal tract. If misused and injected intravenously, naloxone takes effect and counteracts the opioid canceling out the effect (Brent et al., 2017).

Clinical Features

Opiate and opioid toxicity has a classical triad: respiratory depression, extremely small pupils, and loss of consciousness (Brent et al., 2017). Opiates and opioids are responsible for most severe outcomes in recreational drug poisonings (Heier et al., 2022; Miro et al., 2023). While most drug deaths in Europe are due to opiates and opioids, the situation in Europe and the United States is not comparable. While countries like Germany are at an all-time high in drug deaths, the number is 2.227 deaths in a population of 85 million (Bundeskriminalamt, 2024). At the same time, 107,543 Americans out of 343 million died of drug overdose in 2023, mostly due to opiate or opioid toxicity (National Center for Health Statistics–, 2024).

Treatment

The treatment of acute opiate or opioid toxicity is either respiratory and consciousness surveillance, intubation, and mechanical ventilation, or antidote treatment with naloxone (Brent et al., 2017). Naloxone (Narcan®) can be used intramuscularly or intranasally, also by laymen via auto-injector or nasal spray. A full antagonization should only be used in life-threatening events because patients will go into full withdrawal and could get aggressive as a result. In synthetic opioid toxicity, higher naloxone doses may be required.

Total abstinence and harm reduction are the main treatment modalities for OUD. MI and CBT are the psychotherapy of choice. However, there are more treatment options. Strang and Stimson first suggested opioid substitution treatment in 1990 (Strang & Stimson, 1990). This idea was and is still discussed, but substitution has been established as an effective treatment. The idea is to give or prescribe the patients opioids so that they will not go intro withdrawal, have no overdoses, and drug criminality is reduced. Usually, methadone, buprenorphine, or morphine are given due to their pharmacological characteristics. In specialized ambulances, heroin is injected as substitution treatment.

Other harm reduction concepts are safe consumer spaces. In these facilities, drug addicts can consume their drugs in the presence of medical personnel. In case of overdose, a quick reaction is possible. Police need to respect these spaces and not arrest clients in the vicinity.

Another concept is the implantation of naloxone-releasing chips subcutaneously. These devices are not approved in most countries, and sophisticated devices releasing naloxone only in case of overdose are still in development (Dhowan et al., 2019).

Sedatives

In the *DSM-5-TR*, benzodiazepine and Z-substances use disorder is categorized under sedative-, hypnotic-, or anxiolytic-related disorders (SHARD). These disorders are characterized by a problematic pattern of use of sedative, hypnotic, or anxiolytic substances leading to significant impairment or distress. GHB and its precursor GBL are discussed in the *DSM-5-TR* under the category of "Other (or Unknown) SUD." GHB/GBL use disorder is characterized by a problematic pattern of use that leads to significant impairment or distress. The pharmacology, clinical features, and treatment are however quite similar.

Benzodiazepine and Z-Substances Use Disorder

The diagnostic criteria for this disorder require the presence of at least 2 of the following symptoms within a 12-month period: The substances are often taken in larger amounts or over a longer period than intended; there is a persistent desire or unsuccessful efforts to cut down or control use; a great deal of time is spent in activities necessary to obtain, use, or recover from the effects of the substances; craving or a strong desire to use the substances; recurrent use resulting in failure to fulfill major role obligations at work, school, or home; continued use despite persistent or recurrent social or interpersonal problems caused or exacerbated by the effects of the substances; important social, occupational, or recreational activities are given up or reduced because of use; recurrent use in physically hazardous situations; continued use despite knowledge of having a persistent or recurrent physical or psychological problem that is likely to have been caused or exacerbated by the substances; tolerance; and withdrawal symptoms (American Psychiatric Association, 2022).

The *DSM-5-TR* classifies the severity of SHARD as mild if 2–3 symptoms are present, moderate if 4–5 symptoms are present, and severe if 6 or more symptoms are present. Withdrawal symptoms associated with these substances may include autonomic hyperactivity (e.g., sweating or pulse rate greater than 100 bpm); hand tremor; insomnia; nausea or vomiting; transient visual, tactile, or auditory hallucinations or illusions; psychomotor agitation; anxiety; and grand mal seizures. The ICD-10-CM codes for these disorders are F13.10 for mild cases, F13.20 for moderate to severe cases, and F13.239 when withdrawal is present (American Psychiatric Association, 2022).

Gamma Hydroxybutyrate/Gamma Butyrolactone

The diagnostic criteria for a SUD involving GHB/GBL require the presence of at least 2 of the following symptoms within a 12-month period: The substance is often taken in larger amounts or over a longer period than intended; there is a persistent desire or unsuccessful efforts to cut down or control its use; a significant amount of time is spent obtaining, using, or recovering from the effects of the substance; craving or a strong desire to use the substance; recurrent use resulting in a failure to fulfill major role obligations at work, school, or home; continued use despite persistent or recurrent social or interpersonal problems caused or exacerbated by the effects of the substance; important social, occupational, or recreational activities are given up or reduced because of use; recurrent use in physically hazardous situations; continued use despite knowledge of a physical or psychological problem likely caused or exacerbated by the substance; tolerance; and withdrawal symptoms (American Psychiatric Association, 2022).

The severity of the disorder is categorized as mild if 2–3 symptoms are present, moderate if 4–5 symptoms are present, and severe if 6 or more symptoms are present. The corresponding ICD-10-CM codes are generally under the broader category of "Other Substance Use Disorders," with specific codes determined by the presence and severity of symptoms. The *DSM-5-TR* highlights that GHB and GBL, though sometimes used medically, are frequently misused for their sedative and euphoric effects, with a significant risk of dependency and the development of tolerance. Withdrawal from these substances can be severe, potentially leading to symptoms such as anxiety, tremors, and, in extreme cases, delirium (American Psychiatric Association, 2022).

History and Epidemiology

Sedating drugs like benzodiazepines are frequently consumed, and approximately the same number of patients are addicted to sedatives as to alcohol (Institut für Therapieforschung München, 2022). Benzodiazepines are marketed as sedatives or sleeping pills. Diazepam (Valium®), lorazepam

(Ativan®), clonazepam (Klonopin®), or alprazolam (Xanax®) are essential drugs (World Health Organization, 2013). Z-Substances like zopiclone (Imovane®) or zolpidem (Ambien®) have the same mechanism of action and effect. GHB or GBL, also known as "liquid ecstasy" or date rape drugs, have a similar mechanism of action. It has a fast wash-in and wash-out with unconsciousness and amnesia as effects and is consumed orally. Pregabalin is an antiepileptic drug but has been misused more frequently in the last years (Zellner et al., 2017). Synthetic benzodiazepines have been found on the drug market (European Drug Agency, 2024).

Pathophysiology, Pharmacology, and Effect

Benzodiazepines and GHB/GBL directly bind to the $GABA_A$ receptor in the brain. Pregabalin inhibits certain calcium channels in the same neurons carrying $GABA_A$ receptors causing similar effects.

Flumazenil is a direct $GABA_A$ receptor antagonist with a higher receptor affinity. It therefore counteracts benzodiazepines and, to some extent, GHB/GBL and pregabalin toxicity. Since all sedatives have an anticonvulsant effect, the application of flumazenil can cause seizures (Penninga et al., 2016).

Clinical Features

Benzodiazepine, GHB/GBL, and pregabalin effects are sedative, hypnotic (sleep-inducing), anxiolytic (anti-anxiety), anticonvulsant, and muscle relaxing. High doses can also cause anterograde amnesia and dissociation. In mono ingestion, benzodiazepines are viewed as safe drugs. In overdose, benzodiazepines, GHB/GBL, and pregabalin can cause dangerous deep unconsciousness. This is most prominent in GHB/GBL toxicity (Brent et al., 2017; Heier et al., 2022).

Treatment

The treatment of acute sedative toxicity is either respiratory and consciousness surveillance or intubation and mechanical ventilation or antidote treatment with flumazenil (Brent et al., 2017). The routine use of flumazenil is not recommended (Penninga et al., 2016).

Total abstinence and harm reduction are the main treatment modalities for SHARD like BZUD, GUD, and pregabalin use disorder. MI and CBT are the psychotherapy of choice.

Stimulants

Amphetamine and methamphetamine use disorders are both classified under stimulant-related disorders (SRD) in the *DSM-5-TR*. Cocaine use disorder (CUD) is also classified within SRDs in the *DSM-5-TR* and involves a pattern of cocaine use that leads to significant impairment or distress. Synthetic cathinones are potent stimulants that can cause significant physical and psychological effects. In the *DSM-5-TR*, the use of synthetic cathinones is also categorized under SRD. While the pharmacology is different, the clinical features and treatment are quite similar.

Amphetamine and Methamphetamine Use Disorder

These disorders are characterized by a problematic pattern of amphetamine or methamphetamine use that leads to significant impairment or distress. The diagnostic criteria for both disorders require the presence of at least 2 of the following symptoms within a 12-month period: The substances are often taken in larger amounts or over a longer period than intended; there is a persistent desire or unsuccessful efforts to cut down or control use; a significant amount of time is spent obtaining, using, or recovering from the substances; craving or a strong desire to use the substances; recurrent use resulting in failure to fulfill major role obligations; continued use despite persistent or recurrent social or interpersonal problems; giving up important social, occupational, or recreational activities because of use; recurrent use in physically hazardous situations; continued use despite knowledge of a physical or psychological problem likely caused or exacerbated by the substances; tolerance; and withdrawal symptoms (American Psychiatric Association, 2022).

The severity of both is categorized as mild if 2–3 symptoms are present, moderate if 4–5 symptoms are present, and severe if 6 or more symptoms are present. The ICD-10-CM codes for these disorders include F15.10 for mild cases and F15.20 for moderate or severe cases. While both amphetamines (such as Adderall® and Dexedrine®) and methamphetamine are potent stimulants, methamphetamine is known for its particularly severe effects, including significant health risks such as severe dental problems, skin sores, and cognitive deficits. Both substances carry a high risk of developing tolerance and dependence, with withdrawal symptoms that often include severe depression, anxiety, fatigue, and intense cravings, making these disorders particularly challenging to treat (American Psychiatric Association, 2022).

Cocaine Use Disorder

The diagnostic criteria require at least 2 of the following symptoms within a 12-month period: Cocaine is often taken in larger amounts or over a longer period than intended; there is a persistent desire or unsuccessful efforts to cut down or control cocaine use; a great deal of time is spent obtaining, using, or recovering from cocaine; craving or a strong desire to use cocaine; recurrent use resulting in failure to fulfill major role obligations; continued use despite persistent or recurrent social or interpersonal problems; giving up important social, occupational, or recreational activities because of use; recurrent use in physically hazardous situations; continued use despite knowledge of a physical or psychological problem likely caused or exacerbated by cocaine; tolerance; and withdrawal symptoms (American Psychiatric Association, 2022).

The severity of CUD is categorized as mild if 2–3 symptoms are present, moderate if 4–5 symptoms are present, and severe if 6 or more symptoms are present. The ICD-10-CM codes for this disorder are F14.10 for mild and F14.20 for moderate or severe cases. Cocaine, a powerful stimulant, poses a high risk for addiction and is associated with numerous health problems, including cardiovascular issues, nasal damage, and severe psychological effects such as paranoia and anxiety. The development of tolerance and the risk of overdose are significant concerns, with withdrawal symptoms often including fatigue, depression, and intense cravings (American Psychiatric Association, 2022).

Synthetic Cathinones Use Disorder (Bath Salts)

The diagnostic criteria for SRD applicable to synthetic cathinones require the presence of at least 2 of the following symptoms within a 12-month period: The substance is often taken in larger amounts or over a longer period than intended; there is a persistent desire or unsuccessful efforts to cut down or control use; a great deal of time is spent in activities necessary to obtain, use, or recover from the effects of the substance; craving or a strong desire to use the substance; recurrent use resulting in a failure to fulfill major role obligations at work, school, or home; continued use despite persistent or recurrent social or interpersonal problems caused or exacerbated by the effects of the substance; important social, occupational, or recreational activities are given up or reduced because of use; recurrent use in physically hazardous situations; continued use despite knowledge of a physical or psychological problem likely caused or exacerbated by the substance; tolerance; and withdrawal symptoms (American Psychiatric Association, 2022).

The severity of SRD related to synthetic cathinones is categorized as mild if 2–3 symptoms are present, moderate if 4–5 symptoms are present, and severe if 6 or more symptoms are present. The corresponding ICD-10-CM codes are F15.10 for mild cases and F15.20 for moderate or severe cases.

Synthetic cathinones can produce effects similar to those of other stimulants, such as amphetamines and MDMA, including increased sociability, euphoria, and energy, but also severe agitation, paranoia, and hallucinations. The *DSM-5-TR* recognizes the high potential for abuse of synthetic cathinones, with the development of tolerance and dependence being common. Withdrawal symptoms may include fatigue, depression, and anxiety (American Psychiatric Association, 2022).

Epidemiology

The effect of amphetamines, methamphetamine, cocaine, and "Bath salts" is exactly opposite of sedatives. They cause emotional and cognitive effects such as euphoria, increased libido and desire for sex, increased wakefulness, and improved cognitive control. Amphetamine was discovered in 1887 by Lazăr Edeleanu and is used as treatment of attention deficit hyperactivity disorder (ADHD), narcolepsy, and obesity. It also has a military use. Methamphetamine has similar effects but different pharmacokinetics. Cocaine is a tropane alkaloid extracted from *Erythroxylum coca* and *Erythroxylum novogranatense.* "Bath salts" are synthetic phenethylamines, usually cathinone derivatives like methylenedioxypyrovalerone, methylone, or mephedrone. The name "Bath salts" derives from instances in which the drugs were disguised as bath salts with packaging often stating "not for human consumption."

Pathophysiology, Pharmacology, and Effect

Amphetamine and methamphetamine target the norepinephrine and dopamine neurotransmitter systems. Amphetamine, also known as "Speed," can be snorted or ingested orally, methamphetamine, also known as "Crystal" or "Crystal Meth," can be smoked or injected. Cocaine can be snorted or injected, Crack cocaine, also known as "crack," is the free base of cocaine and can be smoked. "Bath salts" can be snorted or injected.

Clinical Features

In overdose, anxiety, agitation/aggression, seizures, fever, rhabdomyolysis, hypertension, and in extreme cases intracerebral bleedings are common symptoms (Brent et al., 2017; Dines, Wood, Yates, et al., 2015). In bath salt toxicity, psychosis was also frequent (Vallersnes et al., 2016). Delusional parasitosis has been observed.

Treatment

Regularly in acute poisonings, sedation with benzodiazepines or even narcosis with mechanical ventilation is necessary (Brent et al., 2017). In extreme agitation and aggression, patients need to be restrained mechanically and heavily sedated (Ghosh et al., 2024). Fluid replacement may be necessary. Antipsychotic treatment may also be necessary.

Total abstinence and harm reduction are the main treatment modalities for SRD like AMUD, CUD, and SCUD. MI and CBT are the psychotherapy of choice.

Hallucinogens

Psilocybin (magic mushrooms), MDMA, LSD, and ketamine are not listed as specific substances in the *DSM-5-TR*; however, they can be classified under hallucinogen-related disorders. Hallucinogen use disorder (HUD) involves a problematic pattern of hallucinogen use leading to significant impairment or distress. The diagnostic criteria for HUD require the presence of at least 2 of the following symptoms within a 12-month period: The substance is often taken in larger amounts or over a longer period than intended; there is a persistent desire or unsuccessful efforts to cut down or control use; a significant amount of time is spent obtaining, using, or recovering from the substance; craving or a strong desire to use the substance; recurrent use resulting in failure to fulfill major role obligations; continued use despite persistent or recurrent social or interpersonal problems; important social, occupational, or recreational activities are given up or reduced because of use; recurrent use in physically hazardous situations; continued use despite knowledge of a physical or psychological problem likely caused or exacerbated by the substance; tolerance; and, in some cases, withdrawal symptoms (American Psychiatric Association, 2022).

The severity of HUD is categorized as mild if 2–3 symptoms are present, moderate if 4–5 symptoms are present, and severe if 6 or more symptoms are present. The ICD-10-CM codes for this disorder include F16.10 for mild and F16.20 for moderate or severe cases. Psilocybin is known for its hallucinogenic effects, which may include altered perceptions of time and space, visual distortions, and changes in thought processes. While physical dependence and withdrawal symptoms are not commonly associated with hallucinogens, psychological impacts can be significant, potentially leading to conditions such as hallucinogen persisting perception disorder (American Psychiatric Association, 2022).

Epidemiology

MDMA, LSD, also known as "Acid," and magic mushrooms are used for different purposes. MDMA was first synthesized in 1912 and is nowadays usually consumed in the partying or raving scene. It promotes a feeling of loving and being loved by the whole world.

LSD was first synthesized by Albert Hofmann in 1938 and is a psychedelic drug causing hallucinations that may end in "horror trips" or trigger psychosis. LSD was described as a "window to the soul" and used widely by psychiatrists in the 1960s until it was regulated by the United Nations in 1971 as a Schedule 1 controlled substance.

Magic mushrooms, also known as "shrooms," are hallucinogenic mushrooms of the genus *Psilocybe azurescens*, *Psilocybe semilanceata*, and *Psilocybe cyanescens*. They contain psilocybin, also known as 4-phosphoryloxy-N,N-dimethyltryptamine (4-PO-DMT), which is a naturally occurring psychedelic drug. Psilocybin has been suggested as a potent antidepressant; however, research is still ongoing (Van Court et al., 2022).

Ketamine is a dissociative anesthetic used medically for induction and maintenance of anesthesia but is used as a recreational drug for its hallucinogenic and dissociative effects. It is known as "Special K" or "K" and was first synthesized in 1962. In medical use, esketamine is preferred due to its reduced dissociative effect. It is an essential drug (World Health Organization, 2013). Recently, ketamine has been approved as an effective antidepressant drug (Sachdeva et al., 2023). Recreational ketamine has been associated with mortality (European Drug Agency, 2024).

Pathophysiology, Pharmacology, and Effect

MDMA acts primarily in the brain by increasing the release of serotonin, dopamine, and noradrenaline. It causes euphoria, increased self-confidence, sociability, and perception of facilitated communication and has entactogenic effects (increased empathy or feelings of closeness with others and oneself). It also causes dilated pupils; relaxation and reduced anxiety; increased emotionality; a sense of inner peace; hallucinations; enhanced sensation, perception, or sexuality; and an altered sense of time. It is consumed orally (Brent et al., 2017).

LSD is a serotonin receptor agonist. Its effects are not fully understood, but it is known to alter the brain's default mode network, leading to its powerful psychedelic effects. LSD can cause mystical, spiritual, or religious experiences. At higher doses, it induces visual and auditory hallucinations. It can lead to anxiety, paranoia, and delusions and may trigger "flashbacks," also known as hallucinogen persisting perception disorder. It is consumed as a liquid, usually as "White on White blotters (WoW)" for sublingual administration.

In 1957, R. Gordon Wasson described the psychedelic visions that he experienced during the ritual use of psychoactive mushrooms in Mexico. The effect of psilocybin had not been understood completely. However, it affects brain regions known as the "theory of mind network" and the default mode network (Soares et al., 2023). Magic mushrooms are consumed orally.

Ketamine is an NMDA receptor antagonist. In sub-anesthetic doses, ketamine produces a dissociative state, characterized by a sense of being separate from the physical body and the external world which is recognized and known as depersonalization. In extensive doses, users may experience the "K-hole," a mental state resulting in visual and auditory distortions and hallucinations. It can be snorted or injected.

Clinical Features

Patients may present with agitation, aggression, and psychosis. In MDMA toxicity, diaphoresis and electrolyte disorders among amphetaminergic effects may appear. Nevertheless, acute intoxications with hallucinogens are rare (Brent et al., 2017).

Treatment

Sedation with benzodiazepines may be necessary (Brent et al., 2017). In extreme agitation and aggression, patients need to be restrained mechanically and heavily sedated (Ghosh et al., 2024). Antipsychotic treatment may also be necessary. Schizophrenia can be triggered by using hallucinogens that might require lifelong psychiatric treatment. Total abstinence and harm reduction are the main treatment modalities for HUD. MI and CBT are the psychotherapy of choice.

Positive Psychology for Substance Use Disorder

It is essential to recognize the positive rewards that are established during recovery for individuals. Scholars have noted that recovery can be challenging, and, to maintain sobriety, positive experiences should be attainable throughout the journey (Hoeppner et al., 2019). Some barriers are the following: lack of financial resources (e.g., insurance); fear of shame and discrimination; public health prevention and screening gaps; minimal trained and qualified addictions practitioners; and consistent misconceptualization and stigma among individuals, communities, programs, and healthcare providers (Smith & Borden, 2020). With such profound challenges on a societal level, positive psychology can be one method to assist clients to redshift their focus to the strengths and positive elements of their lives.

Positive psychology may be a viable treatment approach when assisting individuals with SUD. Highlighting the positive aspects of an individual's life is an extremely different approach from 12-step programs, but perhaps an effective approach to existing treatments, which some clients have noted as being attainable and easily implemented (Krentzman et al., 2023). Counselors and healthcare professionals need to be open to a variety of treatment approaches in order to match their clients' needs. Some of the advantages of positive psychology as a supplemental treatment approach is that it is universal to all populations, and it can be used with other traditional treatment modalities when treating SUD.

Counselors can begin to work with individuals in recovery by focusing on a holistic and comprehensive approach to promote abstinence. Individuals who are either on the road to recovery, considering therapy, or are in the maintenance phase of abstinence often face stigma on a variety of levels. SUDs are connected with significant shame and several challenges that prevent individuals from accessing vital prevention, treatment, and recovery services (Smith & Borden, 2020).

Mindfulness and Self-efficacy and Substance Use Disorder

Mindfulness has gained extreme popularity as a treatment approach to assisting individuals with SUD. In regards to addiction treatment, mindfulness can increase awareness of external and internal triggers for addictive behaviors and enhance tolerance for disturbing emotional, cognitive, and physical experiences (Holas et al., 2021). There are specific techniques that may be highly effective, valuable, and feasible for individuals to implement into their newfound lifestyle of health and recovery. Mindfulness-based intervention is recognized for facilitating long-term health behavior change (Korecki et al., 2020). Furthermore, mindfulness-based recovery prevention (MBRP) is also a prominent intervention within the substance use recovery field. MBRP is a formally structured protocol within a group format with eight, 120-min sessions that combines formal meditation practices with the cognitive behavioral approach of relapse prevention treatment (Korecki et al., 2020). It has been noted that cognitive and behavioral treatment approaches are typical when assisting individuals with addictive behaviors (Bayır & Aylaz, 2021).

Also, mindfulness can be an opportunity for individuals to increase self-efficacy and self-concept as they are in recovery or challenged with addictive behaviors. There is evidence in the literature that mindfulness-based education fosters the positive effect of SUDs or self-efficacy (Bayır & Aylaz, 2021). Self-efficacy, originally coined by Bandura (1977), is an individual's confidence in the capability to accomplish tasks successfully. Strong self-efficacy also includes believing that an individual is able to perform the necessary behaviors in order to attain their desired outcomes (Galacgac &

Tarrojo, 2019). In the context of SUD treatment, self-efficacy is correlated to an individual's belief in their ability to implement and maintain desired positive behaviors that are targeted within their substance use patterns (Moniz-Lewis et al., 2022). As such, mindfulness-based interventions focused on SUD heighten awareness and tolerance of cravings with an elevated ability to sustain present-moment awareness of both positive and negative internal emotional situations and experiences (Mallik et al., 2021). Individuals may begin to recognize emotional dysregulation and become aware of cravings. However, by staying in the present moment and working through the distress, they may be able to refute the temptation of engaging in the substance. Mindfulness-based interventions for SUD with a component of psychological flexibility may be advantageous (Mallik et al., 2021). The benefits to implementing mindfulness into the treatment plan for clients with SUD are numerous, and the literature suggests that this is a viable and effective way to assist to increase self-efficacy, promote self-awareness, and recognize triggers, all of which can decrease the risk of relapse and foster an increase in overcoming SUD.

Conclusion

Overall, individuals with SUD often face extreme challenges, unique adversities, limited resources, and some negative psychosocial factors that can influence their ability to remain abstinent. This chapter provided specific details on the most common substances being abused, pathophysiology, pharmacological effects, common treatments, and etiology of highly addictive substances. It is important to note that this list is not exclusive, and, unfortunately, substances are continuing to be abused everyday with different trends. As counselors work with individuals diagnosed with SUD, it is imperative that they remain current with the best evidence-based treatments, common trends, and overall statistics related to individuals' drugs of choice.

As we progress into more holistic approaches in therapy, we propose that within the positive psychology approach, there are unique treatment modalities that are specifically developed to assist individuals with SUD. Of course, it is also important to consider individual traits and characteristics when assessing, diagnosing, or providing therapy to clients. Upholding a person-centered approach is highly encouraged as it allows for the therapist and client to work collaboratively to develop a treatment plan that feels right for the client. This chapter provided an overview of clinical definitions related to SUD as well as specific pharmacology and treatment approaches for a selected variety of substances. It is important for rehabilitation, mental health, and all healthcare practitioners to be mindful of how SUD can impact individuals in a variety of ways.

References

American Psychiatric Association. (2010). *Practice guideline for the treatment of patients with major depressive disorder.* http://psychiatryonline.org/content.aspx?bookid=28&sectionid=1667485

American Psychiatric Association. (2022). *Diagnostic and statistical manual of mental disorders (5th ed., text rev.).* American Psychiatric Association Publishing.

Bandura, A. (1977). *Social learning theory.* Englewood Cliffs.

Bayır, B., & Aylaz, R. (2021). The effect of mindfulness-based education given to individuals with substance-use disorder according to self-efficacy theory on self-efficacy perception. *Applied Nursing Research, 57*, 151354. https://doi.org/10.1016/j.apnr.2020.151354

Bramness, J. G., Pandey, S., Moe, J. S., Toft, H., Lien, L., & Bolstad, I. (2022). History of delirium tremens in AUD patients in treatment: Relationship to AUD severity and other factors. *Substance Abuse and Rehabilitation, 13*, 65–72. https://doi.org/10.2147/SAR.S361810

Brent, J., Burkhart, K., Dargan, P. I., Hatten, B., Megarbane, B., Palmer, R., & White, J. (2017). *Critical care toxicology.* Springer.

Bundeskriminalamt. (2024). *Bundeslagebild Rauschgiftkriminalität 2023: Zahl der Rauschgiftdelikte gestiegen.* Retrieved on September 2024, from https://www.bka.de/DE/Presse/Listenseite_Pressemitteilungen/2024/Presse2024/240626_PM_BLB_Rauschgift.html#:~:text=Im%20Jahr%202023%20wurden%20in,(17%2C2%20Prozent)

Bundesministerium für Gesundheit. (2016). *Das Neue-psychoaktive-Stoffe-Gesetz (NpSG).* Retrieved on July 2024, from https://www.bundesgesundheitsministerium.de/service/begriffe-von-a-z/n/npsg

Dhowan, B., Lim, J., MacLean, M. D., Berman, A. G., Kim, M. K., Yang, Q., Linnes, J., Lee, C. H., Goergen, C. J., & Lee, H. (2019). Simple minimally-invasive automatic antidote delivery device (A2D2) towards closed-loop reversal of opioid overdose. *Journal of Controlled Release, 306*, 130–137. https://doi.org/10.1016/j.jconrel.2019.05.041

Dines, A. M., Wood, D. M., Galicia, M., Yates, C. M., Heyerdahl, F., Hovda, K. E., Giraudon, I., Sedefov, R., Euro, D. E. N. R. G., & Dargan, P. I. (2015). Presentations to the emergency department following Cannabis use—a multi-centre case series from ten European countries. *Journal of Medical Toxicology, 11*(4), 415–421. https://doi.org/10.1007/s13181-014-0460-x

Dines, A. M., Wood, D. M., Yates, C., Heyerdahl, F., Hovda, K. E., Giraudon, I., Sedefov, R., Dargan, P. I., & Euro, D. E. N. R. G. (2015). Acute recreational drug and new psychoactive substance toxicity in Europe: 12 months data collection from the European Drug Emergencies Network (Euro-DEN). *Clinical Toxicology (Phila), 53*(9), 893–900. https://doi.org/10.3109/15563650.2015.1088157

Esser, M. B., Sherk, A., Liu, Y., Naimi, T. S., Stockwell, T., Stahre, M., Kanny, D., Landen, M., Saitz, R., & Brewer, R. D. (2020). Deaths and years of potential life lost from excessive alcohol use - United States, 2011–2015. *Morbidity and Mortality Weekly Report (MMWR), 69*(39), 1428–1433. https://doi.org/10.15585/mmwr.mm6939a6

European Drug Agency. (2024). *European Drug Report 2024: Trends and Developments*. Retrieved on July 2024, from https://www.emcdda.europa.eu/publications/european-drug-report/2024_en

Fairbanks, J., Umbreit, A., Kolla, B. P., Karpyak, V. M., Schneekloth, T. D., Loukianova, L. L., & Sinha, S. (2020). Evidence-based pharmacotherapies for alcohol use disorder: Clinical pearls. *Mayo Clinic Proceedings*, *95*(9), 1964–1977. https://doi.org/10.1016/j.mayocp.2020.01.030

Galacgac, N. B., & Tarroja, M. C. H. (2019). Dispositional mindfulness and relapse vulnerability as mediated by self-efficacy among persons in recovery from substance use disorders (SUDs). *Philippine Journal of Psychology*, *52*(1), 185–208.

Ghosh, S. M., Kung, J. Y., Crockford, D., Harpur, L., Tanguay, R., Dyer, D., Lang, E., Ayas, T., Feng, G., & VandenBerg, S. D. (2024). Systematic review protocol to determine the most effective pharmacological and non-pharmacological interventions for the management of acute methamphetamine toxicity. *BMJ Open*, *14*(8), e083089. https://doi.org/10.1136/bmjopen-2023-083089

Heier, E. C., Eyer, F., Rabe, C., Geith, S., Dargan, P. I., Wood, D. M., Heyerdahl, F., Dines, A. M., Giraudon, I., Erik Hovda, K., Yates, C., Vallersnes, O. M., Miro, O., Liechti, M. E., Zellner, T., & Euro, D. E. N. R. G. (2022). Clinical effect of ethanol co-use in patients with acute drug toxicity involving the use of central nervous system depressant recreational drugs. *European Journal of Emergency Medicine, 29*(4), 291–300. https://doi.org/10.1097/MEJ.0000000000000932

Henssler, J., Muller, M., Carreira, H., Bschor, T., Heinz, A., & Baethge, C. (2021). Controlled drinking-non-abstinent versus abstinent treatment goals in alcohol use disorder: A systematic review, meta-analysis and meta-regression. *Addiction*, *116*(8), 1973–1987. https://doi.org/10.1111/add.15329

Hoch, E., Volkow, N. D., Friemel, C. M., Lorenzetti, V., Freeman, T. P., & Hall, W. (2024). Cannabis, cannabinoids and health: A review of evidence on risks and medical benefits. *European Archives Psychiatry Clinical Neuroscience*. https://doi.org/10.1007/s00406-024-01880-2

Hoeppner, B. B., Schick, M. R., Carlon, H., & Hoeppner, S. S. (2019). Do self-administered positive psychology exercises work in persons in recovery from problematic substance use? An online randomized survey. *Journal of Substance Abuse Treatment*, *99*, 16–23. https://doi.org/10.1016/j.jsat.2019.01.006

Holas, P., Draps, M., Kowalewska, E., Lewczuk, K., & Gola, M. (2021). A pilot study of mindfulness-based relapse prevention for compulsive sexual behaviour disorder. *Journal of Behavioral Addictions*, *9*(4), 1088–1092.

Huang, S., Xiao, P., & Sun, J. (2020). Structural basis of signaling of cannabinoids receptors: Paving a way for rational drug design in controlling multiple neurological and immune diseases. *Signal Transduction and Target Therapy*, *5*(1), 127. https://doi.org/10.1038/s41392-020-00240-5

Institut für Therapieforschung München. (2022). *Jahresbericht der Deutschen Suchthilfestatistik (DSHS), Suchthilfe in Deutschland 2021*. https://www.suchthilfestatistik.de/fileadmin/user_upload_dshs/05_publikationen/jahresberichte/DSHS_DJ2021_Jahresbericht.pdf

Jung, Y. C., & Namkoong, K. (2014). Alcohol: Intoxication and poisoning—diagnosis and treatment. *Handbook Clinical of Neurology*, *125*, 115–121. https://doi.org/10.1016/B978-0-444-62619-6.00007-0

Kelly, J. F., Abry, A., Ferri, M., & Humphreys, K. (2020). Alcoholics anonymous and 12-step facilitation treatments for alcohol use disorder: A distillation of a 2020 cochrane review for clinicians and policy makers. *Alcohol and Alcoholism*, *55*(6), 641–651. https://doi.org/10.1093/alcalc/agaa050

King's College Hospital NHS Foundation Trust. (2022). *E-cigarettes (vapes) explained*. https://www.kch.nhs.uk/wp-content/uploads/2023/01/pl-1007.1-e-cigarettes-vapes-explained.pdf

Korecki, J. R., Schwebel, F. J., Votaw, V. R., & Witkiewitz, K. (2020). Mindfulness-based programs for substance use disorders: A systematic review of manualized treatments. *Substance Abuse Treatment, Prevention, and Policy*, *15*, 51 (2020). https://doi.org/10.1186/s13011-020-00293-3

Krentzman, A. R., Hoeppner, B. B., Hoeppner, S. S., & Barnett, N. P. (2023). Development, feasibility, acceptability, and impact of a positive psychology journaling intervention to support addiction recovery. *The Journal of Positive Psychology*, *18*(4), 573–591. https://doi.org/10.1080/17439760.2022.2070531

Mallik, D., Kaplan, J., Somohano, V., Bergman, A., & Bowen, S. (2021). Examining the role of craving, mindfulness, and psychological flexibility in a sample of individuals with substance use disorder. *Substance Use & Misuse*, *56*(6), 782–786. https://doi.org/10.1080/10826084.2021.1899220

Manthey, J., Hayer, T., Jacobsen, B., Kalke, J., Klinger, S., Rehm, J., Rosenkranz, M., Verthein, U., Wirth, M., Armstrong, M., Myran, D., Pacula, R., Queirolo, R., & Zobel, F. (2023). *Technical report—Effects of legalizing cannabis*. Institut für interdisziplinäre Sucht- und Drogenforschung (ISD).

Miller, W. R., & Rollnick, S. (1991). *Motivational interviewing: Preparing people to change addictive behavior*. Guilford Press.

Miro, O., Burillo-Putze, G., Schmid, Y., Salgado, E., Liechti, M. E., Dines, A. M., Giraudon, I., Heyerdahl, F., Hovda, K. E., Vallersne, O. M., Eyer, F., Wood, D. M., Yates, C., Dargan, P. I., Galicia, M., & Euro, D. E. N. P. R. G. (2023). Severity of emergency department presentations due to acute drug toxicity in Europe: A longitudinal analysis over a 6-year period (2014–2019) stratified by sex. *European Journal of Emergency Medicine*, *30*(1), 21–31. https://doi.org/10.1097/MEJ.0000000000000978

Mohan, G., Bhide, P., Abu-Shanab, A., Ghose, M., Rajamohan, A., Muhammad, T., Khan, A. A., Khan, M., Khalid, F., Padappayil, R. P., & Du, D. (2023). Predictors of escalation to intensive care unit level of care among admissions for alcohol withdrawal. *Journal of Community Hospital Internal Medicine Perspective*, *13*(5), 8–14. https://doi.org/10.55729/2000-9666.1241

Moniz-Lewis, D. I., Stein, E. R., Bowen, S., & Witkiewitz, K. (2022). Self-efficacy as a potential mechanism of behavior change in mindfulness-based relapse prevention. *Mindfulness*, *13*(9), 2175–2185.

National Center for Health Statistics. (2024). *U.S. Overdose Deaths Decrease in 2023, First Time Since 2018.* https://www.cdc.gov/nchs/pressroom/nchs_press_releases/2024/20240515.htm#:~:text=Provisional%20data%20from%20CDC's%20National,111%2C029%20deaths%20estimated%20in%202022

Nelson, J. M. (2009). *Psychology, religion, and spirituality*. Springer.

Ozluk, P., Cobb, R., Sylwestrzak, G., Raina, D., & Bailly, E. (2022). Alcohol-attributable medical costs in commercially insured and Medicaid populations. *AJPM Focus*, *1*(2), 100036. https://doi.org/10.1016/j.focus.2022.100036

Palpacuer, C., Duprez, R., Huneau, A., Locher, C., Boussageon, R., Laviolle, B., & Naudet, F. (2018). Pharmacologically controlled drinking in the treatment of alcohol dependence or alcohol use disorders: A systematic review with direct and network meta-analyses on nalmefene, naltrexone, acamprosate, baclofen and topiramate. *Addiction*, *113*(2), 220–237. https://doi.org/10.1111/add.13974

Pattison, E. M., Sobell, M. B., & Sobell, L. C. (1977). *Emerging concepts of alcohol dependence*. Springer.

Penninga, E. I., Graudal, N., Ladekarl, M. B., & Jurgens, G. (2016). Adverse events associated with flumazenil treatment for the management of suspected benzodiazepine intoxication—A systematic review with meta-analyses of randomised trials. *Basic & Clinical Pharmacology & Toxicology*, *118*(1), 37–44. https://doi.org/10.1111/bcpt.12434

Pomerleau, O. F. (1992). Nicotine and the central nervous system: Biobehavioral effects of cigarette smoking. *American Journal of Medicine*, *93*(1A), 2S–7S. https://doi.org/10.1016/0002-9343(92)90619-m

Sachdeva, B., Sachdeva, P., Ghosh, S., Ahmad, F., & Sinha, J. K. (2023). Ketamine as a therapeutic agent in major depressive disorder and posttraumatic stress disorder: Potential medicinal and deleterious effects. *Ibrain*, *9*(1), 90–101. https://doi.org/10.1002/ibra.12094

Smith, C. H., & Borden, K. A. (2020). Introduction to the special issue on substance use disorders and addictions. *Professional Psychology: Research and Practice*, *51*(1), 1. https://doi.org/10.1037/pro0000299

Soares, C., Gonzalo, G., Castelhano, J., & Castelo-Branco, M. (2023). The relationship between the default mode network and the theory of mind network as revealed by psychedelics—A meta-analysis. *Neuroscience & Biobehavioral Reviews*, *152*, 105325. https://doi.org/10.1016/j.neubiorev.2023.105325

Stahre, M., Roeber, J., Kanny, D., Brewer, R. D., & Zhang, X. (2014). Contribution of excessive alcohol consumption to deaths and years of potential life lost in the United States. *Preventing Chronic Disease*, *11*, E109. https://doi.org/10.5888/pcd11.130293

Strang, J., & Stimson, G. (1990). *AIDS and drug misuse*. Routledge.

U.S. Centers for Disease Control and Prevention. (2022). *Smoking and tobacco use*. https://www.cdc.gov/tobacco/data_statistics/fact_sheets/fast_facts/cost-and-expenditures.html

U.S. Centers for Disease Control and Prevention. (2024). *Addressing excessive alcohol use: State fact sheets*. https://www.cdc.gov/alcohol/fact-sheets/states/excessive-alcohol-use-united-states.html

Vallersnes, O. M., Dines, A. M., Wood, D. M., Yates, C., Heyerdahl, F., Hovda, K. E., Giraudon, I., Euro, D. E. N. R. G., & Dargan, P. I. (2016). Psychosis associated with acute recreational drug toxicity: A European case series. *BMC Psychiatry, 16*, 293. https://doi.org/10.1186/s12888-016-1002-7

Van Court, R. C., Wiseman, M. S., Meyer, K. W., Ballhorn, D. J., Amses, K. R., Slot, J. C., Dentinger, B. T. M., Garibay-Orijel, R., & Uehling, J. K. (2022). Diversity, biology, and history of psilocybin-containing fungi: Suggestions for research and technological development. *Fungal Biology, 126*(4), 308–319. https://doi.org/10.1016/j.funbio.2022.01.003

Waters, M. L., Dargan, P. I., Yates, C., Dines, A. M., Eyer, F., Giraudon, I., Heyerdahl, F., Hovda, K. E., Liechti, M. E., Miro, O., Vallersnes, O. M., Anseeuw, K., Badaras, R., Bitel, M., Bonnici, J., Brvar, M., Caganova, B., Calyskan, F., Ceschi, A., . . . Wood, D. M. (2024). Clinical effects of cannabis compared to synthetic cannabinoid receptor agonists (SCRAs): A retrospective cohort study of presentations with acute toxicity to European hospitals between 2013 and 2020. *Clinical Toxicology (Phila)*, 1–7. https://doi.org/10.1080/15563650.2024.2346125

Witkiewitz, K., Litten, R. Z., & Leggio, L. (2019). Advances in the science and treatment of alcohol use disorder. *Science Advances, 5*(9), eaax4043. https://doi.org/10.1126/sciadv.aax4043

World Health Organization. (2013). WHO Model List of Essential Medicines, 18th list, http://www.who.int/medicines/publications/essentialmedicines/en/

World Health Organization. (2018). *Global status report on alcohol and health.* https://www3.paho.org/hq/index.php?option=com_docman&view=download&slug=who-s-global-status-report-on-alcohol-and-health-2018-1&Itemid=270&lang=en

World Health Organization. (2023). *Tobacco.* https://www.who.int/news-room/fact-sheets/detail/tobacco

Zakhari, S. (2006). Overview: How is alcohol metabolized by the body? *Alcohol Research & Health, 29*(4), 245–254. https://www.ncbi.nlm.nih.gov/pubmed/17718403

Zellner, N., Eyer, F., & Zellner, T. (2017). Alarming pregabalin abuse in Munich: Prevalence, patterns of use and complications. *Dtsch Med Wochenschr, 142*(19), e140–e147. https://doi.org/10.1055/s-0043-104228

Author Affiliations

Michele Mahr: *Texas Tech University Health Science Center, Lubbock, Texas, U.S.A.; Michele.M.Mahr@ttuhsc.edu*

Monica Wilson: *National University, JFK School of Psychology and Behavioral Sciences, La Jolla, California, U.S.A.; mwilson2@nu.edu*

Tobias Zellner: *Division of Clinical Toxicology and Poison Centre Munich, Department of Internal Medicine II, TUM School of Medicine and Health, Technical University of Munich, Ismaninger Str. 22, 81675 Munich, Germany; tobias.zellner@tum.de*

Depression and Anxiety

David S. Pfaff, PhD, LPC

6

KEYWORDS AND DEFINITIONS:

A good life: The act of living a life of well-being and fulfillment by creating pleasant experiences, engaging valued activities, and pursuing meaning.

Anxiety or **anxiety disorders**: A *DSM-5-TR* category of affective disorders exhibiting symptoms of disproportionate worry, perceived intense danger, skeletal muscle tension, and restlessness resulting in clinically significant distress and functional impairment.

Depression or **depressive disorders**: A *DSM-5-TR* (*Diagnostic and Statistical Manual of Mental Disorders*, Fifth Edition, Text Revision) category of mood disorders exhibiting core symptoms of low mood, diminished life satisfaction, decreased psychomotor activity, and social isolation resulting in clinically significant distress and functional impairment.

Internalizing disorders: A grouping of mental diagnoses characterized by the "internalization" of problems, stressors, and emotions, resulting in attempts to over-control situations and behaviors. Depression and anxiety are prototypical examples of internalizing disorders.

Positive psychology interventions (PPIs): Evidence-based therapeutic interventions aligning with the fundamentals of positive psychology. PPIs need not be exclusive to positive psychology and can be adapted from other approaches.

LEARNING OBJECTIVES:

1. Learn core characteristics of depressive and anxiety disorders, including but not limited to *DSM-5-TR* criteria, etiology, developmental factors, and comorbidity.

2. Recognize as well as analyze both differences and similarities shared by depressive and anxiety disorders.
3. Learn how to apply core concepts from positive psychology in the conceptualization and treatment of depressive and anxiety disorders.
4. Practice knowledge gleaned from this chapter by completing review questions and case study exercise.

Introduction

Many of us crucify ourselves between two thieves—regret for the past and fear of the future.
—Fulton Oursler

From a mental health standpoint, it is fair to wonder if Oursler's quote personifies a natural, albeit painful, human proclivity. That is, feeling caught between depressing over past hurts and missteps, while also anxious and expecting the worst is yet to come. Yet, portraying the experience of depression and anxiety as thievery? Feeling pitted in the middle of an emotional tug-of-war between depression and anxiety thieves from the capacity for living a good life. For instance, internalizing negative experiences and narratives related to the past steals from pleasant experiences in the now. Also stolen are opportunities to engage and connect with life, contributing to a slow and painful drain on the sense of purpose and meaning. Self-efficacy and agency are heisted too, leaving passivity and hopelessness in their absence. Preoccupation with either the past or the future relegates little awareness, time, or energy for living in the present. Perhaps the greatest thievery of all is the loss of living within the present. Make no mistake—the point is not blaming depression and anxiety. These are natural and universal human experiences. Such is the significance of the "crucifying ourselves" aspect, for as challenging and hopeless as depression and anxiety appear, there is the potential for hopefulness and resilience on route to regulating these uncomfortable feelings.

Enter positive psychology, a therapeutic modality channeling the positives to turn the tide on this thievery by cultivating a life of wellness and fulfillment. This chapter illustrates the benefits of positive psychology within the context of depression and anxiety. In doing so, key characteristics of depression and anxiety are analyzed, including the relationship shared by these frequently comorbid disorders. This chapter then frames depression and anxiety through the lens of positive psychology, providing counselors with a host of clinical tools and interventions. The chapter concludes with the opportunity to apply knowledge gleaned from the chapter via review questions and a case study exercise.

Overview of Depression and Anxiety Disorders

The Oursler metaphor is by no means a comprehensive depiction of depression or anxiety. If anything, depression and anxiety are broad terms denoting two separate typologies, or categories, of mental health symptoms and disorders (American Psychiatric Association, 2022). Each category is comprised of individual disorders sharing core features. Different core features make for markedly different symptoms between depression and anxiety. Imagine a stoplight, wherein depressive disorders act as a proverbial "red light" bringing us to stop by lowering mood, decreasing motivation, slowing physical activity, and triggering social withdrawal. Conversely, anxiety disorders are a call to action, or a "yellow light" urging us to hurriedly rush the intersection to avoid danger by controlling all that should, must, have to, or cannot happen. And these examples only begin to scratch the surface of these two different types of mental health disorders. Let us take a closer look at these two categories of mental health disorders.

Depressive Disorders

The poet Atticus (2021) describes depressive disorders as "being color blind and constantly told how colorful the world is." Put into clinical terms, depressive disorders are conditions marked by symptoms of low mood, loss of enjoyment, isolation, emptiness, psychomotor agitation, and hopelessness (American Psychiatric Association, 2022; El-Gabalawi, 2020). Circumstances arise where it is natural to experience these symptoms and they are not ascribed to depression. For instance, feeling sad or a loss of joy upon losing a loved one or when deprived of needs is to be expected. Symptoms are deemed disordered when they lead to clinically significant distress and/or functional impairment. Simply put, symptoms interfere with wellness and the ability to effectively perform in life. Furthermore, depressive symptoms cannot originate from substance use, medical condition, or other mental health condition.

Fundamental criteria aside, the *DSM-5-TR* delineates the following depressive disorders: major depressive disorder; persistent depressive disorder; premenstrual dysphoric disorder (PMDD); substance/medication-induced depressive disorder; depressive disorder due to another medical condition; unspecified depressive disorder; and other specified depressive disorder (Fang & Mao, 2019). Of these disorders, the most frequent occurring is major depressive disorder (MDD). MDD is an episodic disorder, manifesting as acute and periodic depressive episodes contrasting from standard functioning (American Psychiatric Association, 2022). The *DSM-5-TR* stipulates a major depressive episode must contain at least one of two core symptoms: depressed mood and/or loss of enjoyment in life. Other MDD symptoms are substantive weight loss or gain, insomnia or hypersomnia, psychomotor agitation, fatigue, worthlessness, or excessive guilt, diminished cognitive function, and recurrent thoughts of death or suicidal behavior (American Psychiatric Association, 2022). Subsequently, an MDD diagnosis requires demonstrating at least five symptoms over a 2-week period.

Healthcare professionals are also inclined to encounter another common depressive disorder—formerly dysthymia and now persistent depressive disorder (PDD). While similar to MDD, PDD symptoms are persistent and of lower acuity than MDD. A chronic disorder, PDD's symptoms are displayed consistently for least a 2-year period prior to diagnosis. It is common for PDD symptoms to be folded into the experiencer's daily presentation and personality (American Psychiatric Association, 2022). Eeyore from the children's series *Winnie the Pooh* is a familiar simile depicting the depressed mood, slowed activity, and pessimism associated with PDD.

Anxiety Disorders

Kahlil Gibran is often credited with poetically musing—"Our anxiety does not come from thinking about the future, but from wanting to control it." Life is satiated with ambiguity and unknowns, which can be scary if not hard to accept. For these reasons, it is not surprising that we resist these realities by worrying about what should or not should not be in course of trying to control the uncontrollable. Gibran's quote speaks to core symptoms within anxiety disorders, mainly the intense worry and tension accompanying an unwinnable fight for control (Toner & Robinaugh, 2020). Additionally, Gibran illustrates the point that anxiety alone is not *the* problem. Anxiety is vital to survival in that it rouses psychological and physiological reactions to possible threats (Majeed et al., 2020). In this aspect, anxiety compares to another protective emotion—fear.

Nonetheless, it is crucial that counselors appreciate the difference between the two emotions. Consider anxiety "the snake not in the room." Fear manifests when facing realistic and tangibles threats, like coming face-to-face with a hostile poisonous snake. Anxiety reacts to abstract threats that are neither immediate nor materialized. Akin to worrying about going outside for the possibility of encountering poisonous snakes, anxiety reacts to the "snake not in the room." Again, and despite the lack of immediacy, anxiety's role is part of the human self-preservation mechanisms (Majeed et al., 2020). That is not to say anxiety reactions are always accurate or effective. Anxiety reactions can be in disproportion to the level of threat posed, with consequences ranging from the problematic to the disordered.

In alignment with the *DSM-5-TR*, diagnosing an anxiety disorder requires distress and impairment. Symptoms cannot be attributed to substances and other medical or mental health conditions. The *DSM-5-TR* lists the following anxiety disorders: generalized anxiety disorder (GAD); social anxiety disorder; separation anxiety disorder; specific phobia, panic disorder; agoraphobia, selective mutism; substance/medication-induced anxiety disorder; anxiety disorder due to another medical condition; unspecified anxiety disorder; and other specified anxiety disorder (American Psychiatric Association, 2022). GAD is undoubtedly the most prevalent of anxiety disorders, with a global incidence rate higher than any other mental health diagnosis (World Health Organization, 2022). A diagnosis of GAD requires experiencing 2 core symptoms for a period of at least 6 months: excessive general worry and difficulty regulating worry (American Psychiatric Association, 2022). After which at least 3 of the following 6 subsequent symptoms need to be present: restlessness or edginess, easily fatigued, cognitive impairment, irritability, tension, and poor sleep.

Connecting Depressive and Anxiety Disorders

In lieu of their differences, depressive and anxiety disorders share a well-documented connection. Both are labeled as internalizing disorders, a grouping of mental conditions characterized by the "internalizing" of problems, emotions, and behaviors in times of distress (Huberty, 2017). Internalization is fueled by an exaggerated sense of personal control over problems and adversities, effectively leading to over-controlling behaviors (Kamper-DeMarco et al., 2023). The subsequent internalizing effect and attempts at over-control sets off a cascade of distress emotionally, cognitively, and somatically (Kamper-DeMarco et al., 2023). Affective symptoms feature prominently in internalizing disorders, as are experiences of clinically significant distress and functional impairment (Huberty, 2017; Kamper-DeMarco et al., 2023). While not the only ones within the grouping, depressive and anxiety disorders are certainly emblematic of the internalizing disorders.

It is factual that depression and anxiety are so prevalent that combined they represent the majority of the roughly 970 million global mental health diagnoses (World Health Organization, 2022). The World Health Organization (2022) estimates upwards of 280 million people meet criteria for a depressive disorder, second only to 301 million with anxiety disorders. If by sheer prevalence alone, there is little surprise to finding that these disorders share high comorbidity rates with one another (Kalin, 2020). Look no further than the MDD diagnoses and its "with anxious distress" specifier (American Psychiatric Association, 2022).

Granted, prevalence and comorbidity rates are likely a consequence than explanation for the depression/anxiety connection. It is true depression and anxiety are both internalizing disorders, although they are not the only ones within the group. It is apparent that there is a connection shared by depression and anxiety that runs deeper, the product of a confluence of biological, etiological, and development factors.

Etiological and Development Factors

Fang and Mao (2019) label depression and anxiety "multifactor" disorders that can originate from a variety of possible sources. Additionally, Fang and Mao (2019) caution that much remain to be understood about these disorders, leaving more questions than answers as to etiology and development. What is known is that depression and anxiety originate from a complex network of intersecting biopsychosocial factors.

Biological

Biological models of depressive and anxiety disorders are widespread, if not also predominate, within the healthcare professions. According to the model, depressive and anxiety disorders are pathologies born of organic-based dysfunction and/or abnormality (Fang & Mao, 2019). With a range of potential organic causeways, theories focusing on neurochemical dysfunction are commonplace within clinical practice. In quintessence, these theories link depression and anxiety to neurotransmitter dysregulation and imbalances (El-Gabalawi, 2020; Melaragno et al., 2020). This includes the monoamine deficiency theory, wherein depressive symptoms are credited to underutilizations or deficiencies of neurotransmitters for regulating mood, physical and cognitive functioning, and motivation (Parish et al., 2023; Remes et al, 2021). In similar fashion, exaggerated anxiety reactions are attributed to dysregulations in inhibitory and excitatory neurotransmitters (Melaragno, 2020; Parish et al., 2023). The neurotransmitters serotonin, norepinephrine, dopamine, and GABA are linked to depression and anxiety (Herzallah et al., 2021; Melaragno, 2020). The efficacy of antidepressant medications in treating depression and anxiety symptoms affords credibility to neurochemical dysfunction theories (Parish et al., 2023). Still, these theories fall short in addressing all the biopsychosocial nuances found within these disorders.

The study of genetics and intergeneration transmission of symptoms are other angles within the biological model of depression and anxiety. Simply put, depressive and anxiety disorders seemingly "run in families." Studies suggest both categories of disorders demonstrate moderate heritability rates (Kalin, 2020). The genetic markers for depression and anxiety are found to be similar, as are the inherent risks including trait-factors for temperament and personality (Kalin, 2020; Majeed et al., 2020).

Last, physiological health and function also contribute to the presentation of depressive and anxiety disorders. Illness or injury to organs responsible for neurological, emotional, and endocrine functioning can all be cause for depression or anxiety (Daffre et al., 2020; Remes et al., 2021). Research also suggests a strong correlation between gastrointestinal health and emotional wellness, with the gut referred to as a second brain of sorts (Appleton, 2018; Remes et al., 2021). Therefore, what is ingested and is metabolized by way of diet, medication, supplements, and chemical or herbal substances stands to trigger or exacerbate depression and anxiety. In addition, dietary and nutritional deficiencies pose significant risk factors. Physical activity and exercise demonstrate positive and negative correlations to depressive and anxious symptoms (Appleton, 2018; Hong & Zhang, 2021; Mofatteh, 2021). The human body also requires adequate physical rest and sleep, with a lack thereof contributing to risk for depressive or anxiety symptoms as well.

Psychological

Since the creation of the mental health profession, theorists and clinicians have argued over the psychological basis of mental health disorders. Starting with the earliest of theories, Freudian Psychoanalysis, emotional disorders were conceptualized as unconscious conflicts over repressed feelings and experiences (Corey, 2024; Majeed et al., 2020). Conscious neurosis and emotion disturbances were thought to occur when the self-defense mechanisms failed to hold unconscious conflicts at bay (Corey, 2024). Freud's theories came to be inevitably challenged, with continuous advances in theory and science shaping how counseling theories explained depression and anxiety. Cognitive behavioral theories are widely embraced within the counseling profession, which emphasizes conscious dynamics such as dysfunctional thought patterns, schemas, and personal narratives in depression and anxiety (El-Gabalawi, 2020; Majeed et al., 2020).

With respect to positive psychology, the theory of learned helplessness was once a dominantly held approach to the development of depressive and anxiety disorders (Tomasulo, 2020). This theory postulated prolonged exposure to continual stressors and problems caused a "learned" passive response (Tomasulo, 2020). Subsequent research shows passivity is not learned but is in fact an inherent human response (Maier & Seligman, 2016). Focus has now shifted from a learned helpless model to one of learned hopelessness to emotional distress and problems. Operating from learned hopelessness involves negativistic and inflexible attitudes toward the past and future (Maier & Seligman, 2016; Tomasulo, 2020). A person judges themselves as not in control or responsible for their experiences, effectively losing hope for regulating depression or anxiety as well as having a better life.

Social

Psychosocial factors feature prominently into the etiology and development of depression and anxiety, factors acting as a proverbial double-edged sword. For example, psychosocial factors related to stress and adversity pose risk for depressive or anxiety symptoms, while others tied to social connectedness are protective (Cozolino, 2017; Remes et al., 2021). Ultimately, the effects of a psychosocial factor are dependent on a combination of individual and social variables. Individual variables consist of baseline functioning, attitudes, resilience, and inherent traits to name a few. Social variables are comprised of the type of psychosocial factor, where or when it occurs, intensity, frequency, and access to support. Regarding the interplay between the two, Epictetus' said it best: "It's not what happens to you, but how you react to it that matters."

While a litany of psychosocial factors exists, among the more pronounced are adverse childhood experiences (ACEs) and traumatic events (Mofatteh, 2021; Remes et al., 2021). These consist of experiences of emotional neglect, abuse, needs deprivation, or other situations that exceeded one's ability to cope. In a similar vein, exposure to acute or chronic life stressors risks depression or anxiety as well (Mofatteh, 2021; Remes et al., 2021). Examples of common life stressors are relationship conflict, isolation, loss or separation, lifestyle changes, social strife, school, work, and health issues. The number of people experiencing financial strain as a stressor continues to increase, which can lead to poor resource access and diminished quality of life. Oft-overlooked stressors are the effects of social bias, discrimination, and prejudice. Members of racial, gender, sexual, and other social minority groups are at an increased risk for these stressors (Rodgers et al., 2021). Finally, composition and quality of social support influence the progression of depression and anxiety. Poor quality to nonexistent social support places a person at risk for developing and complicating prognoses of depressive and anxiety disorders (Weziak-Bialowolska et al., 2022). Equally, quality social connections can be profoundly protective with respect to these disorders (Weziak-Bialowolska et al., 2022).

Positive Psychology in the Treatment of Depression and Anxiety

Overview

Reminiscent of the Oursler metaphor, positive psychology posits people rely on subjective interpretations of the past in forming expectations for the future (Duckworth et al., 2005). In turn, people then preemptively adapt behavior to align with their expectations. For instance, if past experiences are filtered through regret and depression, a person is primed to expect only disappointment to come and align behavior in the present accordingly. If this behavior or reaction becomes habitual, the person risks being mired within the inherent passivity response and learned hopelessness (Tomasulo, 2020). In effect, feelings of helplessness and hopelessness replace any sense of control, resilience, and self-efficacy. As such, depression and anxiety are elevated to dominant experiences within their life.

The manner with which positive psychology approaches treatment of depression and anxiety can be encapsulated within the question—*does life happen for you, or happen to you?* Life *happening to you* implies being a passive spectator to a life controlled by uncontrollable aspects, including negative experiences or emotional distress. Inherent passivity runs amuck as learned hopeless takes hold as a dominant attitude. On the other hand, life *happening for you* is an empowered perspective to depression and anxiety embracing optimism, growth potential, and learned hopefulness. Depression and anxiety are explored for how they might *happen for you* as well. Notably, depression or anxiety happening *for you* is not invalidating or countering these experiences with toxic positivity (Hart, 2021; Peseschkian & Remmers, 2021). Positive psychology recognizes negative situations are as inevitable as they are essential to growth and well-being (Hart, 2021). Perceiving depression and anxiety as happening *for you* opens the door to regulating and finding meaning in otherwise painful experiences.

Conceptualization

The idea that depression and anxiety happen *for you* illustrates positive psychology's wellness-based treatment approach. Deviating from problem-focused models, positive psychology addresses distress and suffering within the broader scope of well-being and fulfillment. Positive psychology challenges the notion that the royal road to well-being is paved with problems (Peseschkian & Remmers, 2021; Seligman, 2018). Instead of concentrating on only negatives, positive psychology strives for balance on the continuum of human experiences (Peseschkian & Remmers, 2021; Seligman, 2018). Treating depression and anxiety is not just the resolution of symptoms but empowering clients to create positives within their lives (Seligman, 2012). Acknowledging personal strengths and hopefulness is as valuable as addressing problems. A wellness-based approach to depression and anxiety communicates life can *happen for you* in manner that even the negative contributes to wellness and fulfillment. Depression and anxiety may be part of this journey, and while painful and trying, they are also necessary growing pains (Seligman, 2012).

All of this is to say, positive psychology does not regard depressive or anxious symptoms as *the* problems per se. The problem is with how human beings adapt and react to depression and anxiety. Depressive and anxiety disorders are not necessarily "thieves" outright; nor are they inherently bad or abnormal. Quite the contrary, depression and anxiety are universal human experiences. For as peculiar as it sounds, both depression and anxiety were evolutionarily adaptive (Constant et al., 2021; Mermelstein, 2022). Take depression, for instance, which serves the function of warning of unmet needs, withdrawing from stressors or conflict, and signaling our need for social support (Constant et al., 2021). Anxiety is a self-preservation mechanism for keeping us safe and bonded to others (Mermelstein, 2022). To not experiencing depression or anxiety risks losing touch with present experience, our needs or safety, and what is meaningful.

Certainly, the world has changed from where depression and anxiety evolved. Increasingly organized and insular societies furnish modern humans with comparatively more safety and comfort, as well as endless opportunities for getting trapped within our own heads. Still, human beings navigate modern societies with a brain designed for the far-more-threatening world where they originated. This is where positive psychology encourages framing depression and anxiety functionally and contextually, seeing these conditions for what they are as opposed to judgmentally or problem-centrically.

Treatment Approach

A superordinate goal of positive psychology is appreciating life happens *for you* in route to cultivating **a good life** (Hart, 2021). This begs to question, what exactly is a good life, let alone when struggling with depression and anxiety? Answering this question starts with Seligman's **three keys** to a good life (Pan et al., 2022):

1. **The pleasant life**—Acknowledging and constructing positive experiences in the here and now. Doing so is an intentional undertaking consisting of curiosity, optimism, encouragement, and acceptance. The inherent passivity, learned hopelessness, and negativity that are characteristic to depressive and anxiety disorders create barriers to the pleasant life. Therapeutic processes promoting curiosity, contextual awareness, insight, positive emotions, and mindfulness all reinforce the pleasant life.
2. **The engaged life**—Establishing the type of fulfilling life, both personally and socially, that a client wants to be present in. The negative expectations, internalizations, and isolation accompanying unregulated depressive and anxiety disorders thieves that dampen the want to engage life. Therapeutic processes tapping into personal strengths, regulating emotions, and intentional social interaction target the engaged life.
3. **The meaningful life**—Feeling purposeful and deeply connected to the world. Feeling isolation, meaninglessness, and hopelessness are exemplary of how unregulated depression and anxiety drain the meaningful life. In fact, these disorders can be such a drain on purpose and meaning that suicidality becomes a risk. Therapeutic processes for the meaningful life may include personal values, action planning, meaning-making, and forming authentic connections.

As for working toward a good life, Seligman's (2018) **PERMA Model** affords counselors with dynamic therapeutic framework. The PERMA Model functions as a tool for problem conceptualization, treatment planning, and therapeutic intervention. The model is an acronym representing five domains, each with a target construct and objectives for behavioral practice (Seligman, 2018).

1. **Positive emotions**—This first domain emphasizes identifying, generating, and embracing positive emotions, be that happiness, excitement, or contentment, to name a few. Positive emotions can have a profoundly therapeutic effect with respect to the negativity and discomfort that pervade depressive and anxiety disorders.
2. **Engagement**—This domain entails contacting the present by dedicating full attention and engagement to personally meaningful activities. Reaching a state of total engagement is to ex-

perience flow, wherein focus and joy are fully dedicated to the activity at hand. Sense of time and differentiation of self are lost within these flow-states. This domain is expressly relevant as engagement and flow are impaired as internalizations mount with depression and anxiety.

3. **Relationships**—The third PERMA domain is establishing social-connectedness and social-responsibility so that relationships happen *for you*. Depressive and anxiety disorders can have isolating effects, as well as diminish confidence or security within relationships. The relationship domain counters by stressing the importance of forming deep, quality social connections.
4. **Meaning**—Deriving self-regard and meaning from life is challenging when besieged by depression or anxiety. If anything, one may reach the point that emotional distress and hopelessness appear as the meaning of life. The fourth PERMA domain stresses self-value by establishing a purposeful and personally meaningful life. Meaning can also be found in negative or uncomfortable experiences, effectively reframing their meaning to happening *for you* than *to you*.
5. **Accomplishment**—The final PERMA domain is committing to and acting upon a life that happens *for you*. Spotting progress and experiencing accomplishment are important steps in therapy. As for depression or anxiety, these disorders bear a resemblance to a hamster wheel of life happening *to you*.

There are important reminders when applying positive psychology to depressive and anxiety disorders. First, and while positive psychology advocates for living a good life, the therapeutic process requires addressing both negatives and positives. Negatives and symptom recovery are not focal points but are constituents within the grander ambition of life happening *for you*. Treatment intervention is essentially balancing act of meeting a client where they are at with regard to symptoms while challenging them to progress forward with building a good life.

Positive Psychology Interventions

Positive psychology interventions (PPIs) are evidence-based techniques aligning with the fundamentals of positive psychology. PPIs need not be exclusive to positive psychology and can be adapted from other approaches, and interventions from other orientations are adaptable so long as practitioners are holding on to the fidelity of the approach. PPIs address depressive and anxiety disorders by improving awareness, emotional regulation, resilience, mindset, and overall well-being. Below is a sampling of PPIs from several positive psychology resources for intervening with depressive or anxiety disorders (El-Gabalawi, 2020; Hart, 2021; Majeed et al., 2020; Rashid & Seligman, 2018; Tomasulo, 2020).

- **Goal-setting interventions**—Setting behavioral based, realistic, and collaborative therapeutic goals are critical to positive outcomes in counseling. The SMART method is a popular technique that checks all the boxes. Being an acronym, the SMART method frames therapeutic goals as specific, measurable, achievable, relevant, and time-bound. In addition, therapeutic goals are bolstered when composed in additive terms, referred to as "positive language." Additive or positive terms highlight what a client wants, as opposed subtractive or negative terms concentrating on what is not wanted. Goal-setting starts at the onset of counseling and remains ongoing throughout the therapy cycle.

- **Strengths-based interventions**—Strengths-based PPIs counter negativity, feelings of inadequacy, and hopelessness by encouraging clients to recognize and lean into their own strengths. These strengths are a client's personal capabilities and qualities in the form of skillsets, traits, virtues, and values. Strengths-based techniques are focal to positive psychology, and there is an assortment of PPIs like strengths assessments, self-inventories, values questionnaires or card sorts, self-reflective exercises, exploring problem exceptions, and drawing upon past solutions.
- **Gratitude interventions**—The practice of self-appreciation and gratitude is grounding and reparative for those struggling with depression or anxiety. Gratitude-based PPIs foster curiosity and thankfulness for the positives within life, be that within ourselves or others. Examples of these PPIs are gratitude journaling, 3-daily gratitude statements, notes of appreciation to self and others, and gratitude meditation.
- **Self-validating and affirming interventions**—Self-validations and affirmations reframe negative narratives in ways that are positive and nurturing of self-compassion, kindness, and self-regard. PPIs for self-validations and affirmations include self-affirmation cards, self-validating mantras, self-compassion meditations, self-acceptance affirmations or exercises, and affirming self-reflective practices. Overt behavioral exercises are also beneficial, be that acts of kindness or treating oneself as a best friend.
- **Learned hopefulness/optimism interventions**—Acute and chronic depression and anxiety can correlate to learned hopelessness and, hence, the benefits to learning hopefulness and optimism. Among the options of PPIs for learning hopefulness and optimism are psychoeducation, Dweck's (2007) Growth Mindset, Duckworth's (2018) Grit construct, cognitive restructuring and reframing, positive appraisals, positive selective attention, visualizations, and humor.
- **Engagement/connectedness interventions**—Clients battling with internalizations and isolation stand to benefit from PPIs prompting engagement and connection with life. Connecting with activities and relationships that are purposeful and meaningful can be markedly fulfilling. Exploring and assessing values, hobbies, faith/spirituality, and personal interests increase awareness for meaningful and fulfilling engagement. Social skills training, scheduling social engagements, outward demonstrations of gratitude, and practicing social interest nurture connectedness and quality relationships.
- **Interventions for emotional intelligence**—As previously discussed, the world from where emotions evolved is quite different from the one today. In facing this reality, human beings need to adapt how they perceive and utilize emotional experiences. Emotional intelligence is an evidence-based approach to achieving well-being by improving emotional awareness and regulation. Further information on the benefits and integration of emotional intelligence with positive psychology is available in Chapter 7 of this volume.

Practicing Mindfulness

The Oursler metaphor is testament to depression and anxiety's greatest thievery: the ability to experience life happening *for you* within the present. Admittedly, engaging the present is far easier said than done. Connecting with the now requires practice and intentionality, not to mention healthy doses of grace and self-compassion. Fortunately, mindfulness-based PPIs are designed for this very reason (Hart, 2021; Majeed et al., 2018). Despite popular belief, mindfulness-based interventions are not simply for achieving calm or contentment. Mindfulness is also not a static state or achievement, but a process created from repetition and skill. Mindfulness interventions support nonjudgmentally engaging the present by focusing awareness and attention (Hart, 2021). Should attention drift or judgment creep into consciousness, mindfulness calls for a compassionate return to the present moment. Furthermore, mindfulness-based interventions are empirically validated treatments for depressive and anxiety disorders (Goldberg et al., 2018; Majeed et al., 2020; Saeed et al., 2019).

Depressing over the past and worrying about the future unquestionably leave little time or energy for living a pleasant, engaged, or meaningful life. As a PPI, mindfulness-based practices disentangle the past and future to create space for focusing attention on a good life within the present. Counselors integrating mindfulness-based PPIs into treatment provide clients with hands-on training and practical applications for these skills. Importantly, effective mindfulness-based intervention hinges on frequent skills practice. Regular mindfulness skills practice refines skills and commits them to muscle memory, improving the likelihood they will not be an afterthought in times of escalated distress. There is a bevy of mindfulness-based PPIs available to counselors, of which a handful are cataloged below.

- **Formal mindfulness practices**—Mindfulness as a formal meditative practice is a structured exercise directing attention to a specific focal point, be that a mantra, visualization, or other directive. Should attention or engagement drift from that focal point, the instruction is gently and nonjudgmentally return. Formal mindfulness practices transpire within individual and group settings, so long as the setting is relaxed and free from distraction. Last, these structured and directive mindfulness practices are particularly beneficial for those just learning these skills. Sources of formal mindfulness practices include in-person or virtual training modules, books and workbooks, prefabricated scripts, guided recordings, and Apps such as Headspace and Calm. Counselors are also encouraged to provide mindfulness skills training and modeling within sessions.
- **Mindfulness-based yoga**—Mindfulness-based yoga marries the cognitive practices of mindfulness meditation with the physical activity of yoga (Miao et al., 2023; Saeed et al., 2019). In doing so, clients are afforded the psychological and physiological benefits of holistic mind and body mindfulness practice. Mindfulness-based yoga demonstrates excellent potential in the treatment of depressive and anxiety disorders (Miao et al., 2023; Saeed et al., 2019). Clients exhibiting somatic symptoms or difficulty connecting with their physiological experiences may especially benefit from mindfulness-based yoga.

- **Informal mindfulness practices**—Mindfulness-based practices do not necessarily need to be formal or directed. Informal practice is a flexible and adaptable strategy for integrating mindfulness into one's daily schedule. Nearly any daily activity or routine is an occasion for mindfulness practice. For instance, the act of eating, walking, listening, observing, or physical sensation acts as the chance to nonjudgmentally focus attention on that present activity. Another strategy is scheduling time to pause for mindful moments during the day.

Conclusion

Nearly 600 million people worldwide receive a diagnosis of at least one depressive and/or anxiety disorder (World Health Organization, 2022). Perhaps of greater concern is these disorders are pound-for-pound among the most disabling among medical conditions (National Center for Complementary and Integrative Health, n.d.). Obscuring matters are depression and anxiety commonly come as a packaged experience, a product of high comorbidity rates and shared etiological factors. Kalin (2020) warns of the complexities of treating comorbid depression and anxiety, beginning with the difficulties of parsing out and isolating symptoms for treatment. Overlapping affective features are further cause for confusion, especially when those are feelings of agitation, hopelessness, or helplessness. Treatment and long-term prognoses to worsen in comorbid cases as well (Kalin, 2020).

The point is not painting a grim picture of depressive and anxiety disorders but underscoring the significance and necessity for quality treatment. With respect to treatment, positive psychology challenges traditional notions and assumptions about depressive and anxiety disorders. Instead of concentrating on resolving symptoms or solving presenting problems, positive psychology turns the tide on feelings of hopelessness and life happening *to you.* By embracing pleasant experiences, engaging life, and creating meaning, clients grappling with unregulated depression or anxiety effectively learn life happens for you en route to improved well-being and fulfillment. Despite misconception, positive psychology does not invalidate presenting problems or suffering. On the contrary, negative experiences are given due diligence in treatment, although they are neither the start nor end point of the therapeutic process. Utilizing PPIs to treat depression and anxiety is about mitigating the thievery of wellness and fulfillment within the present, a critical stepping stone to embracing that experiences in life happen *for you.*

Critical Thinking Questions

1. How would you describe depressive and anxiety disorders? What are notable differences between these types of disorders? Conversely, how are depressive and anxiety disorders related to one another?
2. .How would you describe or frame depressive and anxiety disorders through the lens of positive psychology to a counseling client? What information do you feel is important to share with them to improve their understanding of these disorders as well as facilitate a positive psychology approach to treatment?
3. Explain the concept of learned helplessness, including how understanding of this concept has changed since its introduction. Similarly, describe the concept of learned hopelessness and how it compares and contrasts with learned hopefulness.
4. Of the PPIs outlined within the chapter, which do you see yourself using with clients and why? Which of these PPIs are you reluctant to try and why?
5. Of the mindfulness-based interventions presented within the chapter, which do you find beneficial to clients? Do you see yourself integrating any of these mindfulness-based interventions into your own daily routine?

Case Study: The Case of Michele and MDD

Michele is a 35-year-old African American woman seeking counseling for "feeling down and depressed." When asked when these symptoms started, Michele states depression "seems to always come and go for as long as she can remember." She suggests a long-standing pattern of psychosocial stressors with "everyone goes through problems; it just seems I've had more than others." Michele reports a history of intermittent depressive episodes like this current one, feeling so sad that even her favorite activities are not as enjoyable. Michele also reports lethargy, low motivation, interrupted sleep, poor appetite, inability to concentrate, and seeing herself as worthless. During these episodes, it is hard for Michele to focus on anything else but her past and all the negative things that have happened. Michele's negative conceptualizations of the past leads to her believe that is all the future holds as well. Whether within an episode or not, Michele generally finds it difficult to not feel guilty about experiencing pleasant things. Michele spends the majority her time at work, leaving little time for hobbies or social interests. Other than a couple of friends she talks to occasionally, Michele has limited social connection and does not really feel close to anyone. Michele generally feels lonely and isolated, which are exacerbated when she feels overwhelmed by depression and is unable to work. Overall, Michele is unhappy about her life and does not feel very fulfilled. Michele states life has not gone as she wanted and has little hope that anything will change and largely feels dread regarding her future.

Michele's self-reports are demonstrative of a major depressive disorder. Michele's history includes a lifelong pattern of psychosocial stressors, to which she responds with inherent passivity, learned hopelessness, and trouble regulating emotions. Michele's depressive symptoms and conceptualized past are now the focal point of current experience, inhibiting her capacity for living a good life. Michele's ability to engage and create meaning is also hindered by past rumination and negative expectations for the future. In all, Michele feels disengaged and isolated from others and what brings her joy. So much so that Michele judges her life as meaningless and hopelessness. In effect, Michele's perspective is that life has and will continue happening *to her* and not *for her*.

After conceptualization, the PERMA Model is an excellent framework for addressing Michele's presenting problems and cultivating a good life that happens *for her*.

1. **Positive emotions**—Michele will benefit from learning the value of positive emotions, as well as skills for generating them within her life. Hopefulness and optimism PPIs cultivate positive emotions via exercises in positive appraisals, positive selective attention, and reframing. Gratitude PPI can also be used as strategies for positive emotions, be that journaling or sharing notes of self-appreciation.

2. **Engagement**—Being disengaged from personal interests and hobbies, identifying and engrossing herself in fulfilling activities give Michele reason to engage the present. Strengths-based PPIs aid with finding engaging activities by exploring of personal strengths, resources, and values. Mindfulness-based interventions will teach Michele how to divert focused attention and engage with these activities.
3. **Relationships**—Michele reports loneliness and isolation, compounded by her lack of quality social connections. Establishing social connectedness and quality relationships stands to improve Michele's social-emotional functioning, as well as in building a life she wants to be present in. Engagement and connectedness PPIs aid Michele by advancing work–life balance and relationship intentionality by scheduling social engagements, demonstrating gratitude for others, and practicing social interest.
4. **Meaning**—Assessing personal strengths, exploring values, and other strengths-based PPIs helps Michele distinguish life pursuits and activities yielding purpose and meaning. SMART goals and action plans are also beneficial for making commitments to take intentional action toward purpose and meaning.
5. **Accomplishment**—It is a wonder if Michele feels much accomplishment or success within her current situation. Therefore, Michele would benefit from realizing and embracing her accomplishments during the therapeutic process. For example, self-validating PPIs in the form of reflective practices and self-affirmations can assist Michele with acknowledging therapeutic accomplishments. In addition, strengths-based and gratitude PPIs could be used to challenge Michelle to identify past achievements and successes.

Of course, this is but one example of applying the PERMA Model to the case of Michele. Take a moment to reflect on how you would want to approach this case and consider the following questions:

- Are there other PPIs that you would consider using with Michele to help with regulating depressive symptoms and improving overall well-being?
- Of the three keys to the good life, which one do you feel Michele is struggling with the most? Is there one key that you would focus on more than the others, at least at first?
- In what ways would mindfulness-based interventions help Michele with regulating depression and improving well-being?
- Which of the mindfulness-based interventions would benefit Michele more than others?

References

Appleton J. (2018). The gut-brain axis: Influence of microbiota on mood and mental health. *Integrative Medicine (Encinitas), 17*(4), 28–32. https://pmc.ncbi.nlm.nih.gov/articles/PMC6469458/

American Psychiatric Association. (2022). *Diagnostic and statistical manual of mental disorders* (5th ed., text rev.). https://doi.org/10.1176/appi.books.9780890425787

Atticus [@atticuspoetry]. (2021, November, 20). *Depression is being color blind and constantly told how colorful the world is* [Post]. X. https://x.com/atticuspoetry/status/1462150759194279936

Constant, A., Hesp, C., Davey, C. G., Friston, K. J., & Badcock P. B. (2021). Why depressed mood is adaptive: A numerical proof of principle for an evolutionary systems theory of depression. *Computational Psychiatry, 5*(1), 60–80. https://doi.org/10.5334/cpsy.70

Corey, G. (2024). *Theory and practice of counseling and psychotherapy* (11th ed.). Cengage Learning.

Cozolino, L. (2017). *The Neuroscience of psychotherapy: Healing the social brain* (3rd ed.). W. W. Norton & Company.

Daffre, C., Oliver, K. I., & Pace-Schott, E. F. (2020). Neurocircuitry of anxiety disorders. In E. Bui, M. E. Charney, & A.W. Baker (Eds.), *Clinical handbook of anxiety disorders: From theory to practice* (pp. 15–42). Humana Press.

Duckworth, A. (2018). *Grit: The power and passion of perseverance*. Scribner.

Duckworth, A. L., Steen, T. A., & Seligman, M. E. P. (2005). Positive psychology in clinical practice. *Annual Review of Clinical Psychology, 1*, 629–651. https://doi.org/10.1146/annurev.clinpsy.1.102803.144154

Dweck, C. S. (2007). *Mindset: The new psychology of success* (updated ed.). Ballantine Books.

El-Gabalawi, F. (2020). Positive interventions in depression. In E. Messias, H. Peseschkian, & C. Cagande (Eds.), *Positive psychiatry, psychotherapy, and psychology*. Springer.

Fang, Y., & Mao, R. (2019). Introduction. In Y. Fang (Ed.). *Depressive disorders: Mechanisms, measurements, and management*. Springer.

Goldberg, S. B., Tucker, R. P., Greene, P. A., Davidson, R. J., Wampold, B. E., Kearney, D. J., & Simpson, T. L. (2018). Mindfulness-based interventions for psychiatric disorders: A systematic review and meta-analysis. *Clinical Psychology Review, 59*, 52–60. https://doi.org/10.1016/j.cpr.2017.10.011

Hart, R. (2021). *Positive psychology: The basics*. Routledge.

Herzallah, M., Miezah, D., & Moustafa, A. A. (2021). Neural and genetic correlates of cognitive deficits in major depressive disorder. In A. A. Moustafa (Ed.), *The nature of depression: An updated review* (pp. 17–40). Academic Press.

Hong, W., & Zhang, Q. (2021). Biological rhythms advance in depressive disorder. In A. A. Moustafa (Ed.), *The nature of depression: An updated review* (pp. 117–133). Academic Press.

Huberty, T. J. (2017). Students with emotional and behavioral problems. *Reference Module in Neuroscience and Biobehavioral Psychology*. https://doi.org/10.1016/B978-0-12-809324-5.05547-4

Kalin, N. H. (2020). The critical relationship between anxiety and depression. *The Journal of Psychiatry, 177*(5), 365–367. https://doi.org/10.1176/appi.ajp.2020.20030305

Kamper-DeMarco, K. E., Shankman, J., Fearey, E., Lawrence, H. R., & Schwartz-Mette, R. A. (2020). Linking social skills and adjustment: Internalizing disorders. In D. W. Nangle, C. A. Erdley, & R. A. Schwartz-Mette (Eds.), *Social skills across the life span*. Academic Press. https://doi.org/10.1016/B978-0-12-817752-5.00003-2

Maier, S. F., & Seligman, M. E. (2016). Learned helplessness at fifty: Insights from neuroscience. *Psychology Review, 123*(4), 349–367. https://doi.org/10.1037/rev0000033

Majeed, S., Salman, R., Lau, P., & Cagande, C. (2020). Positive interventions in anxiety disorders. In E. Messias, H. Peseschkian, & C. Cagande (Eds.), *Positive psychiatry, psychotherapy, and psychology*. Springer.

Melaragno, A., Spera, V., & Bui, E. (2020). Psychopharmacology of anxiety disorders. In E. Bui, M. E. Charney, & A.W. Baker (Eds.), *Clinical handbook of anxiety disorders: From theory to practice* (pp. 251–268). Humana Press.

Mermelstein, J. J. (2022). The evolutionary roots of anxiety and its implications for socialization and group cohesion. *Journal of Psychiatry and Psychiatric Disorders, 6*, 247–252. https://www.fortunejournals.com/articles/the-evolutionary-roots-of-anxiety-and-its-implications-.pdf

Miao, C., Gao, Y., Li, X., Zhou, Y., Chung, J. W., & Smith, G. D. (2003). The effectiveness of mindfulness yoga on patients with major depressive disorder: A systematic review and meta-analysis of randomized controlled trials. *BMC Complementary Medicine and Therapies, 23*, 313. https://doi.org/10.1186/s12906-023-04141-2

Mofatteh, M. (2020). Risk factors associated with stress, anxiety, and depression among university undergraduate students. *AIMS Public Health, 8*(1), 36–65. https://doi.org/10.3934/publichealth.2021004

National Center for Complementary and Integrative Health. (n.d.). *Symptoms matter: Leading causes of disability*. https://www.nccih.nih.gov/about/symptoms-matterleading-causes-of-disability

Pan, S., Ali, K., Kahathuduwa, C., Baronia, R., & Ibrahim, Y. (2022). Meta-analysis of positive psychology on the treatment of depression. *Cureus, 14*(2), e21933. https://doi.org/10.7759/cureus.21933

Parish, A. L., Gillis, B., & Anthamatten, A. (2023). Pharmacotherapy for depression and anxiety in the primary care setting. *The Journal for Nurse Practitioners, 19*(4),104556. https://doi.org/10.1016/j.nurpra.2023.104556

Peseschkian, H., & Remmers, A. (2021). Positive psychotherapy: An introduction. In E. Messias, H. Peseschkian, & C. Cagande (Eds.), *Positive psychiatry, psychotherapy, and psychology*. Springer.

Rashid, T., & Seligman, M. (2018). *Positive psychotherapy: Clinical manual*. Oxford University Press.

Remes, O., Mendes, J. F., & Templeton, P. (2021). Biological, psychological, and social determinants of depression: A review of recent literature. *Brain Sciences, 11*(12), 1633. https://doi.org/10.3390/brainsci11121633

Rodgers, R. F., Berry, R., & Fischer, L. E. (2021). Anxiety disorders: A feminist ecological approach. In A. A. Moustafa (Ed.), *The nature of depression: An updated review* (pp. 43–58). Academic Press.

Saeed, S. A., Cunningham, K., & Bloch, R. M. (2019). Depression and anxiety disorders: Benefits of exercise, yoga, and medication. *American Family Physician, 99*(10), 620–627. https://pubmed.ncbi.nlm.nih.gov/31083878/

Seligman, M. E. P. (2012). *Flourish: A new visionary understanding of happiness and well-being.* Free Press.

Seligman, M. E. (2018). *The hope circuit: A psychologist's journey from helplessness to optimism.* Public Affairs.

Tomasulo, D. (2020). *Learned hopefulness: The power of positivity to overcome depression.* New Harbinger.

Toner, E. R., & Robinaugh, D. J. (2020). A casual systems approach to anxiety disorders. In E. Bui, M. E. Charney, & A. W. Baker (Eds.), *Clinical handbook of anxiety disorders: From theory to practice* (pp. 1–14). Humana Press.

Weziak-Bialowolska, D., Bialowolski P., Lee, M. T., Chen, Y., VanderWeele, T. J., & McNeely, E. (2022). Prospective associations between social connectedness and mental health: Evidence from a longitudinal survey and health insurance claims data. *International Journal of Public Health, 67*, 1604710. https://doi.org/10.3389/ijph.2022.1604710

World Health Organization. (2022). *Mental disorders.* https://www.who.int/news-room/fact-sheets/detail/mental-disorders

Integrating Emotional Intelligence, Mindfulness, and Positive Psychology in Counseling Treatment

7

David S Pfaff
Nicole Noble
Logan Winkelman

KEYWORDS AND DEFINITIONS:

Emotional intelligence: Possessing an awareness and understanding of one's and others' emotions as well as possessing skills to regulate one's emotions and social skills to influence other's emotions.

Self-awareness: An ability to identify, recognize, and understand one's thoughts, feelings, emotions, and behaviors as well as the reasoning and motivations behind these areas.

Self-regulation: The ability to engage in productive coping skills necessary to regulate one's thoughts, feelings, emotions, and behaviors to achieve long-term goals and maintain well-being.

Social skills: The ability to engage in effective interpersonal behaviors necessary to influence others' thoughts, feelings, emotions, and behaviors to achieve personal and shared goals.

Social awareness: The ability to identify, recognize, and understand other's thoughts, feelings, emotions, and behaviors as well as the reasoning and motivations behind these areas.

LEARNING OBJECTIVES:

1. Define emotional intelligence
2. Understand the benefits of utilizing emotional intelligence enhancing strategies with clients
3. Identify the benefits of integrating the approaches of emotional intelligence, positive psychology, and mindfulness in a cohesive framework with clients
4. Investigate understanding of emotional intelligence approaches through a case study and activity

Introduction

While Peter Salovey and John D. Mayer (1990) originally introduced the concept of emotional intelligence, Daniel Goleman (1995) popularized the term asserting that emotional intelligence was a stronger predictor of success in life than intelligence in areas including relationships and careers. Furthermore, Goleman contended that emotional intelligence is a teachable skill that can be cultivated through increased emotional awareness, management, and practice. With Goleman's text is available in 40 languages and over 5 million copies of his book have been sold (The Edge, 2023), the subject matter undoubtedly resonated with a global audience and continues to be studied extensively in fields including psychology, business, and education (Ackley, 2016). Emotional intelligence can be defined as "the ability to monitor one's own and other's feelings and emotions, to discriminate among them and to use this information to guide one's thinking and actions" (Salovey & Mayer, 1990, p. 189). In other words, emotional intelligence may be defined as being able "to rein in emotional impulse; to read another's innermost feelings; to handle relationships smoothly" (Goleman, 1995, p. 10).

Humans experience emotional responses to stressors daily, but for individuals experiencing a particularly challenging life experience that might lead them to seek support from a mental health professional, these emotional responses may be even more intense and extreme than their typical emotional responses. Therefore, the need to practice emotional regulation skills may be even more present for individuals navigating these acute and/or chronic life stressors. Through awareness of emotional reactions and regulating with intentional, deliberate responses, individuals navigating these stressors are more likely to achieve their goals. In fact, according to Goleman (1995), "all emotions are, in essence, impulses to act, the instant plans for handling life that evolution has instilled in us. The very root of the word emotion is *motere*, the Latin verb 'to move'" (p. 15). Therefore, viewing emotions from this perspective illustrates that emotions should not be considered something that works against a person's goals, but rather emotions may be used to motivate and improve outcomes. Thus, counselors fostering client emotional intelligence is paramount in supporting clients in achieving their goals.

Overview of the Chapter

This chapter explores emotional intelligence and its role in promoting client well-being. Specifically, this chapter seeks to integrate positive psychology and mindfulness with emotional intelligence into treatment approaches. To provide context, the chapter includes historical development of emotional intelligence theories including a brief overview of theoretical models of emotional intelligence and the relevance of emotional intelligence in counseling settings. Finally, the chapter concludes with a case study, critical thinking questions, and an activity to assist the reader assess their ability to apply the material.

Importance of Emotional Intelligence in Counseling Treatment

As Salovey and Mayer (1990) outlined in their seminal article on emotional intelligence, utilizing emotional intelligence may assist individuals in harnessing "their own emotions in order to solve problems" (p. 198) including enhancing flexible planning, creative thinking, mood redirected attention, and motivating emotions. While emotional responses to circumstances may not be controllable, emotional regulation can be utilized to first identify emotions, select potential responses to those emotions, and engage in the most desirable response that will best facilitate the achievement of a carefully selected goal. This process aligns well with counseling, which involves helping clients gain insight into their own and other's thoughts, feelings, behaviors, and motivations. Furthermore, effective counseling includes supporting clients in developing positive coping strategies to navigate life stressors and challenges. These improved coping strategies can lead to improved decision-making, enhanced interpersonal relationships, and increased motivation. Emotional intelligence also plays a key role in strengthening social and relationship functioning by enhancing empathy, fostering better communication, and promoting conflict resolution. Ideally, throughout the counseling process, clients feel safe and supported enough to explore areas they otherwise might avoid, fostering their resilience and personal growth. Through focusing on supporting clients in enhancing their emotional intelligence, counselors can empower clients to increase their resiliency to life's challenges, improve social connections, and promote their overall well-being.

The Connection Between Emotional Intelligence, Positive Psychology, and Mindfulness

Emotional intelligence, positive psychology, and mindfulness, all share many similarities that make them ideal treatment approaches to integrate to foster client well-being. Specifically, the emotional intelligence component of improving self-awareness aligns both with mindfulness of having a careful attunement to one's present moment and with positive psychology of being aware of one's strengths to help foster them. Furthermore, the areas of social awareness similarly are associated with mindfulness of acknowledging both internal (self-awareness) and external (social awareness) stimuli and gently accepting these current conditions. Through listening, empathy, and understanding, others are more likely to be motivated to change toward some shared values or goal.

Positive psychology also identifies the benefits of social support and having an increased understanding and empathy toward others and is therefore similarly connected to the emotional intelligence component of social awareness. Additionally, mindfulness principles of identifying one's current emotional states often allow the intensity of these states to dissipate and, in turn, help the individuals to become better able to engage in self-regulation, which is another component of emotional intelligence. Finally, despite popular belief, positive psychology does not involve ignoring negative feelings or experiences but, instead, involves an awareness of them and a decision to accept these experiences and view them as an opportunity for change and growth. This positive psychology acceptance for *what is* aligns with mindfulness practices, and, when emotions can be accepted this way, it can improve self-regulation skills and increase social awareness through fostering empathy and enrich social skills. The connections between emotional intelligence, positive psychology, and mindfulness are numerous. Through incorporating these approaches into a holistic framework, counselors can identify clients' unique needs to provide tailored counseling treatment.

Understanding Emotional Intelligence

Definition and Components of Emotional Intelligence

Emotional intelligence (EI) is a multifaceted construct that plays a crucial role in personal and professional success. It encompasses the ability to perceive, regulate, and evaluate emotions—both in oneself and in others. As mentioned previously, the components of emotional intelligence can be broken down into four key areas:

Self-awareness

Self-awareness is the foundational component of emotional intelligence. It involves the capacity to recognize and understand one's own emotions, thoughts, and behaviors. This awareness extends to understanding the motivations and reasons behind these internal states. It enables individuals to identify emotional triggers and understand how their emotions can influence their actions and decisions.

Self-regulation

Self-regulation refers to the ability to manage one's emotions effectively. This involves using coping strategies to adjust thoughts, feelings, and behaviors in a way that aligns with personal values and goals. Self-regulation helps individuals respond to situations with a calm and composed demeanor, enabling them to navigate challenges and maintain well-being over the long term.

Social Awareness

Social awareness is the ability to accurately perceive and understand the emotions and thoughts of others. This involves empathy and the capacity to consider the perspectives and feelings of those around us. By recognizing others' motivations and emotional states, individuals can build stronger, more understanding relationships.

Social Skills

Social skills are the abilities required to interact effectively with others. They include communication, conflict resolution, and the capacity to influence others' emotions and behaviors. Mastery of social skills allows individuals to build and maintain healthy relationships, facilitating both personal and shared goals.

Historical Context and Development of EI Theory

The roots of emotional intelligence can be traced back to the early 20th century when psychologists began exploring the non-cognitive aspects of intelligence. Researchers like Edward Thorndike in the 1920s introduced the idea of "social intelligence," which laid the groundwork for later developments in understanding the emotional aspects of intelligence (Goleman, 1995). The term "emotional intelligence" itself was first coined in 1990 by psychologists Peter Salovey and John D. Mayer. They defined EI as the ability to perceive, understand, manage, and utilize emotions effectively. Their model focused on four key abilities: perceiving emotions, using emotions to facilitate thinking, understanding emotions, and managing emotions.

In 1995, Daniel Goleman popularized the concept with his book *Emotional Intelligence: Why It Can Matter More Than IQ*. Goleman broadened the scope by integrating emotional and social competencies, emphasizing the role of EI in achieving personal and professional success. His work brought widespread attention to the practical applications of emotional intelligence, making it a household term. Following Goleman, various models of emotional intelligence were developed, each offering unique perspectives.

The concept of emotional intelligence has evolved over time, with several influential models contributing to its development. These models enriched understanding of how emotional intelligence influences behavior and coping strategies. These foundational theoretical models of emotional intelligence are identified as follows:

Ability-Based Model (Salovey and Mayer)

Introduced by Peter Salovey and John D. Mayer in 1990, the ability-based model views emotional intelligence as a set of cognitive abilities. These abilities include perceiving emotions accurately, using emotions to facilitate thought, understanding emotional meanings, and managing emotions effectively. This model posits that EI is a form of intelligence that can be measured and developed.

Mixed Model (Goleman)

Daniel Goleman's mixed model, popularized in his 1995 book, expands the concept of emotional intelligence beyond the cognitive abilities outlined by Salovey and Mayer. Goleman's model includes a broader set of emotional and social competencies, such as self-awareness, self-regulation, motivation, empathy, and social skills. This model emphasizes the practical applications of EI in achieving success in personal and professional settings.

Performance Model (Bar-On)

Reuven Bar-On's performance model, often referred to as the Emotional Quotient Inventory (EQ-i), introduces the concept of emotional-social intelligence, which includes a range of non-cognitive capabilities, competencies, and skills (Bar-On, 1997, 2010). Bar-On's model focuses on how these elements influence an individual's ability to cope with environmental demands and pressures. It highlights the importance of emotional expression, interpersonal relationships, stress management, and adaptability.

Relevance of Emotional Intelligence in Counseling Settings

Today, emotional intelligence is recognized as a critical factor in education, leadership, counseling, and organizational development. In counseling settings, emotional intelligence is an invaluable asset for both counselors and clients. For counselors, developing EI can enhance their ability to empathize with clients, understand their emotions, and respond effectively to their needs. For clients, fostering emotional intelligence can lead to improved emotional regulation, better interpersonal relationships, and greater overall well-being.

Counselors can integrate emotional intelligence into their practice by helping clients develop self-awareness, self-regulation, social-awareness, and social skills. These skills can empower clients to navigate life's challenges with resilience and adaptability, ultimately supporting them in achieving their personal and therapeutic goals. By cultivating emotional intelligence, counselors can create a supportive environment that promotes growth, healing, and positive change.

Integrating Positive Psychology and Emotional Intelligence

Synergy Between Emotional Intelligence and Positive Psychology

Synergy is not simply a relationship between concepts, but a coalescence generating effects greater than those concepts alone. Emotional intelligence and positive psychology demonstrate synergy, with metaphors being a valuable tool for illustrating this relationship. Take the rhetorical question—*does life happen to you or happen for you*? While ostensibly a simple play on words, *to* and *for* represent diametrically opposed approaches to life. Starting with positive psychology, a happening *to you* approach implies the attitudes of inherent passivity and learned helplessness. Akin to a marionette puppet, the sense is external circumstances pull the strings on everything from emotions, to thoughts, or even lifestyle. Inversely, happening *for you* cuts the self-manufactured puppet strings. This more empowering approach to life embraces attitudes of optimism, learned hopefulness, and a growth mindset. Make no mistake—this approach is neither about toxic positivity nor about invalidating negative experiences, quite the contrary. The happening *for you* approach recognizes negative events happen throughout life. Negative events are acknowledged as painful realities, as well as opportunities for discovering strength, resilience, and growth. Life happening *for you* is about discovering purpose and meaning within all lived experiences on the journey to cultivating well-being and a fulfilling lifestyle.

This same happening *to you* versus *for you* dynamic applies to emotions as well. Consider that emotions have critical functions in human survival, relationships, well-being, and fulfillment to name a few (Dennison, 2024). Moreover, it is highly suspect whether life can truly happen *for you* without emotions happening *for you* as well. Emotional intelligence is about emotions happening *for you*, which is fully on display within another metaphor *the elephant and the rider* (Haidt, 2006). Suppose emotions were an elephant and logic were a rider seated atop it. In this case, the rider hopes to embark on a journey of wellness and fulfillment. Assumably, the rider is in control of this elephant, an otherwise burden to the rider's will. At least, this is the idealized relationship between logic and emotion. The reality is the elephant is a much larger and imposing force, complete with its own impulses and wants. After all, this is an elephant, and the rider is going nowhere sans its cooperation. When in conflict, the rider's attempts at logic or control are no match for the elephant's emotional authority. Synchronicity is key if the rider hopes to achieve wellness and a fulfilling journey, the product of a cooperative and symbiotic relationship with the elephant. Lacking in synchrony risks facing the consequences of the elephant's emotions, ranging from immobility to being bucked off and trampled. The rider is best served by acknowledging the elephants' emotions and considering how they happen *for them* on this journey. The elephant's emotions may not always align with the rider's aspirations; nor can the journey be easy or linear, but so is the cost of wellness and fulfillment. The rider's emotional intelligence becomes the great equalizer, not simply logic or reason. So is the reality of human nature where, despite the influence of logic, most behavior and success are attributable to emotion and emotional intelligence (Daye, 2016; Natarelli, 2017; Srivastava & Jaiswal, 2022).

Suffice to say, the emotionally intelligent rider stands a greater chance of success in their journey than the logical or controlling one. This is because the emotionally intelligent rider utilizes the elephant's emotional drive *for them*, as opposed to having it happen *to them*. Emotions happening *for you* are instrumental in meeting the positive psychology goals of well-being and fulfillment. In this way, effectively navigating life is mediated by the ability to channel and regulate emotional experiences (Alemdar & Anılan, 2020; Dennison, 2024). Likewise, emotional awareness and recognition are requisite for insight into what are meaningful, purposeful, and satisfying (Alemdar & Anılan, 2020; Dennison, 2024). In turn, positive psychology provides the emotionally intelligent rider with a comprehensive map that pushes the boundary beyond the emotional aspects of life for their journey to well-being and fulfillment.

Seligman's positive psychology construct of *the good life* affords an opportunity for translating this synergy from metaphor into practical application (Pan et al., 2022). Note the good life consists of three key factors, all of which benefit when integrated with emotional intelligence:

1. **The Pleasant Life**—Generating, identifying, and embracing positive experiences are cornerstones to this first key of the good life (Pan et al., 2022). Of course, living the pleasant life is challenging when overwhelmed by negative or dysregulated emotions. Lacking emotional literacy or operating from a restricted emotional range also poses barriers to the pleasant life. Emotional intelligence with its emphasis on self-awareness and self-regulation facilitates openness, curiosity, and acceptance of positive emotions. Additionally, emotional intelligence supports nurturing positive emotions for the sake of balancing and regulating distress.
2. **The Engaged Life**—Engagement through socially significant experiences, interactions, and relationships is the second key to the good life (Pan et al., 2022). Emotions are a profound mechanism for socially engaging and forming relationships (Alemdar & Anılan, 2020; Dennison, 2024). They fuel the drive to engage, act as feedback loops, and are the glue to attachment bonds (Alemdar & Anılan, 2020). They regard emotional intelligence models related to social awareness and social management are expressly relevant to the engaged life. This includes facilitating the engaged life by way of social skill training, intentional social interaction, social regulation skills, and meaningful relationship-building.
3. **The Meaningful Life**—The final key to the good life are deep feelings of purpose and connection to sources of personal meaning and fulfillment (Pan et al., 2022). Given the need for deep feelings, it is fair to ask if the meaningful life is possible without a degree of emotional intelligence. All the four quadrants of Goleman's emotional intelligence model intersect on the

meaningful life. This comprises recognizing, utilizing, and regulating a full range of emotions for identifying and pursuing personal meaning. Furthermore, emotional intelligence recognizes the value of leveraging personal emotional strengths in promoting resilience and well-being.

Strategies for Integrating Emotional Intelligence and Positive Psychology

While the synergy between emotional intelligence and positive psychology is evident, counselors may question how they can transform this synergy into practical application with clients. Coincidentally, emotional intelligence and positive psychology share the common ambition of improving well-being and functioning (Filice & Weese, 2024; Peseschkian & Remmers, 2021). Both approaches, with their focus on well-being, operate from a wellness model emphasizing health and functioning over pathology and dysfunction. However, within these approaches, negative experiences and emotional distress are not overlooked; instead, they are framed as happening *for you*, contributing to the cultivation of health and wellness. In this respect, consider emotional intelligence as a framework for addressing and elevating emotional objectives within positive psychology. Similarly, positive psychology interventions (PPIs) integrate with the process of cultivating emotional intelligence. For example, PPIs designed for learning hopefulness, optimism, and resilience contribute to the capacity for self- and social-emotional regulation. Other suggestions and ideas for integrating PPIs and emotional intelligence are illustrated below.

Self-awareness

- **Emotional Literacy**—A broad construct, emotional literacy is the product of an emotional education on a number of competencies, including recognition, comprehension, vocabulary, and function (Francis et al,, 2020; Hart, 2021). When employed as PPI, emotional literacy stresses the purposeful and intentional application of emotions within the good life (Francis et al., 2020; Hart, 2021). Among the options for emotional literacy interventions are training programs, psychoeducation, bibliotherapy, emotional recognition exercises, and building an emotional vocabulary.
- **Strengths and Values**—Increasing awareness to leverage personal strengths and values is focal to positive psychology (Hart, 2021; Majeed et al., 2018). Unfortunately, neither emotions nor emotional intelligence garner enough appreciation as strengths or values. PPIs open the door to the idea of emotional strengths and values, providing insight into their influence as well as how to leverage them. Numerous interventions exist for developing awareness of personal strengths and values such as inventories, assessments, values sorts, and self-reflective exercises via journaling or exploratory questioning.

- **Achievements and Successes**—In addition to strengths, positive psychology stresses the benefits of insight into personal achievements and success (Carr, 2022; Hart, 2021). If anything, identifying and leveraging achievements or successes creates an opportunity for expanding awareness for positive emotions. Embracing positive emotions is also associated with achievements or successes and reinforces hope for pleasant experiences as well as reinforces past successes and functioning. As for interventions, there are self-reflective practices on accomplishments or milestone moments, exploring problem-exceptions, and identifying past solutions. Counselors can support clients with emotional processing while practicing these interventions.

Self-regulation

- **Emotional Reframing and Restructuring**—Positive psychology promotes flexible perspective by reframing life experiences in hopeful and optimistic ways (Carr, 2022; Rashid & Seligman, 2018). As such, there are PPIs designed for positively reframing life experiences, including emotions, as purposeful opportunities for resilience and growth (Carr, 2022). Applying PPIs for optimistically reframing and restructuring emotional experiences enhances self-regulation and functioning. Emotional reframing and restructuring involve authoring hopeful narratives with respect to emotional experiences (Carr, 2022). So, instead of problems to be avoided or solved, emotions are instead framed as happening *for you*. Examples of interventions are narrative work, Socratic questioning, cognitive reframing and restructuring, and metaphors.
- **Learned Hopefulness and Optimism**—The positive psychology construct of *learned hopefulness* entails enriching a growth-centered mindset in response to hardship with learned optimism, confidence, and curiosity (Tomasulo, 2020). Of course, learning hopefulness and optimism are applicable to emotional experience as well. Hopelessness and emotions happen *to me* are common reactions to emotional distress and hardship (Tomasulo, 2020). Yet, learned hopefulness and optimism empowers clients to examine how their distressing emotions happen *for them*, embracing and improving their ability to regulate a full range of emotions. PPIs for hopefulness and optimism incorporate psychoeducation, positive appraisals, positive selective attention, visualizations, metaphors, and humor. Dweck's (2007) Growth Mindset concept along with Duckworth's (2018) Grit are also beneficial therapeutic tools.

Social Awareness

- **Social-Emotional Education**—The engaged life hinges on effectively using emotions in social contexts, underscoring the need for social emotional awareness skills. Parallel to self-awareness, an emotional education may also teach competencies for applying emotions *for you* socially and relationally. Structured curriculum or courses teaching social emotional awareness skills are available in the form of Emotional Literacy and Social-Emotional Learning (SEL) programs (Lawson et al., 2020). Although popularized in primary and secondary educational settings, SELs are adapted for adults as well (Lawson et al., 2020).

- **Empathy-Building**—Empathy is the skill or ability to understand, validate, and connect with the experiences of others (Rashid & Seligman, 2018). However, none of these skills are possible without a refined sense of social emotional awareness. Positive psychology holds empathy as a powerful agent for positive emotions and wellness (Hart, 2021). Empathy is a focus of respective PPIs promoting recognition, appreciation, and acceptance for others' experiences (Carr, 2022). Among those PPIs are perspective-building, emotion mapping, visualization exercises, skills practice for listening skills and validations, self-reflective exercises, journaling, acts of kindness or gratitude, and empathy-based meditation.

Social Management

- **Expression and Communication**—In addition to self-regulating, emotions happen *for you* to manage and regulate social circumstance. For instance, living the engaged and meaningful life necessitates effectively sharing and receiving emotions as we navigate the social landscape. The capacity to express and communicate on an emotional level is critical in this regard (Rashid & Seligman, 2018). PPIs addressing expression and communication include social skills training on the likes of active listening and feedback, empathy-building exercises, modeling, role-playing, and social skills counseling groups.
- **Engagement and Relationship-Building**—The research is clear that the best predictor of human wellness and fulfillment is the ability to connect and form emotionally close relationships (Waldinger & Schulz, 2023). Emotional management and regulation skills are key determinants to constructive social engagement, interaction, and relationships. Given positive psychology's emphasis on these concepts, there are a variety of PPIs for building and maintaining a fulfilling social lifestyle (Carr, 2022). These include action planning for social engagement, social commitments, social skills training, empathy and compassion skills training, and gratitude exercises.

Integrating Mindfulness and Emotional Intelligence Into Treatment

Connecting Emotional Intelligence and Mindfulness

Mindfulness practices are notably omitted from the above-outlined PPIs. The rationale being mindfulness practices are of such benefit to emotional intelligence that separate distinction is warranted. In keeping with Filice and Weese (2024), mindfulness practices are "paramount" to emotional intelligence. Among the wealth of benefits, mindfulness practices advocate for a present-oriented, nonjudgmental posture with emotional experiences (Majeed et al., 2018). Conventionally pessimistic or avoidant attitudes toward emotions get traded for openness, curiosity, and acceptance.

Mindfulness practices also aid with recognizing and understanding the reality of emotions, seeing them as fluid experiences (Majeed et al., 2018). The capacity for emotional awareness and regulation are heightened by the intentional, dedicated, and conscious approach to experience as practiced through mindfulness (Filice & Weese, 2024). Within relational contexts, mindfulness practices support being fully engaged and nonjudgmentally aware with others. Enriched social awareness, empathy, and deeper connections are among the social emotional benefits of practicing mindfulness.

Mindfulness-Based Practices for Emotional Intelligence

With mindfulness principal to emotional intelligence, let us consider the practical integration of the two. Listed below are a handful of recommendations for counselors incorporating mindfulness interventions into the four quadrants of emotional intelligence:.

Mindfulness for Self-awareness

- **Formal Mindfulness Meditation**—Formal mindfulness meditative practices focus attention on a specific instruction that promotes full engagement with the present moment (Shuman-Olivier, et al., 2020). Commonly, these instructions include guided or themed meditation, mantras, visualizations, and breathing exercises. Formal mindfulness meditative practices focus nonjudgmental contact and awareness upon emotions as they arise in the moment. This includes channeling awareness on the physiological and cognitive influences that emotional experiences have.
- **Mindful Self-Check-Ins**—Another mindful self-awareness practice is emotional self-checks. These practices involve "scanning" the mind and body for emotional experiences as they occur within the moment (Filice & Weese, 2024). The intent is acknowledging emotions in a curious, nonjudgmental manner and leaning into the reality of these experiences.

Mindfulness for Self-regulation

- **Mindful Responding**—Mindful practices establish intentionally responding to emotional experiences, the antithesis to reactivity or impulsivity (Schuman-Olivier et al., 2020). Specifically, mindfulness encourages utilizing the concept of metacognition to self-monitor emotions and impulses (Schuman-Olivier et al., 2020). Therefore, one strategy is relying on mindful breathing to create a pause and "riding the wave" of initial emotional impulse to respond more deliberately.
- **Mindful Stress/Emotion Regulation**—Mindful emotional regulation strategies take mindful responding a step further by focusing on self-soothing exercises to ease stress and tension (Schuman-Olivier, 2020). Examples for these types of exercises are progressive relaxation, meditation, listening, or walking. The objective is mindfully practicing the desired soothing activity for grounding and expanding contextual awareness beyond the points of stress or tension. The intent is experiencing a calming effect while diverting attention from unpleasant thoughts and experiences (Filice & Weese, 2024).

Mindfulness for Social Awareness

- **Mindful Observing:** Mindful observing social landscapes and interactions is an excellent means for increasing social awareness (Filice & Weese, 2024; Spradlin, 2011). The mindful social observer acts much like a researcher or ethnographer does by approaching social interactions nonjudgmentally and with curiosity. Taking intentional pauses to observe and appreciate verbal and nonverbal communication is but one of the many examples of practicing social mindful observations.
- **Mindful Empathy:** Mindfulness practices can aid with cultivating empathy, a key component to social awareness (Hu et al., 2022). For instance, mindfulness empathy meditations foster social awareness via recognizing, understanding, and sitting with others' emotions (Hu et al., 2022). Mindfulness practices encourage expanding contextual awareness to make room for the emotions and experiences of those around us.

Mindfulness for Social Management

- **Mindful Social Engagement**—Mindfulness practices demonstrate effectiveness for deepening the quality and depth of social engagements (Hu et al., 2022). Exercises practicing such social skills as active and reflective listening promote richer interpersonal engagements and interactions. These are also constructive skills for deepening feelings of empathy, compassion, and social connection.
- **Mindful Conflict Management**—Mindful responding skills are adaptable to interpersonal interactions too, namely, distress and conflict. Mindful conflict management is taking pause to intentionally focus on responding constructively as opposed to avoiding or being emotionally reactive (Kay & Skarlicki, 2020). The objective is akin to the "cooler heads prevail" axiom for constructively working through conflict. Mindful breathing and visualizations are helpful for taking pause and nonjudgmentally making room to respond.

Integrating Mindfulness Into Daily Routines for Clients

Mindfulness is less a static state or accomplishment and more a skillset maintained via regular practice. In fact, Filice and Weese (2024) recommend practicing mindfulness daily to receive the full benefits. For one, daily practice primes the mind for being present and contextually aware (Filice & Weese, 2024). Additionally, emotional balance and wellness are maintained through daily mindfulness practices. Finally, daily mindfulness practices help with forming new habits, especially in times of elevated distress and emotional reactivity. Granted, the daily grind may complicate maintaining a consistent schedule for practicing mindfulness. That is where intentionality and having a strategy for integrating mindfulness into daily routines are beneficial.

- **Scheduling Time**—Committing to regular times for mindfulness practice establishes priority, regularity, and habit-forming. About any time from when a person awakens to falling asleep is a mindfulness scheduling opportunity.
- **Everyday Tasks**—Any daily task presents the chance for a mindful moment, be that eating, driving, listening to music, working, breathing, and so on (Spradlin, 2011). Mindful everyday tasks do not require the same provisions as formal mindfulness practices and may occur anywhere, anytime.
- **Physical Activity**—Similar to everyday tasks, almost any physical activity is adaptable into a mindfulness practice. Activities include walking, running, weight training, and yoga to name a few (Schneider, 2019). Depending on the intensity, it may be important to integrate mindful breathing as well.
- **Technology Assisted**—Mindfulness practices have become the subject of portable devices and Apps. Apps like Headspace and Calm provide users with mindfulness skill training, guided meditation, and practice reminders.

Case Example: Exploring the Application of Emotional Intelligence, Positive Psychology, and Mindfulness Techniques

Jeremy is a 24-year-old, cisgender male, diagnosed with autism spectrum disorder (ASD), who is trying to find a full-time job in the field of engineering. He has been looking for an engineering position unsuccessfully for the last year. Jeremy is also wanting to create a social network so that he can have both personal social connections and to improve his job opportunities. Throughout Jeremy's time at college, he performed well in his coursework but did not make the friendship connections he was hoping to make. While in college, he held a part-time position at a restaurant as a dishwasher that he hoped would allow him to advance to a waiter, but he remained in the position as dishwasher for 4 years. Jeremy was unable to obtain an internship in the field of engineering or serve as a teaching assistant or research assistant for any of his professors throughout college. Jeremy is eager to date but has been unsuccessful in his attempts to find a girlfriend with only a few online dates or opportunities one of which turned out to be a catfishing (an online fake identity intended to deceive someone for exploitative gain) interaction.

Jeremy lived in a dorm with a roommate for his first year of college and had an unpleasant experience with his roommate taking advantage of Jeremy and not interacting with Jeremy more than was necessary. Jeremy then moved into a small one-bedroom apartment throughout college where he spent most of his time alone and only interacted with others online, when attending class, or at his part-time job. Because Jeremy has been unsuccessful in his attempts to find a full-time or even part-time job in engineering for the past year, he had to move back home with his mother and stepfather. Jeremy has a supportive relationship with his mother, but his stepfather mocks Jeremy for his social behaviors and inability to get a job. Jeremy lacks assertiveness and avoids interactions with his stepfather and retreats to his room. Jeremy's self-esteem is low, and he is beginning to feel hopeless about his future.

Through applying emotional intelligence principles, positive psychology approaches, and mindfulness techniques to Jeremy's case, he can improve his self-esteem and increase his coping skills to improve his chances of obtaining a position in the field of engineering and making the social connections that he desires. When considering this case from a counseling perspective, beginning with developing rapport with Jeremy and trying to create a strong therapeutic alliance is essential. Based on the information provided, Jeremy's only form of social support is his mother who allows her husband to treat Jeremy in disrespectful ways. Therefore, a counselor establishing a strong working relationship is crucial in helping Jeremy share more about himself and feel connected to someone else. Through this first step toward a human connection with his counselor, Jeremy can begin to increase his self-esteem and feel more normal by having one person who he feels understands him. The counselor continually focuses on Jeremy's strengths, and what is going right in his life, which incorporates positive psychology principles. The counselor asks Jeremy to reflect on his goals and identify what a meaningful life would look like. The positive psychology–minded counselor suggests Jeremy move his goals beyond just surviving to consider what thriving in life would look like for him. Jeremy has been so focused on getting a job and trying to get some social connections that he has not considered what an ideal life would look like; nor has he identified any goals to move toward his ideal life.

To help Jeremy increase his self-awareness, the counselor can begin helping Jeremy recognize his internal thoughts, feelings, emotional states, and behaviors as well as the reasoning behind these behaviors. Instead of judging himself harshly for avoiding his stepfather, Jeremy may begin to recognize that he is engaging in behaviors necessary to allow him to continue to live at home so that he can survive. Through working with his counselor, Jeremy does realize he may lack in assertiveness as evidenced by his experience with his roommate and his inability to move up at his part-time job despite his reliable, hardworking efforts at this position. Also, Jeremy may recognize that he uses online interactions as a substitute for in-person connections with others because he is afraid of experiencing rejection and feeling humiliated.

Regarding self-regulation techniques, while Jeremy is concerned with experiencing rejection and often avoids initiating interactions with others, the counselor attempts to teach Jeremy mindfulness techniques to calm himself so that he is better able to collect himself if he does experience a rejection. These mindfulness techniques of breathing and guided imagery allow Jeremy to improve his ability to engage in emotional regulation activities necessary to avoid taking rejections personally and engage in productive thought processes, such as recognizing rejection is a normal part of the job search and mate search processes. Additionally, to enhance self-regulation techniques, Jeremy begins exercising regularly. These regular workouts allow Jeremy to increase his self-confidence and his window of tolerance for challenging experiences.

Next, Jeremy practices social-awareness through in-depth discussions regarding body language, facial expressions, and motivations for behaviors. The counselor labels Jeremy's emotions throughout sessions, asks Jeremy to label his emotions throughout session, and asks Jeremy to attempt to label the counselors emotions throughout session. The counselor provides constant authentic feedback regarding these labels to help Jeremy recognize, identify, and understand emotional expressions. For homework, Jeremy is also tasked with attempting to notice others' emotions and potential reasons for those emotions outside of session.

Through discussing TV shows, and in-person interactions he has outside of session, Jeremy continues to increase his ability to understand others' emotions and behaviors.

Finally, Jeremy practices social skills through role-plays in session and homework assignments to approach others and report how the experiences went. Jeremy seeks out workshops on networking, joins public speaking organizations, attends job fairs, and speed-dating events. Jeremy even asks his boss at the restaurant for a promotion and is successful at becoming a waiter, which further tests his social skills. By engaging in repeated in vivo experiences that cause him to have to utilize his social skills, Jeremy continues to enhance them. Throughout all these experiences, the counselor continues to focus on the areas of Jeremy's life that are positive and celebrate his continual victories with him along the way. The counselor constantly reminds Jeremy of the progress he is making toward his goals. Through using these techniques, Jeremy can create a large social network that helps him obtain a full-time position in engineering and gives him the opportunity to meet potential romantic partners.

What are additional techniques someone working with Jeremy could use to increase his self-awareness, self-regulation abilities, social-awareness, and social skills? What about Jeremy's case that illustrates the importance of emotional intelligence and how can emotional intelligence be further fostered with Jeremy? How can positive psychology techniques improve Jeremy's self-esteem and social connections? How can mindfulness techniques help Jeremy in his job search process? In what ways can mindfulness techniques be used to help Jeremy in his search for a potential romantic relationship?

Critical Thinking Questions

1. How can emotional intelligence be measured and assessed in a therapeutic setting?
2. What challenges might arise when integrating emotional intelligence and positive psychology principles into traditional treatment methods?
3. In what ways can mindfulness practices be adapted for clients with varying levels of emotional intelligence?
4. In what ways can positive psychology and mindfulness principles reinforce emotional intelligence development?
5. How can counselor providers maintain their own emotional intelligence and mindfulness to better support their clients

Assessment of Knowledge Activity

This end-of-chapter activity is designed to help you apply the concepts covered in this chapter and deepen your understanding of how emotional intelligence, mindfulness, and positive psychology can be integrated into counseling treatment.

Part 1: Emotional Intelligence Self-assessment Exercise

Instructions for Clients and Counselors

1. Complete an emotional intelligence self-assessment using a validated tool, such as the Emotional Quotient Inventory (EQ-i), The Mayer-Salovey-Caruso Emotional Intelligence Test (MSCEIT), Emotional Intelligence Appraisal Self-Edition by TalentSmart EQ, or a similar online assessment.
2. Reflect on your results and identify areas of strength and areas for improvement.

Self-reflection Prompts

- How accurately do your results reflect your self-perception?
- In what situations do you notice your emotional intelligence strengths being most evident?
- Which areas of emotional intelligence do you find most challenging, and why?

Part 2: Developing a Strengths-Based Action Plan

Identifying Personal Strengths and Areas for Growth

1. Use your assessment results to pinpoint your top three emotional intelligence strengths and three areas that could benefit from development.
2. Discuss these with a partner to gain additional insights and perspectives.

Creating Specific, Measurable Goals

1. Develop at least two actionable goals for enhancing your emotional intelligence. Ensure each goal is specific, measurable, achievable, relevant, and time-bound (SMART).
2. Outline a plan to achieve these goals, including resources or support you might need.

Part 3: Mindfulness Practice Worksheet

Guided Mindfulness Meditation Exercise

1. Follow a guided mindfulness meditation session, focusing on self-awareness and self-regulation. A session could be audio or video-based, lasting about 10 to 15 minutes.
2. Pay attention to your thoughts and emotions during the practice, noting any patterns or insights.

Reflection on Emotional Responses and Insights

- After the meditation, write down any emotional responses you observed.
- Reflect on how mindfulness practice may help you enhance your emotional intelligence skills.

Discussion Questions

1. How did engaging in these activities impact your understanding of emotional intelligence and its role in counseling?
2. What challenges did you face in the self-assessment and mindfulness practice, and how did you address them?
3. How can you incorporate these practices into your daily routine to foster continuous growth in emotional intelligence?

Conclusion

"Emotional intelligence is the ability to make our emotions work for us, instead of against us."

—Peter Salovey

Integrating emotional intelligence, mindfulness, and positive psychology in counseling provides a holistic approach to enhancing clients' ability to navigate life's challenges, from everyday stressors to life's tragedies. By cultivating self-awareness, self-regulation, social awareness, and relationship management, mental health professionals empower clients to build emotional resilience and foster meaningful connections. Mindfulness can assist individuals in all emotional intelligence areas, including awareness of self and others and the ability to engage in emotion regulation skills to respond to challenges instead of reacting to them. This helps individuals shift from reactive responses to thoughtful, intentional actions. For instance, improving self-awareness allows clients to recognize and address negative emotions, enabling them to choose constructive coping strategies. Similarly, fostering gratitude and social awareness creates a foundation for healthier relationships and improved social management. The synergy between emotional intelligence and positive psychology lies in their shared emphasis on health and wellness rather than pathology and dysfunction. Together, these frameworks inspire clients to pursue personal growth, embrace positivity, and develop skills that enhance well-being. By combining these approaches, counselors can help clients not only overcome challenges but also thrive.

References

Ackley, D. (2016). Emotional intelligence: A practical review of models, measures, and applications. *Consulting Psychology Journal: Practice and Research, 68*(4), 269–286. https://doi.org/10.1037/cpb0000070

Alemdar, M., & Anılan, H. (2020). The development and validation of the emotional literacy skills scale. *International Journal of Contemporary Educational Research, 7*(2), 258–270. https://doi.org/10.33200/ijcer.757853

Bar-On, R. (1997). *BarOn emotional quotient inventory* (Vol. 40). Multi-health systems.

Bar-On, R. (2010). Emotional intelligence: An integral part of positive psychology. *South African Journal of Psychology, 40*(1), 54–62.

Carr, A. (2022). *Positive psychology: The science of wellbeing and human strengths.* Routledge.

Daye, D. (2016). *Igniting brand growth via emotional connections. Branding Strategy Insider.* https://www.brandingstrategyinsider.com/2016/02/igniting-brand-growth-viaemotional-connections.html#.XNmdsY5Kg2x

Dennison, J. (2024). Emotions: Functions and significance for attitudes, behaviour, and communication. *Migration Studies, 12*(1), 1–20. https://doi.org/10.1093/migration/mnad018

Duckworth, A. (2018). *Grit: The power and passion of perseverance.* Scribner.

Dweck, C. S. (2007). *Mindset: The new psychology of success (updated ed.).* Ballantine Books.

Filice, L., & Weese, W. J. (2004). Developing emotional intelligence. *Encyclopedia, 4*, 583–599. https://doi.org/10.3390/encyclopedia4010037

Francis, J., Chin, T. C., & Vella-Brodrick, D. (2020). Examining emotional literacy development using a brief on-line positive psychology intervention with primary school children. *International Journal of Environmental Research and Public Health, 17*(20), 7612. https://doi.org/10.3390/ijerph17207612

Goleman, D. (1995). *Emotional intelligence: Why it can matter more than IQ.* Bantam Books.

Haidt, J. (2006). *The happiness hypothesis: Finding modern truth in ancient wisdom.* Basic Books.

Hart, R. (2021). *Positive psychology: The basics.* Routledge.

Hu, Z., Wen, Y., Wang, Y., Lin, Y, Shi, J., Yu, Z., Lin, Y., & Wang, Y. (2022). Effectiveness of mindfulness-based interventions on empathy: A meta-analysis. *Frontiers in Psychology, 20*(13), 992575. https://doi.org/10.3389/fpsyg.2022.992575

Kay, A. A. & Skarlicki, D. P. (2020). Cultivating a conflict-positive workplace: How mindfulness facilitates constructive conflict management. *Organizational Behavior and Human Decision, 159*, 8–20. https://doi.org/10.1016/j.obhdp.2020.02.005

Lawson, G. M., McKenzie, M. E., Becker, K. D., Selby, L., & Hoover, S. A. (2019). The core components of evidence-based social emotional learning programs. *Prevention Science, 20*(4), 457–467. https://doi.org/10.1007/s11121-018-0953-y

Majeed, S., Salman, R., Lau, P., & Cagande, C. (2020). Positive interventions in anxiety disorders. In E. Messias, H. Peseschkian, & C. Cagande (Eds.), *Positive psychiatry, psychotherapy, and psychology*. Springer.

Natarelli, M. (2017). How emotion drives brand choices and decisions. *Branding Strategy Insider*. https://www.brandingstrategyinsider.com/2017/11/how-emotion-drives-brandchoices-and-decisions.html#.XNmd2I5Kg2y

Pan, S., Ali, K., Kahathuduwa, C., Baronia, R., & Ibrahim, Y. (2022). Meta-analysis of positive psychology on the treatment of depression. *Cureus, 14*(2), e21933. https://doi.org/10.7759/cureus.21933

Peseschkian, H., & Remmers, A. (2021). Positive psychotherapy: An introduction. In E. Messias, H. Peseschkian, & C. Cagande (Eds.), *Positive psychiatry, psychotherapy, and psychology*. Springer.

Rashid, T., & Seligman, M. (2018). *Positive psychotherapy: Clinical manual*. Oxford University Press.

Salovey, P., & Mayer, J. D. (1990). Emotional intelligence. *Imagination, Cognition and Personality, 9*(3), 185–211. https://doi.org/10.2190/DUGG-P24E-52WK-6CDG

Schuman-Olivier, Z., Trombka, M., Lovas, D. A., Brewer, J. A., Vago, D. R., Gawande, R., Dunne, J. P., Lazar, S. W., Loucks, E. B., & Fulwiler, C. (2020). Mindfulness and behavior change. *Harvard Review of Psychiatry, 28*(6), 371–394. https://doi.org/10.1097/HRP.0000000000000277

Schneider, J., Malinowski, P., Watson, P. M., & Lattimore, P. (2019). The role of mindfulness in physical activity: A systematic review. *Obesity Review, 20*(3), 448–463. https://doi.org/10.1111/obr.12795

Spradlin, S. A. (2011). *Don' let emotions run your life: How dialectical behavioral therapy can put you in control*. New Harbinger Publications.

Srivastava, M., & Jaiswal, S. (2022). Emotional quotient vs intelligence quotient to achieve professional excellence in life: A systematic literature review. *International Journal of Community Medicine and Public Health, 9*(12), 4662–4665. https://dx.doi.org/10.18203/2394-6040.ijcmph20223229

The Edge. (2023). *Daniel Goleman: Psychologist, author (with Richard Davidson), altered traits*. https://www.edge.org/memberbio/daniel_goleman#:~:text=His%201995%20book%2C%20Emotional%20Intelligence,best%20seller%20in%20many%20countries

Tomasulo, D. (2020). *Learned hopefulness: The power of positivity to overcome depression*. New Harbinger.

Waldinger, R., & Schulz, M. (2023). *The good life: Lessons from the world's longest scientific study of happiness*. Simon & Schuster.

Using a Positive Psychology and Mindfulness Approach for Individuals Diagnosed With Bipolar Disorder

8

Lynn Jennings
Nicole Noble

KEYWORDS AND DEFINITIONS:

Bipolar disorder: A mental health condition characterized by alternating mood states of depression and mania (elevated mood), causing unusual shifts in a person's energy, activity levels, concentration, and ability to function (National Institute of Mental Health, 2022).

Circadian rhythms: Physiological processes that follow a 24-hour day and are influenced by light–dark cycles and involve sleep–wake patterns, hormone levels, and body temperature.

Molecular clock: The regulatory mechanism that controls subcellular processes, producing circadian rhythms.

Positive psychological interventions (PPIs): Interventions that "primarily target the development of resources that support the patient with personal recovery and maintaining mental health" (Geerling et al., 2022, p. 2).

LEARNING OBJECTIVES:

1. Understand the symptoms related to bipolar disorder.
2. Recognize the potential application of positive psychology and its benefits for individuals who experience bipolar disorder.
3. Explore the use of positive psychology exercises with a case example of an individual who experiences bipolar disorder.

Introduction

Bipolar disorder, also referred to as manic-depressive disorder or manic depression, is a mental disorder that can be episodic or chronic in nature. It is characterized by recurrent manic and depressive episodes, often initially exhibited in early adulthood and extending over a person's lifetime (Goodwin & Jamison, 2007). It is estimated to affect 2.8% of the population in the United States (NIH, 2022) and an estimated 40 million people worldwide (World Health Organization [WHO], 2024). "Bipolar disorder has the highest rate of suicide of all psychiatric conditions and is approximately 20–30 times that of the general population" (Miller & Black, 2020, p. 1). In addition, it is one of the leading causes of disability, globally (WHO, 2024). Emotional distress, decreased quality of life, negative social consequences, and increased caregiver burden are associated with bipolar disorder (Kraiss et al., 2020). In addition, the societal burden of bipolar disorder per capita per year is estimated at $881.00 to $27,617.00 direct cost per capita per year and $1,568.00 to $116,062.00 indirect cost per capita per year (Kraiss et al., 2020). Kraiss et al. (2020) further indicated while this societal investment showed improvement in clinical outcomes and, in some instances, cost-savings in several areas, the societal burden is immense.

Due to this information, there is a desire to increase the use of non-pharmacological methods for treating bipolar disorder. Through the use of positive psychology and mindfulness practices discussed in this chapter, hope exists to improve the overall symptomology of those who experience bipolar disorder, reduce rates of suicidality, make treatment for bipolar disorder more healthy and cost-effective, and enhance overall well-being of individuals with bipolar disorder.

Overview of the Chapter

The purpose of this chapter is to provide information on bipolar disorder, utilize positive psychology and mindfulness as a treatment approach to address the disorder, and attend to the emotional, psychological, and behavioral issues that stem from the disorder. This chapter will give an overview of the definition of bipolar disorder, the framework for applying positive psychology and mindfulness, and share some activities that can aid in the treatment of bipolar disorder. Lastly, the chapter will conclude with a case example, critical thinking questions, and an activity to assess the knowledge acquired in this chapter.

Etiology

Despite bipolar disorder being depicted as early as the fifth century BC (Freund & Juckel, 2019), the exact etiology of bipolar disorder remains unknown, and research indicates that multiple factors may contribute to the disorder (National Institute of Mental Health, 2022). A complex interaction between physiological (Milhiet et al., 2014), genetic (O'Connell & Coombes, 2021), environmental (Akhter et al., 2013), and psychological (McKinnon et al., 2012) factors are hypothesized to contribute to the development of bipolar disorder. More precisely, the factors include (1) genetics (Freund & Juckel, 2019) including clock genes concerns (Muneer, 2017); (2) circadian rhythm disturbance (Freund & Juckel, 2019; Muneer, 2017); (3) neurobiological factors including neurotrophins, neurotransmitters, endocrinology, and neuroanatomy (Freund & Juckel, 2019) as well as molecular clock dysregulation and pharmacological switch processes triggers (Muneer, 2017); (4) chronobiological issues (Muneer, 2017); and (5) psychosocial factors (Freund & Juckel, 2019).

Genetics

Based on several studies comparing rates of bipolar disorders in twins and first-degree relatives with bipolar disorders, there appears to be a genetic component to bipolar disorder (Barnett & Smoller, 2009; Chen et al., 2019; Kieseppä et al., 2004). Variants in clock genes involved in circadian functions may predispose individuals who adapt to changing environmental conditions at a slower speed or with less ease to instability of circadian functioning leaving them prone to additional sleep disturbance and more vulnerable to mood disorders (Mukherjee et al., 2010; Murray & Harvey, 2010).

Circadian Rhythm Disturbance

Circadian rhythms are physiological processes that follow a 24-hour day and are influenced by light–dark cycles and involve sleep–wake patterns, hormone levels, and body temperature, and changes in a person's circadian rhythms have been correlated with bipolar disorder (Milhiet et al., 2014).

Neurobiological Factors

Neurobiological factors, whether a lack of neurotrophins resulting in an inability for the brains structures and functions to adapt to change and demonstrate plasticity (Freund & Juckel, 2019) or the influence of thyroid hormones on neurotransmitters (Bauer et al., 2003), illustrate that bipolar disorder likely is influenced by these neurobiological mechanisms. The molecular clock is located at the suprachiasmatic nucleus (SCN) in the hypothalamus and governs the subcellular events that result in circadian rhythms (Muneer, 2017). Dysregulation in the molecular clock can create a negative feedback loop, influencing the expression of gene that regulates rhythmic functions such as the "sleep-wake cycle, feeding behavior, core body temperature, release of hormones, and metabolic regulation" (Milhiet et al., 2014, p. 121). The mechanisms underlying the shift process of cycling from one state of manic or depressive to another suggests that neural processes are involved in triggering these shifts and likely are involved in the manifestation of bipolar disorder (Young & Dulcis, 2015). Pharmacological interventions, including antidepressants and tricyclic antidepressants, have been associated with mood switching and may be related to the onset or exacerbation of bipolar disorder symptoms (Koszewska & Rybakowski, 2009; Muneer, 2017).

Chronobiological Issue

Chronobiological issues refers to social rhythm disruptions such as stressful life events or irregular daily schedules causing a sequence of social and biological rhythm disruptions that result in induced affective episodes in individuals who are vulnerable to bipolar disorder (Levenson et al., 2015).

Psychosocial Factors

Psychosocial factors involving the psychological thought processes and connection of those thoughts to social factors may be relevant in the vulnerability of a person for entering into a manic or depressive state (Freund & Juckel, 2019). Specifically, setting high goals and daydreaming have been associated with mania (Meyer et al., 2011), and the research that supports that cognitive behavior therapy strategies addressing extreme positive and negative appraisals of internal thoughts indicates that psychosocial factors may be involved in the development or continuation of bipolar disorder (Searson et al., 2012). Therefore, many factors contribute to bipolar disorder.

Based on many of the factors that cause the conditions for bipolar disorder being related to environmental circumstance or being exacerbated by lifestyle behaviors, a positive psychology approach may be beneficial in reducing bipolar symptoms and improving overall well-being (Kraiss, 2021). Due to the positive psychology approach focusing on achieving healthy lifestyle behaviors and improving quality of life (Seligman & Csikszentmihalyi, 2000) as well as focusing on strengths and promoting positive internal thoughts and social relationships (Seligman, 2002), PPIs can help individuals with bipolar disorder in addressing many of the aspects of their behaviors that can contribute to manic or depressive states and aid individuals in maintaining a more balanced lifestyle to optimize their internal states (Burke et al., 2023). Specifically, by recognizing strengths, setting and pursuing meaningful goals, and fostering positive relationships, individuals with bipolar disorder can develop protective factors that help reduce depressive symptoms (Celano et al., 2022; Geerling et al., 2022). The goal with positive psychology is to improve overall mental health and, therefore, create the conditions necessary to protect against psychopathology (Seilgman, 2002; Seligman & Csikszentmihalyi, 2000). Additionally, promoting supportive relationships can enhance psychosocial functioning, improve daily life, and assist in the long-term management of the disorder, including preventing recurrences (Kraiss et al., 2018). While depressive or manic state changes can profoundly disrupt an individual's life, these challenging experiences may also serve as opportunities to identify a deeper sense of meaning and purpose (Bohlmeijer & Westerhof, 2021).

Application of Positive Psychology for Individuals Diagnosed With Bipolar Disorder

While treatment for individuals with bipolar disorder has traditionally focused on reducing depressive and manic episodes, a positive psychology approach would emphasize enhancing areas of life that bring meaning, intrinsic satisfaction, and a sense of fulfillment (Kraiss, 2021). Bipolar disorder is characterized by triggers that cause switching between manic and depressive states; therefore, PPIs that focus on promoting resiliency can aid in reducing the frequency and length of these state-switching behaviors. PPIs "primarily target the development of resources that support the patient with personal recovery and maintaining mental health" (Geerling et al., 2022, p. 2). Because "mental wellbeing represents a related but separate dimension of mental health" (Bohlmeijer & Westerhof, 2021, p. 1) and "mental wellbeing reduces the risk of future incidence of mental illness" (Bohlmeijer & Westerhof, 2021, p. 1), interventions focusing on promoting mental well-being have been shown to support individuals with bipolar disorder (Kraiss, 2021). Among PPIs for individuals with bipolar disorder, curriculum has focused on the themes of personal strengths (Celano et al., 2020; Geerling et al., 2022; Kraiss et al., 2018, 2023), gratitude (Celano et al., 2020; Geerling et al., 2022), positive relationships (Geerling et al., 2022; Kraiss et al., 2018 2023), and positive focus/ positive emotions (Geerling et al., 2022; Kraiss et al., 2018, 2023). Through promoting positive attitudes and incorporating positive psychology activities with individuals with bipolar disorder, mental health providers assisting individuals with bipolar disorder can have a framework to not only avoid manic and depressive states but also promote well-being and improved states of being.

Positive Attitudes for Individuals With Bipolar Disorder

Through striving for positive attitudes and states of mind, individuals with bipolar disorder can focus on improving their satisfaction and savor positive experiences to help them enjoy life more fully. Some of these positive goals states may include:

- "Life is characterized by moments of suffering as well as flourishing" (Bohlmeijer & Westerhof, 2021, p. 3). Therefore, in moments of suffering with state changes of bipolar disorder, individuals may wish to recognize that is a part of life, but so is the flourishing that likely will follow at some point in the future.
- Galvez et al. (2011) found evidence that individuals with bipolar disorder had enhancement of the positive psychological traits of spirituality, empathy, creativity, realism, and resilience, and mental health providers may wish to support their clients in preserving and enhancing these traits to improve client outcomes. Furthermore, through recognizing that individuals with bipolar disorder are more prone to creativity during their manic states and realism during their depressive states (Galvez et al., 2011), clients can begin to reframe their mental health disorder and recognize that while there are many potential additional challenges to living with bipolar disorder symptoms, there are also some benefits that they may not have considered.
- Strengthening personal resources, including self-compassion, recognizing one's strengths, positive emotions, hope for future, and positive relationships may assist individuals with bipolar disorder in living a satisfying life (Kraiss, 2021; Kraiss et al., 2018).
- Although fear of relapse is common among individuals with bipolar disorder, these negative emotions can be tolerated and/or accepted as an important part of life that can coexist with positive traits such as focusing on strengths and cultivating positive traits and learning to be compassionate toward one's self (Kraiss et al., 2018).
- Enhancing self-compassion can help to reduce rumination as well as self-criticism, which can improve areas of kindness and positive emotions life (Kraiss, 2021; Kraiss et al., 2018).
- Identifying hope and engaging in goal-directed thinking and behaviors can assist both looking forward to the future and in creating a more desirable future than the present for individuals with bipolar disorder (Geerling et al., 2022).
- Mindfulness-based interventions may assist individuals with bipolar disorder in adapting to the disorder and in moving toward meaningful goals (Murray et al., 2017).
- Seeking to acquire environmental mastery, including fitting in with others, increasing self-acceptance, and applying autonomy, can promote psychological functioning (Del Trevino-Zuniga, 2021).

Positive Psychology Activities for Individuals Diagnosed With Bipolar Disorder

Below are some of the positive psychology activities that may support individuals with bipolar disorder in increasing their personal strengths, positive emotions, relational supports, and overall satisfaction:

- Because lower annual income may be associated with a bipolar disorder diagnosis (Fowler & Dooley, 2023), mental health providers may wish to have their clients with bipolar disorder consider their occupations and earning potential to help serve as protective factors to reduce their chances of future bipolar disorder symptoms.
- Individuals with bipolar disorder commonly report less social support than their non-bipolar disorder peers, including in areas of marital status and social support; adults with bipolar disorder who reported having higher levels of social support also reported higher positive mental health particularly in the areas of "reassurance of their worth" and "social integration" (Fowler & Dooley, 2023); therefore, mental health providers may seek to help support their clients in establishing and maintaining positive social support.
- Utilizing a web-based PPI can assist clients in acquiring "hope, increasing self-esteem, expressing feelings, acceptance, and preventing social isolation" (Geerling et al., 2022, p. 1). This web-based positive psychology app prompted participants to make mantras for themselves, exercise mindfulness, care for others, write a "stoic journal" daily, read about positive psychology, recognize positive moments, view their involvement on the app as a positive activity, and think about possibilities (Geerling et al., 2022).
- Individuals with bipolar disorder may benefit from considering their ideal future self and write about their visions for themselves if everything in their life went as well as it possibly could (Kraiss et al., 2018; Meevissen et al., 2011) and list three good things in their life each day and why those things are good and meaningful (Bolier et al., 2013; Kraiss et al., 2018). Furthermore, any activities focusing on "positive emotions, positive relationships or personal goals" may facilitate psychological well-being and improve depressive, manic, and anxiety symptoms to foster positive euthymic states, which consist of tranquil mental states free from significant distress (Kraiss et al., 2018).

Application of Mindfulness Exercises for Individuals Diagnosed With Bipolar Disorder

Bipolar disorder, as discussed earlier in this chapter, can present some daily challenges for those who experience this disorder. Fluctuations in mood swings can be of the most challenging issues for those affected by bipolar disorder. Mindfulness activities can aid in managing these fluctuations by adding support through emotional regulation thereby reducing the intensity and frequency of mood swings. Four of these exercises are discussed below.

Breathing Exercises. There are many types of breathing exercises available: box breathing, diaphragmatic breathing, pursed lip breathing, and so on. The basic premise is to breathe in deeply and slowly through the nose, then either hold the breath for several seconds, then breathe out through the mouth slowly; or immediately breathe out through the mouth slowly. For example, in the pursed lip breathing exercise, you breathe in through your nose slowly, and then purse your lips and slowly blow out as if you are blowing out a candle. These exercises are intended to be done multiple times in a row until a calming effect is achieved.

Progressive muscle relaxation. Progressive muscle relaxation is a mindfulness technique that can help manage mood swings experience with bipolar disorder. This exercise involves tensing and relaxing muscle groups in the body; generally starting at the feet and moving up the body toward the head. Each muscle group is tensed for approximately 10 seconds, then released. When released, the idea is to concentrate on the feeling of the muscle relaxing for 10 to 20 seconds, then moving to the next muscle group until each muscle group has been tensed and released. By doing this, a person can achieve a deep sense of calmness and relaxation. An additional benefit of this exercise relates to increased body awareness allowing one to more easily identify early signs of mood or tension changes in the body that then will subsequently signal the implementation of earlier coping strategies, helping a person to successfully manage challenges in life (Muhammad Khir et al., 2024).

Mindful Walking. Mindful walking implements physical movement into present-moment awareness, also referred to a *meditation in motion* (Gotink et al., 2016). The feeling of walking allows a person to feel more grounded in the present moment and makes a person more aware of their body sensations (Segal et al., 2002). While participating in mindful walking, the person is instructed to pay attention to their senses, emotions, and thoughts and to let go of their daily, automatic behaviors of hurrying, busyness, and so on. Both physical movement and mindfulness, especially when done together, can increase overall functioning and decrease depressive symptoms and feelings of anxiety (Gotink, et al., 2016).

Mindful Self-compassion. Mindful self-compassion involves being kind to oneself and giving oneself grace, even when frustrated, or when experiencing other negative emotions like rumination, sadness, and so on. It is essential to practice self-compassion especially during those times. Self-compassion is more than self-care; it is a state of mind allowing one to see oneself through the lens of acknowledgment and movement beyond those negative thoughts and feelings (Flanigan, 2023). It is a future-focused practice that allows for problem-solving from positive or more loving perspective. Questions like—*What do I need in this moment? What am I feeling?*—can aid a person into moving in the direction of restructuring automatic negative thoughts into productive, helpful, and self-compassionate thoughts (Flanigan, 2023).

Precautions When Considering a Positive Psychological Perspective With Individuals Diagnosed With Bipolar Disorder

While numerous studies indicate the benefits of positive psychology for individuals diagnosed with bipolar disorder (Celano et al., 2018; Kraiss, 2021; Kraiss et al., 2023), some research has indicated other interventions may be more effective (Hanssen et al., 2024; Miura et al., 2014), and other research has lacked in detecting significant improvements in mania and other symptoms (Geerling et al., 2023; Painter et al., 2019) indicating that additional research should explore the efficacy of PPIs for individuals with bipolar disorder (Del Trevino-Zungia, 2021; Geerling et al., 2022). Furthermore, individuals with bipolar disorder who participated in a web-based positive psychology app noted that when the app prompted them to give "themselves a positive message," they feared forcing positive statements might push their goal setting too far and "foresaw further mood dysregulation toward manic states when they are already hypomanic owing to exercises that stimulate positive emotions, feelings, or happiness" (Geerling et al., 2022, p. 5). Additionally, gender and marital status may influence the effectiveness of treatment interventions. Research suggests that males with bipolar disorder tend to benefit more from PPIs, while unmarried individuals with bipolar disorder also show the greatest benefits from such interventions. In contrast, married individuals with bipolar disorder are more likely to benefit from Mindfulness-Based Cognitive Therapy (Hanssen et al., 2024). Therefore, caution should be used when considering the individual with bipolar disorder's current mood state and selecting an intervention that will not exacerbate any mania or depressive episodes. Furthermore, it should be noted that treatment may need to vary for individuals experiencing an acute episode of bipolar disorder versus individuals seeking long-term management of bipolar disorder (Grande et al., 2015). Additionally, personalized and tailored interventions may offer support in individuals' daily life and resilience (Kraiss, 2021).

Case Example: Exploring Positive Psychological Interventions and Techniques With an Individual Diagnosed With Bipolar Disorder

John, a 45-year-old male, has been experiencing some distress related to his bipolar disorder. John has been married for 25 years, and his only child is a college senior at a nearby university. His chief complaint includes feeling like he's lacking energy and feeling depressed. He's reporting difficulty in paying attention, organizing his day, and completing tasks at work. He reports these symptoms seemed to "come from out of nowhere." Within the past month, he reports functioning better than usual, getting more accomplished and requiring less sleep than he does now. He reports only feeling this way twice in the past three years, each time these feelings only lasted about 1 to 2 months. The only changes he reports in his life include increased psychosocial stress due to a recent job change and the death of a close family member within the past month. He reports he continues to find enjoyment talking to friends and feels he has a good support system.

Let's look at how applying positive psychology and mindfulness can aid in helping John manage his recent distress complicated by his bipolar disorder. As mentioned previously, bipolar disorder affects a person on a psychosocial and individual level. When looking at this from a positive psychology perspective, a counselor could begin by focusing on John's view of himself while experiencing these issues. As mentioned earlier in this chapter, men tend to respond well to PPI exercises, so let's begin by utilizing the exercise of self-compassion. Self-compassion can help mitigate his feelings of depression by focusing on how he feels about those negative feelings. As previously stated, self-compassion involves giving oneself grace when having negative feelings by accepting those feelings and asking questions like—*What do I need in this moment? What am I feeling?*—to help oneself to meet the need that is prompting the feeling of, in this case, depression. By asking these questions, John can move in a direction of restructuring his negative, depressive thoughts into productive thoughts that may lead to an improvement in his feelings about his depressive thoughts.

In addition, a counselor could implement mindful walking to not only get his body moving but also create a heightened sense of his environment and his internal sensations the mindful walking can produce. This exercise will also help him to stop in his day; take a break from his automatic thoughts, which likely involve job stress, deadlines, and so on; and focus on the smells, scenery, and sensations of his body as he walks and stays mindful in the here and now.

These are just a couple of ideas on how to implement mindfulness and positive psychology with a person experiencing distress due to bipolar disorder. What are others that came to mind as you were considering this case study? In what ways could you implement these additional exercises and in what setting?

Conclusion

"It's our challenges and obstacles that give us layers of depth and make us interesting. Are hey fun when they happen? No. But they are what make us unique." —Ellen DeGeneres

For individuals who live with bipolar disorder, there can be certain challenges faced in life as bipolar disorder affects many parts of a person's life. While there may be challenges, there are also ways to manage these issues in a manner that allows for a person to increase their personal strengths, positive emotions, and relational supports through the implementation of mindfulness and positive psychology exercises. This shift can be accomplished through the positive psychology and mindfulness focus of moving the negative feelings and thoughts often associated with bipolar disorder to a positive focus of life fulfillment, meaning-making, and value. This allows a person experiencing bipolar disorder to live a fuller life by embracing positive attitudes and states of mind, improving their overall life satisfaction. Finally, through the use of a positive psychology framework with individuals who experience bipolar disorder, counselors can support these individuals with the goal of allowing them to thrive in their lives.

Critical Thinking Questions

1. How can professionals support individuals who are experiencing bipolar disorder?
2. When implementing a positive psychology approach, what are specific techniques that you would suggest for working with individuals who have experienced bipolar disorder?
3. Which positive psychology activities resonate most with your counseling style and approach?
4. How can mindfulness be an opportunity for helping individuals with bipolar disorder to more effectively cope with their bipolar symptoms?

Assessment of Knowledge Activity

After reading this chapter on integrating positive psychology and mindfulness to support individuals who have experienced bipolar disorder, let's take some time to reflect back on the application of integrating positive psychology and mindfulness on the following scenario. Read the hypothetical situation and address the remaining prompts.

Hypothetical Situation: Tamara is a 52-year-old divorced female with bipolar disorder. She lives alone with her cat, Marcy. She is experiencing feelings of sadness followed by feelings of anger. She has a good support system in a group of friends with whom she works.

1. What activity can you utilize to help Tamara regulate the emotions she is experiencing? Refer back to the sections referring to positive psychology and mindfulness activities and chose an activity or exercise that you feel may be beneficial to Tamara.
2. Consider how the exercise you chose could benefit Tamara. What are the potential benefits you see in implementing this exercise?
3. What challenges do you foresee in implementing this exercise? What are some steps you could take in managing these challenges to help the exercise to be more effective for Tamara?

References

Akhter, A., Fiedorowicz, J. G., Zhang, T., Potash, J. B., Cavanaugh, J., Solomon, D. A., & Coryell, W. H. (2013). Seasonal variation of manic and depressive symptoms in bipolar disorder. *Bipolar Disorders, 15*(4), 377–384. https://doi.org/10.1111/bdi.12072

Barnett, J. H., & Smoller, J. W. (2009). The genetics of bipolar disorder. *Neuroscience*, *164*(1), 331–343. https://doi.org/10.1016/j.neuroscience.2009.03.080

Bauer, M., London, E. D., Silverman, D. H., Rasgon, N., Kirchheiner, J., & Whybrow, P. C. (2003). Thyroid, brain and mood modulation in affective disorder: Insights from molecular research and functional brain imaging. *Pharmacopsychiatry*, *36*(3), S215–S221. https://doi.org/10.1055/s-2003-45133

Bohlmeijer, E., & Westerhof, G. (2021). The model for sustainable mental health: Future directions for integrating positive psychology into mental health care. *Frontiers in Psychology, 12,* 747999, 1–10. https://doi.org/10.3389/fpsyg.2021.747999

Bolier, L., Haverman, M., Westerhof, G. J., Riper, H., Smit, F., & Bohlmeijer, E. (2013). Positive psychology interventions: A meta-analysis of randomized controlled studies. *BMC Public Health, 13*, 119. https://doi.org/10.1186/1471-2458-13-119

Burke, J., Dunne, P. J., Meehan, T., O'Boyle, C., & Nieuwerburgh, C. (2023). *Positive health: 100+ research-based positive psychology and lifestyle medicine tools to enhance your wellbeing.* Routledge.

Celano, C. M., Gomez-Bernal, F., Mastromauro, C. A., Beale, E. E., DuBois, C. M., Auerbach, R. P., & Huffman, J. C. (2020). A positive psychology intervention for patients with bipolar depression: A randomized pilot trial. *Journal of Mental Health, 29*(1), 60–68. https://doi.org/10.1080/09638237.2018.1521942

Chen, M. H., Hsu, J. W., Huang, K. L., Su, T. P., Li, C. T., Lin, W. C., Tsai, S. J., Cheng, C. M., Chang, W. H., Pan, T. L., Chen, T. J., & Bai, Y. M. (2019). Risk and coaggregation of major psychiatric disorders among first-degree relatives of patients with bipolar disorder: A nationwide population-based study. *Psychological Medicine*, *49*(14), 2397–2404. https://doi.org/10.1017/S003329171800332X

Del Trevino-Zungia, M. (2021). Positive well-being and satisfaction with life: Variables affecting the quality of life of people with bipolar disorder (Publication No. 985) [Doctoral dissertation, The University of Texas Rio Grande Valley]. ScholarWorks@UTRGV. https://scholarworks.utrgv.edu/etd/985

Flanigan, R. (2023). Important lessons about self-compassion and bipolar disorder. https://www.bphope.com/bipolar-buzz/important-lessons-about-self-compassion-and-bipolar-disorder/

Fowler, K., & Dooley, K. E. (2023). Positive mental health in adults with bipolar disorder: Exploring social support subtypes, negative social interactions and potential to flourish. *BMC Psychiatry, 23*(759), 1–12. https://doi.org/10.1186/s12888-023-05244-3

Freund, N., Juckel, G. (2019). *Bipolar disorder: Its etiology and how to model in rodents. In: Kobeissy, F. (eds) Psychiatric disorders: Methods in molecular biology, vol 2011. Humana.* https://doi.org/10.1007/978-1-4939-9554-7_4

Galvez, J. F., Thommi, S., & Ghaemi, S. N. (2011). Positive aspects of mental illness: A review in bipolar disorder. *Journal of Affective Disorders, 128*(3), 185–190. https://doi.org/10.1016/j.jad.2010.03.017

Geerling, B., Kelders, S., Klooster, P., Stevens, A., Kupka, R., & Bohlmeijer, E. (2023). Can digital positive psychology interventions improve the quality of life in bipolar disorder? *Authorea.* https://doi.org/10.22541/au.167541845.58088187/v1

Geerling, B., Kelders, S. M., Stevens, A. W. M. M., Kupka, R. W., Bohlmeijer, E. T. (2022). A Web-based positive psychology app for patients with bipolar disorder: Development study. *JMIR Formative Research, 6*(9), e39476, 1–18. https://doi.org/10.2196/39476

Goodwin, F., & Jamison, K. (2007). *Manic-depressive illness: Bipolar disorders and recurrent depression.* Oxford University Press

Gotink, R. A., Hermans, K. S., Geschwind, N., De Nooij, R., De Groot, W. T., & Speckens, A. E. (2016). Mindfulness and mood stimulate each other in an upward spiral: A mindful walking intervention using experience sampling. *Mindfulness, 7*(5), 1114–1122. https://doi.org/10.1007/s12671-016-0550-8

Grande, I., Berk, M., Birmaher, B., & Vieta, E. (2015). Bipolar disorder. *The Lancet, 387*(10027), 1561–1572. https://doi.org/10.1016/S0140-6736(15)00241-X

Hanssen, I., Klooster, P., Kraiss, J., Huijbers, M., Regeer, E., Kupka, R., Bohlmeijer, E., & Speckens, A. (2024). Predicting which intervention works better for whom: Moderators of treatment effect of mindfulness-based cognitive therapy and positive psychology Intervention in patients with bipolar disorder. *Journal of Affective Disorders, 360,* 79–87. https://doi.org/10.1016/j.jad.2024.05.110

Muhammad Khir, S., Wan Mohd Yunus, W. M. A., Mahmud, N., Wang, R., Panatik, S. A., Mohd Sukor, M. S., & Nordin, N. A. (2024). Efficacy of progressive muscle relaxation in adults for stress, anxiety, and depression: A systematic review. *Psychology Research and Behavior Management, 17,* 345–365. https://doi.org/10.2147/PRBM.S437277

Kieseppä, T., Partonen, T., Haukka, J., Kaprio, J., & Lönnqvist, J. (2004). High concordance of bipolar I disorder in a nationwide sample of twins. *The American Journal of Psychiatry, 161*(10), 1814–1821. https://doi.org/10.1176/ajp.161.10.1814

Koszewska, I., & Rybakowski, J. K. (2009). Antidepressant-induced mood conversions in bipolar disorder: A retrospective study of tricyclic versus non-tricyclic antidepressant drugs. *Neuropsychobiology, 59*(1), 12–16. https://doi.org/10.1159/000202824

Kraiss, J. T. (2021). *Living well with bipolar disorder: Integrating positive psychology and personal recovery into the treatment of bipolar disorders* [Doctoral dissertation]. University of Twente. https://research.utwente.nl/en/publications/living-well-with-bipolar-disorder-integrating-positive-psychology

Kraiss, J. T., ten Kloster, P. M., Chrispijn, M., Stevens, A., Doornbos, B., Kupka, R. W., & Bohlmeijer, E. T. (2023). A multicomponent positive psychology intervention for euthymic patients with bipolar disorder to improve mental well-being and personal recovery: A pragmatic randomized controlled trial. *Bipolar Disorder, 25*(8), 683–695. https://doi.org/10.1111/bdi.13313

Kraiss, J. T., ten Klooster, P. M., Chrispijn, M., Trompetter, H. R., Stevens, A. W. M. M., Neutel, E., Kupka, R. W., & Bohlmeijer, E. T. (2018). B-positive: A randomized controlled trail of a multicomponent positive psychology intervention for euthymic patients with bipolar disorder—Study protocol and intervention development. *BMC Psychiatry, 18*(335), 1–13. https://doi.org/10.1186/s12888-018-1916-3

Kraiss, J. T., Wijnen, B., Kupka, R. W., Bohlmeijer, E. T., & Lokkerbol, J. (2020). Economic evaluations of non-pharmacological interventions and cost-of-illness studies in bipolar disorder: A systematic review. *Journal of Affective Disorders, 276,* 388–401. https://doi.org/10.1016/j.jad.2020.06.064

Levenson, J. C., Wallace, M. L., Anderson, B. P., Kupfer, D. J., & Frank, E. (2015). Social rhythm disrupting events increase the risk of recurrence among individuals with bipolar disorder. *Bipolar Disorders, 17*(8), 869–879. https://doi.org/10.1111/bdi.12351

McKinnon, M. C., Cusi, A. M., & MacQueen, G. M. (2012). Psychological factors that may confer risk for bipolar disorder. *Cognitive Neuropsychiatry, 18*(1–2), 115–128. https://doi.org/10.1080/13546805.2012.702505

Meevissen, Y. M., Peters, M. L., & Alberts, H. J. (2011). Become more optimistic by imagining a best possible self: Effects of a two week intervention. *Journal of Behavior Therapy and Experimental Psychiatry, 42*(3), 371–378. https://doi.org/10.1016/j.jbtep.2011.02.012

Meyer, T. D., Finucane, L., & Jordan, G. (2011). Is risk for mania associated with increased daydreaming as a form of mental imagery? *Journal of Affective Disorders, 135*(1–3), 380–383. https://doi.org/10.1016/j.jad.2011.06.002

Miller, J. N., & Black, D. W. (2020). Bipolar disorder and suicide: A review. *Current Psychiatry Reports, 22*(6), 1–10. https://doi.org/10.1007/s11920-020-1130-0

Milhiet, V., Boudebesse, C., Bellivier, F., Drouot, X., Henry, C., Leboyer, M., & Etain, B. (2014). A complex mutual influence between physiological, genetic, environmental and psychological considerations are hypothesized to contribute to the development of bipolar disorder. *Frontiers in Bioscience-Scholar, 6*(1), 120–137. https://doi.org/10.2741/S419

Miura, T., Noma, H., Furukawa, T. A., Mitsuyasu, H., Tanaka, S., Stockton, S., Salanti, G., Motomura, K., Shimano-Katsuki, S., Leucht, S., Cipriani, A., Geddes, J. R., & Kanba, S. (2014). Comparative efficacy and tolerability of pharmacological treatments in the maintenance treatment of bipolar disorder: A systematic review and network meta-analysis. *The Lancet Psychiatry, 1*(5), 351–359. https://doi.org/10.1016/S2215-0366(14)70314-1

Mukherjee, S., Coque, L., Cao, J. L., Kumar, J., Chakravarty, S., Asaithamby, A., Graham, A., Gordon, E., Enwright, J. F., DeLeone, R. J., Birnbaum, S. G., Cooper, D. C., & McClung, C. A. (2010). Knockdown of clock in the ventral tegmental area through RNA interference results in a mixed state of mania and depression-like behavior. *Biological Psychiatry: A Journal of Psychiatric Neuroscience and Therapeutics, 68*(6), 503–511. https://doi.org/10.1016/j.biopsych.2010.04.031

Muneer, A. (2017). Mixed states in bipolar disorder: Etiology, pathogenesis and treatment. *Chonnam Medical Journal, 53*(1), 1–13. https://doi.org/10.4068/cmj.2017.53.1.1

Murray, G., & Harvey, A. (2010). Circadian rhythms and sleep in bipolar disorder. *Bipolar Disorders, 12*(5), 459–472. https://doi.org/10.1111/j.1399-5618.2010.00843.x

Murray, G., Leitan, N. D., Thomas, N., Michalak, E. E., Johnson, S. L., Jones, S., Perich, T., Berk, L., & Berk, M. (2017). Towards recovery-oriented psychosocial interventions for bipolar disorder: Quality of life outcomes, stage-sensitive treatments, and mindfulness mechanisms. *Clinical Psychology Review, 52*, 148–163. https://doi.org/10.1016/j.cpr.2017.01.002

National Institute of Mental Health. (2022). *Bipolar disorder.* https://www.nimh.nih.gov/health/publications/bipolar-disorder

O'Connell, K. S., & Coombes, B. J. (2021). Genetic contributions to bipolar disorder: Current status and future directions. *Psychological Medicine, 51*(13), 2156–2167. https://doi.org/10.1017/S0033291721001252

Painter, J. M., Mote, J., Peckham, A. D., Lee, E. H., Campellone, T. R., Pearlstein, J. G., Morgan, S., Kring, A. M., Johnson, S. L., & Moskowitz, J. T. (2019). A positive emotion regulation intervention for bipolar I disorder: Treatment development and initial outcomes. *General Hospital Psychiatry, 61*, 96–103. https://doi.org/10.1016/j.genhosppsych.2019.07.013

Searson, R., Mansell, W., Lowens, I., & Tai, S. (2012). Think Effectively About Mood Swings (TEAMS): A case series of cognitive-behavioural therapy for bipolar disorders. *Journal of Behavior Therapy and Experimental Psychiatry, 43*(2), 770–779. https://doi.org/10.1016/j.jbtep.2011.10.001

Segal, Z. V., Williams, J. M. G., & Teasdale, J. D. (2002). *Mindfulness-based cognitive therapy for depression: A new approach to relapse prevention.* Guilford.

Seligman, M. E. P. (2002). *Authentic happiness: Using the new positive psychology to realize your potential for lasting fulfillment.* Free Press.

Seligman, M. E. P., & Csikszentmihalyi, M. (2000). Positive psychology: An introduction. *American Psychologist, 55*(1), 5–14. https://doi.org/10.1037/0003-066X.55.1.5

World Health Organization. (2024). https://www.who.int/news-room/fact-sheets/detail/bipolar-disorder

Young, J. W., & Dulcis, D. (2015). Investigating the mechanism(s) underlying switching between states in bipolar disorder. *European Journal of Pharmacology, 75*, 151–162. https://doi.org/10.1016/j.ejphar.2015.03.019

Using a Positive Psychology and Mindfulness Approach for Individuals Who Experienced a Stroke

9

Nicole Noble
Logan Winkelman
Lynn Jennings

KEYWORDS AND DEFINITIONS:

Hemorrhagic strokes: Strokes that occur due to a sudden blood vessel in the brain breaking open and creating pressure on surrounding brain cells due to the leaked blood.

Ischemic strokes: Strokes that occur due to blocked vessels that supply blood flow to the brain, which deprives brain cells of oxygen and nutrients.

PERMA Framework: Stands for Positive emotions, Engagement of feeling and being engrossed in a task, Relationship forming and maintenance, Meaning-making and purpose, and Accomplishment of goals.

PURE Model: Stands for Purpose, Understanding, Responsibility, and Enjoyment through seeking each of these areas and further meaning can be identified from the difficult event of a stroke.

RISE Model: Stands for Relational, Interpersonal, Social, and Environmental (RISE) Model of resilience for individuals following the onset of a disability or a chronic illness and explores the factors influencing resilience.

State reaction: Involves an emotional experience surrounding an event such as the onset of a chronic illness or disability that is distinct and different from a personality trait. Negativity and emotional turmoil following a stroke should be viewed as a state reaction and not a personality trait.

LEARNING OBJECTIVES:

1. Identify the signs of a stroke.
2. Understand the two major types of strokes and the broad causes for a stroke.
3. Recognize the potential application of positive psychology and its benefits for individuals who experienced a stroke.
4. Explore the use of positive psychology attitudes and activities with a case example of an individual who experienced a stroke.

Within a matter of minutes, a stroke can occur, potentially forever damaging the brain and creating any number of disabilities (American Stroke Association, 2024b), or even resulting in death (Mayo Clinic, 2024). A stroke consists of blocked blood flow or sudden bleeding in the brain (American Stroke Association, 2024a). There are two main types of strokes: ischemic and hemorrhagic. Ischemic strokes involve blocked vessels that supply blood flow to the brain, which deprives brain cells of oxygen and nutrients. Hemorrhagic strokes strike due to a sudden blood vessel in the brain breaking open and creating pressure on surrounding brain cells due to the leaked blood. In both types of strokes, the surrounding brain cells are damaged or die within minutes. Further classification of strokes includes the type of blockage and duration of blockage to the brain, as well as the location of the blockage or bleeding within the brain. Depending on how quickly the individual who experienced a stroke received medical intervention and the severity of the stroke, they may recover and even return to their previous functioning with a rehabilitation plan (Mayo Clinic, 2024).

The American Stroke Association (2024e) lists the below symptoms as indicators a person is currently experiencing a stroke and needs immediate emergency medical attention:

- F = Face Drooping
- A = Arm Weakness
- S = Speech Difficulty
- T = Time to call 911
- Numbness
- Confusion
- Trouble Seeing
- Trouble Walking
- Severe Headache

Awareness of these symptoms of a stroke and immediate, emergency medical attention can save lives and prevent death. To assess if someone is having a stroke, (1) ask them to smile and notice if one side of their face is drooping, (2) ask them to raise both of their arms and legs and notice if they are unable to raise one of them, (3) ask them to talk and notice if they are slurring their speech. If any of these signs are suspected, immediate medical attention should be sought to prevent damage and save lives.

Following a stroke, lasting brain damage may lead to challenges such as physical impairments, communication issues including aphasia (difficulty understanding or expressing speech), vision and hearing problems, cognitive difficulties, and emotional and behavioral changes. Fortunately, both physical disabilities and emotional and behavioral changes frequently improve over time. Common mental health concerns following a stroke include depression, anxiety, and grief. Personality changes related to a stroke could consist of impulsivity, apathy, anxiety, Pseudobulbar Affect (PBA) or uncontrollable bouts of crying, laughter or anger, and delirium or confusion and altered states of awareness and attention (American Stoke Association, 2024a). Any of these changes following a stroke can be disruptive to the person experiencing them.

Overview of the Chapter

The purpose of this chapter is to provide information concerning utilizing the approach of positive psychology to aid in adjustment post-stroke, particularly concerning the mental health and emotional and behavioral changes that ensued as a result of a stroke. This chapter will provide information concerning the etiology of strokes, a basic framework of the benefits of positive psychology and its application with stroke survivors, and specific positive psychology goal states and activities for the treatment of individuals' adjustment from a stroke. To assess the knowledge acquired, the chapter will conclude with a case example, critical thinking questions, and finally an activity.

Etiology

Depending on the type of stroke that occurred, ischemic or hemorrhagic, there are different factors involved that create the conditions necessary for the stroke to occur. For an ischemic stroke, which is caused by an artery in the brain being blocked, the reason for the stroke likely involves blocked and narrowed blood vessels lodged in the brain from fatty deposits that built up in blood vessels or from blood clots that travel through the bloodstream, often from the heart (Mayo Clinic, 2024). For a hemorrhagic stroke, which is caused by a bleeding blood vessel in the brain, the reason for the stroke is a condition that affects the blood vessels. These conditions might include: uncontrolled high blood pressure, overuse of blood thinners, aneurysm or a bugle in the artery that can stretch and burst, head trauma, and cerebral amyloid angiopathy or protein deposits that weaken blood vessel walls in the brain (Mayo Clinic, 2024). Risk factors for a stroke include both lifestyle factors—such as physical inactivity, poor diet, obesity, smoking, and illegal drug use (American Stroke Association, 2024d), and medical risk factors, which include high blood pressure, high cholesterol, heart diseases, diabetes, sleep apnea, kidney disease, family history of strokes, mental health conditions including anxiety and depression, migraines, pollution, viral infections, and inflammation (National Heart, Lung, & Blood Institute, 2023). Due to many of the factors that contribute to the risk of having a stroke being lifestyle-related as well as the factors that can improve a person's chances of recovering following a stroke being oriented toward their ability to set and achieve goals related to their well-being (American Stroke Association, 2024c), a positive psychological approach may be an ideal intervention to assist this population (Evans & Cullen, 2019). A positive psychological approach fosters resilience, optimism, and a sense of purpose (Seligman, 2002), which are essential for overcoming the emotional and psychological challenges that survivors of a stroke encounter post-stroke (Evans & Cullen, 2019). Furthermore, through focusing on a strength and growth mindset, positive psychology can help enhance motivation, support the development of healthy habits, and improve overall quality of life (Seligman & Csikszentmihalyi, 2000).

Application of Positive Psychology for Individuals Who Experienced a Stroke

Using positive psychology for stroke survivors at initial consideration appears paradoxical. Individuals who experienced a stroke may experience disruption to many of the areas of their life in which they previously enjoyed pleasure, engagement, and meaningful fulfillment, challenging mental health and well-being (Evans, 2011). Impaired areas include cognitive, physical, communication, and sensing areas, including taste and smell, as well as social aspects. As a result of these transformations, the stroke survivor's sense of identity and purpose may suffer. To state these changes in a positive psychology framework, stroke "may change membership of positive institutions and the opportunity to serve positive institutions (i.e., removes roles within those institutions) and hence reduces access to a source of personal meaning" (Evans, 2011, p. 121). Therefore, following a stroke, psychological distress is unfortunately common, and this distress can negatively impact long-term outcomes (Devereux & Berns, 2023). While psychological distress may seem almost inevitable, due to either a shift in priorities, living in the moment, or experiencing gratitude for a second chance, positive growth and even increased satisfaction occur for many people post-stroke (Evans, 2011). Traditional approaches to stroke recovery would recommend treating the depression, anxiety, or the specific psychological distress the individual is encountering in the hopes of improving recovery outcomes (Cullen et al., 2018). Even the use of the term "recovery" may be limiting in terms of adaption following a stroke, and this term might be better replaced with the word "adjustment" to foster resilience (Sarre et al., 2013). In contrast to other approaches, positive psychological approaches would not focus on the psychological distress or recovery but, instead, on thriving.

Rather than focusing on reduction in symptomatology of anxiety and depression, a positive psychological approach would utilize measures illustrating satisfaction with life or happiness. Instead of a focus on medical approach of healing and recovery (White & Johnstone, 2000), positive psychology focuses on building positive qualities (Seligman & Csikszentmihalyi, 2000) to aid in the adjustment of an individual following their stroke. For individuals following a stroke, this would mean focus on things that are going well instead of what is going wrong in their lives (Seligman, 2011). Furthermore, a noteworthy criticism of positive psychology is that it disregards physiological aspects of health and human flourishing (Burke et al., 2023); however, health involves more than physical and cognitive areas that may be negatively impacted by a stroke (World Health Organization, 2024). While health and disease are frequently viewed as a binary measure, health is more than the absence of a disease (Burke et al., 2023). Rather than merely seeking to remove limitations caused by the stroke, a positive psychological approach would focus on a sense of complete health and well-being, including experiencing pleasure and achieving a happy, meaningful life. Furthermore, this definition of health would indicate that while a person may have limited physical or cognitive abilities as a result of a stroke, they may still be able to achieve other positive markers of health including mental, social, and emotional wellness.

When considering the use of positive psychology for a disability or experience such as a stroke, the distinctions of traits versus personal states and positive qualities not diminishing human loss should be acknowledged (Livneh & Martz, 2016). This means although an individual who experienced a stroke may possess negative emotions surrounding the stroke, they can still focus on their positive character strengths and their human strength and not disregard the enormous loss and suffering that the stroke may have created in their life. The negative emotional state or affectivity that is regularly "experienced after the onset of a chronic illness or disability should be viewed (with some exceptions) as a 'state' reaction, not an inherent personality 'trait', to a stressful, if not traumatic, event related to one's body and/or mind" (Livneh & Martz, 2016, p. 16). By recognizing the common negativity and emotional turmoil following a stroke, the individual's suffering can be acknowledged and their emotions surrounding it can be accepted, ***and*** the individual can still shift their focus away from their sorrow to their strengths, using this change as a catalyst to reevaluate their priorities and intentions for their future, fostering optimism and hope for a life in which they can flourish.

Although currently limited due to few studies, research on the use of positive psychology interventions (PPIs) for individuals who have experienced a stroke or similar brain injury indicates promising results (Andrewes et al., 2014; Cullen et al., 2018; Evans, 2011; Evans & Cullen, 2019; Mavaddat et al., 2017; Terrill et al., 2018, 2022; Wang et al., 2019). Not only is a PPI helpful for an individual post-stroke, but couples who engaged in PPIs together following one partner's stroke were able to increase their coping skills and positively redefine their relationship following the stroke (Einerson et al., 2023). However, when participants have severe impairments from their stroke such as executive dysfunction, or memory impairments, it may make learning or even remembering any of the components of PPI challenging (Andrewes et al., 2014).

Optimizing Attitudes and Experiences Through Positive Psychology Goal States

To practice positive psychological principles, the following list provides quick reference language for the goal states that an individual and their family members may want to strive for in their thoughts, behaviors, and states of being to aid them in their ability to thrive in life. To support an individual who experienced a stroke, the individual who experience the stroke and their family members should focus on:

- Understanding that "enhancing wellbeing and happiness are not destinations but, rather, a process" (Burke et al., 2023, p. 12).
- Recognizing that a stroke can impact an individual's sense of identity. Its negative impact can either make the individual feel that the stroke is all-consuming in their identity or they may wish to deny its impact altogether. It can have a positive impact for individuals who accept the stroke and themselves following it and view the experiences as enriching their identity as they learned new information about themselves as a result of the deeply challenging experience.
- Focusing on realizing potential achievement and lasting fulfillment (Seligman, 2004) following a stroke instead of simply recovering from the stroke and getting back to the life a person once experienced.
- Avoiding focusing on merely relieving the negative symptoms from a stroke; a more fulfilling goal might be to seek to achieve lasting purpose, high self-esteem, and happiness.
- Seeking to use strengths instead of improving weaknesses.
- Striving for a positive mood, which allows individuals to be generous, creative, and tolerant.
- Pursuing play, happiness, positive emotions, and achievement as these pursuits allow for human flourishing.
- Working to improve factors that are under the individual's volunteer level of control as these areas can help to improve and maintain happiness even when encountering adversity.
- Aiming to accomplish tasks as "good enough" rather than attempting to "try harder" as cognitive abilities may be limited post-stroke, and this good enough approach may reduce cognitive mistakes, promote self-acceptance, and enhance well-being following a stroke.

- Pursuing optimism, hope, and growth, through a belief that although the stroke has altered the individual's functioning, there is potential for continued improvement and that something positive likely will come from the experience.
- Increasing social support, resilience, self-efficacy, and hope as these factors were shown to be protective factors against anxiety and depression (Wang et al., 2019).
- Avoiding "ignoring or denying negative aspects of life post-injury but rather focusing more attention to experiences that give a sense of wellbeing and learning to act in a way that promotes wellbeing" (Evans & Cullen, 2019, p. 104).
- Adopting a compassion for oneself as a human being and savoring life's little and big positive moments to promote gratitude.
- Adopting an accepting attitude rather than a judgment preference for one's current moment.
- Finding general life meaning and support to discover the meaning of suffering and recognizing this process a part of the human condition.
- Seeking to engage in benefit finding "to see the silver lining in the darkest clouds" (Burke et al., 2023, p. 138).
- Engaging in prospecting to create the future in which the individual wants to flourish. These tools include:
  1. Anticipation
  2. Goal Setting
  3. Best Possible Self
  4. Hope

The above list is ordered to establish the foundational principles involved in positive psychology and later provide actionable strategies to practice positive psychological principles.

Practical Positive Psychology Activities for Individuals Who Experienced a Stroke

Instead of approaching the aftermath of a stroke as a recovery process, which by its nature emphasizes deficits, through incorporating the following positive psychology activities, individuals who experienced a stroke can focus on their well-being, happiness, and personal fulfillment:

- Benefits Finding: What Went Well Exercise involves writing down three things in the day that went well and the reasons for why these things happened (Seligman, 2011).
- Strength Identification and Maximization: Focusing on character strengths may be beneficial in helping an individual who is struggling to recognize their identity and value following a stroke due to changes in functioning and mental states and may enhance their sense of self. Therefore,

completing a strengths survey, such as the Character Strengths Survey (VIA Institute on Character, 2024), may be beneficial in identifying and maximizing character strengths.

- Gratitude for Current Abilities: Because many aspects of a person's abilities and personality may be limited following a stroke, stroke survivors may focus on what the stroke took away from them and tasks in which they are no longer capable; however, rejoicing in the activities they are currently doing is beneficial in recognizing their strengths and promoting continued growth (Anderson et al., 2022).
- Enhanced Well-being: As recommended by Cullen et al. (2018), a PERMA Framework (Seligman, 2011) may be utilized to assist stroke survivors in simplistically incorporating positive psychology into their lives. PERMA stands for:
  P = Positive emotions, which are not solely about pleasant feelings but are an indicator that psychological growth is occurring.
  E = Engagement or feeling completely engrossed in a task with some level of frequency.
  R = Relationships or forming meaningful, enduring social connections with others.
  M = Meaning including identifying a sense of purpose and fulfillment in one's life.
  A = Accomplishment involves pursuing a goal for its own sake rather than for some specific outcome.
- Social Support and Savoring: Engage in leisure activities can help support well-being following a stroke (Department of Veterans Affairs and Department of Defense, 2019). Reengagement in activities that were previously valued prior to a stroke is facilitated by social support (Jellema et al., 2017). Because "community participation, particularly re-engagement in recreation and leisure is difficult for many individuals after sustaining a stroke" (Porter et al., 2023, p. 98), post-stroke survivors who received leisure education and leisure counseling had reduced depression and perceived barriers (Porter et al., 2023). These social activities enhance their social connections and sense of well-being (Wang et al., 2019).
- Relationship-Building: Couples engaging in the following attitudes through an intentional consistent schedule enhanced their relationships and individual well-being: "expressing gratitude, practicing acts of kindness, fostering relationships, focusing on the positive, savoring, working toward a goal, and spirituality" (Einerson et al., 2023, p. 2613). While there are some structured activities—such as writing letters of gratitude for others, performing an act of kindness for someone else, setting aside time to devote to specific relationships, listing three good things that happened throughout the day, or selecting meaningful goals and devoting time and effort to pursue them—other aspects of these recommendations are more of a mindset, such as focusing on the positive through reflection on positive experiences, savoring life through focusing on all five senses to more fully experience one's environment, and identifying meaning and purpose that is greater than one's self (Terrill et al., 2018, 2022). Furthermore, if the stroke survivor has a partner, focusing on the existing relationship strengths can help promote resilience in the couple and potentially improve both the stroke survivors' mental health and their caregiver's mental health (Terrill et al., 2018). Interventions for post-stroke well-being should focus on not

only the individual who experienced the stroke but also on their supportive caregivers as these relationship-fostering interventions can best aid in their resiliency and prosperity (Anderson et al., 2022). In addition to individuals who experienced a stroke needing to focus on enhancing their health and well-being through engaging in lifestyle changes, caregivers of stroke survivors should also engage in activities to enhance their well-being as this promotes the well-being of the social support available to others with whom they interact.

- Resiliency Training: Anderson et al. (2022) propose a Relational, Intrapersonal, Social, and Environmental (RISE) Model of resilience that explores interconnection and constructs that affect both quality of life and resilience.
- Mindfulness Techniques: Focusing on breathing, body scans, the five senses, and relaxation.
- Enriched Environments: Include sunlight, music, meditation, and social interaction that improve recovery after a stroke (Conley, 2023).
- Goal-setting: Although commonly used in rehabilitation settings with sometimes limited success, intentional person-centered and person-oriented goal-setting is helpful for increasing engagement and improving sense of purpose. Working with the person who experienced a stroke to co-construct a well-being plan is more beneficial for the individual's sense of competence and autonomy than the professional alone creating the plan (Burke et al., 2023). Although a novice assignment might view positive psychology as a focus solely on pleasure, self-discipline and sacrificing one's present moment for their future are actually pillars in the theory (Seligman, 2011).
- Meaning-Making: Writing a letter of forgiveness to self for changes since the stroke, gratitude following the stroke, or even forgiveness for the stroke may assist in positive growth after the trauma of the stroke event (Evans, 2011).
- Tool 71: Purpose, Understanding, Responsibility, Enjoyment (PURE) Model (Burke et al., 2023, p. 132). Through identifying a purpose for one's life, understanding more about self—including the narratives that help or hinder one's life—accepting responsibility for the things one does to fulfill their potential, and enjoying one's life through focusing on tasks that help one enhance their well-being, an individual who encountered a stroke can seek to identify and create further meaning and purpose in their life and possibly even the event of the stroke.

Application of Mindfulness for Individuals Who Experienced a Stroke

As mentioned previously, individuals who experienced a stroke may experience difficulties in many areas of their life. The stress and trauma experienced often with the stroke as well as temporary or sometimes permanent physical impairment can lead to heightened levels of depression, anxiety, and overall emotional distress due to financial, social, interpersonal, and environment factors (Hackett et al., 2005; Vohora & Ogi, 2008). When approaching these difficulties, much like with positive psychology, taking a mindful approach may be helpful to promote healing, happiness, and a fulfilling recovery (Dahlgren, 2016).

Meditation. A mindfulness technique that can be especially helpful in stroke recovery is the practice of meditation. Not only can meditation reduce fatigue and depressive feelings, it can also improve balance, emotional regulation, and focus (Dahlgren, 2016). Meditation is able to accomplish this through the process of neuroplasticity, which is the process of creating and strengthening neural pathways. This process is achieved through learning or relearning new skills and practicing them consistently. The premise is the more you practice these skills, the better these skills will get. Building or rebuilding these skills can be attributed to not only healing the brain after a stroke but also to increasing happiness in an individual who has had a stroke (Gray, 2020).

Mindfulness-Based Stress Reduction. Mindfulness-Based Stress Reduction (MSBR) is an 8-week, mindfulness-based, evidence-based adjunct treatment protocol designed by Dr. Kabat-Zinn (1979). Dr. Kabat-Zinn (2013) defines mindfulness as "the awareness that arises by paying attention on purpose, in the present moment, and non-judgmentally" (iiiv). MSBR is considered an educational intervention that, when utilized, is associated with lowered stress levels and increased psychological health and well-being in patients with a myriad of medical concerns to include stroke and trauma recovery. Like meditation, it works with rewiring the brain through neuroplasticity.

Yoga. Mind and body connection is an essential part of stroke recovery. Yoga can assist in stroke recovery due to the intense focus and attention required. Each movement is deliberate, slow, and relies on breathing regulation. This helps to stimulate the brain, and as in the aforementioned mindfulness activities, helps to rewire the brain (Mak et al., 2023, Pande, 2012). It can also improve range of motion, posture, and endurance, which aids in improved walking and balance. The most helpful concept of the use of yoga is the accessibility of it. Yoga can be progressively implemented in most stages of stroke recovery, even in patients who are experiencing stroke paralysis, and can be done from the bed, a chair, the floor, and so on.

Mindfulness activities can be useful in stroke recovery through the use of many of the activities mentioned; however, there are many other mindfulness activities that can also be helpful. What are some other mindfulness activities that you can identify that may be helpful in stroke recovery that are not covered in the text? When considering these other activities, what makes them helpful when recovering from stroke? In what stage(s) of stroke recovery do you see the activity being implemented?

Precautions When Considering a Positive Psychological Perspective With an Individual Who Experienced a Stroke

Due to stigma and misleading information concerning positive thinking interventions, professionals utilizing positive psychology approaches with individuals who experienced a stroke may wish to begin their relationship with the client by acknowledging that realistic goals and action plans should be integrated into the approach (Cullen et al., 2018). The intervention should not merely rely on thinking positively about this life-altering event or being happy but should, instead, focus on the individual's overall well-being. Furthermore, professionals utilizing positive psychology need to be aware of the approach's limitations and potential for an "imbalanced perspective on the human condition, and particularly life following the onset of severe and life-threatening disabilities" (Livneh & Martz, 2016, p. 17). Finally, as when using any therapeutic approach, professionals should be sensitive to their client's agenda and honor their experience as the fundamental process of any intervention (White & Johnstone, 2000).

Case Example: Exploring Positive Psychological Interventions and Techniques With Someone Who Experienced a Stroke

Evelyn is a 79-year-old widow with a history of hypertension who recently suffered an ischemic stroke, while on an outing with her best friend, Lily. Her symptoms were right facial aphasia (facial drooping), speech difficulty, and confusion. Lily called 911 and Evelyn was taken to the hospital immediately by ambulance. She was treated at the hospital and subsequently moved to a rehabilitation facility for a few weeks to help her relearn tasks necessary for independent living. Within a short period of time, her aphasia ceased, and her confusion and speech difficulties seemed to return to normal. However, she continued to navigate post-stroke fatigue, difficulty concentrating, and impulsivity. Despite these challenges, she appeared to be healing well. While she received immediate, excellent medical treatment and has a good support system from her family and friends, she is struggling to recover from the effects of the stroke on her body and is experiencing some post-stroke depression as a result.

Let's look at how applying positive psychology can aid in helping Evelyn manage her post-stroke depressive episode. As mentioned in the text, a stroke can cause changes in the brain, thought patterns, as well as lifestyle and social changes. Looking at this from a counseling perspective and utilizing some of the fundamental aspects of positive psychology, let's begin by focusing on Evelyn's strengths, values, and self-compassion. One practice to get her started would be to encourage her to keep a gratitude journal. A gratitude journal gives a person the opportunity to identify and reflect on things in their life for which they are grateful. As a counselor, for a few weeks you assign Evelyn the prompt of identifying three things per day (different things each day, not repeating) that she is grateful for. For 3 weeks, Evelyn discusses what she has written in the gratitude journal in her sessions with you. Although at first identifying, writing down, and consistently completing the gratitude journal each day was a struggle, it eventually appeared that her mood was improving as well as her life perspective. Over time, she will likely experience an increase in her overall well-being as well as an increase in her feelings of gratitude through this practice.

Another practice that can be helpful is to focus on personal strengths; what she can do versus what she cannot do or is not as well-suited to do. As mentioned previously, positive psychology focuses on strength-building to help build success while looking for increased opportunities to practice those strengths. As a counselor, you could help Evelyn identify her strengths, build on them, and help her to create or identify more opportunities to utilize those strengths. For example, if she loves to bake, she could bake cookies for a person who is temporarily homebound in lieu of personally visiting them due to Evelyn's lessened mobility. The focus would be on baking the cookies even though she struggled to concentrate on the task and experienced fatigue while attempting to bake the cookies. By focusing on the positive, she was able to complete the challenging task of baking cookies and sending them to a person who had surgery or was ill. Instead of dwelling on her decreased ability to visit in person, she found a sense of purpose and accomplishment. When focusing on strength identification and implementation, her overall well-being should improve over time.

These are just a couple of ideas on how to implement positive psychology with someone who has had a stroke. What are some others you can think of? How would you implement them in a therapeutic or counseling setting?

Conclusion

"I like to think that maybe one day you'll be an old man like me, talking a younger man's ear off, explaining to him how you took the sourest lemon that life has to offer and turned it into something resembling lemonade."

—Dr. Nathan Katowski, *This Is Us* (Fogelman et al., 2016)

For individuals who survive a stroke and for their families, the stroke frequently constitutes one of the most challenging life events they will ever navigate. Through using this life-altering event to incorporate a focus on well-being, optimism, and happiness, positive psychology can provide these individuals negotiating an exceptionally challenging life event with an enduring framework to view each of the day-to-day issues they encounter with positive intention and meaningful purpose. Recognizing the challenge and still confronting it with a sense of gratitude, courage, and appreciation can optimize personal well-being and promote community resilience. A stroke survivor's health and well-being can be best improved not by viewing their stroke as a deficit to be overcome but, instead, by appreciating the growth that is required by the experience, admitting their personal strengths, and remaining positive and hopeful about their future. In fact, for some individuals who experience a stroke, this can lead to positive psychological growth (Evans, 2011). Through using a positive psychology framework with individuals who encountered a stroke and with their families, professionals can support these individuals with the goal of allowing them to savor their lives and flourish.

Critical Thinking Questions

1. How can a professional supporting an individual in adjusting to their new abilities following a stroke both acknowledge their suffering and engage in positive psychological interventions (PPIs) with the individual?
2. Regarding the use of positive psychological language with an individual who experienced a stroke, what are some words that the provider might wish to avoid with the client, and what words should they strive to incorporate in their work?
3. Which of the positive psychology activities listed would be most beneficial for someone who experienced a stroke that influenced their ability to focus and increased their impulsivity?

Assessment of Knowledge Activity

After reading this chapter on integrating positive psychology and mindfulness techniques to support stroke survivors and their caregivers, take some time to reflect on how you can apply this knowledge in a real-life scenario. Write a short reflection (approximately 200–300 words) addressing the following prompts:

1. Describe a Hypothetical Situation: Imagine a stroke survivor named John, a 65-year-old man who has recently returned home after a 2-month stay in a rehabilitation center. John is experiencing feelings of frustration and helplessness due to his limited mobility and speech difficulties. He lives with his daughter, who is his primary caregiver.
2. Identify an Activity: Refer back to the "Practical Positive Psychology Activities for Individuals Who Experienced a Stroke" section in this chapter. Choose one activity that you think would be particularly beneficial for John.
3. Discuss Potential Outcomes and Benefits: Consider how the selected positive psychology intervention (PPI) could help John. What are the potential positive outcomes and benefits for him?
4. Reflect on Challenges and Solutions: What challenges might arise when implementing this intervention with John? How could these challenges be addressed to ensure the effectiveness of the positive psychology technique?

References

American Stroke Association. (2024a). *Effects of stroke*. https://www.stroke.org/en/about-stroke/effects-of-stroke

American Stroke Association. (2024b). *How to qualify for social security disability benefits after a stroke*. https://www.stroke.org/en/life-after-stroke/recovery/managing-your-stroke/finances-insurance-and-assistance/social-security-disability-benefits-after-a-stroke

American Stroke Association. (2024c). *Life after stroke: Our path forward*. https://www.stroke.org/-/media/Stroke-Files/life-after-stroke/Life-After-Stroke-Guide_7819.pdf

American Stroke Association. (2024d). *Stroke risk factors*. https://www.stroke.org/en/about-stroke/stroke-risk-factors

American Stroke Association. (2024e). *Stroke symptoms*. https://www.stroke.org/en/about-stroke/stroke-symptoms

Anderson, M. A., Buffo, C., Ketcher, D., Nguyen, H., MacKenzie, J. J., Reblin, M., & Terrill, A. L. (2022). Applying the RISE Model of resilience in partners post-stroke: A qualitative analysis. *Annals of Behavioral Medicine: A Publication of the Society of Behavioral Medicine, 56*(3), 270–281. https://doi.org/10.1093/abm/kaab053

Andrewes, H. E., Walker, V., & O'Neill, B. (2014). Exploring the use of positive psychology interventions in brain injury survivors with challenging behaviour. *Brain Injury, 28*(7), 965–971. https://doi.org/10.3109/02699052.2014.888764

Burke, J., Dunne, P. J., Meehan, T., O'Boyle, C., & Nieuwerburgh, C. (2023). *Positive health: 100+ research-based positive psychology and lifestyle medicine tools to enhance your wellbeing*. Routledge.

Conley, J. (2023). Neurorecovery and neuroplasticity after stroke: Harnessing the power of enriched environments. *American Physical Therapy Association Magazine, 15*(9), 1–2. https://link.gale.com/apps/doc/A771436869/HRCA?u=txshracd2580&sid=bookmark-HRCA&xid=688eb7ae

Cullen, B., Pownall, J., Cummings, J., Baylan, S., Broomfield, N., Haig, C., Kersel, D., Murray, H., & Evans, J. J. (2018). Positive psychotherapy in ABI Rehab (PoPsTAR): A pilot randomized control trail. *Neuropsychological Rehabilitation, 28*(1), 17–33. https://doi.org/10.1080/09602011.2015.1131722

Dahlgren, K. (2016). *Healing and happiness after stroke: How to get back up after life turned upside-down*. Flint Rehabilitation Devices LLC.

Department of Veterans Affairs and Department of Defense. (2019). *VA/DoD clinical practice guidelines for the management of stroke rehabilitation*. https://www.healthquality.va.gov/guidelines/Rehab/stroke/VADoDStrokeRehabCPGFinal8292019.pdf

Devereux, N., & Berns, A. M. (2023). Evaluation and treatment of psychological effects of stroke. *Delaware Journal of Public Health, 9*(3), 62–69. https://doi.org/10.32481/djph.2023.08.011

Einerson, J., Lundstrom, L. K., Allen, B. K., Sefandonakis, A., & Terrill, A. L. (2023). Learning to flourish in a new reality: A thematic analysis of couples' experience of participation in a positive psychology intervention post-stroke. *Disability and Rehabilitation, 45*(16), 2612–2619. https://doi.org/10.1080/09638288.2022.2102256

Evans, J. J. (2011). Positive psychology and brain injury rehabilitation. *Brain Impairment, 12*(2), 117–127. https://doi.org/10.1375/brim.12.2.117

Evans, J. J., & Cullen, B. (2019). Positive psychotherapy for neurological conditions. In G. Yeates & F. Ashworth (Eds.), *Psychological therapies in acquired brain injury.* Routledge.

Fogelman, D. (Writer), Ficarra, G., & Requa, J. (Directors). (2016, September 20). Pilot (Season 1, Episode 1) [TV series episode]. In S. Beers, G. Ficarra, D. Fogelman, C. Gogolak, J. Requa, & J. Rosenthal (Executive Producers), *This Is Us*. Rhode Island Ave. Productions; Zaftig Films; 20th Century Fox Television.

Gray, L. A. (2020). Living the full-catastrophe: A mindfulness-based approach to recovery from stroke. *Healthcare, 8*(4), 498. https://doi.org/10.3390/healthcare8040498

Hackett, M. L., Yapa, C., Parag, V., & Anderson, C. S. (2005). Frequency of depression after stroke: A systematic review of observational studies. *Stroke, 36*(6), 1330–1340. https://doi.org/10.1161/01.STR.0000165928.19135.35

Jellema, S., Hees, S. V., Zajec, J., Sande, R. V. D., Sanden, M. W. G. N., & Steultjens, E. M. J. (2017). What environmental factors influence resumption of valued activities post stroke: A systematic review of qualitative and quantitative findings. *Clinical Rehabilitation, 31*(7), 936–947. https://doi.org/10.1177/0269215516671013

Kabat-Zinn, J. (2013). *Full catastrophe living, revised edition: how to cope with stress, pain and illness using mindfulness meditation*. Hachette UK.

Livneh, H., & Martz, E. (2016). Psychosocial adaptation to disability within the context of positive psychology: Philosophical aspect and historical roots. *Journal of Occupational Rehabilitation, 26*(1), 13–19. https://doi.org/10.1007/s10926-015-9601-6

Mak, T. C. T., Wong, T. W. L., & Ng, S. S. M. (2023). The use of mindfulness-based interventions in stroke rehabilitation: A scoping review. *Rehabilitation Psychology*, *68*(3), 221–234. https://doi.org/10.1037/rep0000505

Mayo Clinic. (2024, April 30). *Stroke.* https://www.mayoclinic.org/diseases-conditions/stroke/symptoms-causes/syc-20350113

Mavaddat, N., Ross, S., Dobbin, A., Williams, K., Graffy, J., & Mant, J. (2017). Training in positivity for stroke? A qualitative study of acceptability of use of Positive Mental Training (PosMT) as a tool to assist stroke survivors with post-stroke psychological problems and in coping with rehabilitation. *NeuroRehabilitation, 40*(2), 259–270. https://doi.org/10.3233/NRE-161411

National Heart, Lung, & Blood Institute. (2023, May 26). *Stroke: Causes and risk factors.* https://www.nhlbi.nih.gov/health/stroke/causes#:~:text=Strokes%20are%20caused%20by%20blocked,a%20stroke%20or%20future%20strokes

Pande, R. L. (2012). Yoga may aid in stroke recovery. *Harvard Health Publishing. Harvard Medical School.* https://www.health.harvard.edu/blog/yoga-may-aid-stroke-recovery-201207285073thestrokefoundation.org

Porter, H. R., Goodno, H., W., Bowman, E., Titlow, C., Opitz, A., Maher, C., Swingle, I., & Roth, S. (2023). Leisure education and leisure counseling in adult stroke. *Therapeutic Recreation Journal, LVII*(2), 97–115. https://doi.org/10.18666/TRJ-2023-V57-I2-11775

Sarre, S., Redlich, C., Tinker, A., Sadler, E., Bhalla, A., & McKevitt, C. (2013). A systematic review of qualitative studies on adjusting after stroke: Lessons for the study of resilience. *Disability and Rehabilitation, 36*(9), 716–726. https://doi.org/10.3109/09638288.2013.814724

Seligman, M. E. P. (2002). *Authentic happiness: Using the new positive psychology to realize your potential for lasting fulfillment.* Free Press.

Seligman, M. E. P. (2011). *Flourish: A visionary new understanding of happiness and well-being.* Nicholas Brealey Publishing.

Seligman, M. E. P., & Csikszentmihalyi, M. (2000). Positive psychology: An introduction. *American Psychologist, 55*(1), 5–14. https://doi.org/10.1037/0003-066X.55.1.5

Terrill, A. L., Reblin, M., MacKenzie, J. J., Baucom, B. R. W., Einerson, J., Cardell, B., Richards, L. G., & Majersik, J. J. (2022). Intimate relationships and stroke: Piloting a dyadic intervention to improve depression. *International Journal of Environmental Research and Public Health, 19*(3), 1804. https://doi.org/10.3390/ijerph19031804

Terrill, A. L., Reblin, M., MacKenzie, J. J., Cardell, B., Einerson, J., Berg, C. A., Majersik, J. J., & Richards, L. (2018). Development of a novel positive psychology-based intervention for couples post-stroke. *Rehabilitation Psychology, 63*(1), 43–54. https://doi.org/10.1037/rep0000181

VIA Institute on Character. (2024). *The VIA character strengths survey: Get to know your greatest strengths.* https://www.viacharacter.org/account/register

Vohora, R., & Ogi, L. (2008). Addressing the emotional needs of stroke survivors. *Nursing Times, 104*(42), 32–35. https://www.nursingtimes.net/clinical-archive/neurology/addressing-the-emotional-needs-of-stroke-survivors-21-10-2008/

Wang, X., Shang, S., Yang, H., Ai, H., Wang, Y., Chang, S., Sha, X., Wang, L., & Jiang, X. (2019). Associations of psychological distress with positive psychological variables and activities of daily living among stroke patients: A cross-sectional study. *BMC Psychiatry, 19*(1), 381. https://doi.org/10.1186/s12888-019-2368-0

White, M. A., & Johnstone, A. S. (2000). Recovery from stroke: Does rehabilitation counselling have a role to play? *Disability and Rehabilitation, 22*(3), 140–143. https://doi.org/10.1080/096382800296999

World Health Organization. (2024). *Health and well-being.* https://www.who.int/data/gho/data/major-themes/health-and-well-being#:~:text=The%20WHO%20constitution%20states%3A%20%22Health,of%20mental%20disorders%20or%20disabilities

Cultivating Positive Psychology and Mindfulness in Dementia Care

10

Fernando Hinostroza Balmaceda
Logan Winkelman

KEYWORDS AND DEFINITIONS:

Dementia: a decline in cognitive function that disrupts daily life, commonly seen in Alzheimer's disease and other types.

Positive psychology: studies human strengths and well-being, focusing on factors like happiness and resilience.

Mindfulness: the practice of being present and aware without judgment, often developed through meditation.

Caregiving strategies: techniques used to support individuals needing assistance, focusing on communication and emotional support.

Ethical considerations: principles guiding moral conduct in various fields, ensuring respect for individuals' rights and integrity.

LEARNING OBJECTIVES:

1. Students will be able to define dementia and describe the different types, including Alzheimer's, frontotemporal, vascular, and Lewy body dementia, along with their etiologies, risk factors, and symptoms.
2. Students will learn about the principles of positive psychology and identify its benefits for individuals with dementia, as well as strategies for promoting a supportive and optimistic environment in dementia care settings.

3. Students will gain knowledge on the concepts and benefits of mindfulness for dementia patients and their families and develop practical skills for implementing mindfulness techniques in caregiving scenarios.
4. Students will examine the ethical implications and challenges associated with integrating positive psychology and mindfulness into dementia care and formulate strategies for addressing these ethical concerns and overcoming potential barriers.

Introduction

Dementia is a complex and multifaceted condition that affects millions of individuals worldwide. Characterized by a decline in cognitive function beyond what might be expected from normal aging, dementia encompasses a range of symptoms including memory loss, impaired reasoning, and difficulties with communication (Arvanitakis et al., 2019). The impact of dementia extends beyond the individual, profoundly affecting caregivers, families, and communities. As the global population ages, the prevalence of dementia is expected to rise, making it increasingly crucial to explore and implement effective care strategies (Arvanitakis et al., 2019).

In this chapter, we delve into the integration of positive psychology and mindfulness in dementia care—a progressive approach that not only addresses the cognitive and emotional needs of individuals with dementia but also enhances the well-being of caregivers and families. Positive psychology, with its focus on fostering positive emotions, strengths, and virtues, offers valuable tools for improving quality (Seligman & Csikszentmihalyi, 2000). Mindfulness, on the other hand, emphasizes present-moment awareness and acceptance, providing a means to reduce stress and enhance emotional resilience (Siegel et al., 2009).

Understanding dementia in its various forms is essential for tailoring care approaches. We begin by examining the definitions and types of dementia, including Alzheimer's disease, frontotemporal dementia, vascular dementia, and Lewy body dementia. This foundational knowledge will help us appreciate the unique challenges faced by individuals with different types of dementia and the corresponding impact on their caregivers and families (Cheng et al., 2019, 2020). The chapter then explores the power of positive psychology, highlighting its benefits and strategies for promoting positivity in dementia care settings. We will discuss the importance of gratitude, a supportive environment, and positive communication techniques. Following this, we delve into the concept of mindfulness, examining how it can be incorporated into care practices to enhance emotional and cognitive well-being.

To illustrate the practical application of these concepts, we present case studies that demonstrate the transformative impact of positive psychology and mindfulness on individuals with dementia. Additionally, we offer practical examples for students and educators on how to apply these approaches in caregiving and academic settings. As with any innovative approach, there are ethical considerations and challenges to implementing positive psychology and mindfulness in dementia care. We will address these concerns and offer strategies for overcoming potential barriers. Finally, the chapter concludes with a discussion on future directions and potential avenues for further research. By summarizing key points and emphasizing the importance of integrating positive psychology and mindfulness into caregiving practices, we aim to inspire and inform those involved in the care of individuals with dementia.

Understanding Dementia

Definition and Types of Dementia

Dementia is a collective term that describes a decline in cognitive function severe enough to interfere with daily life. This condition affects memory, thinking, behavior, and the ability to perform everyday activities. The cognitive deterioration observed in dementia is caused by neuronal loss and reduced neuronal connections.

Dementia affects individuals and their families, and the number of people with this condition is continuously rising. According to the World Health Organization (WHO), 55 million people suffered from dementia in 2019, and this number is expected to increase to 139 million in 2050. Additionally, the global cost was estimated at US$1.3 trillion per year in 2019 and is projected to rise to US$2.8 trillion by 2030 (Alzheimer's Disease International, 2023). Dementia encompasses various disorders such as Alzheimer's disease, frontotemporal dementia, vascular dementia, and Lewy body dementia, among others, with Alzheimer's disease being the most common.

Alzheimer's Disease

Alzheimer's disease (AD) is a neurodegenerative disease that primarily affects elderly individuals. Memory problems, language impairments, executive dysfunction, personality changes, agnosia, and impaired visual-spatial ability characterize this condition. Over a century ago, Alois Alzheimer was the first to describe the senile plaques and neurofibrillary tangles in postmortem brains of affected individuals.

Risk factors

Age is the most significant risk factor for AD, and the likelihood of developing the condition increases substantially as individuals age. Additionally, alterations in the DNA can cause AD, though genetic mutations account for only a small number of cases. The genes *APP* (encoding for ß-amyloid precursor protein; Tcw & Goate, 2017), *PSEN1* (encoding for the presenilin-1 protein; Shen & Kelleher, 2007; Sun et al., 2017), and *PSEN2* (encoding for the presenilin-2 protein; Zekanowski et al., 2003) are responsible for nearly all inherited cases of AD. Often, individuals younger than 65 years old develop AD due to a mutation in one of the mentioned genes. Polymorphisms in the *APOE* gene (encoding for the apolipoprotein-E) are genetic risk factors for developing AD symptoms after age 65 (Strittmatter et al., 1993).

To date, 12 modifiable risk factors for dementia have been identified. Factors such as diabetes, obesity, hypertension, alcohol abuse, hearing loss, traumatic brain injury, physical inactivity, obesity, smoking, social isolation, less education, and air pollution are associated with an increased risk of developing late-life AD (Alzheimer's Disease International, 2023).

Symptoms

AD patients exhibit a spectrum of cognitive impairment severity, ranging from no cognitive impairment to dementia. The earliest symptoms can be a decline in mental abilities (Jessen et al., 2014). Then, the disease progresses to mild cognitive impairment, where the patient suffers alterations in one or more domains to a mild extent (Petersen, 2004). Mild cognitively impaired patients can suffer from memory and language problems, spatial cognition alterations, or executive function impairments, which negatively impact daily life. Other neuropsychiatric conditions such as social isolation, anxiety, and depression can co-occur in these individuals. Finally, significant amnestic symptoms start (McKhann et al., 2011). For individuals with advanced AD, emotional alterations, aggressive behavior, hallucinations, or delusions are also present (D'Onofrio et al., 2012).

Individuals with AD can begin the condition with a non-amnestic impairment (Lehmann et al., 2013; Ossenkoppele et al., 2016). They can sometimes present non-fluent aphasia and long pauses when finding words or have difficulty with repetition (Bergeron et al., 2018). Others may exhibit visuospatial alterations, including difficulty recognizing faces, reading, and processing complex visual scenes (Crutch et al., 2017). In some cases, patients have deficits in multitasking, executive function, and decision-making (Townley et al., 2020).

Frontotemporal Dementia

Frontotemporal dementia (FTD) is a progressive neurodegenerative condition characterized by neurodegeneration of the frontal and temporal lobes. It primarily presents with behavior, language, or overall executive function changes. The FTD term comprises a condition with language impairment, including non-fluent aphasia (nfvFTD), semantic variant (svFTD), behavioral variant (bvFTD), right lobe variant (rtvFTD), and FTD related to motorneuron disease (FTD-MND).

Symptoms

FTD presents several variants with different symptomatology: the behavioral variant (bvFTD), semantic variant (svFTD), non-fluent aphasia (nfvFTD), right lobe variant (rtvFTD), and a variant related to a motorneuron disease (FTD-MND). The bvFTD is the most frequent variant of the disease (Logroscino et al., 2023). bfFTD individuals exhibit altered executive functions, disinhibition, loss of empathy, apathy, stereotyped attitude, and altered behavior (Seeley, 2019). The svFTD is characterized by language impairments, such as circumlocutions, semantic paraphasia, and anomie. As the disease progress, individuals lose the ability to recognize the meaning of words and exhibit spared speech production (Younes & Miller, 2020). Irritability, social isolation, sleep disturbances, appetite, and libido alterations are also observed. When the right anterior temporal lobe is mainly affected, behavior changes also occur, such as obsessive-compulsive behavior, disinhibition, and eating behavior alterations (Josephs et al., 2009). nfvFTD is the second most frequent variant (Botha & Josephs, 2019). It is characterized by progressive speech impairment. Particularly, non-fluent speech, hesitant, short sentences, phonemic errors, and omissions of articles, verb tenses, and prepositions (Ghosh & Lippa, 2015; Grossman, 2012; Marshall et al., 2018). Individuals diagnosed with rtvFTD exhibit obsessive personality, spatial disorientations, alterations in episodic memory, disinhibition, and prosopagnosia (Chan et al., 2009; Snowden et al., 2018; Veronelli et al., 2017). FTD-MND displays progressive impairments in language and behavior, and individuals also exhibit muscle atrophy and weakness (Burrell et al., 2016; Rodríguez de Rivera et al., 2014).

Vascular Dementia

Vascular dementia (VaD) is the second most common type of dementia after Alzheimer's disease, accounting for approximately 15% to 20% of all dementia cases (Akhter et al., 2021; Plassman et al., 2007). It is characterized by cognitive decline due to cerebrovascular damage, such as strokes or small vessel disease, which leads to insufficient blood flow to the brain. Unlike Alzheimer's, which primarily affects memory, vascular dementia presents a more heterogeneous clinical picture, often including deficits in attention, processing speed, and executive functions (Bir et al., 2021). The progression and symptoms of VaD can vary significantly depending on the location and extent of the vascular lesions, making it a particularly challenging condition to diagnose and manage. Currently, the term "vascular neurocognitive disorder" has been employed by the Fifth Edition of the *Diagnostic and Statistical Manual and Mental Disorders* (American Psychiatric Association, 2013).

Symptoms

The clinical presentation of vascular dementia varies widely depending on the size, location, and number of vascular lesions (Korczyn et al., 2012). Common cognitive symptoms include slowed thinking, difficulty with problem-solving and planning (executive dysfunction) (Sudo et al., 2017), and reduced attention (Tu et al., 2020). Memory impairment is typically less severe in the early stages compared to Alzheimer's disease but may worsen over time (Graham et al., 2004). Non-cognitive symptoms, such as mood changes (depression or apathy) (Ballard et al., 2000), emotional lability, and psychomotor slowing (Macoir, 2024), are also frequent. Neurological signs, like gait disturbances, motor weakness, or focal neurological deficits, may be present, reflecting the underlying cerebrovascular pathology (Lee, 2011; Moretti et al., 2011). The progression of symptoms can be stepwise, with periods of stability followed by sudden declines after new vascular events.

Lewy Body Dementia

Lewy Body Dementia (LBD) is a progressive neurodegenerative disorder and is considered the third most common type of dementia, after Alzheimer's disease and vascular dementia. LBD encompasses two related conditions: Dementia with Lewy Bodies (DLB) and Parkinson's Disease Dementia (PDD), differentiated by the timing of cognitive and motor symptoms (Jellinger, 2003). DLB is characterized by cognitive decline, fluctuating attention, visual hallucinations, and motor symptoms similar to Parkinson's disease (Emre et al., 2007; McKeith et al., 2017), while PDD presents with dementia in the context of established Parkinsonism. The hallmark of LBD is the presence of Lewy bodies—abnormal aggregates of the protein alpha-synuclein—in the brain's cortex and subcortical structures, which disrupt neuronal function and communication (Taylor et al., 2020; Walker et al., 2015).

Symptoms

The clinical presentation of Lewy Body Dementia is characterized by a combination of cognitive, neuropsychiatric, and motor symptoms. Core cognitive symptoms include fluctuating attention and alertness, executive dysfunction, and visuospatial impairments, often more pronounced than memory deficits in the early stages. Visual hallucinations—typically vivid, well-formed images of people or animals—are a key diagnostic feature and occur in up to 80% of patients. Other neuropsychiatric symptoms include delusions, REM sleep behavior disorder (acting out dreams), and depression. Motor symptoms similar to Parkinsonism, such as bradykinesia, rigidity, tremors, and postural instability, are common and may precede or follow cognitive decline. Autonomic dysfunction, including orthostatic hypotension, urinary incontinence, and constipation, is also frequently observed. The progression of LBD is typically gradual, with symptoms worsening over time, but fluctuating cognitive function and alertness can make the clinical course unpredictable (Auning et al., 2011; Choudhury et al., 2022).

Common Symptoms and Challenges Faced by Individuals With Dementia

Although Alzheimer's disease (AD), frontotemporal dementia (FTD), vascular dementia (VaD), and Lewy body dementia (LBD) have distinct underlying pathologies and patterns of symptom progression, they share several common symptoms due to the generalized impact on brain function. Cognitive impairment is a central feature across all these dementias, often affecting memory, attention, and executive functioning. Memory loss, particularly of recent events, is most prominent in Alzheimer's but can also occur in later stages of FTD, VaD, and LBD (Chan et al., 2009; Graham et al., 2004; McKhann et al., 2011). Impaired executive functioning—difficulties with planning, organizing, and problem-solving—is common across all forms of dementia, though it may manifest differently; for example, it may present early in FTD and VaD, whereas in AD and LBD, it often appears later (Bir et al., 2021; Choudhury et al., 2022; Seeley, 2019; Townley et al., 2020). Language difficulties, such as aphasia, are seen in AD and FTD, though FTD may more often feature profound language disturbances due to its impact on the frontal and temporal lobes (Bergeron et al., 2018; Younes & Miller, 2020).

Behavioral and neuropsychiatric symptoms are also common across these dementias, although their prevalence and nature can differ. Mood disturbances, such as depression and anxiety, are frequent in AD, VaD, and LBD (Ballard et al., 2000; Choudhury et al., 2022; McKhann et al., 2011), while apathy is a common symptom in both AD and FTD (D'Onofrio et al., 2012; Seeley, 2019). Hallucinations and delusions are more characteristic of LBD but can also occur in AD, particularly in the later stages (Choudhury et al., 2022; D'Onofrio et al., 2012). Sleep disturbances and fluctuating alertness are hallmarks of LBD but can also be observed in AD and other dementias (Choudhury et al., 2022; D'Onofrio et al., 2012). Additionally, all forms of dementia may lead to impairments in social and occupational functioning, contributing to a loss of independence and increased caregiver burden.

Individuals with dementia face numerous challenges that significantly impact their quality of life. Cognitive impairments, such as memory loss and executive dysfunction, can make it difficult for them to perform activities of daily living, such as managing finances, preparing meals, or maintaining personal hygiene. These deficits can lead to a loss of independence and an increased reliance on caregivers, often resulting in feelings of frustration, helplessness, and anxiety. Behavioral changes, such as aggression, agitation, and impulsivity, can further complicate care and strain relationships with family members and caregivers (Collins & Kishita, 2019; Molero Jurado et al., 2020; Weisman de Mamani et al., 2018).

Social isolation and stigma are also significant challenges for individuals with dementia. As their symptoms progress, they may withdraw from social activities due to difficulties communicating or following conversations, fear of embarrassment, or lack of understanding from others. This isolation can exacerbate feelings of depression and anxiety (Riley et al., 2014). Additionally, individuals with dementia may face misunderstandings or misperceptions from the public, who may attribute their behavior to laziness, rudeness, or lack of intelligence rather than recognizing it as a symptom of their illness (Siette et al., 2023). Access to appropriate medical care, support services, and tailored interventions can also be limited, especially in underserved areas, making it difficult for individuals and their families to cope with the complexities of the disease.

Impact on Caregivers and Families

Caring for a loved one with dementia can have a profound and multifaceted impact on caregivers and families, often resulting in significant emotional, physical, and financial burdens. The progressive nature of dementia means that caregiving responsibilities typically increase over time, requiring more hours of direct care and supervision, which can lead to chronic stress and burnout. Emotionally, caregivers may experience a range of feelings, including sadness, frustration, guilt, and grief, as they witness the gradual decline of their loved one's cognitive and functional abilities. This emotional toll is often compounded by the unpredictable nature of dementia symptoms, such as behavioral changes, aggression, or agitation, which can be particularly challenging to manage and can create tension within the caregiving relationship.

The physical demands of caregiving are also considerable. Many caregivers, especially those who are older, may face their own health issues while managing the daily needs of someone with dementia, including assistance with mobility, personal hygiene, and feeding. The constant vigilance required to ensure the safety of a person with dementia, who may be prone to wandering or falls, can result in sleep disturbances and fatigue for the caregiver. Financially, caregiving can be a substantial burden, particularly if it necessitates reducing work hours, taking unpaid leave, or paying for additional support services, medical expenses, or home modifications. Over time, these challenges can lead to significant caregiver strain, increased risk for depression, anxiety, and other health problems, and diminished quality of life.

The impact on families extends beyond the primary caregiver. Family members may experience strained relationships due to differing opinions on care decisions or the division of caregiving duties, leading to conflict and feelings of resentment. Children or younger relatives may struggle with the emotional weight of seeing a loved one change so drastically, which can affect their own mental health and academic or social functioning. Moreover, families often face difficult decisions regarding long-term care, such as whether to transition the individual to a residential facility, which can evoke feelings of guilt or uncertainty. However, the caregiving experience can also foster resilience and strengthen bonds within families as they navigate these challenges together, often finding new ways to connect and support each other through shared adversity (Collins & Kishita, 2019; Molero Jurado et al., 2020; Weisman de Mamani et al., 2018).

The Power of Positive Psychology

Exploring the Concept of Positive Psychology

Positive psychology, in psychological terms, refers to a cognitive and emotional orientation that emphasizes optimism, constructive interpretation of events, and adaptive coping mechanisms in the face of stressors or challenges. It involves a tendency to focus on positive outcomes, beliefs, and expectations, while minimizing or reappraising negative thoughts in a more realistic or growth-oriented context (Seligman & Csikszentmihalyi, 2000). From a cognitive-behavioral perspective, positive psychology aligns with the idea that our thoughts significantly influence our emotions and behaviors; by cultivating positive thought patterns, individuals can potentially enhance their emotional well-being, resilience, and problem-solving capabilities. This concept is closely linked to constructs such as cognitive reappraisal, self-efficacy, and hope, all of which play a crucial role in psychological health and therapeutic processes (Brockman et al., 2017; McRae et al., 2012; Riepenhausen et al., 2022).

Research in psychology supports the idea that positive psychology can lead to various beneficial outcomes, including lower levels of stress, reduced symptoms of depression and anxiety, and better overall health (Bolier et al., 2013; Carr et al., 2021; Pione et al., 2021; Santos et al., 2013). Positive psychology is thought to activate adaptive coping strategies, such as seeking social support, engaging in problem-solving, and maintaining persistence in goal-directed behavior despite adversity. However, it is essential to differentiate positive psychology from unrealistic optimism or denial of reality; effective positive psychology involves a balanced approach that recognizes real challenges while maintaining a focus on potential solutions and personal strengths. For psychologists, fostering positive psychology in clients may involve techniques like cognitive restructuring, mindfulness, and encouraging behaviors that align with clients' values and goals, ultimately promoting a more adaptive and resilient response to life's difficulties (Hofmann & Gómez, 2017; Lim & Tierney, 2023).

Benefits of Positive Psychology for Individuals With Dementia

For individuals with dementia, positive psychology can play a significant role in enhancing quality of life, emotional well-being, and overall functioning. While cognitive decline is an inevitable part of dementia, fostering a positive outlook can help mitigate some of the emotional and psychological challenges that accompany the disease, such as anxiety, depression, and frustration (Tan et al., 2023). Positive psychology can encourage a sense of self-efficacy and agency, even in the face of declining cognitive abilities, by helping individuals focus on what they can still do, rather than what they have lost (Moniz-Cook et al., 2016; Pione et al., 2021). This approach aligns with cognitive-behavioral principles, where modifying negative thought patterns can lead to improvements in mood and adaptive behavior, reducing feelings of hopelessness and helplessness (Stoner et al., 2019).

Positive psychology can also contribute to better management of behavioral and psychological symptoms of dementia (BPSD), such as agitation, apathy, and aggression. Research suggests that a positive environment, where optimism and hope are reinforced, can reduce the frequency and intensity of these symptoms (Moniz-Cook et al., 2016; Stoner et al., 2019). This can be facilitated through psychosocial interventions that emphasize strengths-based approaches, encourage engagement in meaningful activities, and promote social connections. These interventions help individuals with dementia maintain a sense of purpose, dignity, and social inclusion, which in turn supports more positive psychology patterns.

For caregivers and healthcare professionals, promoting positive psychology involves creating a supportive, person-centered care environment that acknowledges the emotional and psychological needs of individuals with dementia. Techniques such as validation therapy, reminiscence therapy, and the use of positive reinforcement can help reinforce positive thoughts and emotions (Chen et al., 2020; Woods et al., 2018). By focusing on positive aspects of experience, practitioners can help individuals with dementia cope more effectively with their condition, ultimately contributing to improved mental health outcomes and a more meaningful experience of life despite the progression of cognitive decline.

Strategies for Promoting Positive Psychology in Dementia Care Settings

Encouraging Gratitude and Appreciation

Encouraging gratitude and appreciation in dementia care settings involves creating opportunities for individuals to focus on positive experiences and moments, which can help counterbalance feelings of loss or frustration. Simple, structured gratitude exercises can be incorporated into daily routines. For example, caregivers can prompt residents to share or write down something they are grateful for each day, such as a favorite meal, a meaningful conversation, or the beauty of the garden. Even brief reflections on positive experiences can activate emotional areas of the brain that are associated with well-being. Using tools like a "gratitude board" or a "thankfulness jar," where residents and staff write down things they appreciate, can create a sense of community and shared positivity, reinforcing a culture of gratitude.

Reminiscence therapy is another effective strategy to foster gratitude and appreciation (Chen et al., 2020; Woods et al., 2018). By encouraging individuals to recall and talk about positive past experiences, accomplishments, and cherished memories, caregivers help to reinforce a positive self-identity and personal worth. These sessions can be structured around specific themes, such as "favorite holidays" or "proud moments," using photographs, music, or objects to prompt memory recall. This not only helps individuals with dementia focus on positive memories but also strengthens social bonds and enhances mood by sharing these experiences with others. Ultimately, cultivating a mindset of gratitude helps maintain a more optimistic outlook, which can reduce stress, improve mood, and enhance overall quality of life for those with dementia (Moniz-Cook et al., 2016; Stoner et al., 2019).

Fostering a Supportive and Optimistic Environment

Fostering a supportive and optimistic environment in dementia care settings involves creating both a physical and emotional space where individuals feel valued, safe, and encouraged. One way to achieve this is by training staff to adopt a person-centered care approach, which emphasizes understanding and responding to each individual's unique preferences, abilities, and needs. This can include offering choices in daily activities, celebrating personal milestones, and providing regular positive reinforcement to acknowledge achievements, no matter how small. The goal is to create an environment where individuals feel competent and motivated, reducing anxiety and enhancing overall engagement and well-being.

In addition to these interpersonal strategies, the physical environment plays a critical role in fostering positivity. Care settings can be designed to promote calmness and comfort, with ample natural light, cheerful and familiar décor, and safe spaces for movement and relaxation. Creating areas where individuals can engage in enjoyable activities—such as gardens for light gardening, cozy reading nooks, or spaces for music and art therapy—can help maintain a sense of purpose and joy. Group activities, like singing, storytelling, or gentle exercise, can help build social connections, reduce feelings of isolation, and promote an atmosphere of camaraderie and shared optimism. A supportive and positive environment, both in its social and physical aspects, is essential for enhancing the emotional and psychological well-being of individuals with dementia.

Using Positive Language and Communication Techniques

Using positive language and effective communication techniques is essential in dementia care settings, as it directly impacts how individuals perceive themselves and their abilities. Caregivers should aim to use language that is affirmative, encouraging, and focused on what the person can do, rather than their limitations. For example, instead of saying, "Don't do that," a caregiver might say, "Let's try this together." This not only maintains dignity but also fosters a sense of collaboration and capability. Communication should be clear, slow, and accompanied by nonverbal cues, such as smiling and maintaining eye contact, which can help convey warmth, reassurance, and understanding.

Positive communication techniques also include active listening and validating the feelings of individuals with dementia. When a person expresses distress or confusion, instead of dismissing their concerns, caregivers can acknowledge their feelings by saying, "I understand you're feeling upset; let's see how we can make this better together." This approach validates their experience, which can reduce anxiety and promote trust. Additionally, using humor, when appropriate, and offering gentle compliments can uplift mood and enhance social interactions. By maintaining a focus on positive language and supportive communication, caregivers can significantly impact the emotional health and quality of life for individuals with dementia, helping them feel more connected, respected, and secure.

Understanding and Implementing Mindfulness

Benefits of Mindfulness for Dementia Patients and Their Families

Implementing mindfulness strategies can yield numerous benefits for dementia patients and their families. For patients, mindfulness can help reduce agitation, anxiety, and depression, fostering a greater sense of peace and improving cognitive functioning. By focusing on the present moment, patients may experience enhanced emotional regulation and a stronger connection to their surroundings.

Family members, often acting as caregivers, also stand to gain significantly from mindfulness practices (Shim et al., 2021). Mindfulness can alleviate caregiver stress, prevent burnout, and improve emotional well-being. By adopting a mindful approach, caregivers can cultivate patience, empathy, and resilience, which are essential qualities when providing long-term care for a loved one with dementia. Additionally, mindfulness can enhance communication and strengthen the emotional bond between the patient and their family.

Strategies for Implementing Mindfulness Techniques

To effectively incorporate mindfulness into dementia care, the following strategies can be employed:

1. **Mindful Breathing**: Simple breathing exercises can help both patients and caregivers develop a sense of calm. Encouraging patients to take slow, deep breaths while focusing on the sensation of the breath can reduce anxiety and bring attention to the present moment. Caregivers can practice mindful breathing during stressful moments to regain composure and clarity.
2. **Guided Imagery**: This technique involves guiding patients through a series of visualizations to evoke a sense of peace and relaxation. Caregivers can describe serene scenes, such as a walk on a beach or a quiet forest, helping patients to mentally escape from their immediate stressors.
3. **Body Scan Meditation**: This practice involves directing attention to different parts of the body, noticing sensations without judgment. It can help patients become more attuned to their physical state and reduce discomfort. Caregivers can guide patients through the body scan or use it themselves to manage their own stress.
4. **Mindful Activities**: Incorporating mindfulness into daily activities can make the practice more accessible. Activities such as mindful eating, where participants focus on the taste, texture, and aroma of food, or mindful walking, where attention is placed on the sensations of movement, can be beneficial. These activities encourage patients to engage with their environment in a meaningful way.
5. **Mindful Listening**: Encouraging mindful listening during conversations can enhance communication. Caregivers can practice being fully present and attentive to the patient without interrupting or planning their response. This fosters a deeper connection and understanding.

By integrating these mindfulness strategies into dementia care, both patients and their family members can experience improved emotional well-being, reduced stress, and a stronger sense of connection (Berk et al., 2018; Shim et al., 2021). Mindfulness offers a compassionate approach to navigating the challenges of dementia, promoting a more positive and fulfilling caregiving experience.

Case Studies and Practical Applications

Case Studies Illustrating the Impact of Positive Psychology and Mindfulness on Individuals With Dementia

Positive psychology and mindfulness (Innis et al., 2021) have shown promising results in enhancing the well-being of individuals with dementia. Consider the case of Mrs. Thompson, an 80-year-old woman diagnosed with Alzheimer's disease. Her caregivers introduced mindfulness practices such as guided imagery and deep breathing exercises to help manage her anxiety and agitation. Over time, Mrs. Thompson exhibited a noticeable reduction in stress levels, as evidenced by fewer episodes of confusion and an improved sleep pattern. Additionally, incorporating elements of positive psychology, such as gratitude journaling and reminiscing about cherished memories, significantly uplifted her mood. Mrs. Thompson began to express more joy and contentment, even in the face of cognitive decline.

Similarly, Mr. Garcia, a 75-year-old man with vascular dementia, benefited from a combined approach of mindfulness and positive psychology. His caregivers implemented a routine of mindful walking and sensory awareness exercises, which helped ground him in the present moment. Coupled with strengths-based interventions like focusing on his artistic abilities, Mr. Garcia experienced an enhanced sense of purpose and self-worth. These strategies not only improved his cognitive function but also strengthened the emotional bond with his family members, who participated in art sessions and mindfulness activities together.

Practical Examples of How Students Can Apply These Concepts in Caregiving Settings

Students in counseling and related fields can play a pivotal role in integrating positive psychology and mindfulness strategies in caregiving settings. One practical example is the implementation of a "Mindful Moments" program in residential care facilities, where students lead short, daily mindfulness sessions for residents. These sessions can include breathing exercises, body scans, and mindful listening activities, tailored to the cognitive abilities of individuals with dementia. By creating a calm and supportive environment, students help reduce anxiety and promote relaxation among residents.

In addition to mindfulness practices, students can facilitate positive psychology interventions by encouraging residents to engage in activities that foster positive emotions and social connections. For instance, they can organize "Gratitude Circles," where residents share things they are thankful for, or "Memory Lane" sessions, where they reminisce about past experiences and achievements. These activities not only enhance emotional well-being but also provide opportunities for meaningful interactions between residents and their families.

Furthermore, students can collaborate with caregivers to develop personalized care plans that incorporate strengths-based approaches. By identifying and leveraging each individual's unique skills and interests, students can help create a more engaging and fulfilling daily routine for patients with dementia. For example, if a resident has a passion for gardening, students can assist in setting up a small garden space where the resident can actively participate in planting and nurturing plants. This not only promotes a sense of accomplishment but also provides therapeutic benefits through connection to nature.

Integrating positive psychology and mindfulness strategies offers a holistic approach to improving the quality of life for individuals with dementia and their families. These interventions can significantly enhance emotional well-being, cognitive function, and social relationships. By applying these concepts in caregiving settings, we can foster a compassionate and supportive environment for those affected by dementia.

Ethical Considerations and Challenges

Ethical Implications Positive Psychology and Mindfulness in Dementia Care

Implementing positive psychology and mindfulness in dementia care may bring forth ethical implications. One primary concern is ensuring that interventions are person-centered and respect the autonomy and dignity of patients. Given the cognitive impairments associated with dementia, obtaining informed consent can be complex; patients might not fully grasp the nature of these interventions or their potential benefits and risks (Paller et al., 2015). Therefore, it is crucial to engage family members and caregivers in the decision-making process while prioritizing the patient's best interests and expressed wishes. Additionally, there is an ethical responsibility to ensure that these practices are evidence-based and tailored to the individual's needs, avoiding a one-size-fits-all approach that could inadvertently cause harm (Cheng et al., 2019, 2020).

Challenges and Barriers in Adopting These Approaches

Challenges and barriers may hinder the adoption of positive psychology and mindfulness in dementia care. First, there is a general lack of awareness and understanding among healthcare providers and caregivers about the benefits of these practices. Additionally, the progressive nature of dementia means that patients' abilities to engage in mindfulness exercises may diminish over time, requiring constant adaptation of approaches. Cultural and individual differences also play a significant role; what works for one patient might not resonate with another, necessitating a highly personalized approach. Moreover, limited resources and training opportunities for caregivers can impede the effective implementation of these interventions, leaving many ill-equipped to incorporate them into daily care routines.

Strategies for Addressing Ethical Concerns and Overcoming Challenges

To address these ethical concerns and overcome the challenges, several strategies can be employed. Developing comprehensive training programs for healthcare providers and caregivers is essential to enhance their understanding and ability to apply positive psychology and mindfulness techniques effectively. This training should include ethical guidelines and practical skills for obtaining informed consent and tailoring interventions to individual needs (Bisson et al., 2024). Creating interdisciplinary teams that include psychologists, social workers, and medical professionals can ensure a holistic approach to care, where ethical considerations are continuously monitored and addressed. Additionally, fostering open communication and collaboration between caregivers, family members, and patients can help in customizing interventions that respect the patient's preferences and cultural background. Finally, advocating for increased funding and resources dedicated to dementia care can help bridge the gap in accessibility and support the sustainable integration of these beneficial practices (Bisson et al., 2024).

While integrating positive psychology and mindfulness into dementia care presents ethical challenges and practical barriers, a thoughtful, inclusive, and well-resourced approach can help mitigate these issues. Through prioritizing person-centered care and fostering a collaborative environment, we can enhance the quality of life for patients with dementia and their families (Vespa et al., 2022).

Future Directions and Conclusion

Potential Avenues for Further Research

The integration of positive psychology and mindfulness in dementia care presents a promising landscape for enhancing the quality of life for individuals with dementia, their caregivers, and the healthcare systems that support them. As the prevalence of dementia continues to rise globally, there is an increasing need for innovative strategies that go beyond traditional medical and pharmaceutical interventions. Therefore, it is imperative to thoughtfully consider the future of dementia care and identify avenues for further scholarly investigation.

Efficacy of Positive Psychology Interventions

Research could focus on developing and testing specific positive psychology interventions (PPIs) tailored to the needs of people with dementia. This includes exploring strategies such as gratitude exercises, strengths-based approaches, and fostering positive emotions. Studies could aim to measure the impact of these interventions on mental health outcomes, such as depression and anxiety, as well as on cognitive decline.

Mindfulness Practices and Cognitive Function

Further research is needed to evaluate the impact of mindfulness practices on cognitive functions in individuals with dementia. Investigating the potential for mindfulness exercises to slow cognitive decline or enhance cognitive reserve would provide valuable insights. Studies could examine the neurological mechanisms underlying these effects and explore the role of mindfulness in neuroplasticity.

Caregiver Well-being and Support

The well-being of caregivers is crucial in dementia care. Research could further explore how positive psychology and mindfulness interventions can reduce caregiver stress and burnout. This may include assessing the benefits of mindfulness training programs for caregivers, as well as interventions designed to enhance their resilience and emotional well-being.

Social and Emotional Connections

Exploring how mindfulness and positive psychology can foster social and emotional connections among individuals with dementia is another rich area for research. This could involve studying group-based interventions that encourage social interaction, empathy, and compassion, potentially improving quality of life and reducing feelings of isolation.

Cultural and Contextual Adaptations

Cultural and contextual factors play a significant role in the acceptance and effectiveness of interventions. Research could focus on adapting positive psychology and mindfulness practices to diverse cultural contexts within dementia care. This includes understanding how cultural differences influence perceptions of mindfulness and positivity and tailoring interventions accordingly.

Longitudinal Studies on Quality of Life

Longitudinal research is essential to assess the long-term effects of integrating positive psychology and mindfulness in dementia care. Studies could track changes in quality of life, emotional well-being, and cognitive functioning over extended periods, providing insights into the sustainability and cumulative benefits of these interventions.

Integration Into Standard Care Practices

Investigating how positive psychology and mindfulness can be seamlessly integrated into standard dementia care practices is another important research avenue. This includes examining the feasibility, cost-effectiveness, and scalability of implementing these approaches in various care settings, from home-based care to institutional environments.

Technology-Enhanced Interventions

With the advancement of technology, there is potential to develop innovative, technology-enhanced interventions that incorporate positive psychology and mindfulness. Research could explore the use of apps, virtual reality, and online platforms to deliver these interventions, making them more accessible to a broader audience.

The integration of positive psychology and mindfulness into dementia care holds great promise for enhancing the well-being of individuals with dementia and their caregivers. Exploring these research avenues would allow for the development of evidence-based practices that improve care outcomes and contribute to a more compassionate and supportive care environment.

Summary of Key Points

The integration of positive psychology and mindfulness into dementia care marks a transformative shift in addressing the comprehensive needs of individuals with dementia and their caregivers. This chapter has underscored the profound impact that fostering positive emotions, strengths, and virtues through positive psychology can have on enhancing the quality of life for those affected by dementia. By creating an environment that emphasizes present-moment awareness and acceptance, mindfulness practices offer a meaningful way to support cognitive and emotional well-being.

Understanding the diverse manifestations of dementia, including Alzheimer's disease, frontotemporal dementia, vascular dementia, and Lewy body dementia, is crucial for developing tailored care approaches. This chapter has provided an insightful overview of these conditions, laying the groundwork for the application of positive psychology and mindfulness strategies in various care settings. The power of positive psychology lies in its ability to transform care environments by promoting positivity and resilience. Strategies highlighted in this chapter offer a roadmap for integrating these principles into daily care practices, ultimately leading to improved mental health outcomes for individuals with dementia and reducing caregiver stress and burnout.

Mindfulness, as explored in this chapter, provides a complementary approach that enhances the emotional and cognitive aspects of dementia care. By fostering a sense of calm and acceptance, mindfulness can help individuals with dementia navigate the challenges of their condition with greater ease and grace. Through case studies and practical examples, this chapter has illustrated the tangible benefits of these approaches in both caregiving and educational contexts. By adopting these progressive strategies, caregivers, families, and educators can create compassionate, supportive environments that prioritize the well-being of individuals with dementia. In conclusion, the integration of positive psychology and mindfulness into dementia care offers a promising avenue for enhancing the lives of individuals with dementia and their caregivers. Continuing to explore and refine these approaches can pave the way for more holistic and effective care practices that support the diverse needs of those impacted by dementia.

References

Akhter, F., Persaud, A., Zaokari, Y., Zhao, Z., & Zhu, D. (2021). Vascular dementia and underlying sex differences. *Frontiers in Aging Neuroscience*, *13*, 720715. https://doi.org/10.3389/fnagi.2021.720715

Alzheimer's Disease International. (2023). *World Alzheimer Report 2023: Reducing dementia risk: Never too early, never too late.* https://www.alzint.org/resource/world-alzheimer-report-2023/

American Psychiatric Association. (2013). *Diagnostic and statistical manual of mental disorders* (5th ed.). American Psychiatric Association.

Arvanitakis, Z., Shah, R. C., & Bennett, D. A. (2019). *Diagnosis and management of dementia: Review. JAMA*, *322*(16), 1589–1599. https://doi.org/10.1001/jama.2019.4782

Auning, E., Rongve, A., Fladby, T., Booij, J., Hortobágyi, T., Siepel, F. J., Ballard, C., & Aarsland, D. (2011). Early and presenting symptoms of dementia with lewy bodies. *Dementia and Geriatric Cognitive Disorders*, *32*(3), 202–208. https://doi.org/10.1159/000333072

Ballard, C., Neill, D., O'Brien, J., McKeith, I. G., Ince, P., & Perry, R. (2000). Anxiety, depression and psychosis in vascular dementia: Prevalence and associations. *Journal of Affective Disorders*, *59*(2), 97–106. https://doi.org/10.1016/s0165-0327(99)00057-9

Bergeron, D., Gorno-Tempini, M. L., Rabinovici, G. D., Santos-Santos, M. A., Seeley, W., Miller, B. L., Pijnenburg, Y., Keulen, M. A., Groot, C., van Berckel, B. N. M., van der Flier, W. M., Scheltens, P., Rohrer, J. D., Warren, J. D., Schott, J. M., Fox, N. C., Sanchez-Valle, R., Grau-Rivera, O., Gelpi, E., … Ossenkoppele, R. (2018). Prevalence of amyloid-β pathology in distinct variants of primary progressive aphasia. *Annals of Neurology*, *84*(5), 729–740. https://doi.org/10.1002/ana.25333

Berk, L., Warmenhoven, F., van Os, J., & van Boxtel, M. (2018). Mindfulness training for people with dementia and their caregivers: Rationale, current research, and future directions. *Frontiers in Psychology*, *9*. https://doi.org/10.3389/fpsyg.2018.00982

Bir, S. C., Khan, M. W., Javalkar, V., Toledo, E. G., & Kelley, R. E. (2021). Emerging concepts in vascular dementia: A review. *Journal of Stroke and Cerebrovascular Diseases: The Official Journal of National Stroke Association*, *30*(8), 105864. https://doi.org/10.1016/j.jstrokecerebrovasdis.2021.105864

Bisson, S., Sinclair, C., & Djuraskovic, I. (2024). *Ethics in action: Personal reflections of Canadian psychologists*. University of Calgary.

Bolier, L., Haverman, M., Westerhof, G. J., Riper, H., Smit, F., & Bohlmeijer, E. (2013). Positive psychology interventions: A meta-analysis of randomized controlled studies. *BMC Public Health*, *13*(1), 119. https://doi.org/10.1186/1471-2458-13-119

Botha, H., & Josephs, K. A. (2019). Primary progressive aphasias and apraxia of speech. *Continuum (Minneapolis, Minn.)*, *25*(1), 101–127. https://doi.org/10.1212/CON.0000000000000699

Brockman, R., Ciarrochi, J., Parker, P., & Kashdan, T. (2017). Emotion regulation strategies in daily life: Mindfulness, cognitive reappraisal and emotion suppression. *Cognitive Behaviour Therapy*, *46*(2), 91–113. https://doi.org/10.1080/16506073.2016.1218926

Burrell, J. R., Halliday, G. M., Kril, J. J., Ittner, L. M., Götz, J., Kiernan, M. C., & Hodges, J. R. (2016). The frontotemporal dementia-motor neuron disease continuum. *The Lancet*, *388*(10047), 919–931. https://doi.org/10.1016/S0140-6736(16)00737-6

Carr, A., Cullen, K., Keeney, C., Canning, C., Mooney, O., Chinseallaigh, E., & O'Dowd, A. (2021). Effectiveness of positive psychology interventions: A systematic review and meta-analysis. *The Journal of Positive Psychology*, *16*(6), 749–769. https://doi.org/10.1080/17439760.2020.1818807

Chan, D., Anderson, V., Pijnenburg, Y., Whitwell, J., Barnes, J., Scahill, R., Stevens, J. M., Barkhof, F., Scheltens, P., Rossor, M. N., & Fox, N. C. (2009). The clinical profile of right temporal lobe atrophy. *Brain: A Journal of Neurology*, *132*(Pt 5), 1287–1298. https://doi.org/10.1093/brain/awp037

Chen, J., Xiao, H., Chen, Y., Sun, H., Chen, S., & Zheng, J. (2020). Effect of reminiscence therapy based on positive psychology theory (RTBPPT) on the positive feelings of the spousal caregivers of elderly patients with advanced cancer in China. *European Journal of Cancer Care*, *29*(6), e13324. https://doi.org/10.1111/ecc.13324

Cheng, S.-T., Au, A., Losada, A., Thompson, L. W., & Gallagher-Thompson, D. (2019). Psychological interventions for dementia caregivers: What we have achieved, what we have learned. *Current Psychiatry Reports*, *21*(7), 59. https://doi.org/10.1007/s11920-019-1045-9

Cheng, S.-T., Li, K.-K., Losada, A., Zhang, F., Au, A., Thompson, L. W., & Gallagher-Thompson, D. (2020). The effectiveness of nonpharmacological interventions for informal dementia caregivers: An updated systematic review and meta-analysis. *Psychology and Aging*, *35*(1), 55–77. https://doi.org/10.1037/pag0000401

Choudhury, P., Graff-Radford, J., Aakre, J. A., Wurtz, L., Knopman, D. S., Graff-Radford, N. R., Kantarci, K., Forsberg, L. K., Fields, J. A., Pedraza, O., Chen, Q., Miyagawa, T., Day, G. S., Tipton, P., Savica, R., Botha, H., Lachner, C., Dredla, B., Reichard, R. R., … Ferman, T. J. (2022). The temporal onset of the core features in dementia with Lewy bodies. *Alzheimer's & Dementia : The Journal of the Alzheimer's Association*, *18*(4), 591–601. https://doi.org/10.1002/alz.12411

Collins, R. N., & Kishita, N. (2019). The effectiveness of mindfulness- and acceptance-based interventions for informal caregivers of people with dementia: A meta-analysis. *The Gerontologist*, *59*(4), e363–e379. https://doi.org/10.1093/geront/gny024

Crutch, S. J., Schott, J. M., Rabinovici, G. D., Murray, M., Snowden, J. S., van der Flier, W. M., Dickerson, B. C., Vandenberghe, R., Ahmed, S., Bak, T. H., Boeve, B. F., Butler, C., Cappa, S. F., Ceccaldi, M., de Souza, L. C., Dubois, B., Felician, O., Galasko, D., Graff-Radford, J., … Fox, N. C. (2017). Consensus classification of posterior cortical atrophy. *Alzheimer's & Dementia : The Journal of the Alzheimer's Association*, *13*(8), 870–884. https://doi.org/10.1016/j.jalz.2017.01.014

D'Onofrio, G., Sancarlo, D., Panza, F., Copetti, M., Cascavilla, L., Paris, F., Seripa, D., Matera, M. G., Solfrizzi, V., Pellegrini, F., & Pilotto, A. (2012). Neuropsychiatric symptoms and functional status in Alzheimer's disease and vascular dementia patients. *Current Alzheimer Research*, *9*(6), 759–771. https://doi.org/10.2174/156720512801322582

Emre, M., Aarsland, D., Brown, R., Burn, D. J., Duyckaerts, C., Mizuno, Y., Broe, G. A., Cummings, J., Dickson, D. W., Gauthier, S., Goldman, J., Goetz, C., Korczyn, A., Lees, A., Levy, R., Litvan,

I., McKeith, I., Olanow, W., Poewe, W., … Dubois, B. (2007). Clinical diagnostic criteria for dementia associated with Parkinson's disease. *Movement Disorders: Official Journal of the Movement Disorder Society*, *22*(12), 1689–1707; quiz 1837. https://doi.org/10.1002/mds.21507

Ghosh, S., & Lippa, C. F. (2015). Clinical subtypes of frontotemporal dementia. *American Journal of Alzheimer's Disease and Other Dementias*, *30*(7), 653–661. https://doi.org/10.1177/1533317513494442

Graham, N. L., Emery, T., & Hodges, J. R. (2004). Distinctive cognitive profiles in Alzheimer's disease and subcortical vascular dementia. *Journal of Neurology, Neurosurgery, and Psychiatry*, *75*(1), 61–71.

Grossman, M. (2012). The non-fluent/agrammatic variant of primary progressive aphasia. *The Lancet. Neurology*, *11*(6), 545–555. https://doi.org/10.1016/S1474-4422(12)70099-6

Hofmann, S. G., & Gómez, A. F. (2017). Mindfulness-based interventions for anxiety and depression. *The Psychiatric Clinics of North America*, *40*(4), 739–749. https://doi.org/10.1016/j.psc.2017.08.008

Innis, A. D., Tolea, M. I., & Galvin, J. E. (2021). The effect of baseline patient and caregiver mindfulness on dementia outcomes. *Journal of Alzheimer's Disease: JAD*, *79*(3), 1345–1367. https://doi.org/10.3233/JAD-201292

Jellinger, K. A. (2003). Neuropathological spectrum of synucleinopathies. *Movement Disorders: Official Journal of the Movement Disorder Society*, *18* (Suppl 6), S2–12. https://doi.org/10.1002/mds.10557

Jessen, F., Amariglio, R. E., van Boxtel, M., Breteler, M., Ceccaldi, M., Chételat, G., Dubois, B., Dufouil, C., Ellis, K. A., van der Flier, W. M., Glodzik, L., van Harten, A. C., de Leon, M. J., McHugh, P., Mielke, M. M., Molinuevo, J. L., Mosconi, L., Osorio, R. S., Perrotin, A., … Subjective Cognitive Decline Initiative (SCD-I) Working Group. (2014). A conceptual framework for research on subjective cognitive decline in preclinical Alzheimer's disease. *Alzheimer's & Dementia: The Journal of the Alzheimer's Association*, *10*(6), 844–852. https://doi.org/10.1016/j.jalz.2014.01.001

Josephs, K. A., Whitwell, J. L., Knopman, D. S., Boeve, B. F., Vemuri, P., Senjem, M. L., Parisi, J. E., Ivnik, R. J., Dickson, D. W., Petersen, R. C., & Jack, C. R. J. (2009). Two distinct subtypes of right temporal variant frontotemporal dementia. *Neurology*, *73*(18), 1443–1450. https://doi.org/10.1212/WNL.0b013e3181bf9945

Korczyn, A. D., Vakhapova, V., & Grinberg, L. T. (2012). Vascular dementia. *Journal of the Neurological Sciences*, *322*(1-2), 2–10. https://doi.org/10.1016/j.jns.2012.03.027

Lee, A. Y. (2011). Vascular dementia. *Chonnam Medical Journal*, *47*(2), 66–71. https://doi.org/10.4068/cmj.2011.47.2.66

Lehmann, M., Ghosh, P. M., Madison, C., Laforce, R., Corbetta-Rastelli, C., Weiner, M. W., Greicius, M. D., Seeley, W. W., Gorno-Tempini, M. L., Rosen, H. J., Miller, B. L., Jagust, W. J., & Rabinovici, G. D. (2013). Diverging patterns of amyloid deposition and hypometabolism in clinical variants of probable Alzheimer's disease. *Brain: A Journal of Neurology*, *136*(Pt 3), 844–858. https://doi.org/10.1093/brain/aws327

Lim, W. L., & Tierney, S. (2023). The effectiveness of positive psychology interventions for promoting well-being of adults experiencing depression compared to other active psychological treatments: A systematic review and meta-analysis. *Journal of Happiness Studies*, *24*(1), 249–273. https://doi.org/10.1007/s10902-022-00598-z

Logroscino, G., Piccininni, M., Graff, C., Hardiman, O., Ludolph, A. C., Moreno, F., Otto, M., Remes, A. M., Rowe, J. B., Seelaar, H., Solje, E., Stefanova, E., Traykov, L., Jelic, V., Rydell, M. T., Pender, N., Anderl-Straub, S., Barandiaran, M., Gabilondo, A., … FRONTIERS group. (2023). Incidence of syndromes associated with frontotemporal lobar degeneration in 9 European Countries. *JAMA Neurology*, *80*(3), 279–286. https://doi.org/10.1001/jamaneurol.2022.5128

Macoir, J. (2024). Language impairment in vascular dementia: A clinical review. *Journal of Geriatric Psychiatry and Neurology*, *37*(2), 87–95. https://doi.org/10.1177/08919887231195225

Marshall, C. R., Hardy, C. J. D., Volkmer, A., Russell, L. L., Bond, R. L., Fletcher, P. D., Clark, C. N., Mummery, C. J., Schott, J. M., Rossor, M. N., Fox, N. C., Crutch, S. J., Rohrer, J. D., & Warren, J. D. (2018). Primary progressive aphasia: A clinical approach. *Journal of Neurology*, *265*(6), 1474–1490. https://doi.org/10.1007/s00415-018-8762-6

McKeith, I. G., Boeve, B. F., Dickson, D. W., Halliday, G., Taylor, J.-P., Weintraub, D., Aarsland, D., Galvin, J., Attems, J., Ballard, C. G., Bayston, A., Beach, T. G., Blanc, F., Bohnen, N., Bonanni, L., Bras, J., Brundin, P., Burn, D., Chen-Plotkin, A., … Kosaka, K. (2017). Diagnosis and management of dementia with Lewy bodies: Fourth consensus report of the DLB Consortium. *Neurology*, *89*(1), 88–100. https://doi.org/10.1212/WNL.0000000000004058

McKhann, G. M., Knopman, D. S., Chertkow, H., Hyman, B. T., Jack, C. R., Kawas, C. H., Klunk, W. E., Koroshetz, W. J., Manly, J. J., Mayeux, R., Mohs, R. C., Morris, J. C., Rossor, M. N., Scheltens, P., Carrillo, M. C., Thies, B., Weintraub, S., & Phelps, C. H. (2011). The diagnosis of dementia due to Alzheimer's disease: Recommendations from the National Institute on Aging-Alzheimer's Association workgroups on diagnostic guidelines for Alzheimer's disease. *Alzheimer's & Dementia: The Journal of the Alzheimer's Association*, *7*(3), 263–269. https://doi.org/10.1016/j.jalz.2011.03.005

McRae, K., Ciesielski, B., & Gross, J. J. (2012). Unpacking cognitive reappraisal: Goals, tactics, and outcomes. *Emotion*, *12*(2), 250–255. https://doi.org/10.1037/a0026351

Molero Jurado, M. D. M., Pérez-Fuentes, M. D. C., Barragán Martín, A. B., Soriano Sánchez, J. G., Oropesa Ruiz, N. F., Sisto, M., & Gázquez Linares, J. J. (2020). Mindfulness in family caregivers of persons with dementia: Systematic review and meta-analysis. *Healthcare (Basel, Switzerland)*, *8*(3). https://doi.org/10.3390/healthcare8030193

Moniz-Cook, E., Woods, B., Killick, J., Nolan, M., Ryan, T., Quinn, C., Norris, A., Patterson, K., Harris, P., Irwin, H., Phinney, A., Stirling, E., Bryden, C., Stoner, C., & Spector, A. (2016). *Positive psychology approaches to dementia* (Chris Clarke, Emma Wolverson). Jessica Kingsley Publishers.

Moretti, R., Torre, P., Antonello, R. M., Esposito, F., & Bellini, G. (2011). Gait and equilibrium in subcortical vascular dementia. *Current Gerontology and Geriatrics Research*, *2011*, 263507. https://doi.org/10.1155/2011/263507

Ossenkoppele, R., Schonhaut, D. R., Schöll, M., Lockhart, S. N., Ayakta, N., Baker, S. L., O'Neil, J. P., Janabi, M., Lazaris, A., Cantwell, A., Vogel, J., Santos, M., Miller, Z. A., Bettcher, B. M., Vossel, K. A., Kramer, J. H., Gorno-Tempini, M. L., Miller, B. L., Jagust, W. J., & Rabinovici, G. D. (2016). Tau PET patterns mirror clinical and neuroanatomical variability in Alzheimer's disease. *Brain: A Journal of Neurology*, *139*(Pt 5), 1551–1567. https://doi.org/10.1093/brain/aww027

Paller, K. A., Creery, J. D., Florczak, S. M., Weintraub, S., Mesulam, M.-M., Reber, P. J., Kiragu, J., Rooks, J., Safron, A., Morhardt, D., O'Hara, M., Gigler, K. L., Molony, J. M., & Maslar, M. (2015). Benefits of mindfulness training for patients with progressive cognitive decline and their caregivers. *American Journal of Alzheimer's Disease and Other Dementias*, *30*(3), 257–267. https://doi.org/10.1177/1533317514545377

Petersen, R. C. (2004). Mild cognitive impairment as a diagnostic entity. *Journal of Internal Medicine*, *256*(3), 183–194. https://doi.org/10.1111/j.1365-2796.2004.01388.x

Pione, R. D., Spector, A., Cartwright, A. V., & Stoner, C. R. (2021). A psychometric appraisal of positive psychology outcome measures in use with carers of people living with dementia: A systematic review. *International Psychogeriatrics*, *33*(4), 385–404. https://doi.org/10.1017/S1041610220003464

Plassman, B. L., Langa, K. M., Fisher, G. G., Heeringa, S. G., Weir, D. R., Ofstedal, M. B., Burke, J. R., Hurd, M. D., Potter, G. G., Rodgers, W. L., Steffens, D. C., Willis, R. J., & Wallace, R. B. (2007). Prevalence of dementia in the United States: The aging, demographics, and memory study. *Neuroepidemiology*, *29*(1–2), 125–132. https://doi.org/10.1159/000109998

Riepenhausen, A., Wackerhagen, C., Reppmann, Z. C., Deter, H.-C., Kalisch, R., Veer, I. M., & Walter, H. (2022). Positive cognitive reappraisal in stress resilience, mental health, and well-being: A comprehensive systematic review. *Emotion Review*, *14*(4), 310–331. https://doi.org/10.1177/17540739221114642

Riley, R. J., Burgener, S., & Buckwalter, K. C. (2014). Anxiety and stigma in dementia: A threat to aging in place. *The Nursing Clinics of North America*, *49*(2), 213–231. https://doi.org/10.1016/j.cnur.2014.02.008

Rodríguez de Rivera, F. J., Rambold, H. A., & Díez-Tejedor, E. (2014). Assessment of cognitive impairment in amyotrophic lateral sclerosis. *Journal of the Neurological Sciences*, *337*(1–2), 1–2. https://doi.org/10.1016/j.jns.2013.11.030

Santos, V., Paes, F., Pereira, V., Arias-Carrión, O., Silva, A. C., Carta, M. G., Nardi, A. E., & Machado, S. (2013). The role of positive emotion and contributions of positive psychology in depression treatment: Systematic review. *Clinical Practice and Epidemiology in Mental Health : CP & EMH*, *9*, 221–237. https://doi.org/10.2174/1745017901309010221

Seeley, W. W. (2019). Behavioral variant frontotemporal dementia. *Continuum (Minneapolis, Minn.)*, *25*(1), 76–100. https://doi.org/10.1212/CON.0000000000000698

Seligman, M., & Csikszentmihalyi, M. (2000). *Positive psychology: An introduction.* American *Psychologist*, 55(1), 5–14. https://psycnet.apa.org/record/2000-13324-001

Shen, J., & Kelleher, R. J. (2007). The presenilin hypothesis of Alzheimer's disease: Evidence for a loss-of-function pathogenic mechanism. *Proceedings of the National Academy of Sciences*, *104*(2), 403–409. https://doi.org/10.1073/pnas.0608332104

Shim, M., Tilley, J. L., Im, S., Price, K., & Gonzalez, A. (2021). A systematic review of mindfulness-based interventions for patients with mild cognitive impairment or dementia and caregivers. *Journal of Geriatric Psychiatry and Neurology*, *34*(6), 528–554. https://doi.org/10.1177/0891988720957104

Siegel, R. D., Germer, C. K., & Olendzki, A. (2009). Mindfulness: What is it? Where did it come from? In F. Didonna (Ed.), *Clinical handbook of mindfulness* (pp. 17–35). Springer. https://doi.org/10.1007/978-0-387-09593-6_2

Siette, J., Meka, A., & Antoniades, J. (2023). Breaking the barriers: Overcoming dementia-related stigma in minority communities. *Frontiers in Psychiatry*, *14*, 1278944. https://doi.org/10.3389/fpsyt.2023.1278944

Snowden, J. S., Harris, J. M., Thompson, J. C., Kobylecki, C., Jones, M., Richardson, A. M., & Neary, D. (2018). Semantic dementia and the left and right temporal lobes. *Cortex; A Journal Devoted to the Study of the Nervous System and Behavior*, *107*, 188–203. https://doi.org/10.1016/j.cortex.2017.08.024

Stoner, C. R., Stansfeld, J., Orrell, M., & Spector, A. (2019). The development of positive psychology outcome measures and their uses in dementia research: A systematic review. *Dementia (London, England)*, *18*(6), 2085–2106. https://doi.org/10.1177/1471301217740288

Strittmatter, W. J., Saunders, A. M., Schmechel, D., Pericak-Vance, M., Enghild, J., Salvesen, G. S., & Roses, A. D. (1993). Apolipoprotein E: High-avidity binding to beta-amyloid and increased frequency of type 4 allele in late-onset familial Alzheimer disease. *Proceedings of the National Academy of Sciences*, *90*(5), 1977–1981. https://doi.org/10.1073/pnas.90.5.1977

Sudo, F. K., Amado, P., Alves, G. S., Laks, J., & Engelhardt, E. (2017). A continuum of executive function deficits in early subcortical vascular cognitive impairment: A systematic review and meta-analysis. *Dementia & Neuropsychologia*, *11*(4), 371–380. https://doi.org/10.1590/1980-57642016dn11-040006

Sun, L., Zhou, R., Yang, G., & Shi, Y. (2017). Analysis of 138 pathogenic mutations in presenilin-1 on the in vitro production of Aβ42 and Aβ40 peptides by γ-secretase. *Proceedings of the National Academy of Sciences of the United States of America*, *114*(4), E476–E485. https://doi.org/10.1073/pnas.1618657114

Tan, K. P., Ang, J. K., Koh, E. B. Y., Pang, N. T. P., & Mat Saher, Z. (2023). Relationship of psychological flexibility and mindfulness to caregiver burden, and depressive and anxiety symptoms in caregivers of people with dementia. *International Journal of Environmental Research and Public Health*, *20*(5). https://doi.org/10.3390/ijerph20054232

Taylor, J.-P., McKeith, I. G., Burn, D. J., Boeve, B. F., Weintraub, D., Bamford, C., Allan, L. M., Thomas, A. J., & O'Brien, J. T. (2020). New evidence on the management of Lewy body dementia. *The Lancet. Neurology*, *19*(2), 157–169. https://doi.org/10.1016/S1474-4422(19)30153-X

Tcw, J., & Goate, A. M. (2017). Genetics of β-amyloid precursor protein in Alzheimer's disease. *Cold Spring Harbor Perspectives in Medicine*, *7*(6), a024539. https://doi.org/10.1101/cshperspect.a024539

Townley, R. A., Graff-Radford, J., Mantyh, W. G., Botha, H., Polsinelli, A. J., Przybelski, S. A., Machulda, M. M., Makhlouf, A. T., Senjem, M. L., Murray, M. E., Reichard, R. R., Savica, R., Boeve, B. F., Drubach, D. A., Josephs, K. A., Knopman, D. S., Lowe, V. J., Jack, C. R. J., Petersen, R. C., & Jones, D. T. (2020). Progressive dysexecutive syndrome due to Alzheimer's disease: A description of 55 cases and comparison to other phenotypes. *Brain Communications*, *2*(1), fcaa068. https://doi.org/10.1093/braincomms/fcaa068

Tu, M.-C., Hsu, Y.-H., Yang, J.-J., Huang, W.-H., Deng, J. F., Lin, S.-Y., Lin, C.-Y., & Kuo, L.-W. (2020). Attention and functional connectivity among patients with early-stage subcortical ischemic vascular disease and Alzheimer's disease. *Frontiers in Aging Neuroscience*, *12*, 239. https://doi.org/10.3389/fnagi.2020.00239

Veronelli, L., Makaretz, S. J., Quimby, M., Dickerson, B. C., & Collins, J. A. (2017). Geschwind Syndrome in frontotemporal lobar degeneration: Neuroanatomical and neuropsychological features over 9 years. *Cortex; a Journal Devoted to the Study of the Nervous System and Behavior*, *94*, 27–38. https://doi.org/10.1016/j.cortex.2017.06.003

Vespa, A., Fabbietti, P., & Giulietti, M. V. (2022). Study of the effects of mindfulness training on quality of life of patients with Alzheimer's disease and their caregivers (Dyad Mindfulness Project). *Aging Clinical and Experimental Research*, *34*(1), 65–71. https://doi.org/10.1007/s40520-021-01907-x

Walker, Z., Possin, K. L., Boeve, B. F., & Aarsland, D. (2015). Lewy body dementias. *Lancet (London, England)*, *386*(10004), 1683–1697. https://doi.org/10.1016/S0140-6736(15)00462-6

Weisman de Mamani, A., Weintraub, M. J., Maura, J., Martinez de Andino, A., & Brown, C. A. (2018). The interplay among mindfulness, caregiver burden, and mental health in family members of individuals with dementia. *Professional Psychology: Research and Practice*, *49*(2), 116–123. https://doi.org/10.1037/pro0000181

Woods, B., O'Philbin, L., Farrell, E. M., Spector, A. E., & Orrell, M. (2018). Reminiscence therapy for dementia. *Cochrane Database of Systematic Reviews*, *3*. https://doi.org/10.1002/14651858.CD001120.pub3

Younes, K., & Miller, B. L. (2020). Neuropsychiatric aspects of frontotemporal dementia. *The Psychiatric Clinics of North America*, *43*(2), 345–360. https://doi.org/10.1016/j.psc.2020.02.005

Zekanowski, C., Styczyńska, M., Pepłońska, B., Gabryelewicz, T., Religa, D., Ilkowski, J., Kijanowska-Haładyna, B., Kotapka-Minc, S., Mikkelsen, S., Pfeffer, A., Barczak, A., Łuczywek, E., Wasiak, B., Chodakowska-Zebrowska, M., Gustaw, K., Łaczkowski, J., Sobów, T., Kuźnicki, J., & Barcikowska, M. (2003). Mutations in presenilin 1, presenilin 2 and amyloid precursor protein genes in patients with early-onset Alzheimer's disease in Poland. *Experimental Neurology*, *184*(2), 991–996. https://doi.org/10.1016/S0014-4886(03)00384-4

11

Positive Psychology and Mindfulness for Childhood Trauma

Lynn Jennings
Robert Paul Maddox II
Michele M. Mahr

KEYWORDS AND DEFINITIONS:

Abuse: Intentional, harmful, cruel, or violent, demeaning, and/or invasive interactions with another person (Tracy, 2021).

Adverse childhood experiences (ACEs): Traumatic events that occur in the life of a child prior to the age of 18 years old. These adverse experiences can be defined as child abuse or neglect, other forms of violence to or around the child, or exposure to substance use or abuse. ACEs are linked to increased physiological, mental, psychological, and relational issues throughout the lifespan (King-White, 2024).

Domestic violence: "A pattern of abusive behavior (physical, emotional, sexual) in any relationship that is used by one partner to exert power and control over another partner" (U.S. Department of Justice, 2024, para. 1). Children, until the mid-1980s, were not considered victims of domestic violence, but it is now clear that they are affected by domestic violence and show symptoms of trauma when raised in these environments (Edwards, 2019),

Neglect: The failure to adequately meet the primary physical and emotional needs of a child. These needs include the following: housing, food, clothing, education, medical care, and so on (Centers for Disease Control and Prevention, 2024).

PERMA model: A model in positive psychology developed by Martin Seligman. This model provides a framework to understand and enhance well-being through the following: positive emotions, engagement, relationships, meaning, and accomplishment (Seligman, 2011).

Posttraumatic stress disorder: "A mental health condition that's caused by an extremely stressful or terrifying event—either being part of it or witnessing it. Symptoms may include flashbacks, nightmares, severe anxiety and uncontrollable thoughts about the event" (Mayo Clinic, 2024).

Traumatic experiences: Intensely stressful events or situations that affect a person(s) on an emotional and physical level. These kinds of events can include, but are not limited to: natural disasters, acts of violence, and car accidents or crashes or other accidents (National Institute of Mental Health, 2024).

Traumatic shock: A defense mechanism your body enacts when faced with any sudden, terrible experience that disrupts your well-being and overwhelms you. Physical symptoms can include, but are not limited to: reduction of awareness of emotional or physical pain, numbness, reduction of cognizance of situation, and so on (Kleber, 2019).

LEARNING OBJECTIVES:

1. Identify childhood trauma.
2. Understand the types of childhood trauma.
3. Recognize the potential application of positive psychology and its benefits for individuals who experienced childhood trauma.
4. Explore the use of positive psychology attitudes and activities with a case example of an individual who experienced childhood trauma.

Overview of the Chapter

The purpose of this chapter is to provide information on childhood trauma and utilizing positive psychology and mindfulness as a treatment approach to childhood trauma and the emotional, psychological, and behavioral issues that stem from these experiences. This chapter will provide information concerning what childhood traumatic experiences that form part of the framework of how positive psychology and mindfulness could be applied and activities that can be utilized in the treatment of childhood trauma events. Last, the chapter will conclude with a case example, critical thinking questions, and an activity to assess the knowledge acquired in this chapter.

Throughout history, childhood traumatic experiences have been a growing topic of discussion in our society. However, until recently the impact, long term and short term, has been underrepresented or unstated altogether. Traumatic experiences are defined as events or situations that threaten the physical or the emotional well-being of a child that overwhelms their ability to cope with the situation (American Psychiatric Association, 2022). Navigating these traumatic experiences can be challenging for children and their caregivers as environmental, developmental, psychological, and psychosocial factors must be considered when planning a course of treatment for these trauma responses. Utilizing positive psychology and mindfulness, children and caregivers can more easily manage the symptoms exhibited, ideally shorten the length of time the symptoms are present, and improve the outcome for the child, overall.

Etiology of Childhood Trauma

Trauma is a profound psychological and physiological response to overwhelming experiences that exceed an individual's capacity to cope. It results in intense negative emotions linked to the perceived threat level (Blaustein, 2013; Van der Kolk, 2014). While trauma can affect anyone at any age, Adverse Childhood Experiences (ACEs) specifically refer to events that occur before age 18 that are potentially traumatic and can include abuse, neglect, exposure to violence, and familial experiences with substance use or mental health issues (Centers for Disease Control and Prevention, 2021).

While there are some shared similarities between ACEs and general trauma, there are also distinct differences in their characteristics. ACEs are limited to occurrences that take place in childhood and adolescence and focus on specific categories such as abuse, neglect, and household dysfunction. By contrast, trauma is often viewed as being broader in scope, occurring at any stage of life. Additionally, the ACEs framework emphasizes the potential cumulative impact of multiple adversities, while trauma can refer to single events or recurring experiences. ACEs research has often highlighted connections to adult health and behavior, while trauma studies have frequently focused more on immediate and mid-term impacts for survivors.

Both ACEs and general trauma share systemic consequences (Perry & Szalavitz, 2017), potentially leading to population-wide effects (Bender & Sims, 2007). These effects can include complex trauma and secondary or vicarious trauma resulting from community-wide events (Cénat & Dalexis, 2020; Collin-Vézina et al., 2020; Guessoum et al., 2020). Repeated exposure to traumatic events, whether classified as ACEs or not, can result in complex trauma with far-reaching developmental implications (National Child Traumatic Stress Network, 2012). The prevalence of both ACEs and trauma among children is significant. Felitti and Anda (2010) report that one in six school-aged children experience complex trauma, while over 50% have faced traumatic events or ACEs.

This high prevalence underscores the critical need for professionals to understand ACEs, trauma, overall human development, and the impact on children's physical, functional, and cognitive development. By recognizing the distinctions and overlaps between ACEs and general trauma, professionals can better tailor their approaches to support affected children and create trauma-informed environments.

Positive Psychology Through a Developmental Trauma Informed Lens—Integrating Creativity, Play, and Play-based Interventions

Experiencing ACEs and trauma can impact a child's overall development (Bender & Sims, 2006; Maddox et al., 2024; Perry & Szalavitz, 2017; Van der Kolk, 2014). Because of the potential developmental effects of ACEs and trauma, it is important to approach interventions from a developmental and trauma-informed perspective. The integration of creativity, play, and play-based interventions represents a developmentally appropriate approach for working with children. Play can be considered a form of communication, where play is viewed as a child's first language with toys or objects serving as their words (Landreth, 2023). Utilizing play and play-based interventions can help foster open communication and understanding between clinicians and children who have experienced ACEs and/or trauma. Facilitating greater understanding between children and adults, play as a natural form of communication for children can help facilitate an environment that aligns with the six core principles of trauma-informed care: (a) safety; (b) trustworthiness; (c) peer support; (d) empowerment, voice, and choice; (e) recognition of the potential impacts of cultural, historical, and gender issues; and (f) collaboration and mutuality (Centers for Disease Control and Prevention, 2018). Through play in the therapeutic process, children can experience (a) greater safety, (b) build trust, (c) engage in mutual self-help and peer support, (d) collaborate and have mutuality in their relationship with a clinician, (e) exercise their ability to have a greater voice and choice within the therapeutic process, and (f) participate in a culturally and developmentally responsive therapeutic process.

Play also represents a vital factor in the cognitive and social-emotional development of children (Pearson & Cordiano, 2010). As such, incorporating play and play-based positive psychology interventions (PPIs) within a trauma-informed care framework can be a developmentally responsive approach for addressing the impacts of trauma and ACEs in children. Pretend-play in particular has been shown to have connections with numerous developmental processes concerning adaptive functioning (Pearson & Cordiano, 2010; Russ, 2004). Through play, children engage in processes related to cognitive, affective, and interpersonal development that can contribute to their optimal functioning. The processes involved in play, such as creativity, emotional regulation, self-awareness, empathy, and coping (Pearson et al., 2008), can also relate to areas that align well with core elements of PPIs and the PERMA Model.

Application of Positive Psychology for Individuals Who Experienced Childhood Trauma

Positive psychology may be an effective practice to implement when working with individuals who have experienced past childhood trauma. The repercussions of childhood trauma have been mentioned above in great length. As counselors, psychologists, and healthcare providers begin to work with this vulnerable population, positive psychology can provide a foundation to assist clients in moving forward in healing as they process past trauma. That said, positive changes in an individual's life as a result of facing adversity started to gain popularity in trauma-related literature during the mid-1990s (Taheri et al., 2024).

When an individual experiences trauma, this event can be overwhelming and skew their perception that the world and society are both good and safe (Berry Street Victoria, 2013). Unfortunately, the mind and body are both severely impacted when individuals are experiencing high-intensity stress and trauma. The dysregulated stress response associated with trauma specifically alters the body (Brunzell et al., 2016). The body responds to trauma equivalently to the way it processes extensive toxic stress: either fast-acting to stabilize neurobiological system responses in less than 20 minutes or prolonged stress when body functions slow down (Brunzell et al., 2016).

Positive psychology is the scholarly examination of highest human functioning; the goals of this concept are to better understand and then incorporate specific factors that assist individuals and communities to excel and flourish (Seligman & Csikszentmihalyi, 2000). As counselors and mental health providers assist individuals on how to handle and overcome life stressors and obstacles, it is essential to equip their clients with a flexible life attitude and mental resilience that can help them cope with the harsh reality from losses, grief, and sorrows (Leung, 2023). Furthermore, helping clients to comprehend that life circumstances are held in polarity as strengths and vulnerability may coincide and that healing and wellness relies upon our competence to steer ourselves with a healthy balance of the positives and negatives (Leung, 2023).

The ideology of experiencing both positive and negative situations in optimal balance without judgment has been termed as "tragic optimism" (TO). Viktor Frankl (1985) suggested that there is an optimism that can stand within the direct situation, as he experienced in his own and other inmates' survival during the Nazi concentration camps event. Frankl (1985) noted that TO is "optimism in the face of tragedy" (p. 162) that can result in validation of an accomplishment and achievement and life-changing growth and intentional control over one's life and decisions (Leung, 2023, p. 2). With TO, individuals may view their traumatic experience with a positive perspective as they recognize the mental toughness, resilience, and strength they developed due to the trauma. Individuals who face trauma and, specifically, childhood trauma, may struggle to see the "good" after such experiences. However, TO is the trust that individuals can still obtain a happy, peaceful, and pleasurable life regardless of the "Tragic Triad" known as pain, guilt, and death in life (Ward, 2024).

Instead of escaping from negative emotions and experiences, tragic optimists lean into them as opportunities to develop a more profound feeling of life's meaning and purpose (Ward, 2024). This viewpoint may be highly valuable for individuals who are struggling to find meaning or value in life after experiencing trauma, neglect, abuse, or other unsettling experiences. TO encourages people to face their fears and to be with the uncomfortable feelings as this will allow for growth, gratitude, and purpose for one's life. The correlation between trauma and optimism has been examined in a variety of settings where individuals have been challenged with adversity (Alex et al., 2024). Some research has suggested that when individuals with traumatic pasts demonstrate hope and optimism, it may indicate that these individuals are more likely to develop posttraumatic growth (PTG) (Alex et al., 2024). PTG has been categorized as a person's higher levels of personal functioning and overall wellness in comparison to how this same individual was prior to their experience of the traumatic event (Alex et al., 2024). Finally, tragic optimists strongly resonate with the idea that there is such an intrinsic value to life that breathing alone is enough to feel worthy for living (Ward, 2024).

Resilience, Hope, and Positive Psychology for Trauma Survivors

In more recent trauma literature, there has been research focused on what factors may impact the psychological wellness for individuals who have experienced childhood trauma in order for clinicians to best assist child abuse survivors in coping with their trauma (Munoz et al., 2019). The two variables that have been correlated to positive well-being after childhood trauma are hope and resilience, and constructs that have been linked to well-being after childhood trauma are resilience and hope (Munoz et al., 2019). Furthermore, positive psychology approaches suggest interventions that are advantageous not only for treating individuals with psychological conditions or who are at-risk but also for increasing the well-being for typically developing children (Owens & Waters, 2020). The following section will target how the characteristics of hope and resilience within positive psychology principles can positively impact the well-being for trauma survivors.

Resilience and Trauma Survivors

When understanding resilience, it is important to recognize the individual's assets, strengths, internal resources, emotional self-efficacy, and positive attributes (Türk-Kurtçal & Kocatürk, 2020). One term that is vital to conceptualizing how individuals cope with trauma is psychological resilience. Psychological resilience is recognized as a robust process in which individuals adapt healthily regardless of experiencing drastic difficulties or trauma (Luthar et al., 2000). Trauma survivors may build psychological resilience as a result of their previous negative experiences which can be useful in future events or unforeseen challenges. Variables that decrease or remove the impact of risk or struggle and increase healthy adaptability and individual strengths are defined as protective factors (Masten et al., 1994). Within the trauma literature when investigating psychological resilience, the factors that impact the creation of psychological resilience were "protective factors" (Türk-Kurtça &

Kocatürk, 2020). This is important information for clinicians who are working with trauma survivors because they can work with clients to focus on their protective factors that may help in building their psychological resiliency.

Positive psychology proposes that the individual will embrace and transform suffering through meaning as the core for personal development in resilience and psychological wellness (Yıldırım et al., 2022). As a result, resilience relies on both positive individual strengths and the courage and mental toughness to tackle and survive suffering (Yıldırım et al., 2022). Therefore, individuals who are also coping with past childhood trauma may develop resilience in times of hardship without even knowing that they are creating this strength. Another area in which resilience and positive psychology may be beneficial for trauma survivors is during times of self-isolation. Unfortunately, a maladaptive coping mechanism for some individuals who experience trauma is self-isolation. As a result of the negative consequences on their well-being, survivors may desire to isolate themselves in response to the complicated emotions that they may feel after a distressing event (Brand et al., 2017). Often, this behavior can feel comforting and soothing for some survivors as they have isolated themselves from others as a protective barrier from past adversities (Downey & Crummey, 2022).

Hope and Trauma Survivors

The characteristic of "hope" has been increasingly recognized within positive psychology literature and studies. The idea of hope has attracted the attention of philosophers, poets, artists, and scholars throughout history (Colla et al., 2022). However, some scholars also suggest optimism, which also includes hope, may not all be advantageous for individuals. For example, unrealistic optimism can be advantageous for protecting well-being (it helps to normalize and cope with fear); however, it could also be detrimental for one's health (Dolinski et al., 2021). Typically, individuals trust and hope that their own personal future will be superior, optimistic, and more successful in comparison to others, and this is often referred to as unrealistic optimism or biased optimism (Salgado & Berntsten, 2021). Schneider (2001) separates unrealistic optimism that has been defined as remaining positive regardless of the conditions, whereas realistic optimism consists of flourishing, hoping, and striving for positive experiences while being mindful of limitations. Also, realistic optimism highlights hoping and also putting forth effort and not just dreaming for a positive outcome (Dursun, 2021).

Recently, scholars have brought awareness to the expansion of positive psychology with a more sophisticated understanding of the variables and relevant contexts that impact an individuals' well-being (Colla et al., 2022). With this new approach, comes not only complexity but also an opportunity for researchers and practitioners to develop a robust understanding of how clients may benefit from tenets embedded in positive psychology. As such, throughout the previous 30 years, Snyder et al.'s (1991) two-factor model of hope has prevailed in the psychological literature and is one of the foundational theories within the premise of positive psychology (Colla et al., 2022). Snyders et al.'s (1991) hope theory recognizes hope as an influential motivating experience that is developed from two very different types of cognition—pathway thinking and agency thinking. This theory suggests that hope is a result from an individuals' perception to create a variety of adaptable paths to reach their goals, providing them with the opportunity to distinguish the challenges and techniques to conquer these barriers in order to reach their desired outcome (Colla et al., 2022). For example, if a trauma survivor is utilizing the mechanisms that are within hope theory, they may have the ability to recognize healthy options on how to handle the stressors versus going back to apply maladaptive coping mechanisms that they may have used in the past.

Furthermore, hope is often interwoven with the concepts of resilience, anticipation, and longing (Bandieri et al., 2024). It is important to recognize that hope and optimism are not terms to be used interchangeably. Although optimism can also be an excellent emotional resource for trauma survivors, it is not the same as hope. Optimism is a heightened vague expectation of a positive future and positive outcomes will occur regardless of a person's behaviors. Whereas hope specifically includes expectancies that positive desired outcomes will happen by a person's pathways and agency (Corn et al., 2020). Both optimism and hope can be extremely beneficial for trauma survivors during times of healing, treatment, and recovery.

Practical Positive Psychology Exercises for Individuals Who Have Experienced Childhood Trauma

Mental Subtraction is when one imagines their life in the absence of one of their key strengths. The purpose for engaging in such an activity is to facilitate more gratitude for our strengths, fostering happiness and well-being (Niemiec, 2018). Visualize how you apply this strength currently in your life. Be specific and imagine what your life would be if you did not use this strength any longer. For example, if a key strength for you is complimenting others, how would your daily living change if you no longer applied this strength.

Journaling—this strategy is simple, inexpensive, and creative. The individual simply writes down any thought that comes to their mind or what has happened to them during the day. This practice allows the individual to express how they are feeling and what emotions come up after intentionally thinking about their day. It is an opportunity for self-reflection.

Self-love and Self-compassion

Developing habits that focus on caring for yourself with positive affirmations, vision boards, or connecting with others that validate your self-care habits are all very simple ways to become mindful of how to increase your mood, happiness, and positive well-being.

Considerations for a Positive Psychological Perspective With an Individual Who Experienced Childhood Trauma

Trauma is a subjective experience for each child; therefore, not all traumatic events should be approached in the same manner with every child. As previously mentioned, the field of positive psychology is conceptually linked to trauma-informed care (Brunzell et al., 2016). When utilizing positive psychology with a child who has experienced trauma, there are two perspectives from which well-being is considered. The first, subjective well-being, involves positive affect, negative experiences, and life satisfaction (Benoit et al., 2021). The second, psychological well-being, involves positive relationships, autonomy, and life purpose (Benoit et al., 2021). Due to these things being somewhat unmeasurable, a counselor may interpret a child's state of being incorrectly if the counselor does not fully understand or grasp the effect of the traumatic event on the child. As such, it is important to listen carefully to how the child is expressing the impact of the trauma on their lives, souls, and psyche to be able to determine the treatment plan moving forward in a manner that does not adversely affect the child. Asking open-ended questions can be a trusted step in this process as it avoids yes/no answers that can mask deeper issues that the child is unable to express verbally or conceptually. Congruence or incongruence between answers and behavior can also help the counselor to identify areas that may need more attention than others (immediately, short term and long term) in the treatment plan development for that child.

Application of Mindfulness for Individuals Who Experienced Childhood Trauma

The American Psychological Association (n.d.) defines *mindfulness* as an awareness of the individual's internal states and surroundings. Mindfulness is often used in therapeutic interventions with those individuals who have been traumatized and has been utilized in multiple settings to include schools, hospitals, prisons, hospital settings, and businesses. Mindfulness practices can be especially helpful in those situations where the traumatized individual has a multitude of trauma reminders, also often called sensory reminders (Miller-Karas, 2023). Mindfulness activities can be helpful in reducing traumatic symptoms through different platforms, to include standardized and unstandardized practices. Standardized practices include: Mindfulness Based Stress Reduction (MBSR), Mindfulness Based Cognitive Therapy (MBCT), and Mindfulness Based Relapse Prevention (MBRP). Unstandardized practices may include: educational sessions, art therapy, group therapy, yoga, or other interventions that focus on mind–body connections (Ortiz et al., 2017). Implementing mindfulness practices using either platform can bring significant decreases in trauma-related symptoms such as depression, anxiety, stress, posttraumatic stress disorder (PTSD), and other short-term and long-term-related symptoms, as well as increase mental health outcomes, resilience, and overall quality of life.

There are many creative mindfulness activities that are effective when working with children. The activities below are among the many creative ways to help children with mindfulness practices.

Grounding with colors. This activity involves using colors to help a child ground themselves in the world around them. The activity typically requests the child to look around and name all of the colors around them, to include the subtle differences in the colors; for example, the different colors of green in the grass, the trees, weeds, flowers, and so on. This exercise will help ground them to their environment in the here and now.

Grounding with sound. Much like grounds with colors, grounding with sound involves paying attention to and naming the sounds they hear in their current environment. As a counselor you can also create sound by using a sound machine or a bell. The child will listen to the sound and then when it is completely quiet they can describe the sounds they heard. Again, this activity will help a child to ground themselves to their environment in the here and now.

Box breathing. Box breathing can be done in many ways: with objects, without objects, with body movements, without body movements, and so on. The basic idea, overall, in box breathing is to breathe in for a count, hold for a count, and breathe out for a count. Many counselors use the 4/4/4 method while others may use different counts. Either way, this relaxation technique, adapted from yoga, is a breathing technique that can be done multiple times in a row that is designed to return your breathing to a normal pattern when the person feels stressed or overwhelmed (Swiner, 2023).

Meditation. Meditation can be helpful when teaching a child about mindfulness, decreasing stress, headaches, and other symptoms that can be attributed to traumatic events. The goal of meditation is not to ignore our feelings and sensations in our bodies but to identify them and acknowledge them while gaining insight and awareness of them (Selva, 2017). Meditation can be done in a structured manner at particular times of the day or in a more impromptu manner. It can also be used through a manner where another person is leading you through the meditation exercise, which is referred to as guided meditation, or a person can use unguided meditation, or meditation is done without any external tools. Both have benefits for lowering anxiety, depression, and stress. When speaking specifically about childhood trauma, the body scan exercise is reportedly one of the more effective meditation activities for children. In this exercise, each part of the body is isolated typically from feet to head and each part is felt individually, which allows the person to sense any discomfort they are experiencing due to a stressful or traumatic event (Scott, 2024).

Mindful Jar. This activity is designed to help children put perspective on strong emotions and bring peace into their lives. It involves filling a clear jar with a lid (like a mason jar) with water, and adding a spoonful of glitter glue (or dry glitter and glue) to the water, replacing the lid on the jar, then shaking the jar, making the glitter swirl around in the water.

The instruction is given (some version of this) for the child to imagine their thoughts when stressed, angry, or sad, being like the glitter in the jar. It is messy, hard to see clearly, hard to think clearly, and so on. Then the jar is placed back on a hard surface. As the glitter mixture settles and the water becomes clearer, the inference can be made that when we are able to calm ourselves/our minds for a while, our thoughts will clear and we can see the issues in front of us more clearly (Ackerman, 2017). Other activities like deep breathing or box breathing can be implemented in addition when using this object lesson to help children calm their minds while they try to calm their emotions. Additionally, if the opportunity presents itself, helping the child separate their emotions during this activity can be helpful. Mindfulness practices of focusing on the swirling of the contents in the jar can also be implemented here (Ackerman, 2017).

While contemplating other mindfulness activities that can be implemented, consider making a list of mindfulness activities that have been effective in the past and creatively think of others that could be implemented to include the aforementioned activities. Then get to work implementing these into practice! As we move on to putting this into practice with the case examples below, ask yourself: Which mindfulness activities might work best in each scenario? Why would you choose that activity over another activity?

Case Example 1: Exploring Positive Psychological Interventions and Mindfulness Techniques With Adults Who Experienced Childhood Trauma

Charlie is a 25-year-old graduate student who was sexually assaulted by a family member from ages 11 to 14 years old. Though she told a trusted adult about these occurrences around the age of 16 and was offered counseling and other resources to help her heal from these events, she is having some traumatic stress-related symptoms, currently. She recently got out of a long-term relationship involving domestic violence that she believes has exacerbated her symptoms of re-experiencing, hypervigilance, and overall feelings of anxiety.

Let's look at how applying positive psychology can aid in helping Charlie manage her trauma symptoms of re-experiencing, hypervigilance, and overall feelings of anxiety. As mentioned in the text, childhood trauma can cause changes in the brain, thought patterns, as well as lifestyle and social changes. Looking at this from a counseling perspective and utilizing some of the fundamental aspects of positive psychology, let's begin by focusing on Charlie's strengths, values, and felt safety. The use of guided meditation or meditation may help Charlie to ground herself into the here and now and slow down or cease the re-experiencing issues while mitigating the anxiety and feelings of fear that lead to the hypervigilance. As mentioned earlier in the text, guided meditation would enlist the use of an in-person or an audio- or video-led meditation by another person. Unguided meditation or meditation is done without any external tools so duration, space, and silence are determined by the individual. No matter which one you choose to use, the exercise of meditation can be helpful in lowering stress levels, as well as levels of anxiety and depression.

Another practice that can be helpful is to focus on grounding with colors, sounds, or another method that involves her surroundings. In doing this, she will slow down or cease the fear and anxiety of potential flashbacks or intrusive memories she is experiencing and be aware of her environment and her current state of safety and well-being. When experiencing intrusive thoughts or memories, or in the situation where a person is experiencing a flashback, it can overwhelm the person to feel or believe they are back in the traumatic situation, which threatens their safety and well-being. Utilizing the grounding technique, it reorients them to their current state and environment allowing them to feel safe once again.

These are just a couple of ideas on how to implement positive psychology with someone who has experienced childhood trauma. What are some others you can think of? How would you implement them in a therapeutic or counseling setting?

Case Example 2: Exploring Positive Psychological Interventions and Mindfulness Techniques With Children Who Experienced Childhood Trauma

Jeremiah is a 6-year-old cis-gendered male who has experienced multiple adverse childhood experiences (ACEs). Having lived in a household marked by domestic violence, with his mother who struggled with substance abuse and a father who has been incarcerated, Jeremiah exhibits symptoms associated with a history of trauma, including difficulties sleeping due to recurring nightmares, struggles concentrating in school, increased anxiety, and troubles forming healthy social relationships. He has frequent emotional outbursts, is often withdrawn socially, and appears to be underperforming academically at school.

Utilizing an integrative approach combining positive psychology and mindfulness-based interventions within a trauma-informed framework can provide Jeremiah with needed tools for coping. Given his age, it is important to utilize developmentally appropriate means, such as play, to facilitate the implementation of interventions. Through the implementation of a developmentally responsive, trauma-informed approach that integrates mindfulness practices that increase emotional awareness and positive psychology techniques that highlight personal empowerment and resilience, Jeremiah will be able to engage in a process that will help him shift his perspective from a trauma response that is an attempt of simply survive to one of potential growth and empowerment.

This represents one way to potentially approach working with a child who has experienced multiple ACEs and trauma. What factors do you need to be mindful of when determining appropriate interventions in such cases? How would you implement developmentally appropriate positive psychology and mindfulness-based interventions for children in a therapeutic or counseling setting?

Conclusion

When examining the various factors associated with childhood trauma along with the potential utilization of positive psychology and mindfulness, recognizing that the therapeutic process needs to involve more than just responding to symptoms is important. Healing from ACEs and trauma can include factors such as increasing emotional awareness, cultivating resilience, and promoting personal growth. Implementing positive psychology and mindfulness-based interventions can help foster and facilitate a therapeutic healing process. Through the tools provided by such interventions, survivors who have experienced ACEs and trauma can begin to redefine their past experiences, engage in greater self-compassion, and increase their sense of self-control and self-determination. In this chapter, the information, activities, case examples, and critical thinking questions provided are intended to connect theoretical conceptualization with real-world applications. The implementation of positive psychology and mindfulness-based interventions can help to empower individuals in understanding the impacts of ACEs and trauma while also acknowledging that they do not have to allow their past experiences to determine their future path in life.

> *Nine times out of ten, the story behind the misbehavior won't make you angry; it will break your heart.—Annette Breaux*

> *When it feels disheartening to learn that trauma changes the brain, remember that healing changes the brain, too.—@howhumansheal*

Critical Thinking Questions

1. How can professional support children who have experienced childhood trauma?
2. What are some similarities and differences in treatment approaches when working with adults who have experienced childhood trauma versus children who have undergone trauma?
3. When implementing a positive psychology approach, what are specific techniques that you would suggest for working with individuals that have experienced childhood trauma?
4. Which positive psychology activities resonate most with your counseling style and approach?
5. How can mindfulness be an opportunity for healing trauma children?

Assessment of Knowledge Activity

After reading this chapter on integrating positive psychology and mindfulness to support individuals who have experienced childhood traumatic events, let's take some time to reflect back on the application of integrating positive psychology and mindfulness on the following scenario. Read the hypothetical situation and address the remaining prompts.

Hypothetical Situation: Imagine a childhood trauma survivor named Cindi, a 20-year-old woman who has recently disclosed childhood abuse from the ages of 10 to 12 years of age by a close family member. She is experiencing feelings of sadness, hypervigilance, and anxiety. She has moved back in with her parents for support during this time.

1. Refer back to the "Application of Mindfulness for Individuals Who Experienced Childhood Trauma" section in this chapter and choose an activity that you think may be beneficial for Cindi.
2. Consider how the selected positive psychology intervention (PPI) could help Cindi. What can you foresee as some potential positive benefits and outcomes for her?
3. What challenges may arise when implementing this intervention with Cindi? How could these challenges be mitigated to ensure the chosen technique is effective when working with Cindi?

https://positivepsychology.com/positive-psychology-worksheets-activities/

References

Akerman, C. (2017). *21 Mindfulness exercises, techniques & activities for adults* (+pdf) :// positivepsychology.com/mindfulness-exercises-techniques-activities/

Alex, J., Bhatia, J. K., & Marakwar, A. (2024). Optimism and PTSD: A review. *International Journal of Indian Psychology*, *12*(1). https://doi.org/10.25215/1201.025

American Psychiatric Association. (2022). *The diagnostic and statistical manual* (5th ed., text rev.). Author.

American Psychological Association. (n.d.). *Mindfulness*. American Psychological Association. https://www.apa.org/topics/mindfulness

Bandieri, E., Borelli, E., Bigi, S., Mucciarini, C., Gilioli, F., Ferrari, U., Eliardo, S., Luppi, M., & Potenza, L. (2024). Positive psychological well-being in early palliative care: A narrative review of the roles of hope, gratitude, and death acceptance. *Current Oncology*, *31*(2), 672–684. https://doi.org/10.3390/curroncol31020049

Bender, W. M., & Sims, R. (2006). Katrina kids! Helping kids exposed to population-wide trauma. *Teaching Exceptional Children, 40*(1), 40–47. https://doi.org/10.1177/004005990704000105

Benoit, V., & Gabola, P. (2021). Effects of positive psychology interventions on the well-being of young children: A systematic literature review. *International Journal of Environmental Research and Public Health*, *18*(22), 12065. https://doi.org/10.3390/ijerph182212065

Berry Street Victoria. (2013). *Foundations for practice: Trauma module*. Author.

Blaustein, M. E. (2013). Childhood trauma and a framework for intervention. In E. Rossen & R. Hull (Eds.), *Supporting and educating traumatized students: A guide for school-based professionals* (pp. 3–21). Oxford University Press.

Brand, B. L., Schielke, H. J., & Brams, J. S. (2017). Assisting the courts in understanding and connecting with experiences of disconnection: Addressing trauma-related dissociation as a forensic psychologist, part I. *Psychological Injury and Law*, *10*, 283–297. https://doi.org/10.1007/s12207-017-9304-8

Breaux, A. (n.d.). *Backpack, backpack . . . What's in it?—The Sensory Path*. https://thesensorypath.com/backpack-backpack-whats-in-it/

Brunzell, T., Stokes, H., & Waters, L. (2016). Trauma-informed positive education: Using positive psychology to strengthen vulnerable students. *Contemporary School Psychology Journal*, 20, 63–83. https://doi.org/10.1007/s40688-015-0070-x

Cénat, J. M., & Dalexis, R. D. (2020). The complex trauma spectrum during the COVID-19 pandemic: A threat for children and adolescents' physical and mental health. *Psychiatry Research*, *293*, 113473. https://doi.org/10.1016/j.psychres.2020.113473

Centers for Disease Control and Prevention (2024). https://www.cdc.gov/

Centers for Disease Control and Prevention. (2018, June 28). *6 Guiding principles to a trauma-informed approach*. Centers for Disease Control and Prevention. https://stacks.cdc.gov/view/cdc/56843

Centers for Disease Control and Prevention. (2021, August 23). *Adverse childhood experiences (aces)*. Centers for Disease Control and Prevention. https://www.cdc.gov/vitalsigns/aces/index.html

Colla, R., Williams, P., Oades, L. G., & Camacho-Morles, J. (2022). "A new hope" for positive psychology: A dynamic systems reconceptualization of hope theory. *Frontiers in Psychology, 13*, 809053. https://doi.org/10.3389/fpsyg.2022.809053

Collin-Vézina, D., Brend, D., & Beeman, I. (2020). When it counts the most: Trauma-informed care and the COVID-19 global pandemic. *Developmental Child Welfare, 2*(3), 172–179. https://doi.org/10.1177/2516103220942530

Corn, B. W., Feldman, D. B., & Wexler, I. (2020). The science of hope. *The Lancet Oncology*, *21*(9), e452–e459. www.thelancet.com/oncology

Dolinski, D., Dolinska, B., Zmaczynska-Witek, B., Banach, M., & Kulesza, W. (2020). Unrealistic optimism in the time of coronavirus pandemic: May it help to kill, if so—whom: Disease or the person? *Journal of Clinical Medicine*, *9*(5), 1464. https://doi.org/10.3390/jcm9051464

Downey, C., & Crummy, A. (2022). The impact of childhood trauma on children's wellbeing and adult behavior. *European Journal of Trauma & Dissociation*, *6*(1), 100237. https://doi.org/10.1016/j.ejtd.2021.100237

Dursun, P. (2021). Optimism, hope and subjective well-being: A literature overview. Çatalhöyük *Uluslararası Turizm ve Sosyal Araştırmalar Dergisi*, (6), 61–74.

Edwards, B. G. (2019). *Alarming effects of children's exposure of domestic violence.* https://www.researchgate.net/publication/360176979_Alarming_effects_of_children's_exposure_to_domestic_violence

Felitti, V. J., & Anda, R. F. (2010). The relationship of adverse childhood experiences to adult medical disease, psychiatric disorders, and sexual behavior: Implications for healthcare. *The Impact of Early Life Trauma on Health and Disease: The Hidden Epidemic*, *77*, 87.

Frankl, V. E. (1985). *Man's search for meaning: Revised and updated.* Washington Square Press.

Guessoum, S. B., Lachal, J., Radjack, R., Carretier, E., Minassian, S., Benoit, L., & Moro, M. R. (2020). Adolescent psychiatric disorders during the COVID-19 pandemic and lockdown. *Psychiatry Research*, *291*, 113264.

Hollingsworth, M. (2023, March 31). Backpack, backpack . . . what's in it? *The Sensory Path.* https://thesensorypath.com/backpack-backpack-whats-in-it/

King-White, D. (2024). *Childhood trauma: Types, causes signs & treatments.* https://www.choosingtherapy.com/childhood-trauma/

Kleber, R. J. (2019). Trauma and public mental health: A focused review. *Front Psychiatry, 10*, 451. https://doi.org/10.3389/fpsyt.2019.00451

Landreth, G. L. (2023). *Play therapy: The art of the relationship* (4th ed.). Routledge.

Leung, M. M. (2023). Tragic optimism: An integrative meaning-centred approach to trauma treatment. In *A Second-Wave Positive Psychology in Counseling Psychology* (pp. 259–277). Routledge.

Luthar, S. S., Cicchetti, D., & Becker, B. (2000). The construct of resilience: A critical evaluation and guidelines for future work. *Child Development, 71*(3), 543–562. https://doi.org/10.1111/1467-8624.00164

Maddox, R. P., II, Rujimora, J., Nichols, L. M., Williams, M. K., Hunt, T., & Carter, R. A., Jr., (2024). Trauma-informed schools: Implications for special education and school counseling. *TEACHING Exceptional Children, 56*(6), 510–520.

Masten, A. S., Wang, M. C., & Gordon, E. W. (1994). Resilience in individual development: Successful adaptation despite risk and adversity. In M. Wang & E. Gordon (Eds.), *Educational resilience in inner-city America: Challenges and prospects* (pp. 3–25). Lawrence Erlbaum.

Mayo Clinic. (2024). https://www.mayoclinic.org/

Miller-Karas, E. (2023). *Mindfulness through a trauma-informed lens.* https://www.psychologytoday.com/us/blog/building-resiliency-to-trauma/202312/mindfulness-through-a-trauma-informed-lens

Munoz, R. T., Hanks, H., & Hellman, C. M. (2019, October 10). Hope and resilience as distinct contributors to psychological flourishing among childhood trauma survivors. *Traumatology. Advance online publication.* http://dx.doi.org/10.1037/trm0000224

National Child Traumatic Stress Network. (2012). https://www.nctsn.org/interventions/child-and-family-traumatic-stress-intervention

Niemiec, R. M. (2018). *Character strengths interventions: A field guide for practitioners.* Hogrefe.

National Institute of Mental Health. (2024). https://www.nimh.nih.gov/

Ortiz, R., & Sibinga, E. M. (2017). The role of mindfulness in reducing the adverse effects of childhood stress and trauma. *Children (Basel, Switzerland), 4*(3), 16. https://doi.org/10.3390/children4030016

Owens, R. L., & Waters, L. (2020). What does positive psychology tell us about early intervention and prevention with children and adolescents? A review of positive psychological interventions with young people. *The Journal of Positive Psychology, 15*(5), 588–597. https://doi.org/10.1080/17439760.2020.1789706

Pearson, B. L., & Cordiano, T. S. (2010). Can we play again? Applying positive psychology principles in cognitive-behavioral play therapy. In G. W. Burns (Ed.), *Happiness, healing, enhancement: Your casebook collection for applying positive psychology in therapy* (pp. 267–278). John Wiley & Sons.

Pearson, B. L., Russ, S. W., & Cain Spannagel, S. A. (2008). Pretend play and positive psychology: Natural companions. *Journal of Positive Psychology, 3*, 110–119.

Perry, B. D., & Szalavitz, M. (2017). *The boy who was raised as a dog* (rev. ed.). Basic Books.

Russ, S. W. (2004). *Play in child development and psychotherapy: Toward empirically supported practice.* Lawrence Erlbaum Associates.

SAMHSA. (2014). Trauma. https://ncsacw.samhsa.gov/userfiles/files/SAMHSA_Trauma.pdf

SAMHSA. (2020). *Understanding child trauma.* https://www.samhsa.gov/child-trauma/understanding-child-trauma

Salgado, S., & Berntsen, D. (2021). "It won't happen to us": Unrealistic optimism affects COVID-19 risk assessments and attitudes regarding protective behaviour. *Journal of Applied Research in Memory and Cognition*, *10*(3), 368–380. https://doi.org/10.1016/j.jarmac.2021.07.006

Scott, E. (2024). *What is body scan meditation?* https://www.verywellmind.com/body-scan-meditation-why-and-how-3144782

Schneider, S. L. (2001). In search of realistic optimism: Meaning, knowledge, and warm fuzziness. *American psychologist*, *56*(3), 250.

Seligman, M. E. (2011). *Flourish: A visionary new understanding of happiness and well-being.* Simon and Schuster.

Seligman, M. E. P., & Csikszentmihalyi, M. (2000). Positive psychology: An introduction. *American Psychologist, 55*, 5–14.

Selva, J. (2017). The history and origins of mindfulness.*Positivepsychology.com.* https://positivepsychology.com/history-of-mindfulness/

Swiner, N. (2023). Box breathing: Getting started with box breathing, how to do it, benefits and tips. *WebMD.* https://www.webmd.com/balance/what-is-box-breathing

Taheri, M., Harding, N., Stettaford, T., Fitzpatrick, S., & McCormack, L. (2024). Female-specific refugee trauma impacting psychological wellbeing post-settlement: A scoping review of research. *Journal of Loss and Trauma*, 1–30. https://doi.org/10.1080/15325024.2024.2325077

Tracy, N. (2021, December 17). What is abuse? Abuse definition. *HealthyPlace.* https://www.healthyplace.com/abuse/abuse-information/what-is-abuse-abuse-definition

Türk-Kurtça, T., & Kocatürk, M. (2020). The role of childhood traumas, emotional self-efficacy and internal-external locus of control in predicting psychological resilience. *International Journal of Education and Literacy Studies*, *8*(3), 105–115. https://dx.doi.org/10.7575/aiac.ijels.v.8n.3p.105

U.S. Department of Justice. (2024, October 15). *Domestic violence.* Office on Violence Against Women (OVW). https://www.justice.gov/ovw/domestic-violence

Van der Kolk, B. (2014). *The body keeps the score: Brain, mind and body in the healing of trauma.* Viking.

Ward, S. (2024). Do physicians need tragic optimism? *Internal Medicine Journal*, *54*(2), 348–351. https://doi:10.1111/imj.16315

Yıldırım, M., Arslan, G., & Wong, P. T. (2022). Meaningful living, resilience, affective balance, and psychological health problems among Turkish young adults during coronavirus pandemic. *Current Psychology*, *41*(11), 7812–7823. https://doi.org/10.1007/s12144-020-01244-8

12

Positive Psychology and Mindfulness: Eating Disorders

Michele Mahr
Lindsey Nichols
Michelle Kelley Shuler
Jonathan W. Carrier

KEYWORDS AND DEFINITIONS:

Anorexia nervosa: Significantly low body weight in the context of age, sex, developmental trajectory, and physical health

Body dysmorphia: A mental health condition that makes one view their appearance unfairly and negatively

Body image: How a person sees and feels about their body and appearance

Bulimia nervosa: Recurrent episodes of binge eating, followed by inappropriate compensatory behaviors to prevent weight gain

Eudaimonia: The pursuit, manifestation, and/or experience of virtue, personal growth, self-actualization, flourishing, excellence, and meaning

Orthorexia: When an individual has obsessive attention to healthy eating that then results in physical and psychosocial impairments and a potential eating disorder termed orthorexia nervosa (ON).

LEARNING OBJECTIVES:

1. Understanding the etiology of eating disorders (EDs) as well as specific criteria noted in the *DSM* (American Psychiatric Association [APA], 2022, *Diagnostic and Statistical Manual of Mental Disorders*; 5th ed., text rev.)

2. Evaluating the most common types of EDs and the manifestation of symptoms
3. Conceptualize how positive psychology can be a potential treatment modality for individuals with EDs
4. Applying mindfulness techniques when assisting individuals with EDs
5. Creating safe and nonjudgmental spaces for practicing mindfulness and meditation when working with individuals with EDs

Anorexia Nervosa, Bulimia Nervosa, and Binge-Eating Disorder

Eating disorders (EDs) are serious mental health conditions characterized by persistent disturbances in eating behaviors, weight, and related thoughts and emotions (Schmidt et al., 2016). These disorders can have severe physical and psychological consequences and affect millions of individuals worldwide (Galmiche et al., 2019). EDs have a complex etiology, involving biological, psychological, and sociocultural factors. They often co-occur with other mental health conditions, such as depression, anxiety, and obsessive-compulsive disorder (Ulfvebrand et al., 2015). EDs have a lifetime prevalence estimated at 8.4% for women and 2.2% for men (Galmiche et al., 2019). Research has highlighted the increasing frequency of these disorders across diverse populations (Mohler-Kuo et al., 2016). This trend underscores the need for continued research and improved treatment strategies. This chapter focuses on three primary EDs: Anorexia Nervosa (AN), Bulimia Nervosa (BN), and Binge-Eating Disorder (BED). In this section, we explore the diagnostic criteria, symptoms, causes, and common treatment approaches for AN, BN, and BED.

Anorexia Nervosa

Characteristics of anorexia nervosa (AN) include "significantly low body weight in the context of age, sex, developmental trajectory, and physical health" (American Psychiatric Association [APA] 2022, p. 381). Individuals with AN experience an intense and persistent fear of gaining weight or becoming fat, even when underweight (APA, 2022). There is also a "disturbance in the way one's body weight or shape is experienced, [with] undue influence of body weight or shape on self-evaluation, or persistent lack of recognition of the seriousness of current low body weight" (APA, 2022, p. 381). AN has two subtypes: (1) restricting and (2) binge eating/purging (APA, 2022). Researchers have highlighted the importance of considering cultural variations in presenting AN symptoms (Bhattacharya et al., 2022).

Diagnostic Criteria and Symptoms

Symptoms of AN extend beyond the diagnostic criteria and can manifest in various ways. Individuals with AN typically engage in severe restriction of food intake and may exhibit excessive exercise behaviors (Young et al., 2017). They also often have a distorted body image and show a preoccupation with food and weight (APA, 2022). Social withdrawal is common as individuals become increasingly isolated due to their eating behaviors and body image concerns (Schmidt et al., 2016).

Physical symptoms of AN can be severe and wide-ranging. These may include fatigue, dizziness, hair loss, dry skin, cold intolerance, and the growth of fine body hair (lanugo) (APA, 2022; Wholihan, 2015). In females, amenorrhea (cessation of menstruation) is expected, although it is not a diagnostic criterion in the *DSM-5* (Zipfel et al., 2015) or *DSM-5-TR* (APA, 2022). Cardiovascular complications, electrolyte imbalances, and bone-density loss are medically severe consequences of prolonged AN (Mehler & Brown, 2015). Research has also highlighted the impact of AN on cognitive functioning (Tchanturia et al., 2019; Westwood & Tchanturia, 2017).

Causes

The etiology of AN involves a complex interplay of genetic, neurobiological, psychological, and sociocultural factors (APA, 2022). Twin studies have demonstrated a significant genetic component, with heritability estimates ranging from 16% to 74% (Watson et al., 2021). Genome studies have identified specific genes associated with AN (Hübel et al., 2019; Yilmaz et al., 2015). Neurobiological research has implicated alterations in neurotransmitter systems, most notably serotonin and dopamine, in developing and maintaining AN (Kaye et al., 2013). Neuroimaging studies have revealed structural and functional brain changes in individuals with AN, particularly reward processing and body image (King et al., 2018).

Psychological factors also play a role in AN. Traits such as perfectionism, low self-esteem, and body dissatisfaction are commonly associated with the disorder (Dakanalis et al., 2016). Research has also highlighted the role of emotion regulation difficulties in AN (Haynos et al., 2017). Additionally, sociocultural influences, including exposure to idealized body images and societal pressure for thinness (Culbert et al., 2015), as well as social media content (Fardouly & Vartanian, 2016), have been found to contribute to the development of AN.

Common Treatments

Treatment for AN typically involves a multidisciplinary approach, combining psychological, nutritional, and sometimes pharmacological interventions. Cognitive Behavioral Therapy (CBT) is a widely used psychological treatment that helps patients challenge distorted thoughts about food, weight, and body image (Dalle Grave et al., 2013). Recent adaptations of CBT, such as Enhanced

CBT (CBT-E) and family therapies, have shown positive results in treating AN across different age groups (Dalle Grave et al., 2019).

Nutritional rehabilitation is a crucial component of AN treatment. This process involves supervised weight restoration and normalization of eating patterns, often requiring the expertise of registered dietitians specializing in EDs (Marzola et al., 2013). Much research has focused on optimizing re-feeding protocols while promoting efficient weight gain (Garber et al., 2016). While there are no specific medications approved for AN, antidepressants may be used to treat comorbid conditions such as depression or anxiety (Attia et al., 2019). Pharmacological research has explored the potential of atypical antipsychotics and hormonal treatments in AN, although results have been mixed (Himmerich & Treasure, 2018).

Bulimia Nervosa

Characteristics of bulimia nervosa (BN) include recurrent episodes of binge eating, followed by inappropriate compensatory behaviors to prevent weight gain (APA, 2022; McDonald, 2019). These compensatory behaviors may include self-induced vomiting, misuse of laxatives or diuretics, fasting, or excessive exercise (APA, 2022). Additionally, self-evaluation in BN is "unduly influenced by body shape and weight" (APA, 2022, p. 387). Studies have highlighted the importance of considering presentations of BN that do not meet full diagnostic criteria, as they may still cause significant distress and impairment (Stice et al., 2013).

Diagnostic Criteria and Symptoms

Meeting BN diagnostic criteria includes binge–purge cycles occurring at least once a week for 3 months (APA, 2022). The primary symptoms of BN revolve around the binge–purge cycle. During binge episodes, individuals discretely consume large amounts of food, often experiencing a lack of control over eating (APA, 2022), followed by compensatory behaviors aimed at preventing weight gain (APA, 2022). Individuals with BN often experience intense feelings of guilt and shame after binge episodes (APA, 2022). The frequency and intensity of these episodes can vary, with some individuals engaging in multiple binge–purge cycles per day (Smink et al., 2013).

Physical symptoms of BN can be severe and can include dental erosion from frequent vomiting, electrolyte imbalances, and gastrointestinal problems (APA, 2022). Swelling of the salivary glands, calluses on the back of the hands (from induced vomiting), and menstrual irregularities are also common (Mitchell, 2016). There are long-term cardiovascular complications associated with BN, including an increased risk of cardiovascular disease and stroke (Tith et al., 2020).

Psychological symptoms of BN often include preoccupation with food, weight, and body shape, as well as mood disturbances such as depression and anxiety (Mitchell, 2016). Many individuals with BN report using binge eating as a maladaptive coping mechanism for dealing with negative emotions or stress (Lavender et al., 2015). The cyclical nature of BN can lead to feelings of helplessness and loss of control, further exacerbating psychological distress (Bottera & De Young, 2024).

Causes

The development of BN includes genetic, neurobiological, psychological, and sociocultural factors (APA, 2022). Genetic studies have demonstrated a significant heritable component, with twin studies suggesting heritability of at least 40% for BN (McDonald, 2019; Trace et al., 2013; Wade, 2019). Neurobiological research has identified dysregulation in reward and impulse control circuits in individuals with BN, possibly contributing to the binge–purge cycle (Berner & Marsh, 2014). Neurological studies of BN have revealed brain structure and function alterations, particularly in emotion regulation and impulse control (Westwater et al., 2017; Westwater et al., 2021).

Psychological factors play an essential role in the development and maintenance of BN. Low self-esteem, perfectionism, and difficulties in emotion regulation are common in individuals with BN (Wonderlich et al., 2014). Body image disturbance and weight-related self-worth perpetuate bulimic symptoms (Linardon, 2018). Sociocultural influences, including the internalization of the thin ideal and exposure to media and social media promoting unrealistic body standards, also contribute to the development of BN (Fardouly & Vartanian, 2016; Keel & Forney, 2013).

Common Treatments

Evidence-based treatments for BN primarily focus on CBT and nutritional counseling (Fairburn et al., 2015; Schebendach et al., 2012). Nutritional counseling involves working with patients to establish regular eating patterns and challenge food-related beliefs that contribute to the binge–purge cycle (Brauhardt et al., 2014; Schebendach et al., 2012). CBT-E has been found to be particularly effective as a treatment for BN (Fairburn et al., 2015; Wonderlich et al., 2014). This approach addresses dysfunctional thoughts and behaviors related to eating, weight, and shape and has shown significant efficacy in reducing binge–purge behaviors (Fairburn et al., 2015).

Binge-Eating Disorder

Unlike AN and BN, individuals with binge-eating disorder (BED) are often overweight or obese, which can lead to additional health complications such as Type 2 diabetes, cardiovascular disease, and metabolic syndrome (Wilfley et al., 2016). However, it is essential to note that not all individuals with BED are overweight and not all overweight individuals have BED (Wilfley et al., 2016). BED harms an individual's quality of life, including physical health, psychological well-being, and social functioning (Udo & Grilo, 2018). BED-affected individuals often present with conditions such as low self-esteem, body dissatisfaction, and mood disturbances, such as depression and anxiety (Leehr et al., 2015).

Diagnostic Criteria and Symptoms

Characteristics of BED include recurrent episodes of binge eating without the compensatory behaviors seen in BN (APA, 2022). During episodes of binge eating, individuals eat large amounts of food in a discrete period, which they have difficulty controlling (APA, 2022). Binge eating in BED is associated with eating much more rapidly than usual, eating until feeling uncomfortably full, eating large amounts of food when not feeling physically hungry, eating alone due to embarrassment, and feeling disgusted, depressed, or guilty after overeating (APA, 2022; Goldschmidt, 2017). The frequency and intensity of these episodes can vary, with some individuals engaging in binge eating multiple times per week (Hudson et al., 2017). To meet the diagnostic criteria for BED, binge-eating episodes must occur at least once a week for 3 months and cause marked distress (APA, 2022).

Causes

"Little is known about the development of BED" (APA, 2022, p. 394), but research shows some similarities in the characteristics of BED, AN, and BN. For example, studies suggest a genetic component, with twin studies indicating the heritability of the disorder (Munn-Chernoff et al., 2021; Thornton et al., 2011). Neurobiological research has identified alterations in reward-processing and impulse-control circuits in individuals with BED, which may contribute to the compulsive eating behaviors characteristic of the disorder (Kessler et al., 2016). Additionally, studies have revealed differences in brain responses to food cues and cognitive control processes in individuals with BED compared to healthy controls (Balodis et al., 2015).

Psychological factors play a clear role in BED. Low self-esteem, depression, and difficulties in emotion regulation are common in individuals with BED (Grilo et al., 2013). Triggers of binge-eating episodes include negative affect and impulsivity (Leehr et al., 2015). Furthermore, studies have suggested that individuals with BED may use binge eating as a maladaptive coping mechanism for dealing with stress (Razzoli et al., 2017). Environmental influences, such as childhood trauma, weight-based teasing, and exposure to restrictive dieting practices may also contribute to the development of BED (Hilbert et al., 2014).

Common Treatments

Evidence-based treatments for BED primarily involve psychological interventions, with some role for pharmacotherapy. Cognitive Behavioral Therapy (CBT) has shown significant efficacy in reducing binge-eating episodes and improving associated psychopathology (van Riel et al., 2023). CBT for BED focuses on identifying and modifying dysfunctional thoughts and behaviors related to eating, weight, and shape (Wilson & Zandberg, 2012). Interpersonal Psychotherapy (IPT) has also shown efficacy comparable to CBT in treating BED (Shafran, 2010).

Positive Psychology and Eating Disorders

The principles embedded in positive psychology align well with assisting individuals who have been diagnosed with an eating disorder (ED). Positive psychology allows individuals the opportunity to focus on their strengths and assets during times of adversity while at the same time acknowledging symptoms related to their ED. Counselors need to create a safe, nonjudgmental space for clients to process their disordered thoughts, behaviors, and compulsions related to their ED. The working alliance (WA) supports the nonverbal contract between the therapist and client, including the emotional bond between client and therapist, the desired results for treatment, and the strategies to reach those goals (Bordin, 1979). Within this safe space, clients begin to trust their counselors, a collaborative working relationship begins to develop, clients begin to open up, and counselors can initiate some positive psychology techniques if deemed appropriate. The skills to develop a therapeutic environment that facilitates growth in the therapeutic relationship and produces prosperous outcomes is a primary goal of psychotherapists (Dixon et al., 2022). ED treatment is recognized as a specialty area in counseling; however, all counselors should be aware of gaps within ED treatment which will guide them to make the necessary referrals for patients to receive ethical and culturally sensitive treatment for the condition (Labarta et al., 2023).

Increasing political initiatives bring more attention and awareness to the positive consequences of healthy eating. For example, the increase in obesity rate in adults and children due to unhealthy eating behaviors (e.g., substantial intake of fast food and sugary drinks) has facilitated public health legislation and promotion of healthy eating campaigns (He et al., 2020). Unfortunately, this has also led some individuals to obsess over healthy eating, and it has been counterproductive for individuals with an ED.

This targeted awareness in excessive amounts can also sometimes be referred to as healthy orthorexia (Barthels et al., 2019). Orthorexia refers to individual's obsessive attention to healthy eating, which then results in physical and psychosocial impairments and a potential ED termed orthorexia nervosa (ON) (He et al., 2020). The heightened focus on positive health behaviors and healthy eating may be counterproductive for some individuals mentally. It often becomes questionable as to what is "healthy" versus "unhealthy" in the ED world. Many factors impact this thought process, such as genetics (biology), psychological, environmental, cultural, social, and even the spiritual aspects of individuals. Research has indicated that the concept of positive psychology may be a viable option to assist individuals in finding that balance of positive health behaviors without exceeding to the point of becoming obsessive.

The concepts within positive psychology and positive psychology interventions (PPIs) may be effective on several levels for individuals with EDs. Aside from the target population, PPIs can enhance positive thoughts, behaviors, and overall daily functioning in real-life experiences (Allen et al., 2021). Leaning into this mindset, specific literature focusing on conceptualizing positive body attitudes is vital for informing practitioners' work to foster clients' strengths and facilitate a healthy relationship with their bodies (Koller et al., 2020). The approving body image construct is separate from body image negativity; it eliminates negative thoughts about an individual's body and reinforces positive thoughts (Koller et al., 2020). Furthermore, eudaimonia is a Greek term translated as "happiness" or "flourishing" (Waterman et al., 2010) and often represents an array of concepts. Generally speaking, it is related to a meaningful life filled with self-actualization focused on pleasure, which contrasts with hedonia (Huta, 2020).

Specific PPIs may produce successful outcomes for individuals with ED. For example, gratitude interventions are one component of PPIs. As such, gratitude interventions may develop positive and valuable resources that foster adaptation and positively impact an individual's mental health (Bohlmeijer & Westerhof, 2021). A positive psychology perspective may be valuable regarding ED by identifying factors and beneficial individual characteristics connected to lower maladaptive eating behaviors and concerns (Voica et al., 2021). A recent meta-analysis conducted by Koydemir et al. (2021) exploring PPIs and their effects on subjective well-being and psychological well-being revealed that the interventions using technology were less effective than those that implemented non-technological strategies equally in the short and long term. However, the implementation of technology-assisted PPIs has been reported to be effective in other research studies (e.g., Koydemir & Sun-Selışık, 2016). It appears that there is still a gap in empirical studies that have targeted the effectiveness of well-being and mental health treatment modalities through technology (Koydemir et al., 2021).

Contrary to "normal" clinical psychology, which aims to treat adverse mental and emotional pathology, positive psychology focuses on the positive aspects, strengths, and abilities that foster individuals' flourishing (Jeong et al., 2020). Resilience and emotional intelligence are topics addressed within PPIs (Csikszentmihalyi & Larson, 2014). Counselors can work with clients on building resiliency, increasing emotional intelligence, and increasing positive self-concept, all of which may enhance a positive body image, potentially decreasing the development or ongoing symptoms related to an ED.

Critical Thinking Questions

1. What are two specific tools based on the positive psychology concept that you would implement with a client who has been diagnosed with bulimia? Why did you choose these techniques?
2. How can you foster a healthy balance of eating healthy and positive body image without fostering a potential opportunity for your client to begin obsessing over healthy eating which may lead to orthorexia nervosa (ON)?
3. What is visualization and how can you help clients with eating disorders (EDs) to use this exercise? What are some challenges that you may face when working with clients during this exercise?

Mindfulness and Eating Disorders

Although meditation techniques and mindfulness have been around for decades, they are now being even more recognized as potential treatment options when assisting individuals with eating disorders (EDs). Mindfulness is often defined as a state of consciousness that emerges through intentional attention to the present moment without judgment (Barbosa et al., 2020). Prior literature suggests that both mindful eating behavior and self-compassion impact healthy eating, resulting in a healthier body mass index (BMI) and, more importantly, the result of disordered eating. In a recent study conducted by Shaw and Cassidy (2022) about self-compassion and mindful eating, the findings revealed that participants who are self-compassionate and practice mindful eating are more unlikely to develop an ED. Furthermore, they found that self-kindness was correlated to an increase in positive eating attitudes (Shaw & Cassidy, 2022). Recent literature implies that mindfulness may play a critical role in ED psychopathology (Sala et al., 2020). Creative strategies to address dysfunctional eating behaviors have manifested, intentionally focusing on mindfulness, mindful eating, and intuitive eating (Barbosa et al., 2020).

Mindful eating (ME) focuses attention on food during consumption and self-awareness of the participation with food (Nelson, 2017). The goal of mindful eating is not to lose weight or calorie restriction; however, it is common for individuals to lose weight when they adhere to this practice. As noted earlier, individuals with EDs often struggle to remain in the present moment and enjoy the process of eating versus the consequence of ingesting the food. ME can benefit this vulnerable population because this practice aims to assist individuals in embracing the moment and the food while encouraging them to remain present while eating (Nelson, 2017). For example, Mercado and colleagues (2021) published a meta-analysis on randomized controlled studies examining binge-eating disorder (BED) and obesity by applying mindful-based interventions (MBIs). All studies in this meta-analysis investigated the efficacy of MBIs with control groups primarily encouraging either dietary or exercise-based behavioral change in individuals with overweight, obesity, and/or BED. The findings of this analysis reported that symptoms decreased for individuals with BED, and there was an inclination for a significant increase in mindfulness scores after the intervention (Mercado et al., 2021).

Another facet of mindfulness is self-compassion. When individuals are kind to themselves while remaining aware of their thoughts, this may result in more mindful, healthy eating behaviors. Neff (2003) describes self-compassion as having three ingredients, each with opposing beliefs: self-kindness versus self-judgment, common humanity versus isolation, and mindfulness versus over-identification. The last dimension of mindfulness versus over-identification is relevant to this chapter. In a recent study conducted by Shaw and Cassidy (2022) regarding self-compassion and ED, the findings propose that mindful eating behavior and self-compassion may represent both healthier eating and decreased obesity, in addition to a healthier perception toward food resulting in less of a chance of developing an ED. Also, this study noted that more healthy eating habits were positively correlated to self-kindness (Shaw & Cassidy, 2022). Individuals who have been diagnosed with an ED may benefit from an increase in positive self-talk, positive body image, and self-love, which are practices that appear viable during times of mindfulness.

Intuitive Eating and Mindfulness

Last, intuitive eating (IE) has underpinned mindfulness and gained recognition in the ED therapeutic field in the past decade. The diet mentality is when individuals are listening to non-physiological factors, such as cognitions, to decide food intake rather than depend on the body's natural self-regulation system (Grider et al., 2021). With this focus, individuals may be unable to identify true physical hunger versus what they "should" eat. For example, external signals encouraging food intake may include emotions, food availability, seeing or smelling food, eating heightened at social gatherings and setting, serving sizes, or enticing food packaging (Grider et al., 2021).

A recent study by Bennett and Latner (2022) focused on ME, IE, and the loss of control over eating. Notably, the results of this study suggest that both ME and IE patterns can prohibit eating disturbances, and healthier eating choices can disrupt the onset of pathological behaviors at any stage in their development. As clinicians and counselors assist individuals in IE, it is also essential to recognize the stage of recovery that each individual is in during the treatment process. Regardless, sufficient evidence in the literature suggests that ME and IE may positively impact individual psychological well-being around food intake. IE and ME have had increased attention as holistic strategies that reduce eating behaviors not driven by physical hunger while promoting psychological well-being (Denny et al., 2013). Further research and investigation on the benefits of IE for individuals struggling with ED will inform how clinicians implement this holistic practice during treatment.

Conclusion

This chapter provided an overview of specific EDs, etiology, symptomatology, and common treatment modalities for each condition. The intention was to inform and provide specific techniques embedded in positive psychology and mindfulness that may be effective when assisting individuals with an ED. We must consider that all techniques and concepts may not work for all individuals struggling with an ED; however, proposing a variety of progressive strategies and options for clients can positively impact the counseling relationship. Regardless of the specific modality, implementing a person-centered approach while developing a safe rapport with clients is the foundation for effective treatment with a positive outcome.

It is essential to remain multiculturally competent during the counseling experience to allow for open, safe, and trusting conversations between the therapist and the client. That said, research findings provided in this chapter also suggest that there is a need to promote intervention efforts to reach marginalized populations or those with historically minoritized identities, such as Black, Indigenous, People of Color (BIPOC), Lesbian, Gay, Bisexual, Transgender, and Queer (LGBTQ+) individuals, and people of size (Labarta et al., 2023). For example, Goel et al. (2022) noted that it would be highly advantageous if researchers and scientists committed to recruiting more racially diverse samples in all ED studies. This effort should proportionally focus on researchers from underrepresented racial/ethnic populations and individuals who suggest questions that specifically target EDs in marginalized racial/ethnic groups. Within the realm of ED, we hope that the research and clinical implications will continue to expand on potential and advanced treatment options to assist individuals in living their best quality of life.

Mindful Eating Resources and Activities

https://positivepsychology.com/mindful-eating-exercises/

https://nutritionsource.hsph.harvard.edu/mindful-eating/

https://www.thecenterformindfuleating.org/

https://www.fammed.wisc.edu/files/webfm-uploads/documents/outreach/im/handout_mindful_eating.pdf

https://biteoutoflifenutrition.com/mindful-eating-exercises/

https://www.newportacademy.com/?s=positive+psychology+

Case Study

History

James, now a 20-year-old Intercollegiate Wrestler, has been struggling with food since he was 8 years old. His relationship with food was influenced by his parent's concern for James's weight and body image, which his dad often called James "fat" as a child. Despite James's dedication and skill, his relationship with his body has always been complex. Now in college, he faces an unsupportive environment and internal pressures that have led to severe anorexia.

Family Influence

Growing up, James faced persistent body shaming from his father, who often commented on his weight and physique, pushing him into wrestling in hopes it would "keep him lean." These comments left James with lasting self-esteem issues, and he began associating his athletic performance with his physical appearance, especially weight. Over time, James's focus on weight and physique overshadowed his love for wrestling, evolving into an unhealthy obsession. His mother, always a support to James, was also his idol as he grew up an only child. Despite her love and care for her only child, his dad had spent years body-shaming his mother as well, which led to her poor health and dependence on his father for finances and attention.

Current Situation

James's restrictive eating patterns started in elementary school but worsened once he joined the college team. In his freshman year, his college coach regularly praised thinner athletes, reinforcing James's belief that weight loss equates to better performance. Now, as a junior, he's become noticeably underweight, fatigued, and has struggled with recurring injuries, affecting his performance.

Despite these warning signs, James's coach has been dismissive. When James's teammates raised concerns about his health, the coach downplayed it, saying, "He just needs to toughen up and push through." The lack of support from his coach has led James to withdraw further, internalizing his struggles.

Symptoms and Diagnosis

James exhibits classic symptoms of anorexia, including extreme food restriction, an intense fear of gaining weight, distorted body perception, low energy levels, and a fixation on maintaining low body fat. He also lost his best friend on the team who died last year in an auto accident. Despite his deteriorating physical condition, he remains convinced that continued weight loss will improve his wrestling and he keeping pushing himself in honor of the friend who was his number 1 supporter and training partner.

Challenges in Treatment

James's case is complicated by the multiple pressures he faces, including parental influence, his team and his coach, and his self-worth and identity, as he has attached his self-worth to his weight and performance, making it difficult for him to accept help or change his behaviors. His association with a culture obsessed with performance and success.

Treatment Plan

1. **Nutritional Counseling**: A dietitian specialized in sports nutrition would work with James to help him understand the importance of balanced nutrition for athletic performance and comprehensive health.
2. **Therapy**: Cognitive Behavioral Therapy (CBT) to help James address his deep-seated beliefs about body image and self-worth, alongside addressing his father's influence on his self-perception.
3. **Coaching Intervention**: Educating the coach on the effects of negative reinforcement and the importance of mental health in athletics could improve the team's culture.
4. **Individual Counseling**: Including James's father in some counseling sessions would allow a space for both to discuss the impact of past comments and work on building a healthier relationship.

Critical Thinking Questions

- How has James's father's consistent body shaming influenced James's self-perception and his relationship with food and body image?
- In what ways has James's mother's experience with body shaming and dependency on his father possibly impacted James's view of self-worth and relationships?
- Given the father's role in reinforcing negative self-image, what challenges might arise in family counseling, and how could these be approached effectively?
- How might the coach's dismissive attitude toward mental health issues affect the overall team culture, and what impact could this have on James's recovery process?
- What role can the coach realistically play in fostering a healthy environment for athletes struggling with body image and mental health issues?
- How might the loss of his best friend and training partner have influenced James's relationship with wrestling and his drive to continue losing weight?
- In what ways might James be using restrictive eating or intense weight control as a means to cope with his grief, and how can therapy help him find healthier ways to honor his friend's memory?
- What challenges might arise in helping James separate his identity from his performance and body image, and how could a counselor address these challenges?
- How can the counselor help James build a healthy self-image that is not tied solely to his success in wrestling or his physical appearance?
- How do cultural expectations around "toughness" in sports impact athletes' willingness to seek help for mental health or eating disorders (EDs)?
- What steps can athletic programs take to address harmful cultural norms that promote extreme thinness and toughness over health and well-being?
- What ethical challenges might arise when involving James's father in counseling, given his role in contributing to James's body image issues?
- How should the counselor balance respecting James's autonomy with intervening when his health is at serious risk?

References

Allen, J. G., Romate, J., & Rajkumar, E. (2021). Mindfulness-based positive psychology interventions: A systematic review. *BMC Psychology, 9*, 1–18. https://doi.org/10.1186/s40359-021-00618-2

American Psychiatric Association. (2022). *Diagnostic and statistical manual of mental disorders* (5th ed., text rev.). https://doi.org/10.1176/appi.books.9780890425787

Attia, E., Steinglass, J. E., Walsh, B. T., Wang, Y., Wu, P., Schreyer, C., Wildes, J., Yilmaz, Z., Guarda, A. S., Kaplan, A. S., & Marcus, M. D. (2019). Olanzapine versus placebo in adult outpatients with anorexia nervosa: A randomized clinical trial. *The American Journal of Psychiatry, 176*(6), 449–456. https://doi.org/10.1176/appi.ajp.2018.18101125

Balodis, I. M., Grilo, C. M., & Potenza, M. N. (2015). Neurobiological features of binge eating disorder. *CNS Spectrums, 20*(6), 557–565. https://doi.org/10.1017/S1092852915000814

Barbosa, M. R., Penaforte, F. R. D. O., & Silva, A. F. D. S. (2020). Mindfulness, mindful eating and intuitive eating in the approach to obesity and eating disorders. *SMAD. Revista Eletrônica Saúde Mental Álcool e Drogas, 16*(3), 118–135. https://doi.org/10.11606/issn.1806-6976.smad.2020.165262

Barthels, F., Barrada, J. R., & Roncero, M. (2019). Orthorexia nervosa and healthy orthorexia as new eating styles. *PLoS One, 14*(7), e0219609. https://doi.org/10.1371/journal.pone.0219609

Bennett, B. L., & Latner, J. D. (2022). Mindful eating, intuitive eating, and the loss of control over eating. *Eating Behaviors, 47,* 101680. https://doi.org/10.1016/j.eatbeh.2022.101680

Berner, L. A., & Marsh, R. (2014). Frontostriatal circuits and the development of bulimia nervosa. *Frontiers in Behavioral Neuroscience, 8,* 395. https://doi.org/10.3389/fnbeh.2014.00395

Bohlmeijer, E., & Westerhof, G. (2021). The model for sustainable mental health: Future directions for integrating Positive Psychology into mental health care. *Frontiers in Psychology, 12,* 747999. https://doi.org/10.3389/fpsyg.2021.747999

Bhattacharya, A., Cooper, M., McAdams, C., Peebles, R., & Timko, C. A. (2022). Cultural shifts in the symptoms of anorexia nervosa: The case of orthorexia nervosa. *Appetite, 170*, 105869–105869. https://doi.org/10.1016/j.appet.2021.105869

Bottera, A. R., & De Young, K. P. (2024). Loss of control eating exhibits an evening diurnal shift among females with bulimia nervosa and binge-eating disorder. *European Eating Disorders Review, 32*(1), 56–65. https://doi.org/10.1002/erv.3021

Bordin, E. S. (1979). The generalizability of the psychoanalytic concept of the working alliance. *Psychotherapy: Theory, Research & Practice, 16*(3), 252–260. https://psycnet.apa.org/doi/10.1037/h0085885

Brauhardt, A., de Zwaan, M., & Hilbert, A. (2014). The therapeutic process in psychological treatments for eating disorders: A systematic review. *The International Journal of Eating Disorders, 47*(6), 565–584. https://doi.org/10.1002/eat.22287

Csikszentmihalyi, M., & Larson, R. (2014). *Flow and the foundations of positive psychology* (Vol. 10, pp. 978–994). Springer.

Culbert, K. M., Racine, S. E., & Klump, K. L. (2015). Research review: What we have learned about the causes of eating disorders—A synthesis of sociocultural, psychological, and biological research. *Journal of Child Psychology and Psychiatry, and Allied Disciplines, 56*(11), 1141–1164. https://doi.org/10.1111/jcpp.12441

Dakanalis, A., Pla-Sanjuanelo, J., Caslini, M., Volpato, C., Riva, G., Clerici, M., & Carrà, G. (2016). Predicting onset and maintenance of men's eating disorders. *International Journal of Clinical and Health Psychology, 16*(3), 247–255. https://doi.org/10.1016/j.ijchp.2016.05.002

Dalle Grave, R., Calugi, S., Doll, H. A., & Fairburn, C. G. (2013). Enhanced cognitive behavior therapy for adolescents with anorexia nervosa: An alternative to family therapy? *Behaviour Research and Therapy, 51*(1), R9–R12. https://doi.org/10.1016/j.brat.2012.09.008

Dalle Grave, R., Eckhardt, S., Calugi, S., & Le Grange, D. (2019). A conceptual comparison of family-based treatment and enhanced cognitive behavior therapy in the treatment of adolescents with eating disorders. *Journal of Eating Disorders, 7,* 42. https://doi.org/10.1186/s40337-019-0275-x

Denny, K., Loth, K., Eisenberg, M.E., & Neumark-Sztainer, D. (2013). Intuitive eating in young adults. Who is doing it, and how is it related to disordered eating behaviors? *Appetite, 60,* 13–19. https://doi.org/10.1016/j.appet.2012.09.029

Dixon, K. M., Kivlighan, D. M., Jr., Hill, C. E., & Gelso, C. J. (2022). Cultural humility, working alliance, and outcome rating scale in psychodynamic psychotherapy: Between-therapist, within-therapist, and within-client effects. *Journal of Counseling Psychology, 69*(3), 276–286. http://dx.doi.org/10.1037/cou0000590

Fairburn, C. G., Bailey-Straebler, S., Basden, S., Doll, H. A., Jones, R., Murphy, R., O'Connor, M. E., & Cooper, Z. (2015). A transdiagnostic comparison of enhanced cognitive behavior therapy (CBT-E) and interpersonal psychotherapy in the treatment of eating disorders. *Behaviour Research and Therapy, 70,* 64–71. https://doi.org/10.1016/j.brat.2015.04.010

Fardouly, J., & Vartanian, L. R. (2016). Social media and body image concerns: Current research and future directions. *Current Opinion in Psychology, 9,* 1–5. https://doi.org/10.1016/j.copsyc.2015.09.005

Galmiche, M., Déchelotte, P., Lambert, G., & Tavolacci, M. P. (2019). Prevalence of eating disorders over the 2000–2018 period: A systematic literature review. *The American Journal of Clinical Nutrition, 109*(5), 1402–1413. https://doi.org/10.1093/ajcn/nqy342

Garber, A. K., Sawyer, S. M., Golden, N. H., Guarda, A. S., Katzman, D. K., Kohn, M. R., Le Grange, D., Madden, S., Whitelaw, M., & Redgrave, G. W. (2016). A systematic review of approaches to refeeding in patients with anorexia nervosa. *The International Journal of Eating Disorders, 49*(3), 293–310. https://doi.org/10.1002/eat.22482

Goel, N. J., Jennings Mathis, K., Egbert, A. H., Petterway, F., Breithaupt, L., Eddy, K. T., & Graham, A. K. (2022). Accountability in promoting representation of historically marginalized racial and ethnic populations in the eating disorders field: A call to action. *International Journal of Eating Disorders, 55*(4), 463–469. https://doi.org/10.1002/eat.23682

Goldschmidt, A. B. (2017). Are loss of control while eating and overeating valid constructs? A critical review of the literature. *Obesity Reviews, 18*(4), 412–449. https://doi.org/10.1111/obr.12491

Grider, H. S., Douglas, S. M., & Raynor, H. A. (2021). The influence of mindful eating and/or intuitive eating approaches on dietary intake: A systematic review. *Journal of the Academy of Nutrition and Dietetics, 121*(4), 709–727. https://doi.org/10.1016/j.jand.2020.10.019

Grilo, C. M., White, M. A., Gueorguieva, R., Wilson, G. T., & Masheb, R. M. (2013). Predictive significance of the overvaluation of shape/weight in obese patients with binge eating disorder: Findings from a randomized controlled trial with 12-month follow-up. *Psychological Medicine, 43*(6), 1335–1344. https://doi.org/10.1017/S0033291712002097

Haynos, A. F., Berg, K. C., Cao, L., Crosby, R. D., Lavender, J. M., Utzinger, L. M., Wonderlich, S. A., Engel, S. G., Mitchell, J. E., Le Grange, D., Peterson, C. B., & Crow, S. J. (2017). Trajectories of higher- and lower-order dimensions of negative and positive affect relative to restrictive eating in anorexia nervosa. *Journal of Abnormal Psychology, 126*(5), 495–505. https://doi.org/10.1037/abn0000202

He, J., Zhao, Y., Zhang, H., & Lin, Z. (2020). Orthorexia nervosa is associated with positive body image and life satisfaction in Chinese elderly: Evidence for a positive psychology perspective. *International Journal of Eating Disorders, 54*(2), 212–221. https://doi.org/10.1002/eat.23400

Hilbert, A., Pike, K. M., Goldschmidt, A. B., Wilfley, D. E., Fairburn, C. G., Dohm, F. A., Walsh, B. T., & Striegel Weissman, R. (2014). Risk factors across the eating disorders. *Psychiatry Research, 220*(1–2), 500–506. https://doi.org/10.1016/j.psychres.2014.05.054

Himmerich, H., & Treasure, J. (2018). Psychopharmacological advances in eating disorders. *Expert Review of Clinical Pharmacology, 11*(1), 95–108. https://doi.org/10.1080/17512433.2018.1383895

Hübel, C., Marzi, S. J., Breen, G., & Bulik, C. M. (2019). Epigenetics in eating disorders: A systematic review. *Molecular Psychiatry, 24*(6), 901–915. https://doi.org/10.1038/s41380-018-0254-7

Hudson, J. I., McElroy, S. L., Ferreira-Cornwell, M. C., Radewonuk, J., & Gasior, M. (2017). Efficacy of lisdexamfetamine in adults with moderate to severe binge-eating disorder: A randomized clinical trial. *JAMA Psychiatry, 74*(9), 903–910. https://doi.org/10.1001/jamapsychiatry.2017.1889

Huta, V. (2020). How distinct are eudaimonia and hedonia? It depends on how they are measured. *Journal of Well-Being Assessment, 4*(3), 511–537. https://doi.org/10.1007/s41543-021-00046-4

Jeong, S., Alghowinem, S., Aymerich-Franch, L., Arias, K., Lapedriza, A., Picard, R., Park, H. W., & Breazeal, C. (2020). A robotic positive psychology coach to improve college students' wellbeing. In *2020 29th IEEE International Conference on Robot and Human Interactive Communication (RO-MAN)* (pp. 187–194). IEEE. https://doi.org/10.48550/arXiv.2009.03829

Kaye, W. H., Wierenga, C. E., Bailer, U. F., Simmons, A. N., & Bischoff-Grethe, A. (2013). Nothing tastes as good as skinny feels: The neurobiology of anorexia nervosa. *Trends in Neurosciences, 36*(2), 110–120. https://doi.org/10.1016/j.tins.2013.01.003

Keel, P. K., & Forney, K. J. (2013). Psychosocial risk factors for eating disorders. *The International Journal of Eating Disorders, 46*(5), 433–439. https://doi.org/10.1002/eat.22094

Kessler, R. M., Hutson, P. H., Herman, B. K., & Potenza, M. N. (2016). The neurobiological basis of binge-eating disorder. *Neuroscience and Biobehavioral Reviews, 63,* 223–238. https://doi.org/10.1016/j.neubiorev.2016.01.013

King, J. A., Frank, G. K. W., Thompson, P. M., & Ehrlich, S. (2018). Structural neuroimaging of anorexia nervosa: Future directions in the quest for mechanisms underlying dynamic alterations. *Biological Psychiatry, 83*(3), 224–234. https://doi.org/10.1016/j.biopsych.2017.08.011

Koller, K. A., Thompson, K. A., Miller, A. J., Walsh, E. C., & Bardone-Cone, A. M. (2020). Body appreciation and intuitive eating in eating disorder recovery. *International Journal of Eating Disorders, 53*(8), 1261–1269. https://doi.org/10.1002/eat.23238

Koydemir, S., Sökmez, A. B., & Schütz, A. (2021). A meta-analysis of the effectiveness of randomized controlled positive psychological interventions on subjective and psychological well-being. *Applied Research in Quality of Life, 16*(3), 1145–1185. https://doi.org/10.1007/s11482-019-09788-z

Koydemir, S., & Sun-Selışık, E. (2016). Well-being on campus: A pilot study to test the effectiveness of an online strengths-based intervention for first year college students. *British Journal of Guidance and Counselling, 44*(4), 434–446. https://doi.org/10.1080/03069885.2015.1110562

Labarta, A. C., Irvine, T., & Peluso, P. R. (2023). Exploring clinician attitudes towards treating eating disorders: Bridging counselor training gaps. *Journal of Counselor Preparation and Supervision, 17*(1). https://research.library.kutztown.edu/jcps/vol17/iss1/2

Lavender, J. M., Wonderlich, S. A., Engel, S. G., Gordon, K. H., Kaye, W. H., & Mitchell, J. E. (2015). Dimensions of emotion dysregulation in anorexia nervosa and bulimia nervosa: A conceptual review of the empirical literature. *Clinical Psychology Review, 40,* 111–122. https://doi.org/10.1016/j.cpr.2015.05.010

Leehr, E. J., Krohmer, K., Schag, K., Dresler, T., Zipfel, S., & Giel, K. E. (2015). Emotion regulation model in binge eating disorder and obesity: A systematic review. *Neuroscience and Biobehavioral Reviews, 49,* 125–134. https://doi.org/10.1016/j.neubiorev.2014.12.008

Linardon, J. (2018). Meta-analysis of the effects of cognitive-behavioral therapy on the core eating disorder maintaining mechanisms: Implications for mechanisms of therapeutic change. *Cognitive Behaviour Therapy, 47*(2), 107–125. https://doi.org/10.1080/16506073.2018.1427785

Marzola, E., Nasser, J. A., Hashim, S. A., Shih, P. A., & Kaye, W. H. (2013). Nutritional rehabilitation in anorexia nervosa: Review of the literature and implications for treatment. *BMC Psychiatry, 13,* 290. https://doi.org/10.1186/1471-244X-13-290

McDonald, S. (2019). Understanding the genetics and epigenetics of bulimia nervosa/bulimia spectrum disorder and comorbid borderline personality disorder (BN/BSD-BPD): A systematic review. *Eating and Weight Disorders, 24*(5), 799–814. https://doi.org/10.1007/s40519-019-00688-7

Mehler, P. S., & Brown, C. (2015). Anorexia nervosa—medical complications. *Journal of Eating Disorders, 3,* 11. https://doi.org/10.1186/s40337-015-0040-8

Mercado, D., Robinson, L., Gordon, G., Werthmann, J., Campbell, I. C., & Schmidt, U. (2021). The outcomes of mindfulness-based interventions for obesity and binge eating disorder: A meta-analysis of randomized controlled trials. *Appetite, 166,* 105464. https://doi.org/10.1016/j.appet.2021.105464

Mitchell, J. E. (2016). Medical comorbidity and medical complications associated with binge-eating disorder. *The International Journal of Eating Disorders, 49*(3), 319–323. https://doi.org/10.1002/eat.22452

Mohler-Kuo, M., Schnyder, U., Dermota, P., Wei, W., & Milos, G. (2016). The prevalence, correlates, and help-seeking of eating disorders in Switzerland. *Psychological Medicine, 46*(13), 2749–2758. https://doi.org/10.1017/S0033291716001136

Munn-Chernoff, M. A., Johnson, E. C., Chou, Y. L., Coleman, J. R. I., Thornton, L. M., Walters, R. K., Yilmaz, Z., Baker, J. H., Hübel, C., Gordon, S., Medland, S. E., Watson, H. J., Gaspar, H. A., Bryois, J., Hinney, A., Leppä, V. M., Mattheisen, M., Ripke, S., Yao, S., Giusti-Rodríguez, P., … Agrawal, A. (2021). Shared genetic risk between eating disorder- and substance-use-related phenotypes: Evidence from genome-wide association studies. *Addiction Biology, 26*(1), e12880. https://doi.org/10.1111/adb.12880

Neff, K. D. (2003). The development and validation of a scale to measure self-compassion. *Self & Identity, 2*(3), 223–250. https://doi.org/10.1080/15298860309027

Nelson, J. B. (2017). Mindful eating: The art of presence while you eat. *Diabetes Spectrum: A Publication of the American Diabetes Association, 30*(3), 171. https://doi.org/10.2337/ds17-0015

Razzoli, M., Pearson, C., Crow, S., & Bartolomucci, A. (2017). Stress, overeating, and obesity: Insights from human studies and preclinical models. *Neuroscience & Biobehavioral Reviews,* 76(Pt. A), 154–162. https://doi.org/10.1016/j.neubiorev.2017.01.026

Sala, M., Shankar Ram, S., Vanzhula, I. A., & Levinson, C. A. (2020). Mindfulness and eating disorder psychopathology: A meta-analysis. *International Journal of Eating Disorders, 53*(6), 834–851. https://doi.org/10.1002/eat.23247

Schebendach, J., Mayer, L. E., Devlin, M. J., Attia, E., & Walsh, B. T. (2012). Dietary energy density and diet variety as risk factors for relapse in anorexia nervosa: A replication. *The International Journal of Eating Disorders, 45*(1), 79–84. https://doi.org/10.1002/eat.20922

Schmidt, U., Adan, R., Böhm, I., Campbell, I. C., Dingemans, A., Ehrlich, S., Elzakkers, I., Favaro, A., Giel, K., Harrison, A., Himmerich, H., Hoek, H. W., Herpertz-Dahlmann, B., Kas, M. J., Seitz, J., Smeets, P., Sternheim, L., Tenconi, E., van Elburg, A., van Furth, E., & Zipfel, S. (2016). Eating disorders: The big issue. *The Lancet Psychiatry, 3*(4), 313–315. https://doi.org/10.1016/S2215-0366(16)00081-X

Shafran, R. (2010). Interpersonal therapy or guided self-help CBT improve remission from binge eating compared to a behavioural weight-loss programme at 2-year post-treatment. *BMJ Mental Health, 13*(2), 48–48. https://doi.org/10.1136/ebmh.13.2.48

Shaw, R., & Cassidy, T. (2022). Self-compassion, mindful eating, eating attitudes and wellbeing among emerging adults. *The Journal of Psychology, 156*(1), 33–47. https://doi.org/10.1080/00223980.2021.1992334

Smink, F. R., van Hoeken, D., & Hoek, H. W. (2013). Epidemiology, course, and outcome of eating disorders. *Current Opinion in Psychiatry, 26*(6), 543–548. https://doi.org/10.1097/YCO.0b013e328365a24f

Stice, E., Marti, C. N., & Rohde, P. (2013). Prevalence, incidence, impairment, and course of the proposed *DSM-5* eating disorder diagnoses in an 8-year prospective community study of young women. *Journal of Abnormal Psychology, 122*(2), 445–457. https://doi.org/10.1037/a0030679

Tchanturia, K., Adamson, J., Leppanen, J., & Westwood, H. (2019). Characteristics of autism spectrum disorder in anorexia nervosa: A naturalistic study in an inpatient treatment programme. *Autism: The International Journal of Research and Practice, 23*(1), 123–130. https://doi.org/10.1177/1362361317722431

Thornton, L. M., Mazzeo, S. E., & Bulik, C. M. (2011). The heritability of eating disorders: methods and current findings. *Current Topics in Behavioral Neurosciences, 6*, 141–156. https://doi.org/10.1007/7854_2010_91

Tith, R. M., Paradis, G., Potter, B. J., Low, N., Healy-Profitós, J., He, S., & Auger, N. (2020). Association of bulimia nervosa with long-term risk of cardiovascular disease and mortality among women. *JAMA Psychiatry, 77*(1), 44–51. https://doi.org/10.1001/jamapsychiatry.2019.2914

Trace, S. E., Baker, J. H., Peñas-Lledó, E., & Bulik, C. M. (2013). The genetics of eating disorders. *Annual Review of Clinical Psychology, 9*, 589–620. https://doi.org/10.1146/annurev-clinpsy-050212-185546

Udo, T., & Grilo, C. M. (2018). Prevalence and correlates of DSM-5-defined eating disorders in a nationally representative sample of U.S. adults. *Biological Psychiatry, 84*(5), 345–354. https://doi.org/10.1016/j.biopsych.2018.03.014

Ulfvebrand, S., Birgegård, A., Norring, C., Högdahl, L., & von Hausswolff-Juhlin, Y. (2015). Psychiatric comorbidity in women and men with eating disorders results from a large clinical database. *Psychiatry Research, 230*(2), 294–299. https://doi.org/10.1016/j.psychres.2015.09.008

van Riel, L., van den Berg, E., Polak, M., Geerts, M., Peen, J., Ingenhoven, T., & Dekker, J. (2023). Exploring effectiveness of CBT in obese patients with binge eating disorder: personality functioning is associated with clinically significant change. *BMC Psychiatry, 23*(1), 136–136. https://doi.org/10.1186/s12888-023-04626-x

Voica, S. A., Kling, J., Frisen, A., & Piran, N. (2021). Disordered eating through the lens of positive psychology: The role of embodiment, self-esteem and identity coherence. *Body Image, 39*, 103–113. https://doi.org/10.1016/j.bodyim.2021.06.006

Wade, T. D. (2019). Recent research on bulimia nervosa. *The Psychiatric Clinics of North America, 42*(1), 21–32. https://doi.org/10.1016/j.psc.2018.10.002

Waterman, A. S., Schwartz, S. J., Zamboanga, B. L., Ravert, R. D., Williams, M. K., Bede Agocha, V. B., Kim, S. Y., & Brent Donnellan, M. (2010). The Questionnaire for Eudaimonic Well-Being: Psychometric properties, demographic comparisons, and evidence of validity. *The Journal of Positive Psychology*, *5*(1), 41–61. https://doi.org/10.1080/17439760903435208

Watson, H. J., Palmos, A. B., Hunjan, A., Baker, J. H., Yilmaz, Z., & Davies, H. L. (2021). Genetics of eating disorders in the genome-wide era. *Psychological Medicine, 51*(13), 2287–2297. https://doi.org/10.1017/S0033291720005474

Westwater, M. L., Mancini, F., Shapleske, J., Serfontein, J., Ernst, M., Ziauddeen, H., & Fletcher, P. C. (2021). Dissociable hormonal profiles for psychopathology and stress in anorexia and bulimia nervosa. *Psychological Medicine*, *51*(16), 2814–2824. https://doi.org/10.1017/S0033291720001440

Westwater, M. L., Seidlitz, J., Diederen, K. M., Fischer, S., & Thompson, J. C. (2017). Alterations in cortical thickness and structural connectivity are associated with symptom severity in bulimia nervosa. *Psychiatry Research: Neuroimaging. bioRxiv.* https://doi.org/10.1101/127910

Westwood, H., & Tchanturia, K. (2017). Autism spectrum disorder in anorexia nervosa: An updated literature review. *Current Psychiatry Reports, 19*(7), 41. https://doi.org/10.1007/s11920-017-0791-9

Wholihan, D. (2015). Anorexia and cachexia. In J. A. Pace & B. R. Ferrel (Eds.), *Physical aspects of care: Nutritional, dermatologic, neurologic and other symptoms* (pp. 13–21). Oxford University Press.

Wilfley, D. E., Citrome, L., & Herman, B. K. (2016). Characteristics of binge eating disorder in relation to diagnostic criteria. *Neuropsychiatric Disease and Treatment, 12,* 2213–2223. https://doi.org/10.2147/NDT.S107777

Wilson, G. T., & Zandberg, L. J. (2012). Cognitive-behavioral guided self-help for eating disorders: effectiveness and scalability. *Clinical Psychology Review, 32*(4), 343–357. https://doi.org/10.1016/j.cpr.2012.03.001

Wonderlich, S. A., Peterson, C. B., Crosby, R. D., Smith, T. L., Klein, M. H., Mitchell, J. E., & Crow, S. J. (2014). A randomized controlled comparison of integrative cognitive-affective therapy (ICAT) and enhanced cognitive-behavioral therapy (CBT-E) for bulimia nervosa. *Psychological Medicine, 44*(3), 543–553. https://doi.org/10.1017/S0033291713001098

Yilmaz, Z., Hardaway, J. A., & Bulik, C. M. (2015). Genetics and epigenetics of eating disorders. *Advances in Genomics and Genetics, 5,* 131–150. https://doi.org/10.2147/AGG.S55776

Young, S., Touyz, S., Meyer, C., Arcelus, J., Rhodes, P., Madden, S., Pike, K., Attia, E., Crosby, R. D., Wales, J., & Hay, P. (2017). Validity of exercise measures in adults with anorexia nervosa: The EDE, compulsive exercise test and other self-report Scales. *The International Journal of Eating Disorders, 50*(5), 533–541. https://doi.org/10.1002/eat.22633

Zipfel, S., Giel, K. E., Bulik, C. M., Hay, P., & Schmidt, U. (2015). Anorexia nervosa: Aetiology, assessment, and treatment. *The Lancet Psychiatry, 2*(12), 1099–1111. https://doi.org/10.1016/S2215-0366(15)00356-9

Posttraumatic Stress Disorder

13

Demaris Washington
Michele M. Mahr
Michelle Kelley Shuler

KEYWORDS AND DEFINITIONS:

Crisis: An emotionally significant event or radical change of status in a person's life.

Mindfulness: Heightened awareness and acceptance of internal experiences, which may be beneficial for individuals who have experienced trauma.

Positive psychology: A focus on positive subjective experience, individual characteristics, and positive institutions aimed to improve quality of life and decrease or prevent pathology.

Posttraumatic growth (PTG): Positive psychological improvements brought on by traumatic experiences or difficult circumstances.

Posttraumatic stress disorder (PTSD): A complex reaction to trauma with multiple factors involved that can lead to difficulty in individuals struggling to rebuild their lives and coping with stresses and life challenges after going through a traumatic event.

Stress: Stress is the natural reaction of the body when changes or challenges occur. It can result in many different physical, emotional, and behavioral responses.

Trauma: Encompasses experiences that cause intense physical and psychological stress reactions.

LEARNING OBJECTIVES:

1. Learn the definition of PTSD and the typical manifestations of the condition
2. Recognize how to implement positive psychology and mindfulness into the treatment plan when working with individuals with PTSD

3. Understand how finding meaning and purpose can relate to individuals with PTSD
4. Process the elements related to mindfulness and apply to the case study provided in the chapter
5. Conceptualize the definition of posttraumatic growth (PTG) and how it relates to PTSD and positive psychology

Overview of the Chapter

The purpose of this chapter is to provide an overview of the etiology of posttraumatic stress disorder (PTSD), common symptoms of this condition, and research related to PTSD. Furthermore, positive psychology and mindfulness can be viable treatment options to assist individuals who are struggling with this debilitating condition. The authors of this chapter will elaborate and suggest how healthcare professionals can implement these treatment modalities when working with individuals diagnosed with PTSD. Within this chapter, the authors will also focus on finding meaning and purpose related to positive psychology relevant to the most current evidence-based literature. Last, a sample case study presenting an opportunity to incorporate positive psychology and mindfulness when assisting individuals with PTSD is included.

Etiology of Posttraumatic Stress Disorder

It is crucial to look at the etiology of PTSD by examining various contributing factors, as research has highlighted the complexity of the disorder, often recognizing more than just one cause. The research literature on PTSD has identified several contributing factors, such as neurobiological, psychological, and environmental factors, that impact the development of this condition. Evolving on the scientific cause of PTSD is crucial for healthcare professionals as it leads to significant clinical implications. According to SAMHSA (2012), "trauma" refers to experiences that cause intense physical and psychological stress reactions.

> Trauma results from an event, series of events, or set of circumstances that [are] experienced by an individual as physically or emotionally harmful or threatening and that [have] lasting adverse effects on the individual's functioning and physical, social, emotional, or spiritual well-being. (p. 2)

How we define trauma has evolved, as has the diagnosis of PTSD throughout the years. Various movements throughout history have largely influenced this. For instance, research on veterans returning from combat and social movements was instrumental in the development of the diagnosis of PTSD (U.S. Department of Veteran Affairs, 2024). However, symptoms of PTSD were recognized much earlier in the 19th century (Institute of Medicine, 2012). There were early attempts to explain the occurrence of PTSD from medical and psychological perspectives. Over time, PTSD has evolved to encompass all types of traumatic stress and events (see Table 13.1). Historically, there has been a fundamental shift in the etiological factors of PTSD. Researchers have highlighted external factors (i.e., a traumatic experience) and inherent attributes of the individual (i.e., predisposition) and how these factors contribute to the symptomology of PTSD (Hu, 2024). To gain a better understanding of PTSD, let us begin by exploring the various types of trauma.

The *Diagnostic and Statistical Manual of Mental Disorders* (*DSM*) has adapted the diagnostic criteria for PTSD throughout the years. Initially, the *DSM-III* (APA, 1980, third ed.) defined traumatic experiences as catastrophic stressors that are outside the standard tolerance of human experience. These catastrophic occurrences appear to overwhelm the human ability to respond adaptively, leading to symptomology characteristic of PTSD. The expression of these symptoms largely depends on individual coping differences with catastrophic stress, leading to variance in the occurrence of PTSD. The *DSM-IV* (APA, 1994, fourth ed.) diagnostic criteria for PTSD added the history of exposure to a traumatic event and symptoms. The *DSM-V TR* revised the PTSD diagnostic criteria to include conceptual and clinical implications (American Psychiatric Association, 2013). Currently, PTSD falls under a new category, Trauma- and Stressor-Related Disorders, which require exposure to a traumatic or adverse event. *DSM-V-TR* defines posttraumatic stress disorder as a mental health condition that involves symptoms of intrusive memories (e.g., flashbacks), changes in cognition and mood, and physical alteration in reactivity and arousal (e.g., hypervigilance) as well as avoidance of stimuli related to trauma exposure (American Psychiatric Association, 2013). The etiological factors of PTSD are unique and differ from other psychiatric illnesses.

The etiology of PTSD is complicated, and research has offered many pathways of inquiry. Interestingly, research within this area has sought to understand the sequela of mental and physical issues, highlighting why some individuals go on to develop symptoms of PTSD and others do not. According to the National Institute of Health (2024), approximately 6 out of every 10 males (60%) and 5 out of every 10 women (50%) will encounter at least one trauma in their lifetime. Furthermore, between 5% and 8% of those individuals will have PTSD. PTSD has been researched through the lens of its psychological consequences (Jones & Barlow, 1990). Throughout the years, research on PTSD has evolved to gain an understanding of its contributing factors. PTSD research has expanded to examine more than just the psychological consequences and has included examining other contributing factors, such as biological and physiological aspects, psychological responses, and environmental influences. In the next section, we will discuss how biological and neurobiological factors play a role in the occurrence of PTSD.

Biological and Neurobiological Factors

Research indicates that biological and neurobiological factors play a role in susceptibility to PTSD (Toledo & Carson, 2022). For example, studies have identified an increased risk of developing symptoms when there is a family history of PTSD (Hu, 2024). Twin studies contributed significantly to our understanding of the genetic etiology of PTSD by suggesting that some individuals have a genetic predisposition that makes them more vulnerable to developing PTSD (Kremen et al., 2012).

Other links to the occurrence of PTSD include genetic markers and variants. Specific markers, such as those related to serotonin transporter (5 HTT) and brain-derived neurotrophic factor (BDNF), have been associated with an increased risk of PTSD (Al Jowf et al., 2021). These are associated with neurotransmitter regulation and stress response (Nisar et al., 2020). The serotonin transporter gene, 5 HTT, is linked with serotonin levels in the brain. Specifically, gene variation in short (s) and long (l) alleles of the 5 HTT gene promoter have been linked to stress response and vulnerability to disorders like PTSD (Bomyea et al., 2012). Individuals with this genetic predisposition are likely to experience heightened emotional responses, leading to a greater risk of developing PTSD. The gene variant 5 HTT is one of the many factors developing this disorder.

BDNF is associated with PTSD and contributes to the regulation of neuronal survival, neuroplasticity, and stress response (Bathina & Das, 2015; Zhang et al., 2016). The experience of stress and altered levels of BDNF can trigger neuronal death, leading to changes in the brain's ability to cope with traumatic experiences (Pfisterer & Khodosevich, 2017). BDNF supports neuroplasticity, facilitating the growth and survival of neurons in the brain. In general, brain neuroplasticity aids in adaptability and recovery from stress. Altered levels of BDNF also play a critical role in memory formation and extinction of fear response (Mahan & Ressler, 2012). These processes are often crucial aspects involved in PTSD as individuals can struggle with modifying their fear response, and disruption in BDNF may contribute to this difficulty. Conceptualizing the responsibility of the BDNF is necessary in understanding how neurobiological changes impact emotional and cognitive responses to trauma. It is essential to note the complexity of not only genetic factors but also environmental factors that may further influence the risk of PTSD.

Other PTSD studies link neurobiological changes in both the central and autonomic nervous systems (Al Jowf et al., 2023). Changes in the central and autonomic nervous system explain many of the psychological and physical symptoms of PTSD (*Van der Kolk, 2006*). Individuals with PTSD experience significant changes in their central nervous systems (CNS) (Raise-Abdullahi et al., 2023). Stress response, memory, and emotional regulation are critical areas controlled by the CNS. Particularly, studies show activity in three specific areas. One study shows that overactivation in the amygdala increased the fear response demonstrating hyperarousal leading to symptoms of PTSD (Sherin & Nemeroff, 2011). A second study showed prefrontal cortex dysregulation impairs emotional regulation (Bremner, 2006). A third study showed that hippocampal atrophy led to difficulty in differentiating between past and present traumatic experiences (Raise-Abdullahi et al., 2023).

Each structure plays a central role in emotion, stress response, and emotional modulation. The amygdala is a part of the region of the brain that is responsible for processes of emotions like fear and anxiety and can become overactive when an individual has symptoms of PTSD. The prefrontal cortex plays a central role in emotional dysregulation. The hippocampus operates to consolidate memory and is associated with flashbacks and intrusive memories. The hypothalamic-pituitary-adrenal (HPA) axis governs the stress response and the release of cortisol, a stress hormone (Stephens & Wand, 2012). One study shows that lower levels of cortisol modify feedback mechanisms contributing to the occurrence of PTSD symptoms (Al Jowf et al., 2021). In conclusion, research shows that changes in the central and autonomic nervous system support the development of PTSD, and it is crucial to understand the treatment targeting psychological and physiological aspects of PTSD.

Using Magnetic Resonance Imaging (MRI) and functional MRI (fMRI), researchers can study areas of the brain affected by PTSD. As mentioned earlier, crucial brain structures such as the hippocampus, amygdala, and prefrontal cortex have been focal points of these studies. These studies have led to the advancement of understanding of the functional changes in these particular structures. Noteworthy findings in MRI studies have shown that individuals with PTSD tend to have reduced volume in hippocampal and prefrontal cortex brain structures (Bremner, 2007; Bremner et al., 2008; Morey et al., 2012). Reduced volume in the hippocampus responsible for memory leads to difficulty in memory processing associated with re-experiencing trauma memories. Similarly, reduced volume in the prefrontal cortex is linked to difficulty regulating emotional responses, resulting in persistent fear and anxiety (Kredlow et al., 2022).

Altering levels of neurotransmitters such as serotonin, norepinephrine, and glutamate have been associated with the occurrence of PTSD. These neurotransmitters influence mood, arousal, and stress reactivity. Individuals with PTSD with reduced serotonin levels are known to have increased levels of anxiety, particularly affecting an individual's ability to cope effectively (Murrough et al., 2011); all of this leads to an increase in hypervigilance, which is a hallmark symptom of PTSD. The brain's excitatory neurotransmitter glutamate is also shown to sponsor abnormal levels in PTSD patients (Averill et al., 2017). Glutamate changes influence hyperarousal and cognitive dysfunctions. As individuals with PTSD have imbalances of this neurotransmitter, many will see changes in excitatory signaling and stress sensitivities.

Psychological Factors

Studies of psychological factors such as cognitive appraisal and emotional regulation demonstrate how individuals interpret and evaluate stressful and traumatic events. Interpretation and evaluation of a traumatic event can vary from person to person. Most often, these events alter perception, leading to distortion. The initial appraisal of an event has a significant impact on whether the individual will go on to express symptoms of PTSD (SAMHSA, 2012). When a threat is perceived overwhelmingly, and there is evidence of helplessness, one is more likely to experience persistent emotional distress.

Environmental Factors

Environmental factors also influence the occurrence of PTSD. High-risk environmental factors such as occupational hazards, exposure to community violence, crime, and conflict may play a significant role in the development of PTSD symptomatology. However, the severity of the trauma and the person's ability to cope with and regulate stress often modulate such development (Cruz et al., 2022; National Institute of Health, 2024). Notably, chronic exposure to environmental stressors that include poverty and discrimination may have a greater risk of experiencing trauma and a reduced sense of resilience to such events (Cruz et al., 2022). As an individual experiences repeated exposure to their environment, there is an increasing likelihood of PTSD-like symptoms. These experiences, plus unresolved trauma, impact an individual's ability to recover from the initial trauma, leading to the experience of ongoing stress. Other environmental factors, such as home instability and displacement, can also contribute to the lack of emotional and social support during or after the experience of traumatic events. These factors further disrupt an individual's ability to process and heal from their trauma. Combined, trauma and a lack of support have been found to increase the vulnerability of specific populations, leading to the greater occurrence of PTSD (Rhodes et al., 2010). Maladaptive coping and learned responses can further exacerbate PTSD. Some of these learned responses include being on constant alert and hypervigilant. Living in high-crime areas can increase hypervigilance and alertness of harm and threat (Van der Kolk, 2006). This level of activation can lead to a chronic state to dysregulation due to stress and trauma, making it difficult to recover (Sherin & Nemeroff, 2011). As the body remains in a constant state of stress response, the brain's ability to cope effectively increases the risk of developing PTSD.

Dynamic Factors

The occurrence of PTSD is complex and dynamic. Contributing factors such as biology, psychology, and environment play an influential role in the expression of the symptomatology of PTSD. These factors increase vulnerability after a traumatic experience. The interactions of these factors contribute to the variability in the onset, severity, and duration of those exposed to trauma. Stein et al. (2002) found that genetic, familiar, and unique environmental factors best accounted for the variance in the experience of PTSD. It is important to note that understanding how these factors contribute to the experience of PTSD adds critical clinical value to how we move forward with providing treatment and intervention.

Most Common Treatment Modalities

Some of the standard treatment modalities used to alleviate symptoms of PTSD include the following: Cognitive Behavior Therapy (CBT), Eye Movement Desensitization and Reprocessing (EMDR), and Cognitive Processing Therapy (CPT) (Schrader & Ross, 2021). Each of these treatment modalities has been widely researched and found to have a level of efficacy when treating PTSD (Kar, 2011). These various models offer different tools to cope with and heal from PTSD. CBT addresses distorted cognitions and maladaptive behaviors associated with the experience of trauma. The treatment can involve manageable exposures to trauma-related material to help reduce anxiety as well as teach strategies to cope with and manage symptoms. EMDR involves a patient being guided through eye movements while recalling and processing traumatic memories. This technique seeks to reduce any emotional distress and dysregulation associated with the trauma. CPT is a specific type of CBT that focuses on changing negative beliefs related to trauma. It encourages the patients to identify and challenge distorted cognition through a narrative component that facilitates reprocessing and reevaluating cognition and beliefs. These methods approach PTSD and trauma through the lens of pathology and a deficient perspective. The following section will explore how positive psychology builds resilience through a strength-based perspective, leading to optimism, connectedness, and mindfulness.

Positive Psychology

The positive psychology movement began in 1998 and has gained enormous popularity in research, application, and scholarship. Positive psychology seeks to explore what will help an individual thrive and flourish (Kim et al., 2018) as opposed to previous psychological research focused on states of depression and chaos. Generally, the overall quality of life, wellness, and health may impact an individual's mind and body. It is common knowledge that increased well-being promotes many advantages to individuals and the societies in which they reside (Lambert et al., 2019). With this in mind, some healthcare professionals and practitioners resonate with positive psychology and how it may be an effective treatment modality for individuals with PTSD. Facing challenges with optimism and a positive attitude will hopefully result in perceived success and learning opportunities instead of feelings of helplessness and overwhelm. Specifically, researchers within the positive psychology realm examine adaptive constructs such as resilience and mental strength to serve as buffers during adversity (Kim et al., 2018). For example, Lies et al. (2014) found that within 5 and 8 months, survivors of the 2009 Indonesian earthquake who displayed higher levels of hardiness and gratitude tended to report lower levels of global distress and posttraumatic stress than those with lower levels of these qualities. There appears to be a research gap for a more rigorous methodological approach in positive psychology studies, resulting in more robust informative studies (Hendricks et al., 2020). Suppose researchers can examine more specific positive constructs that benefit individuals during stress or crisis. In that case, this may be valuable information for clinicians and healthcare providers to evaluate when assessing for PTSD symptoms.

Specific interventions are deemed positive psychology interventions (PPIs) within positive psychology. Empirically supported, PPIs are intentional activities developed to increase the frequency of positive emotions and experiences, explicitly fostering behaviors and thoughts that result in an individual flourishing (Sin & Lyubomirsky, 2009). Scholars Hendricks et al. (2020) suggest that PPIs heighten positive feelings, behaviors, and cognitions while using theoretically and empirically based strategies to improve well-being. For individuals with PTSD, the PPIs may be viable strategies to assist in reframing the mindset to a more positive approach despite the experience of trauma and its persisting aftermath. PPIs focus on subjective experiences that include ideas correlated with wellness, flow, and beneficial emotions (Donaldson et al., 2019). Positive psychology and PPIs aim to highlight areas naturally seen as strengths within an individual versus focusing on the lack or areas of growth. When we think of attributes individuals may acquire or develop with a positive psychology approach, some may be wisdom, resilience, and purpose (Donaldson et al., 2019).

When evaluating individuals who have experienced trauma, it is essential to determine which factors may increase resiliency, shield from unfortunate outcomes such as PTSD, and/or assist in mitigating symptoms if they do occur (Gallagher et al., 2020). Hope, self-efficacy, and optimism are all relevant characteristics to developing resilience for individuals to maintain favorable expectations (Gallagher et al., 2020). Scholars Doody et al. (2021) reported a systematic review of military and emergency frontline workers that highlighted building resilience before deploying them into situations where they may experience traumatic incidents. Resiliency may be a preventative measure and a coping strategy especially for military and frontline workers to avoid the risk of developing mental health issues after exposure to potentially traumatic events.

Posttraumatic Growth

Without a doubt, trauma can have a significant and pervasive impact on an individual's life. Numerous supporting studies demonstrate the adverse effects of traumatic events leading to the symptoms of PTSD. Such results can present a one-sided perspective as some people do not express symptoms of PTSD and/or go on to recover from symptoms of PTSD to lead healthy and active lives. Recently, research has shifted to examine why this might be the case for some and not others. One area of focus that seeks to explain this experience is posttraumatic growth (PTG). PTG refers to positive psychological improvements brought on by traumatic experiences or challenging circumstances. Psychologists Richard Tedeschi and Lawrence Calhoun initially coined the term "posttraumatic growth" in the mid-1990s (Dell'Osso et al., 2022). PTG involves adjusting one's life philosophy, relational dynamics and interaction, and perception. This growth can increase mindfulness, belief in oneself, and appreciation for life. It is a significant part of psychopathological research, focusing on trauma's impact on illness. However, studies are now exploring the benefits of trauma, arguing that bad experiences do not always lead to adverse outcomes.

PTG is complex and involves a change in a person's core beliefs. It can further lead to perspective-building for individuals who experience it. Trauma can act as a catalyst in challenging belief systems, leading to growth experiences. PTG develops individually and is affected by the person's qualities. PTG research is fundamental as it diverts attention from pathology. For example, PTG is applicable for veterans because believing that growth after traumatic loss is possible gives hope to the individual who has experienced the loss and also provides them with resources for rebuilding their lives by helping them understand how experiencing trauma has changed them (Moore et al., 2022). One of the tools used to examine PTG is the Posttraumatic Growth Inventory (PTGI). The PTGI is a practical tool that can help people identify growth areas and highlight needed support. This inventory has gained momentum in the clinical field when assessing individuals who have experienced trauma or high levels of stress (Tedeschi et al., 2017). Within the PTGI emerged a 5-factor system with the following domains: Personal Strength, New Possibilities, Relating to Others, Appreciation of Life, and Spiritual Change (Tedeschi & Calhoun, 1996).

Domain 1 includes having an increased sense of self-strength and reliance. Domain 2 regards the changed quality of relationships, which entails increased compassion and feelings of connection with others. Domain 3 represents the experience of discovering a new or different journey in life established without adversity. Domain 4 encompasses an overall gratitude and appreciation for life. Finally, Domain 5 contains spiritual and existential changes that may involve deep reflection on philosophical questions (Taku et al., 2021). The Spiritual Change (SC) factor has provoked debate due to its short and restricted content (Tedeschi et al., 2017).

Finding meaning through trauma may help facilitate growth, healing, and recovery from a traumatic event. Using a variety of coping strategies, including passive and active coping strategies, can lead to a reduction in distress (Park, 2021). Some of these strategies can include finding meaning in trauma, reflecting and learning from the experience, reevaluating priorities, and integrating clarified values into daily life. By acknowledging the experience, a person can explore how and what happened during the trauma. This consideration can lead to a change in perspective and a reevaluation of what is important in life. Other strategies can help alleviate the impact of traumatic stress as well, such as practicing self-care, seeking social support, and engaging in mindfulness (Sawyer, 2023). Overall, when individuals can find a purpose or meaning in their experience, it may facilitate a growth mindset versus a fixed mindset, contributing to viewing the traumatic event with a fresh perspective.

Mindfulness and Meditation

Within the counseling research, literature, and clinical application, mindfulness has recently gained positive recognition as an additional tool to assist clients in times of stress. Mindfulness entails intentionally focusing on the present moment, without judgment (Kabat-Zinn & Hahn, 2009). Wellness has a foundation that involves removing the resistance against symptoms (not the symptoms themselves) and relying on gratitude, connectedness, and peace in the present moment (Lang et al., 2012). Mindfulness is an individual's elevated awareness and acceptance of internal experiences, which may benefit individuals who have undergone traumatic experiences (Harper et al., 2022).

The mindfulness practice appears to decrease physiological arousal, expand attentional control, and facilitate the acceptance of undesired experiences, each of which may target activities that regulate PTSD (Lang et al., 2012). In addition to mindfulness, meditation may also be advantageous for individuals coping with and managing PTSD symptoms. Lang and colleagues (2012) suggest that meditation may reduce PTSD symptoms and related functional impairments. Of course, it is essential to note that each individual is unique and may adhere to and respond to different therapeutic tools; however, counselors should be aware of the benefits of meditation and mindfulness. The results of a recent systematic review and meta-analysis by Harper and colleagues (2022) suggest there is a significant correlation between increased mindfulness and a decrease in PTSD symptoms. Notably, this endorses the idea that abilities such as heightened awareness and acceptance of internal experiences practiced during mindfulness-based interventions (Lang, 2017) may be advantageous for individuals who have experienced a traumatic event. There is a need for specific training related to mindfulness for healthcare professionals who are interested in implementing mindfulness into clinical practice for clients who are more at risk of trauma or perhaps do not have adequate access to treatment (Harper et al., 2022).

Conclusion

This chapter provided numerous reasons why positive psychology and mindfulness may be viable options for healthcare professionals and practitioners to implement into the treatment plan when assisting individuals with PTSD. As individuals face adversities, counselors need to reinforce the positive aspect of the experience, regardless of how difficult that may be at the moment. As noted, PTG can help individuals view the challenge or trauma as an experience that allows personal growth and builds resiliency. Furthermore, the PTGI may be a tool that counselors will include in the assessment and evaluation process during intake for clients with significant amounts of stress or adversities. Further research is warranted to understand how positive psychology, mindfulness, and meditation may psychologically, emotionally, and physically impact individuals who experience PTSD. An increased comprehension of the relationship between trait mindfulness and PTSD symptomatology has favorable inferences for elevating skills in mindful acceptance and awareness for individuals who are at an increased risk of developing PTSD symptoms (Harper et al., 2022). Meditation and mindfulness may not attract all individuals with PTSD; however, for those who are seeking complementary and alternative approaches, it would be a supplementation to our knowledge of empirically supported treatment approaches (Lang et al., 2012). This questioning and challenging the status quo of traditional therapy may hopefully inspire individuals to view their traumas from a place of empowerment versus the victim mindset. As we progress in the counseling discipline with new innovative treatments, such as mindfulness, clients with PTSD may move forward to PTG while also feeling empowered to cope with their diagnosis.

Case Study

Tina is a 35-year-old Latinx female, married, with three children. She experienced a car accident approximately 6 months ago. Shortly after her accident, she began experiencing symptoms that include flashbacks, nightmares, and difficulty driving in the car due to high anxiety. Her daily functioning has been impaired leading to difficulties with working and caring for her family. Her spouse has convinced her to start treatment online. She is reluctant to attend therapy as she feels she just needs time to process what happens to her. Prior to the accident, Tina was independent, active, and outgoing. Since the accident, her mood has changed dramatically and she does not want to leave the house. Her mood changes have led to a multitude of adverse effects; she appears to be on the edge, jumpy, most of the times; there are also other adverse effects such as decreased appetite and difficulty with sleep. She also worries when her spouse and children are away that something terrible will happen to them. After starting therapy, she has been able to share her thoughts and feelings related to the car accident. Please answer the following questions to inform her treatment and treatment plan.

1. What are the positive psychology approaches that would be most effective when working with Tina?
2. What strategies, practices, and skills would you like to focus on in the treatment of Tina?
3. How can you incorporate skills such as mindfulness into the treatment of Tina? What might that look like for treatment?

Critical Thinking Questions

1. How can positive psychology interventions (PPIs) be effectively integrated with trauma-informed modalities to treat PTSD symptomology?
2. What are the advantages of integrating the tenets of positive psychology into the treatment of PTSD?
3. What are the disadvantages of integrating the tenets of positive psychology into the treatment of PTSD?
4. What are the long-term effects of integrating positive psychology into the treatment of PTSD?
5. What are the specific tools, techniques, skills, and interventions that have been proven to be the most effective with PTSD?
6. What individual characteristics impact the effectiveness of positive psychology when incorporated into treatment of PTSD?
7. How do individual characteristics impact the effectiveness of positive psychology when incorporated into treatment of PTSD?
8. Is positive psychology proven to be effective when implemented in the treatment of PTSD?
9. How does positive psychology address toxic positivity in the treatment of PTSD?
10. What are the ethical considerations when implementing positive psychology in the treatment of PTSD?
11. What are the outcomes in treatment when positive psychology is integrated in trauma-informed care?

Resources for Positive Psychology and Mindfulness

https://positivepsychology.com/post-traumatic-growth/inventory

https://positivepsychology.com/

https://www.health.harvard.edu/topics/positive-psychology

https://www.health.harvard.edu/mind-and-mood/mindfulness-can-help-you-tame-fears-and-worries

https://www.tandfonline.com/journals/rpos20

https://www.verywellmind.com/what-is-positive-psychology-2794902

References

Al Jowf, G. I., Snijders, C., Rutten, B. P. F., de Nijs, L., & Eijssen, L. M. T. (2021). The molecular biology of susceptibility to post-traumatic stress disorder: Highlights of epigenetics and epigenomics. *International Journal of Molecular Sciences*, *22*(19), 10743. https://doi.org/10.3390/ijms221910743

Al Jowf, G. I., Ahmed, Z. T., Reijnders, R. A., de Nijs, L., & Eijssen, L. M. T. (2023). To predict, prevent, and manage post-traumatic stress disorder (PTSD): A review of pathophysiology, treatment, and biomarkers. *International Journal of Molecular Sciences, 24*(6), 5238. https://doi.org/10.3390/ijms24065238

American Psychiatric Association. (1980). *Diagnostic and statistical manual of mental disorders* (3rd ed.). https://doi.org/10.1176/ajp.145.10.1301

American Psychiatric Association. (1994). *Diagnostic and statistical manual of mental disorders* (4th ed.). https://doi.org/10.1176/ajp.152.8.1228

American Psychiatric Association. (2022). *Diagnostic and statistical manual of mental disorders* (5th ed., text rev.). https://doi.org/10.1176/appi.books.9780890425787

American Psychiatric Association. (2013). *Diagnostic and statistical manual of mental disorders* (5th ed.). Washington, DC: Author.

Averill, L. A., Purohit, P., Averill, C. L., Boesl, M. A., Krystal, J. H., & Abdallah, C. G. (2017). Glutamate dysregulation and glutamatergic therapeutics for PTSD: Evidence from human studies. *Neuroscience Letters*, *649*, 147–155, https://doi.org/10.1016/j.neulet.2016.11.064

Bathina, S., & Das, U. N. (2015). Brain-derived neurotrophic factor and its clinical implications. *Archives of Medical Science, 11*(6), 1164–1178. https://doi.org/10.5114/aoms.2015.56342

Bremner, J. D. (2007). Functional neuroimaging in post-traumatic stress disorder. *Expert Review of Neurotherapeutics*, *7*(4), 393–405. https://doi.org/10.1586/14737175.7.4.393

Bremner, J. D., Elzinga, B., Schmahl, C., & Vermetten, E. (2008). Structural and functional plasticity of the human brain in posttraumatic stress disorder. *Progress in Brain Research, 167*, 171–186. https://doi.org/10.1016/S0079-6123(07)67012-5

Bomyea, J., Risbrough, V., & Lang, A. J. (2012). A consideration of select pre-trauma factors as key vulnerabilities in PTSD. *Clinical Psychology Review*, *32*(7), 630–641. https://doi.org/10.1016/j.cpr.2012.06.008

Cruz, D., Lichten, M., Berg, K., & George, P. (2022). Developmental trauma: Conceptual framework, associated risks and comorbidities, and evaluation and treatment. *Frontiers in psychiatry*, *13*, 800687. https://doi.org/10.3389/fpsyt.2022.800687

Dell'Osso, L., Lorenzi, P., Nardi, B., Carmassi, C., & Carpita, B. (2022). Post traumatic growth (PTG) in the frame of traumatic experiences. *Clinical Neuropsychiatry*, *19*(6), 390–393. https://doi.org/10.36131/cnfioritieditore20220606

Doody, C. B., Robertson, L., Cox, K. M., Bogue, J., Egan, J., & Sarma, K. M. (2021). Pre-deployment programmes for building resilience in military and frontline emergency service personnel. *Cochrane Database of Systematic Reviews*, (12). https://doi.org/10.1002/14651858.CD013242.pub2

Donaldson, S. I., Lee, J. Y., & Donaldson, S. I. (2019). Evaluating positive psychology interventions at work: A systematic review and meta-analysis. *International Journal of Applied Positive Psychology*, *4*(3), 113–134. https://doi.org/10.1007/s41042-019-00021-8

Gallagher, M. W., Long, L. J., & Phillips, C. A. (2020). Hope, optimism, self-efficacy, and posttraumatic stress disorder: A meta-analytic review of the protective effects of positive expectancies. *Journal of Clinical Psychology*, *76*(3), 329–355. http://doi/org/10.1002/jclp.22882

Harper, L., Jones, A., Goodwin, L., & Gillespie, S. (2022). Association between trait mindfulness and symptoms of post-traumatic stress: A meta-analysis. *Journal of Psychiatric Research*, *152*, 233–241. https://doi.org/10.1016/j.jpsychires.2022.05.027

Hendricks, T., Schotanus-Dijkstra, M., Hassankhan, A., De Jong, J., & Bohlmeijer, E. (2020). The efficacy of multi-component positive psychology interventions: A systematic review and meta-analysis of randomized controlled trials. *Journal of Happiness Studies*, *21*(1), 357–390. https://doi.org/10.1007/s10902-019-00082-1

Hu, K. (2024). An analysis of the etiology of post-traumatic stress disorder. In *SHS Web of Conferences* (Vol. 193, p. 03006). EDP Sciences. https://doi.org/10.1051/shsconf/202419303006

Institute of Medicine. (2012). *Treatment for posttraumatic stress disorder in military and veteran populations: Initial assessment*. The National Academies Press. https://doi.org/10.17226/13364

Jones, J. C., & Barlow, D. H. (1990). The etiology of posttraumatic stress disorder. *Clinical Psychology Review*, *10*(3), 299–328. https://doi.org/10.1016/0272-7358(90)90064-H

Kabat-Zinn, J., & Hanh, T. N. (2009). *Full catastrophe living: Using the wisdom of your body and mind to face stress, pain, and illness*. Delta.

Kar, N. (2011). Cognitive behavioral therapy for the treatment of post-traumatic stress disorder: A review. *Neuropsychiatric Disease and Treatment*, *7*, 167–181. https://doi.org/10.2147/NDT.S10389

Kim, H., Doiron, K., Warren, M., & Donaldson, S. (2018). The international landscape of positive psychology research: A systematic review. *International Journal of Wellbeing*, *8*(1), 50–70. https://doi.org/10.5502/ijw.v8i1.651

Kredlow, M. A, Fenster, R. J., Laurent, E. S., Ressler, K. J., & Phelps, E. A. (2022). Prefrontal cortex, amygdala, and threat processing: Implications for PTSD. *Neuropsychopharmacology : Official Publication of the American College of Neuropsychopharmacology*, *47*(1), 247–259. https://doi.org/10.1038/s41386-021-01155-7

Kremen, W. S., Koenen, K. C., Afari, N., & Lyons, M. J. (2012). Twin studies of posttraumatic stress disorder: Differentiating vulnerability factors from sequelae. *Neuropharmacology*, *62*(2), 647–653. https://doi.org/10.1016/j.neuropharm.2011.03.012

Lambert, L., Passmore, H. A., & Joshanloo, M. A. (2019). Positive psychology intervention program in a culturally-diverse university: Boosting happiness and reducing fear. *Journal of Happiness Studies*, *20*, 1141–1162. https://doi.org/10.1007/s10902-018-9993-z

Lang, A. J. (2017). Mindfulness in PTSD treatment. *Current Opinion in Psychology, 14*, 40–43. https://doi.org/10.1016/j.copsyc.2016.10.005

Lang, A. J., Strauss, J. L., Bomyea, J., Bormann, J. E., Hickman, S. D., Good, R. C., & Essex, M. (2012). The theoretical and empirical basis for meditation as an intervention for PTSD. *Behavior Modification, 36*(6), 759–786. https://doi.org10.1177/0145445512441200

Lies, J., Mellor, D., & Hong, R. Y. (2014). Gratitude and personal functioning among earthquake survivors in Indonesia. *The Journal of Positive Psychology, 9*(4), 295–305. https://doi.org/10.1080/17439760.2014.902492

Mahan, A. L., & Ressler, K. J. (2012). Fear conditioning, synaptic plasticity and the amygdala: Implications for posttraumatic stress disorder. *Trends in Neurosciences, 35*(1), 24–35. https://doi.org/10.1016/j.tins.2011.06.007

Moore, M., Palmer, J. K., Cerel, J., & Ruocco, K. (2022). Growth and hope after loss: How TAPS facilitates posttraumatic growth in those grieving military deaths. *Frontiers in Psychology, 13*, 996041. https://doi.org/10.3389/fpsyg.2022.996041

Morey, R. A., Gold, A. L., LaBar, K. S., Beall, S. K., Brown, M. A., Haswell, C. C., Nasser, J. D.,Wagner, H. R., McCarthy, G., & Mid-Atlantic MIRECC Workgroup. (2012). Amygdala volume changes in posttraumatic stress disorder in a large case-controlled veterans group. *Archives of General Psychiatry, 69*(11), 1169–1178. https://doi.org/10.1001/archgenpsychiatry.2012.50

Murrough, J. W., Czermak, C., Henry, S., Nabulsi, N., Gallezot, J. D., Gueorguieva, R., Planeta-Wilson, B., Krystal, J. H., Neumaier, J. F., Huang, Y., Ding, Y. S., Carson, R. E., & Neumeister, A. (2011). The effect of early trauma exposure on serotonin type 1B receptor expression revealed by reduced selective radioligand binding. *Archives of General Psychiatry, 68*(9), 892–900. https://doi.org/10.1001/archgenpsychiatry.2011.91

National Institute of Health. (2024). *Post traumatic stress disorder (PTSD) 2024.* https://hr.nih.gov/working-nih/civil/post-traumatic-stress-disorder-ptsd-2024

Nisar, S., Bhat, A. A., Hashem, S., Syed, N., Yadav, S. K., Uddin, S., Fakhro, K., Bagga, P., Thompson, P., Reddy, R., Frenneaux, M. P., & Haris, M. (2020). Genetic and neuroimaging approaches to understanding post-traumatic stress disorder. *International Journal of Molecular Sciences, 21*(12), 4503. https://doi.org/10.3390/ijms21124503

Park, C. L., Finkelstein-Fox, L., Russell, B. S., Fendrich, M., Hutchison, M., & Becker, J. (2021). Psychological resilience early in the COVID-19 pandemic: Stressors, resources, and coping strategies in a national sample of Americans. *American Psychologist. 76*, 715–728. https://doi.org/10.1037/amp0000813

Pfisterer, U., & Khodosevich, K. (2017). Neuronal survival in the brain: Neuron type-specific mechanisms. *Cell Death & Disease, 8*, e2643. https://doi.org/10.1038/cddis.2017.64

Raise-Abdullahi, P., Meamar, M., Vafaei, A. A., Alizadeh, M., Dadkhah, M., Shafia, S., Ghalandari-Shamami, M., Naderian, R., Afshin Samaei, S., & Rashidy-Pour, A. (2023). Hypothalamus and post-traumatic stress disorder: A review. *Brain Sciences, 13*(7), 1010. https://doi.org/10.3390/brainsci13071010

Rhodes, J., Chan, C., Paxson, C., Rouse, C. E., Waters, M., & Fussell, E. (2010). The impact of hurricane Katrina on the mental and physical health of low-income parents in New Orleans. *American Journal of Orthopsychiatry, 80*(2), 237.

Sawyer, H. (2023). Mindfulness: Strategies to implement targeted self-care. *Journal of Interprofessional Education & Practice, 31*, 100614. https://doi.org/10.1016/j.xjep.2023.100614

Schrader, C., & Ross, A. (2021). A review of PTSD and current treatment strategies. *Missouri Medicine, 118*(6), 546–551.

Sherin, J. E., & Nemeroff, C. B. (2011). Post-traumatic stress disorder: The neurobiological impact of psychological trauma. *Dialogues in Clinical Neuroscience, 13*(3), 263–278. https://doi.org/10.31887/DCNS.2011.13.2/jsherin

Sin, N. L., & Lyubomirsky, S. (2009). Enhancing well-being and alleviating depressive symptoms with positive psychology interventions: A practice-friendly meta-analysis. *Journal of Clinical Psychology, 65*(5), 467–487. https://doi.org/10.1002/jclp.20593

Stein, M. B., Jang, K. L., Taylor, S., Vernon, P. A., & Livesley, W. J. (2002). Genetic and environmental influences on trauma exposure and posttraumatic stress disorder symptoms: A twin study. *American Journal of Psychiatry, 159*(10), 1675–1681. https://doi.org/10.1176/appi.ajp.159.10.1675

Stephens, M. A., & Wand, G. (2012). Stress and the HPA axis: Role of glucocorticoids in alcohol dependence. *Alcohol Research: Current Reviews, 34*(4), 468–483.

Substance Abuse and Mental Health Services Administration [SAMHSA], Trauma and Justice Strategic Initiative. (2012). https://ncsacw.acf.hhs.gov/userfiles/files/SAMHSA_Trauma.pdf

Taku, K., Tedeschi, R. G., Shakespeare-Finch, J., Krosch, D., David, G., Kehl, D., ... & Calhoun, L. G. (2021). Posttraumatic growth (PTG) and posttraumatic depreciation (PTD) across ten countries: Global validation of the PTG-PTD theoretical model. *Personality and Individual Differences, 169*, 110222. https://doi.org/10.1016/j.paid.2020.110222

Tedeschi, R. G., & Calhoun, L. G. (1996). The Posttraumatic growth inventory: Measuring the positive legacy of trauma. *Journal of Traumatic Stress, 9*(3), 455–471. https://doi.org/10.1007/BF02103658

Tedeschi, R. G., Cann, A., Taku, K., Senol-Durak, E., & Calhoun, L. G. (2017). The posttraumatic growth inventory: A revision integrating existential and spiritual change. *Journal of Traumatic Stress, 30*(1), 11–18. https://doi.org/10.1002/jts.22155

Toledo, F., & Carson, F. (2022). Neurobiological features of posttraumatic stress disorder (PTSD) and their role in understanding adaptive behavior and stress resilience. *International Journal of Environmental Research and Public Health, 19*(16), 10258. https://doi.org/10.3390/ijerph191610258

U.S. Department of Veteran Affairs. (2023). *PTSD: National Center for PTSD. How common is PTSD in Adults?* https://www.ptsd.va.gov/understand/common/common_adults.asp

U.S. Department of Veteran Affairs. (2024). *History of PTSD in Veteran: Civil War to* DSM 5. Author. http://va.gov

Van der Kolk, B. A. (2006). Clinical implications of neuroscience research in PTSD. *Annals of the New York Academy of Sciences, 1071*, 277–293. https://doi.org/10.1196/annals.1364.022

Zhang, L., Li, X. X., & Hu, X. Z. (2016). Post-traumatic stress disorder risk and brain-derived neurotrophic factor Val66Met. *World Journal of Psychiatry*, 6(1), 1–6. https://doi.org/10.5498/wjp.v6.i1.1

Implementing Positive Psychology and Mindfulness: The Aging Population

14

Susan L. Williams
Michele M. Mahr

KEYWORDS AND DEFINITIONS:

Chair Yoga: The act of using a chair to guide and support an individual when performing specific yoga poses.

Gratitude: Appreciation for specific things that an individual may have in their life, including a sense of thankfulness (Sansone & Sansone, 2010).

Hope: Recognized as a positive state that relies on three factors: goals (targets to be attained), pathways (action planning to obtain these objectives), and agency (the enthusiasm and intention that is directed toward achieving these goals) (Shehata et al., 2024).

Positive aging: A multifactorial concept that merges several characteristics of aging well, including optimal, successful, productive, and healthy aging (Bar-Tu, 2021).

Wisdom: A complicated multidimensional characteristic and the individual must incorporate several or all subcomponents of wisdom to an extensive amount to be considered wise (Bangen et al., 2013).

LEARNING OBJECTIVES:

1. Identify psychological and physical barriers that the older adult population may encounter during the aging process
2. Recognize potential strategies that can increase positive aging for the older adult population
3. Describe various techniques related to positive psychology and mindfulness that may assist the older adult population in aging with peace

4. Examine two case studies on aging and formulate answers to critical thinking questions based on the information provided in this chapter
5. Define the benefits to mindfulness and how they are connected to improving the lives of the older adult population
6. Be able to distinguish the myths versus facts related to the aging population

The aging population has its own set of developmental challenges to cope with. Beginning in their 60s and the 70s, the cumulative effects of aging become more prominent, and the aging process seems to accelerate. From the wrinkles on the face to the shorter body stature, muscle loss, less visual acuity, hearing, loss, weakened immune system, brain cells dying off at a faster rate, and reflexes slowing down, there are a lot of changes that need to be accommodated in older persons' lives (Kassin et al., 2023). However, Kassin et al. (2023) also state that there is good news to consider about the aging process. In discussing a study by Levy et al. (2002), it was noted that

> Men and women who had a positive view of aging, when measured up to 23 years earlier, lived seven and a half years longer than those with less positive views of aging. Apparently, a positive attitude about aging—which is accompanied by a strong will to live—is more predictive of longevity than gender, wealth, cholesterol level, blood pressure, weight, smoking and exercise. (Kassin et al., 2023, p. 383)

Psychological Challenges to Positive Aging

Growing older can be very difficult for some adults, especially those who make negative assumptions about the aging process and endorse negative stereotypes about aging. Hill (2005) indicated there are specific personality traits as measured by the NEO-PI-R (Costa & McRae, 1992a, 1992b) that indicate when a person may struggle with the aging process. Those scoring low in Openness to Experience are less flexible in their outlook, resist change, and are unable to think outside of the box and look forward to new opportunities and experiences. Those scoring high in Neuroticism feel excessive anxiety and worry and have more negative, rigid, and pessimistic thoughts in their approach to life. Overall, those scoring low in Neuroticism and high in Extraversion have the highest life satisfaction in old age (Hill, 2005). While personality traits tend to be stable over time, one can modify the behavioral manifestations of those traits to a more positive direction through therapy. Counseling techniques that help older adults reduce their rigid thinking, negative outlook, amount of ongoing worry and regrets, and level of self-absorption can promote a more positive view of the aging process.

Cognitive Decline in the Older Population

According to Kassin, et al., (2023) Alzheimer's disease is

> a progressive and irreversible brain disorder that afflicts mostly the elderly and kills brain cells at a terrifying pace. It begins with simple lapses of memory and is soon followed by attention problems and bursts of anger, depression, changes in mood and personality and a deterioration of physical functions. (p. 384)

There is no cure for this disease currently. Once diagnosed, people with Alzheimer's tend to live approximately 8 more years. However, there continue to be breakthroughs in the treatment of Alzheimer's disease through lifestyle changes and research with new medications. Ornish and Ornish (2019) have worked with older adults in numerous research studies to attempt to reverse signs of early-stage dementia where they modified their participants' eating plan/diet to a whole-foods, plant-based diet; incorporated regular moderate aerobic exercise, strength training, and stretching into their weekly activities; taught them to incorporate stress reduction techniques, such as gentle yoga, meditation, breathing techniques, and relaxation techniques into their schedule; and provided a weekly hour-long support group to give them an opportunity to deeply connect with others, experience compassion and empathy in one's interactions, and express their authentic feelings, which is a very healing experience.

To support the positive impact of exercise on brain health and reversal of cognitive impairment, Ornish and Ornish (2019) noted that

> Another study found that men and women with mild cognitive impairment (a precursor to Alzheimer's disease) who exercised four times a week over a six-month period (treadmill, stationary bike, or elliptical machine) experienced an increase in gray matter volume as measured by MRI and an improvement in cognitive function. In contrast, the control group showed some brain atrophy and worsening in cognitive function. Similar findings were documented in another randomized controlled trial. After six months, those doing moderate aerobic exercise had significant increases in brain volume both in gray matter and white matter regions. (p. 107)

Similarly, Sanjay Gupta has noted that the progression of Alzheimer's disease can be slowed, prevented, and possibly reversed.

> Preventing problems down the road is health care, instead of sick care. Today, getting off the road to Alzheimer's disease and other dementias is so much simpler than we previously thought. The decisions we make every day—to eat healthy, to move more, to learn new skills, and to spend time with loved ones—sounds easy, but the evidence is clear. It can, and will, lead to better brain health. (CNN Press Room, 2024, para. 1)

Arthur Kramer, a research psychologist from the University of Illinois has also noted: "It is not just a matter of slowing down the aging process; it's a matter of reversing it" (Ornish & Ornish, 2019, p. 107). Clearly, positive psychology interventions (PPIs) including lifestyle changes provide a lot of hope for the aging process.

Mental Health and Older Adults

According to the APA (2014a), the older adult population is growing in numbers, diversity, and mental health needs. By 2030, older adults will make up 20% of the U.S. population. There is a need for more mental health providers with expertise in working with the older people. It is important for mental health providers to examine any stereotypes or biases they might have about the older adults, so they can unlearn them and not have them negatively impact their treatment with older adult clients (APA, 2014b).

Positive aging involves accommodation to physical changes, functional limitations, as well as changes in social functioning, and most of the older adult clients are able to do that well. Learning the biological changes that occur with aging is an important part of understanding one's older adult clients. The aging population is increasingly diverse, and it is crucial for clinicians to consider all of their client's intersectional identities when working with them (APA, 2014b). While most of the older adults report good mental health, about 20% to 22% have a psychological disorder (APA, 2014a). Depressive symptoms in older adults may present more on a somatic basis rather than via emotional symptoms. Feelings of anxiety tend to be more related to worries that are age related. Older adult clients have typically experienced losses of loved one and may need to do grief work. They are susceptible to alcohol-related problems due to age-related physiological changes. A very small percentage of older adults (2.2% men and 1.4% women) report using illicit drugs. That number is expected to rise as baby boomers age. For the majority of older adults, age-related changes in memory and cognition are quite mild and don't interfere with their daily activities of living. A smaller number who are living with dementia may present with feelings of paranoia, behavioral disturbances, anxiety, and depression. As their functional ability worsens, discerning the best living environment for them, in consultation with their family members, can be an important part of treatment.

Research shows that older adults respond well to a variety of forms of therapy, including interpersonal therapy, cognitive-behavioral therapy, animal-assisted therapy, music therapy, art therapy, exercise training, reminiscence therapy, occupational therapy, laughter therapy, and geriatric group therapy (Lonczak, 2021). Tailoring the treatment approach to the specific needs of each older client is essential. Counselors can always help older clients find continued meaning and purpose in their lives is very important. Giving back to their communities by engaging in volunteer work or spending time with the younger generation may be opportunities for some older adults to find a sense of purpose in their lives.

Myths and Facts About Aging

There are many myths and ageist beliefs about older adult population (American Psychological Association [APA], 2014a; National Institute on Aging 2024; Reid, 2023). It is important for clinicians to be very aware of these stigmas that older clients face and assist them in combatting these stereotypes others impose on them.

Some of these myths include the following:

MYTHS	FACTS
All older people end up with memory problems and many develop dementia.	Risk for dementia does increase with age, but it is not a part of the normal aging process.
Older adults should be more sedentary to avoid falls or accidents.	Exercise is good for people at all ages of life. It helps improve mental and physical health.
Older adults aren't able to learn new things because they are too set in their ways.	The older adults are capable of learning new things and doing so helps keep their memory stronger.
Older adults are stubborn and inflexible.	One's personality traits tend to be stable over time and do not change drastically with age. Older adults do have to cope with functional limitations of aging, and most of them successfully navigate these changes.
Depression and loneliness are an inevitable part of aging.	Younger people have higher rates of depression than older people do. It is important for older adults to maintain positive social contacts and engage in activities that give them joy.
Older adults are no longer interested in intimacy or sex.	Most older adults have meaningful interpersonal and sexual relationships.
Older people need less sleep than their younger counterparts.	All adults need about 7–9 hours of sleep per night. This need for sleep does not decrease with age. Older adults may have a more difficult time falling asleep and staying asleep, but adequate sleep is just as important for them to improve their overall sense of well-being and reduce the risks of falls.

Strategies for Positive Aging

According to Hill (2008), there are seven strategies for positive aging that can be utilized by older adults to improve their aging process.

1. Finding Meaning in Your Life as You Age

While older adults will find that they can't do all of the activities they enjoyed in their youth, instead of looking back with regret over abilities lost, they can seek to create meaningful experiences that give them hope, joy, and fulfillment. That could include volunteer work, giving back to the younger generation via a reading program, joining a senior center and embarking on new experiences and trips, or sharing your life story with younger people, and so on. Even when disability or illness impedes one's life further, there can be ways to continue to find meaning that helps sustain one's spirit and mental well-being.

2. Being a Life-Long Learner

It is never too late to learn something new, whether that is a musical instrument, a new language, cooking new recipes, gardening, taking classes in new subjects, traveling, and learning about other cultures; the possibilities are endless. Learning new information helps improve brain function. Even older adults in assisted living and memory care can explore opportunities for learning that can be adapted to their current abilities.

3. Cultivating Wisdom Through Reflection on Your Past

Older adults are in the unique position to reflect on their life history, understand their past successes and failures, and learn from them to create a present and future that can bring peace of mind. As Hill (2008) stated,

> Positive aging represents a lifestyle which produces a "wise" skill set. Unlike the pessimistic view of age-related decline, wisdom seems to improve as one becomes older. In many respects, wisdom is enhanced by the ability to learn from life experiences and to make more effective life decisions. (p. 65)

One can learn to cultivate wisdom in their older years by learning from past mistakes, being reflective and not impulsive when trying to solve problems, helping others in need, not repeating past negative patterns, and cultivating optimism about yourself and others.

4. Strengthening Your Interpersonal Relationships

"The need to belong is an emotion or a desire to be a part of someone's life; to be connected in some way" (Hill, 2008, p. 67). Older adults can enhance their sense of belongingness by thinking about those in their social group and assessing the quality of their interactions with them. Do they show concern and care for others and is that caring reciprocated? It is important to note that one does not need to be in physical proximity with someone else to feel they belong. Interactions over the phone, email, or social media sites can also convey caring and concern for one another .Being flexible and affirming in one's interactions is important as it conveys that one is thinking about the other's needs. Having a positive social support network and sense of belonging is crucial to one's sense of well-being, and it can be strengthened through intentional positive behaviors.

5. Helping Others and Receiving Help

The act of helping others serves to strengthen bonds to one's family, friends, and the larger community. Research into the impact of volunteering has shown that it makes people "happier, healthier, easier to live with, and better at taking care of yourself and others" (Hill, 2008. p. 93). It has also been shown to increase longevity (Harris & Thoresen, 2005) and is associated with a greater sense of life purpose and meaning. Older adults can evaluate what skills they have to offer to their community and find an organization to become involved with. Another challenge of aging is when one recognizes their need to receive help from others. It is critical to learn how to receive help with flexibility and grace. It is important to acknowledge that someone who cares about you wants to provide needed assistance as a way of showing they care. One can develop a more positive attitude about receiving help by thinking back on times when you helped others when they were in need and how that felt to you. Being a grandparent offers opportunities for both helping out one's grandkids and receiving help from them, which can serve to strengthen the bonds of your relationship. It is also satisfying to know that by allowing one's grandchildren to help out, you are assisting them in learning important life lessons that aid in their maturation.

6. Embracing Forgiveness

Hill (2008) noted that "the propensity to forgive emerges and matures across the lifespan" (p. 113). Forgiveness is associated with both emotional and spiritual healing. Lawler et al. (2005) found that the act of forgiveness serves to reduce hostility, negative emotions, high blood pressure, feelings of chronic anger or depression, susceptibility to disease, and cardiac reactivity.

Forgiveness involves having a compassionate approach to the situation and a worldview that is not idealized, one in which it is acknowledged that bad things can happen to innocent victims and people are capable of heinous acts. When one practices forgiveness, it helps free up inner resources and allows you to think more compassionately and flexibly about the world around you as well as yourself. It increases older adults' capacity to feel happier and live a better life as they age. Self-forgiveness is also a crucial part of positive aging. It starts with recognizing we are all imperfect as humans and will make mistakes. Self-forgiveness, which begins with having compassion for oneself, has been associated with positive emotions and improved personal adjustment (Neff, 2003). Seeking forgiveness from others also frees one up from long-held guilt and shame. Receiving forgiveness can assist the older person in working toward humility, gratitude, reconciliation, and in finding meaning in their past mistakes.

7. Cultivating Gratitude

Fitzgerald (1988) described three elements of gratitude:

> Gratitude is (1) a warm sense of appreciation for somebody or something, (2) a sense of goodwill toward that individual or thing, and (3) a disposition to act which flows from appreciation and goodwill. Gratitude is not merely an emotion; however, we describe it as a virtue when it contributes to living one's life well (p. 120).

Cultivating a sense of gratitude about one's life aids older adults in feeling positive about their life circumstances despite the challenges they may be facing. One can learn to cultivate a more grateful perspective by starting a gratitude journal that involves writing down things they are grateful for on a daily basis with a minimum of five entries per day. This helps you to focus on the positive aspects of life. Emmons and McCullough (2003) found that people who utilized a gratitude journal showed greater well-being on measures of life satisfaction and self-esteem compared with a control group. Writing in a gratitude journal can help you discover you can find things to be grateful for even when in poor health, when coping with loss, or in other challenging situations. It can help you learn to reframe your regrets into opportunities. As Hill (2008) stated,

> We need strategies and techniques to deal with the vicissitudes of growing old. If you are truly grateful, you will not ignore reality, but you will be skilled at finding meaning in the "good and the bad" that you encounter. (p. 143)

That is not to downplay the seriousness of one's situation but rather to highlight that there is always something to be thankful for as well. Gratitude journaling helps shift one's mindset from negative to positive.

Conclusion and Summary

To conclude, this chapter provided an overview of how to foster positive aging for the older adult population with specific techniques and strategies. As noted, positive psychology and mindfulness practices can be highly valuable to assist the aging population in living a higher quality of life, based upon their own individualistic standards. Within the neuroscience literature, one operational definition of mindfulness is having the awareness that stems from focused attention in an intentional and nonjudgmental state to direct the experience within the present moment (Kabat-Zinn, 1982). It is essential that the negative stigma related to aging gracefully and positively be addressed and decreased. This chapter highlighted some of the myths that are often perceived by society related to positive aging. Our hope is that the societal norm will change and we will see a paradigm shift on how living longer can be a healthy, vibrant, and exciting experience. By being intentional to implement mindfulness, yoga, breathing exercises, positive affirmations, journaling, and gratitude exercises into the lives of the aging population, it may lead to overall improved quality of life.

Case Study

Sandra is a 71-year-old widowed female who lost her husband of 35 years three months ago when he had a massive heart attack and died before paramedics arrived at their home. She witnessed his death and has flashback images about his passing, which are highly upsetting to her. Since then, she has lost 20 pounds without trying to do so, as she says she no longer has an appetite. She is 5'5" and currently weighs 120 lbs. Due to her stress, she resumed smoking cigarettes, which greatly upsets her because she quit 10 years ago and was proud of herself for doing so. She is a retired elementary education school teacher. She states since her husband's passing, her days are long, monotonous, and she feels she has no significant meaning or purpose in life. She has three grandchildren, but they live out of state, and she rarely sees them. She is having sleep problems and reports difficulty falling asleep, mid-cycle awakening, and early-morning awakening. Overall, she states she is getting about 4 to 5 hours of sleep per night, when she typically slept 7 to 8 hours per night before her husband's death. She is a member of a local church and used to attend services regularly, but that has lessened since her husband's passing. She feels angry with God about her husband's death and feels a lot of guilt about her anger. She is very motivated to seek help and states her goals are to maintain her weight loss, quit smoking, learn how to cope with her loss, and find meaning in her life again.

Critical Thinking Questions

- What are some specific interventions or strategies based on Positive Psychology you would utilize to begin to assist Sandra?
- What are some assessment tools that might be helpful to use with Sandra at this time?
- What questions would you ask Sandra about her treatment goals?
- How would you help Sandra expand her social support network and reduce her feelings of isolation?
- What resources could you offer for Sandra's ongoing self-care?
- What other forms of treatment (beyond individual counseling) might you recommend?

Suggested Treatment Options

This is a complicated case study that requires a multifaceted and holistic approach to help Sandra heal. There are numerous concerns to address: her grief over her husband's death; the trauma she experienced witnessing his death and the resulting sleep difficulties and flashbacks; her lack of social supports and increased isolation due to rarely seeing her family and not going to church anymore; her loss of faith and anger at God; and resuming the smoking habit and feeling like she has no meaning in her life. All of these symptoms could result in her experiencing a major depression and potential suicidal ideation in the future if not treated adequately. Sandra needs to be further assessed for depression and PTSD. A referral for a medical evaluation is important. If her symptoms do meet the criteria for PTSD, she could benefit from an adjunctive treatment such as EMDR (Shapiro, 2014; Valente-Gomez et al., 2017), brainspotting (Blanchfield, 2013; Corrigan & Grand, 2013), or transcranial magnetic stimulation (Hayes, 2023) for treatment of her trauma. She could be assessed for antidepressant medication, but since her loss is fairly recent, talking about her grief in individual therapy as well as joining a grief support group (if she is amenable to this option) may help to ameliorate her depression without the use of medication. Two potential assessment instruments that could be helpful in her case include the Beck Depression Inventory (Beck et al., 1961) and the Suicide Probability Scale (Cull & Gill, 1982). There are numerous positive psychology interventions (PPIs) that could be utilized in this case. Sandra stated she wanted to find meaning in her life. It would be important to ask her what has given her a sense of meaning throughout her life and work from her responses. Since she is a retired school teacher, one option she might consider would be to volunteer some time in a classroom to help students with their interpersonal skills, encouraging cooperation and respect of others, doing creative art projects with students, reading stories to small groups, or whatever she might feel interested in as a way to continue to give back to the younger generation. If she is not interested in being back in the classroom, one could inquire about her hobbies or things she used to enjoy and brainstorm ways those things could be reintegrated into her life. If she loves animals, for instance, volunteering with a local animal shelter might give her meaning. These activities would also help her strengthen her interpersonal relationships and acquire a sense of connection that is missing in her life. One could inquire about possibly making a plan to visit her grandchildren or have them visit her to nurture those important relationships in her life.

In terms of dealing with her grief and loss, processing those feelings on a deep level is very important, and they can also be intertwined with cultivating gratitude for the life she has lived and the love she shared with her husband, savoring those positive experiences and positive reminiscences of her life. If she enjoys writing, starting a gratitude journal could be very helpful. Using mindfulness and meditation techniques could assist her in working on her goal of smoking cessation. Learning deep breathing techniques to ease her anxiety when she has the urge to reach for a cigarette, as well as setting aside time each day for meditation and calming her mind, would be positive distractions. If she enjoys the outdoors, spending time in nature would be helpful in reducing her feelings of depression. There might be opportunities to join a walking group at a local senior center where she could get exercise, meet new friends, and boost her mood and physical health all at the same time. In terms of her anger at God over her husband's death and the guilt she feels about this, learning to embrace forgiveness for these feelings could assist her in reducing her anger. One potential goal in this area might be to set up a meeting with her minister to further discuss these feelings from a religious perspective and perhaps later on consider attending church services again. Whatever direction she chooses to take in her healing journey, it would always be on her own terms and suited to her needs and desires.

Positive Psychology and Positive Aging

Positive psychology developed by Seligman and Csikszentmihalyi (2000) focuses on highlighting the assets of an individual's strengths while using the available resources to help them live the most optimal life. Leaning into positive psychology and positive aging research and tools, one program has been identified as The Mental Fitness Program for Positive Aging (MFPPA), which is developed for older adults in community settings (Bar-Tur, 2021). This program can heighten seniors' quality of life by increasing their essential participation, help them engage in an active life, and assist them develop the skills and techniques needed to handle challenges (Bar-Tur, 2021). When considering the definition of wellness, we must look at the holistic perspective and not just one dimension of wellness. As such, wellness is not just a life without an illness; it is an active process focused on an individual living a peaceful, healthy, and fulfilling life that also entails bringing improvement into their physical, psychological, and emotional domains (Levine, 2019).

As noted earlier in this chapter, the aging population faces challenges that need specialized attention and intentional effort. Research is also being directed to study how positive psychology can be applied to assist the aging population. For example, in a recent study at a community setting of individuals 65 years of age or older, a study was conducted implementing the Positive Psychology Interaction Group Program. This program was integrated over 10 weeks with the expectation of positive effects on the emotional well-being of older adults and to create positive self-perception, life satisfaction, successful communication, and coping skills for stress (Gümüş Demir et al., 2021).

PPIs have been clinically studied in research with several populations, but only a minimum have targeted the effects of such practices in older adult participants (Gümüş Demir et al., 2021). It can be assumed that the older adult population may also benefit from activities and programs that foster hope. With this in mind, Charles Richard Snyder, known for the Forgiveness and Hope Theory, and a scholar within the positive psychology realm, acknowledges hope to be connected with an individuals' cognitive skill. Snyder's theory entails the following three areas: goals (approaching life with purpose), path (seeking various ways to achieve life goals), and actions (changeable motivation to achieve life goals) (Snyder, 2002).

Mindfulness and Positive Aging

Mindfulness practice can be highly valuable and effective for the aging population as they devote their attention and intention into aging positively. Included in the various Mind–Body Strategies, mindfulness has become the leading practice among health professionals due to its high correlation with health-promoting positive behaviors, such as emotional management, physical well-being, positive sleep quality, and healthy eating (Sala et al., 2020). A recent study examining the efficacy of mindfulness-based interventions for individuals aged 60 years and above to improve cognition revealed positive outcomes for those in the study (Sanchez-Lara et al., 2021). Specifically, the scholars noted that the research and findings imply that implementing mindfulness over a longer timeframe, applying targeted mindfulness-based interventions, could increase the effect size for individuals 60 years or older (Sanchez-Lara et al., 2021). Moreover, the results within this study revealed that mindfulness training being practiced at an earlier age may help prevent cognitive impairment for the future, which is extremely pertinent when working with the aging population. The older adult population often have rich, robust, and many memories from their past lives that they may wish to reflect on in order to find meaning to this stage of their life. Mindfulness allows for an individual to feel safe and secure without judgment, also leading to complete acceptance to whatever they are feeling or thinking in that moment.

The older adult population typically face psychological barriers such as loneliness, anxiety, and depression, which can hinder and decrease their overall wellness (Herdian et al., 2024). Mindfulness may be a viable and feasible option to help the aging population face their psychological and emotional concerns with resiliency while also remaining open to the possibility of hope to achieve positive outcomes despite the challenges. It is essential that healthcare professionals assist the aging population by targeting common mental health issues with effective and culturally relevant interventions (Herdian et al., 2024).

Chair Yoga and Mindfulness

Yoga is often correlated with mindfulness due to the fact that the individual must remain mindful during specific poses and remain focused throughout the practice. Yoga is often recognized as a spiritual discipline, an art, a science, and a philosophy that was derived in ancient India (Chobe et al., 2020). Some individuals may find a sense of peace and overall calmness when practicing yoga, as it helps to calm the mind while focusing on the body. Yoga can also be defined as a lifestyle for an individual when seeking a higher pursuit of being or meaning by combining the individual consciousness with an altered state of consciousness (Chobe et al., 2020). In a broader sense, it is a way of living life to achieve higher pursuit, that is, the union of individual consciousness with cosmic consciousness. Chair yoga is a unique type of yoga practiced while sitting on a chair, or standing using a chair for guidance and support; it is adapted for individuals with limited ability to be able to balance and engage in yoga safely (Gannotti & Veneri, 2022). A recent scoping review conducted by two researchers examined the current published literature related to the use of chair/adapted yoga with the aging population. The scholars suggested that based on the findings in support of chair/adapted yoga, it is recommended that this intervention should be implemented continuously and investigated even more for older adult population (Gannotti & Veneri, 2022). Furthermore, a systematic review conducted by Chobe et al. (2020) suggests that yoga-based interventions have positive impacts on the older adult population, such as improving attention, executive functions, and memory of cognition.

Creativity and Mindfulness

It is important to consider that the older adult population may feel isolated or stagnant as they age because they may not have the level of creativity that they once had in their years of youth. That said, assisting individuals to tap into their creative side may result in positive aging. For example, in one study conducted by Cantu and Fleuriet in 2018 suggested that creative engagement is one road to aging successfully. The participants in this study implied that their creative engagement in activities increased their strength in focusing, which then added to an improved sense of overall wellness (Cantu & Fleuriet, 2018). Counselors may want to suggest various creative activities that may stimulate the older adult population to have increased positive emotions and feelings related to their aging process. Furthermore, the capacity for creativity and artistic expression has been integrated into the field of gerontology and scientific ideas related to the aging process (Galassi et al., 2022). Interestingly, the application of utilizing colors, gestures, and materials excite locations of the brain related to the limbic or emotions system, specifically the hippocampus, which is where new brain cells are developed (Stern, 2009). With this information, it can be assumed that implementing creative activities into the lives of the aging population may lead to elevated moods and emotions.

In order for clients to remain engaged in the creative art activity, being mindful would be expected. It may require a level of intentionality and focus to participate in the creative practices. One pathway to stimulate creativity includes mindfulness training, which has a limited number of examined studies (Cheung & Hui, 2024). Hence, this could be an area that warrants further research and investigation and potential experimental studies that incorporate the aging population as participants in mindfulness trainings while evaluating creativity factors. Essentially, the active engagement of creative activities may be a potential nonpharmacological strategy that may also decrease the cognitive impairment for the aging population (Cantu & Fleuriet, 2018).

Please take time to analyze this case study while applying the aforementioned mindfulness concepts and techniques mentioned above.

Case Study: Mindfulness

Dorothy is an 80-year-old single woman who has been living in assisted care for the past five years. She has a history of chronic debilitating neck and back pain stemming from a severe auto accident 25 years ago. She was a professional musician, playing violin in orchestras all over the world before her pain was too much to continue her musical career. She now spends most of her time in bed since lying down, which lessens her pain somewhat. It is extremely painful for her to sit in a chair or walk with a walker. She has had neck and back surgeries in the past that had minimal impact on her pain level. Her medications are also not very effective at reducing her pain. She has been through a pain management program and did not find it to be helpful. She feels hopeless about her future and states that she just wishes she could die. She does not engage with other residents in her community and takes all of her meals in bed. Her relatives live out of state, and, while they are very supportive of her, they visit infrequently. She primarily spends her time reading and watching TV. She is extremely bright and has very strong cognitive functioning. Before her pain became so severe, she played bridge regularly, frequently won, and really enjoyed that game. She is an avid animal lover, and although pets are allowed in her residence, she does not have any due to feeling she can't physically take care of them. She has friends who visit occasionally, and, although she enjoys their visits, she is in more pain after they leave. She is taking antidepressant medication that has improved her mood only slightly, but she is not currently in therapy. She was offered the opportunity to see a visiting therapist and has agreed to begin treatment. Her goal is to become more mobile via being able to sit in a wheelchair and leave her room on occasion to interact with other residents.

- What are some specific interventions or strategies based on Positive Psychology you would utilize to begin to assist Dorothy?
- What are some assessment tools that might be helpful to use with Dorothy at this time?
- What questions would you ask Dorothy about her current situation?
- How would you help Dorothy expand her social support network and reduce her feelings of isolation?
- What resources could you offer for Dorothy's ongoing self-care?
- What other forms of treatment (beyond individual counseling) might you recommend?
- How can you assist Dorothy in restoring hope in her life?

While working on your responses to the questions above, the following possible interventions could be considered as part of your plan: Dorothy needs to be assessed for depression and suicidality.

Two potential assessment instruments that could be helpful in her case include the Beck Depression Inventory (Beck et al., 1961) and the Suicide Probability Scale (Cull & Gill, 1982). Other areas of potential intervention include a medication evaluation, physical therapy, chair yoga, breathing exercises, meditation, social interaction with residents, reminiscence therapy, animal-assisted therapy, music therapy, cognitive restructuring to reduce negative thoughts and increase positive self-statements, progressive relaxation training, grieving the loss of her career and mobility while challenging herself to find activities she can still enjoy, exploring the beautiful grounds of her residence in a reclining and padded wheelchair, watching comedies so she can engage in laughter, making a gratitude list, face-timing with friends and relatives, and learning a new skill such as a new language or a game that is intriguing and fun.

References

American Psychological Association. (2014a). *Working with older adults. What mental health practitioners should know.* https://www.apa.org/pi/aging/resources/guides/practitioners-should-know

American Psychological Association. (2014b). Guidelines for psychological practice with older adults. *American Psychologist, 69*(1), 34–65.

Bangen, K. J., Meeks, T. W., & Jeste, D. V. (2013). Defining and assessing wisdom: A review of the literature. *The American Journal of Geriatric Psychiatry, 21*(12), 1254–1266. http://dx.doi.org/10.1016/j.jagp.2012.11.020

Bar-Tur, L. (2021). Fostering well-being in the elderly: Translating theories on positive aging to practical approaches. *Frontiers in Medicine, 8*, 517226. https://doi.org/10.3389/fmed.2021.517226

Beck, A. T., Ward, C. H., Mendelson, M., Mock, J., & Erbauch, J. (1961). *Beck Depression Inventory (BDI)* [Database record]. APA PsycTests. https://doi.org/10.1037/t00741-000

Blanchfield, T. (2023, April 24). *Brainspotting therapy: How it works, techniques and efficacy.* Verywellmind. https://www.verywellmind.com/brainspotting-therapy-definition-techniques-and-efficacy-5213947

Cantu, A. G., & Fleuriet, K. J. (2018). "Making the ordinary more extraordinary": Exploring creativity as a health promotion practice among older adults in a community-based professionally taught arts program. *Journal of Holistic Nursing, 36*(2), 123–133. http://doi.org/10.1177/0898010117697863

Cheung, H. N., & Hui, A. N. (2023). Impact of a mindfulness-based program on creativity and mindfulness disposition of school children. *Psychology of Aesthetics, Creativity, and the Arts, 17*(6), 694–704. https://doi.org/10.1037/aca0000598

Chobe, S., Chobe, M., Metri, K., Patra, S. K., & Nagaratna, R. (2020). Impact of yoga on cognition and mental health among elderly: A systematic review. *Complementary Therapies in Medicine, 52*, 102421. https://doi.org/10.1016/j.ctim.2020.102421

Corrigan, F., & Grand, D. (2013). Brainspotting: Recruiting the midbrain for accessing and healing sensorimotor memories of traumatic activation. *Medical Hypotheses, 80*(6), 759–766. https://doi.org/10.1016/j.mehy.2013.03.005

Costa, P. T., & McCrae, R.R. (1992a). Normal personality assessment in clinical practice. The NEO Personality Inventory. *Psychological Assessment, 4*, 5–13.

Costa, P. T., & McCrae, R. R. (1992b). *Revised NEO Personality Inventory professional manual.* Psychological Assessment Resources.

CNN Press Room. (2024, May 13) *CNN's Dr. Sanjay Gupta reports "The last Alzheimer's patient."* https://cnnpressroom.blogs.com/2024/05/13/cnns-dr-sanjay-gupta-reports-the-last-alzheimers-patient-for-the-whole-story-with-anderson-cooper/

Cull, J. G., & Gill, W. S. (1982). *Suicide Probability Scale (SPS)* [Database record]. APA PsycTests. https://doi.org/10.1037/t01198-000

Emmons, R. A., & McCullough, M. E. (2003). Counting blessings versus burdens: An experimental investigation of gratitude and subjective well-being in daily life. *Journal of Personality and Social Psychology, 84*(2), 377–389. https://doi.org/10.1037/0022-3514.84.2.377

Fitzgerald, P. (1998). Gratitude and justice. *Ethics, 109,* 119–153.

Galassi F, Merizzi, A., D'Amen, B., & Santini, S. (2022, Sep 26). Creativity and art therapies to promote healthy aging: A scoping review. *Front Psychol. 13*:906191. doi:10.3389/fpsyg.2022.906191. PMID: 36225688; PMCID: PMC9549330

Gannotti, M., & Veneri, D. (2022). Take a seat for yoga with seniors: A scoping review. *OBM Geriatrics, 6*(2), 1–69. https://doi.org/10.21926/obm.geriatr.2202197

Gümüş Demir, Z., Keskin, R., & Güler, K. (2021). The effect of the positive psychology interaction group program on anger and hope in elderly individuals. *Turkish Journal of Geriatrics, 24*(1). https://doi.org/10.31086/tjgeri.2021.204

Harris, A. H. S., & Thoresen, C. E. (2005). Volunteering is associated with delayed mortality in older people: Analysis of the longitudinal study of aging. *Journal of Health Psychology, 10*(6), 739–752.

Hayes, T. (2023, March 30). FDA clears brain modulation device for PTSD. *Healthcare Packaging.* https://www.healthcarepackaging.com/quick-hits/article/22780424/fda-clears-brain-modulation-device-for-ptsd

Herdian, H., Estria, S. R., Setyawati, R., & Dewi, D. S. E. (2024). Mindfulness therapy training: Efforts to improve mental health of the elderly in the elderly of Pimpinan Daerah Aisyiyah Banyumas Organization. *International Journal of Community Service Implementation*, 2(2), p.164-171.

Hill, R. D. (2005). *Positive aging.* W. W. Norton.

Hill, R. D. (2008). *Seven strategies for positive aging.* W. W. Norton.

Kabat-Zinn, J. (1982). An outpatient program in behavioral medicine for chronic pain patients based on the practice of mindfulness meditation: Theoretical considerations and preliminary results. *General Hospital Psychiatry, 4,* 33–47.

Kassin, S., Privitera, G. J., & Clayton, K. D. (2023). *Essentials of psychology.* Sage.

Lawler, K. A., Younger, J. W., Piferi, R. L., Jobe, R. L., Edmundson, K. A., & Jones, W. H. (2005). The unique effects of forgiveness on health: An exploration of pathways. *Journal of Behavioral Medicine. 28,* 157–167.

Levine, G. N. (2019). The mind-heart-body connection. *Circulation, 140*(17), 1363–1365. https://doi.org/10.1161/CIRCULATIONAHA.119.041914

Levy, B. R., Slade, M. D., Kunkel, S. R., & Kasi, S. V. (2002). Longevity increased by positive self-perceptions of aging. *Journal of Personality and Social Psychology, 83,*(2), 261–270.

Lonczak, H. S. (2021, May 5). *Geriatric therapy: How to help older adults with depression.* https://positivepsychology.com/geriatric-therapy-older-adults-depression/#

National Institute on Aging. (2024, April 10). *10 common misconceptions about aging.* https://www.nia.nih.gov/health/healthy-aging/10-common-mosconceptions-about-aging/

Neff, K. D. (2003). Self-compassion: An alternative conceptualization of a healthy attitude towards oneself. *Self and Identity, 2,* 85–102.

Ornish, D., & Ornish, A. (2019). *UnDo it!* Ballantine Books.

Reid, S. (2023, February 23). *Ageism and age discrimination.* HelpGuide.org https://www.helpguide.org/articles/aging-issues/ageism-and-age-discrimination.htm#

Sala, M., Rochefort, C., Lui, P. P., & Baldwin, A. S. (2020). Trait mindfulness and health behaviors: A meta-analysis. *Health Psychology Review, 14*(3), 345–349. https://doi.org/10.1080/17437199.2019.1650290

Sanchez-Lara, E., Lozano-Ruiz, A., Perez-Garcia, M., & Caracuel, A. (2021). Efficacy of mindfulness-based interventions in cognitive function in the elderly people: A systematic review and meta-analysis. *Aging & Mental Health,* 26(9), 1699–1709. https://doi.org/10.1080/13607863.2021.1976724

Sansone, R. A., & Sansone, L. A. (2010). Gratitude and well-being: the benefits of appreciation. *Psychiatry (edgmont)*, *7*(11), 18.

Seligman, M. E. P., & Csikszentmihalyi, M. (2000). Positive psychology: An introduction. *American Psychologist, 55*(1), 5–14. https://psycnet.apa.org/doi/10.1037/0003-066X.55.1.5

Shapiro, F. (2014). The role of eye movement desensitization and reprocessing (EMDR) therapy in medicine: Addressing the psychological and physical symptoms stemming from adverse life experiences. *The Permanente Journal, 18*(1), 71–77. https://dx.doi.org/10.7812/TPP/13-098

Shehata, H. S. E., Farag, N. A. K., & Mohamed, B. E. S. (2024). Effect of positive psychology interventions on psychological flourishing, optimism, and hope among depressive patients. *Assiut Scientific Nursing Journal, 12*(46), 280–292. https://doi.org/10.21608/asnj.2024.322074.1912

Snyder, C. R. (2002). Hope theory: Rainbows in the mind. *Psychological inquiry, 13*(4), 249–275.

Stern, Y. (2009). Cognitive reserve. *Neuropsychologia, 47*(10), 2015–2028.

Valiente-Gomez, A., Moreno-Alcazar, A., Treen, D., Cedron, C., Colom, F., Perez, V., & Armann, B. (2017, September 26). EMDR beyond PTSD: A systematic literature review. *Frontiers in Psychology, 8,* 1668. https://doi.org/10.3389/fpsyg.2017.01668

www.ingramcontent.com/pod-product-compliance
Lightning Source LLC
La Vergne TN
LVHW080031210926
848481LV00011B/3155

9798385154807